Succeeding Puccini

Luigi Emilio Caldanzano, poster for *L'amore dei tre re*, 1913. *Museo Teatrale alla Scala.*

Succeeding Puccini

The Operatic Career of Italo Montemezzi,
1875–1952

DAVID CHANDLER AND RAFFAELE MELLACE

OXFORD
UNIVERSITY PRESS

Oxford University Press is a department of the University of Oxford.
It furthers the University's objective of excellence in research, scholarship,
and education by publishing worldwide. Oxford is a registered trade mark of
Oxford University Press in the UK and in certain other countries.

Published in the United States of America by Oxford University Press
198 Madison Avenue, New York, NY 10016, United States of America.

© Oxford University Press 2025

All rights reserved. No part of this publication may be reproduced, stored in a retrieval system, transmitted, used for text and data mining, or used for training artificial intelligence, in any form or by any means, without the prior permission in writing of Oxford University Press, or as expressly permitted by law, by license or under terms agreed with the appropriate reprographics rights organization. Inquiries concerning reproduction outside the scope of the above should be sent to the Rights Department, Oxford University Press, at the address above.

You must not circulate this work in any other form
and you must impose this same condition on any acquirer.

Library of Congress Cataloging-in-Publication Data
Names: Chandler, David (David John) author. | Mellace, Raffaele, 1969– author.
Title: Succeeding Puccini : the operatic career of Italo Montemezzi, 1875–1952 /
David Chandler and Raffaele Mellace.
Description: [1.] | New York : Oxford University Press, 2025. |
Includes bibliographical references and index. |
Identifiers: LCCN 2025000578 (print) | LCCN 2025000579 (ebook) |
ISBN 9780197761342 (hardback) | ISBN 9780197761373 | ISBN 9780197761366 (epub)
Subjects: LCSH: Montemezzi, Italo, 1875-1952. | Composers—Italy—20th century. |
Opera—Italy—20th century. | LCGFT: Biographies.
Classification: LCC ML410.M765 C53 2025 (print) | LCC ML410.M765 (ebook) |
DDC 782.1092 [B]—dc23/eng/20250106
LC record available at https://lccn.loc.gov/2025000578
LC ebook record available at https://lccn.loc.gov/2025000579

DOI: 10.1093/9780197761373.001.0001

Printed by Marquis Book Printing, Canada

The manufacturer's authorized representative in the EU for product safety is
Oxford University Press España S.A., Parque Empresarial San Fernando de Henares,
Avenida de Castilla, 2 - 28830 Madrid (www.oup.es/en).

To our parents:
Hugh and Alison Chandler
Ada Somazzi and Luigi Mellace

Contents

List of Illustrations		ix
Acknowledgments		xi
Introduction: Artistic Ends		1
1.	"A simple man of the land": The Apprentice Composer, 1875–1900	10
2.	"The temperament of a born opera composer": *Bianca* and *Giovanni Gallurese*, 1901–1905	37
3.	"How many times I wept": *Héllera* and Illica, 1905–1909	75
4.	"A real Italian music drama": The Making of *L'amore dei tre re*, 1909–1912	110
5.	"The name of Montemezzi": *L'amore dei tre re* on Four Continents, 1913–1928	151
6.	"Enthusiasm for my Homeland": *La nave* and D'Annunzio, 1914–1919	181
7.	"Lost in looking for librettos": America, Marriage, Inertia, 1919–1926	220
8.	"A sort of *loisir*": *Paolo e Virginia* and *La notte di Zoraima*, 1927–1932	251
9.	"A world torn up by war": *L'incantesimo*, 1933–1942	289
10.	"The same Italianate song": *Italia mia! Nulla fermerà il tuo canto!*, 1943–1952	323
Epilogue: "The shining path"		349
Select Bibliography		357
Index		361

Illustrations

Frontispiece: Luigi Emilio Caldanzano, poster for *L'amore dei tre re*, 1913.   ii

I.1   Montemezzi at home in Beverly Hills, December 14, 1946   3

1.1   Villa Montemezzi, Vigasio, mid-1900s   15

1.2   The dramatic scene *Gelosia*, 1898   32

2.1   Stage picture of Act 1 of *Giovanni Gallurese*,
Teatro Dal Verme, Milan, 1905   51

2.2   Set design for Act 2 of *Giovanni Gallurese*,
Teatro Dal Verme, Milan, 1905   58

2.3   Montemezzi and Tullio Serafin, 1905   73

3.1   Frontispiece to *Giovanni Gallurese*, 1905   77

3.2   Set design for Act 3 of *Héllera*, 1909   89

3.3   Caramba, costume design for *Héllera*, Act 2, 1909   99

4.1   Montemezzi, Sem Benelli, and Franco Alfano, ca. 1913   112

4.2   Fernando Autori and Lina Scavizzi as Archibaldo and Fiora,
Teatro La Fenice, 1926   124

4.3   *L'amore dei tre re*, abandoned draft, "il figlio ha trovato il suo bene!"   127

4.4   *L'amore dei tre re*, autograph full score, "Dammi le labbra"   134

5.1   Virgilio Lazzari and Dorothy Kirsten as Archibaldo and Fiora, 1948   169

5.2   Cartoon of Montemezzi by Giovanni Viafora, 1916   171

6.1   Set design for *La nave*, Third Episode, 1918   211

7.1   Mary Garden as Fiora, 1921   228

7.2   Katherine and Italo Montemezzi, January 1925   231

7.3   The Montemezzis' apartment in Milan, 1930s   239

8.1   The crowd scene in *La notte di Zoraima*, Metropolitan Opera
House, 1931   275

8.2   Poster for *La notte di Zoraima*, La Scala, 1931   280

9.1   Marco, Katherine, and Italo Montemezzi in Hallein, Austria,
August 25, 1936   293

10.1 Montemezzi in his Vigasio home, October 15, 1951   345

E.1   Katherine and Marco Montemezzi presenting Montemezzi's bust to
the Opera Guild of California, 1954   354

Acknowledgments

This book was made possible by the assistance and generosity of many people; we are deeply grateful to them all.

Our first expression of thanks goes to the late Renata Donadelli (1930–2022), for long the chatelaine of Villa Montemezzi, Vigasio; she preserved an invaluable collection of manuscripts and other items related to Italo Montemezzi, as well as first- and secondhand recollections of the composer. David was warmly welcomed to the Villa, with lavish Italian hospitality, in 2014 and 2016; these visits involved not just Renata, but her three children, Francesco, Giovanni, and Caterina Sartori, and Caterina's husband, David Mitzman. In 2023, Raffaele was entertained at the Villa by Caterina and David. Stretching the definition, these visits were all "research trips"; more importantly, they were gloriously happy days.

David Mitzman's contribution to making the book possible has been unparalleled. He undertook to scan and catalog the relevant Donadelli family documents, creating a digital archive on which we have regularly, gratefully drawn. Nor did his help stop there; he also read and commented on the book in manuscript, making many useful suggestions that have been incorporated into the final text.

Our major predecessor in the field of Montemezzi studies is Piergiorgio Rossetti of Vigasio, who published the 2002 *Omaggio a Italo Montemezzi*. Back in 2007, having discovered that the Comune of Vigasio had released some CDs of Montemezzi's music, David inquired about the possibility of buying them; in an outstanding example of Italian generosity, Cristiano Marastoni promptly mailed him not just the CDs, but Piergiorgio's book as well, with the compliments of the Comune. That gift led, by degrees, to the idea of the present study. Since then, Piergiorgio has been extremely generous with his time and local knowledge. He has traced various Montemezzi family records in the archives of the Comune of Vigasio, and read through the Verona newspapers for 1904, discovering previously unknown information about the early history of *Giovanni Gallurese* that we have gratefully absorbed into Chapter 2.

xii ACKNOWLEDGMENTS

Monica Cuneo has assisted David with his research since 2011. She has translated and transcribed dozens of Montemezzi-related documents, and many of the translations in the book are hers. The feel she developed for the composer's sometimes virtually illegible handwriting has yielded dividends time and time again. She has also chased up Italian libraries and archives with telephone calls, has helped buy documents in Italy, and has made the whole research process immeasurably easier. Other translations from Italian have been made by Giulia Martino and Ornella Trevisan. For translations from other languages, and help interpreting documents in other languages, we are indebted to Florence Tesmoingt (French), Laura Ball, Yoko Mori, and Dee Kunze (German), Alejandro Aguilar and Monica Sanchez (Spanish), Pedro Ricardo Piccini and Bárbara T. Okazaki (Portuguese), and Anna Granberg (Swedish).

Davide Mingozzi contributed greatly to the book, creating all the music examples; we are deeply grateful for his efforts. His work was supported by the Dipartimento di Italianistica, Romanistica, Antichistica, Arte e Spettacolo (DIRAAS) of the University of Genoa.

A number of people have helped locate records and documents for us, often facing considerable difficulty in the process. In particular, we are very grateful to Simonetta Sargenti for tracing records pertaining to Montemezzi at the Conservatorio Giuseppe Verdi, Milan, along with some of his student compositions still held there. Frederick E. Smith, a professional genealogist, provided invaluable help in solving some of the mysteries around the Levy/ Leith family, most importantly locating Katherine Leith's birth certificate. Romina Dezillio traced Montemezzi's abandoned *Paolo e Virginia* libretto and dug out valuable information relating to its eventual setting by María Isabel Curubeto Godoy. Kris Lipkowski traced and copied many articles on Montemezzi in American newspapers and magazines; Charlotte Lekhal located the Montemezzis' property records in Milan; Marco Pasetto, who has done much to raise awareness of Montemezzi's music, made some crucial discoveries in Villa Montemezzi; and Patrick Swoboda looked for records of Bortolo Montemezzi in the Austrian State Archive.

Many librarians and archivists were generous with their time and in making copies of materials in their collections available, or, in some cases, confirming that records did not exist. In particular, we are very grateful to Pierluigi Ledda and Maria Pia Ferraris of the Archivio Storico Ricordi for undertaking to scan many of the Montemezzi-related documents in their collection in 2011, and for much help with our research since then. Grateful

ACKNOWLEDGMENTS xiii

thanks, too, to Marco Mazzolini and Alessandro Olto of Casa Ricordi for making available the full scores of Montemezzi's operas. We are much indebted to Alan Akers of the Northwestern University Music Library, John Pennino of the Metropolitan Opera House Archive, Andrea Vitalini of the Archivio Storico Teatro alla Scala, Matteo Sartorio of the Museo Teatrale alla Scala, Cesare Freddi of the Archivio Musicale Teatro alla Scala, and Davide Massimiliano and the Archivio fotografico Teatro alla Scala for providing copies of valuable Montemezzi-related documents in their collections. Further abundant thanks goes to: Anna Argentino of the Conservatorio Giuseppe Verdi; Frances Barulich of the Morgan Library and Museum; Robert Busey of U.S. Citizenship and Immigration Services; Paola Capasso of the Biblioteca Comunale di Castel d'Azzano; Fernando de Carvalho of the Teatro Nacional de São Carlos, Lisbon; Yesenia Castro of the New York Public Library; Marco Chiariglione of the Biblioteca Civica Centrale, Turin; Marco De Poli of the University of Padua Archives; Cristina Giordano of the United Nations Office at Geneva Library; Daniela Greco of the Arena di Verona; Edoardo Ferrari of the Biblioteca Civica di Verona; Robert Foster of the Royal College of Music; Helena Iggander of the Royal Swedish Opera; Márton Karczag of the Magyar Állami Operaház; Arin Kasparian of the Los Angeles Public Library; Ellen Keith of the Chicago History Museum; Maurice Klapwald of the New York Public Library; Kaitlyn Krieg of the Morgan Library and Museum; Diane Mallstrom of the Public Library of Cincinnati and Hamilton County; Richard Martin of the Royal College of Music; Beth Ann McGowan of Northern Illinois University Special Collections; Ann Mosher of Temple University Library; Katie Papas of the Rush Rhees Library, University of Rochester; Claudio Quinto of the Comune di Castel d'Azzano; Laura Rebonato of the Biblioteca Civica di Verona; Barbara Rominski of the San Francisco Opera Archive; Curt A. Roesler of the Deutsche Oper Berlin; Claudia Scipioni of the Comune of Milan; Maria Simonella of the Archivio Sem Benelli, Biblioteca della Società Economica di Chiavari; Anita de Souza Lazarim of the Theatro Municipal de São Paulo; and Matthew Stuckings of the National Library of Australia. In addition, David joined the Music Library Association Discussion List (MLA-L) in 2011, and has benefited from numerous acts of kindness, bibliographical and other, from members of that wonderful body in the years since.

Sylvan Barnet, Kate Walter, and Henry Glendon Walter III shared memories of Montemezzi in the last decade of his life and provided information about his American relatives. Maureen Polsby, Steven Schot, and

xiv ACKNOWLEDGMENTS

Mary Gray shared memories of Marco Montemezzi. Peter Dale read and commented on several chapters, and Matteo Paoletti commented on an early draft of Chapter 3. Further advice, support, and assistance of various kinds has come from Andrea Aveto, Silvia Barbantani, Edoardo Buroni, Nancy Carnevale, Livia Cavaglieri, James Doering, Konrad Dryden, Roger Flury, Mark Russell Gallagher, Julian Grant, Patty Greiner, Michael Kaye, Andrew H. King, Marianne Kordas, Elaine Mitchener, Cesare Orselli, Duane D. Printz, Angelo Rusconi, Polina Sandler, Cristi Sauser, Michael Sharp, Douglas W. Smith, Jack Sullivan, Carlo Tremolada, Michael Turnbull, Giada Viviani, Christopher Webber, and the staff at the Hotel Montemezzi, Vigasio.

For scans of the photographs included in the book, and permission to reproduce them, we are grateful to Chiara Gasparini and the Archivio Storico Ricordi © Ricordi & C. S.r.l. Milan; John Tomasicchio and the Metropolitan Opera Archives; Matteo Sartorio and the Museo Teatrale alla Scala; Andrea Vitalini and the Archivio Storico Teatro alla Scala; Tiziana Porro and the Biblioteca Nazionale Braidense; and Simon Elliott and the UCLA Library Special Collections. Many of the digital images were restored and prepared for publication by Neil Rhodes.

We are very grateful to Gurminder Kaur Bhogal for encouraging the project and recommending us to Norman Hirschy, commissioning editor at Oxford University Press, and for Norm's enthusiastic response to our proposal and advice at every stage since. OUP's two readers provided wonderfully sympathetic and useful commentary. Laura Santo guided us through the publication process with kindness and expertise. Dorothy Bauhoff was an exemplary copy editor and Vinothini Thiruvannamalai and Gopinath Anbalagan, supported by Leslie Johnson, expertly took charge of the book's production. Mariia Baturina developed the original cover concept.

We agreed on the plan and scope of the book, and the happy process of coauthorship between Kyoto and Milan involved David writing the biographical and critical reception portions and Raffaele writing all the musical analysis. When it came to the discussion of Montemezzi's librettos and their sources, we worked in close partnership. We are well aware that writing a book like this requires the patience and tolerance of one's family, so our final thanks must go to Kaori and Annie Ashizu, and to Maria Chiara Uboldi and Federico, Emma, and Angelica Mellace, for putting up with years of talk about Italo Montemezzi with love and good humor. *Succeeding Puccini* is dedicated to our parents, who made us what we are.

David Chandler and Raffaele Mellace, 2024

Introduction

Artistic Ends

In his classic *Short History of Opera* (1947), Donald Jay Grout asserted categorically that *L'amore dei tre re* of 1913 was "without doubt the greatest Italian tragic opera since Verdi's *Otello*."[1] A masterpiece wrapping up the great century that began with Rossini's international successes, it was, Grout waxed poetic, "the ripe and languid fruit of a dying age, the sunset of a long and glorious day." That same year, 1947, *Musical America*, one of the world's most widely read music magazines, devoted an editorial to the issue of "More Variety in the Operatic Diet." Nine American opera companies out of ten, it complained, endlessly recycled the same dozen operas—*Aida*, *La traviata*, *Il trovatore*, *Rigoletto*, *Il barbiere di Siviglia*, *Carmen*, *Faust*, *Cavalleria rusticana*, *Pagliacci*, *La Bohème*, *Tosca*, and *Madama Butterfly*: "About the only thing that changes is the order in which these favorites are presented."[2] Yet there were other operas, the editorial urged, which might not be middlebrow favorites in the same way, but had nevertheless abundantly proved themselves with audiences and critics, offering more challenging, elevated pleasure. Four examples were given: *Tristan und Isolde*, *Pelléas et Mélisande*, *Der Rosenkavalier*, and *L'amore dei tre re*. Nearly eight decades on, it may seem astonishing to find *L'amore dei tre re* placed in such company, yet in the first half of the twentieth century it was constantly associated with these canonical works. It was often compared to *Tristan und Isolde* and characterized (sometimes with sarcasm) as "the Italian *Tristan*"; as a *Literaturoper*, it was said to have "done in an Italian way for an Italian drama what Debussy did in a subtly French way for [Maeterlinck]";[3] and in the United States, especially, it was seen as standing in a competitive relationship to Strauss's operas. By 1930, the Metropolitan Opera House, New York,

---

[1] Donald Jay Grout, *A Short History of Opera*, 2 vols. (New York: Columbia University Press, 1947), vol. 2, pp. 444–45.

[2] "Towards More Variety in the Operatic Diet," *Musical America*, July 1947, p. 14.

[3] The formula is Philip Hale's, a notable American champion of Debussy. See "'Love of the Three Kings' Is Seen Here," *Boston Herald*, February 10, 1914, p. 11.

Succeeding Puccini. David Chandler and Raffaele Mellace, Oxford University Press. © Oxford University Press 2025.
DOI: 10.1093/9780197761373.003.0001

2 INTRODUCTION

had given fifty-three performances of *L'amore dei tre re* to forty-eight of *Der Rosenkavalier*: Puccini's works apart, no other modern opera came close.

As if responding to the *Musical America* appeal, the San Francisco Opera celebrated its twenty-fifth anniversary in 1947 with an unprecedentedly ambitious autumn season that included *Tristan*, *Pelléas*, and *L'amore dei tre re*. Between October 10 and 14, opera lovers were given a unique chance to see the three operas performed by the same company in the space of just five days. *Tristan* and *Pelléas* were both well received, but it was *L'amore dei tre re* that most impressed the audience, as well as some of the critics, proving "[o]ne of the major successes of the season," and "receiv[ing] an ovation of overwhelming proportions."[4] This state of affairs was particularly satisfactory to the lean, white-haired, seventy-two-year-old man who had traveled from his home in Beverly Hills to conduct *L'amore dei tre re*, for he happened to be the composer of the opera: Italo Montemezzi (1875–1952) (Figure I.1). He had married a wealthy American woman in 1921 and moved to the United States in 1939; contrary to the misleading claims found in many reference works, he never moved back to his beloved Italy. As he soaked up the "overwhelming" applause in San Francisco, he must have felt assured that his masterpiece had lost none of its power to thrill and exalt a receptive audience. But though Montemezzi, through his marriage—which indirectly resulted from his musical activities—had achieved a level of material prosperity attained by very few opera composers in any period, his was, in many respects, a frustrated career. He had never been able to repeat the success of *L'amore dei tre re*, and he was known to the musical world almost entirely for this score, the fame of which far eclipsed his own. It seems almost incredible that there should be confusion about where the wealthy composer of such a well-known opera lived in the final years of his life, but the obscurity surrounding him only thickened after his death. As Alan Mallach wrote in 2007, "it is hard to imagine anyone but a true specialist who can name another Montemezzi opera, or proffer even the most minimal information that might illuminate who he was, and how this shadowy figure came to write this one notable opera [*L'amore dei tre re*]."[5]

This book brings Italo Montemezzi out of the shadows and into the light. Who was this man who composed an opera which maintained a solid place in the international repertoire for decades, that was often named in the same

---

[4] Marjory M. Fisher, "San Francisco Opera Ends Lustrous Season," *Musical America*, November 1, 1947, p. 26.

[5] Alan Mallach, *The Autumn of Italian Opera: From Verismo to Modernism, 1890–1915* (Boston: Northeastern University Press, 2007), p. 318.

Figure I.1 Montemezzi at home in Beverly Hills, December 14, 1946. *Otto Rothschild photographic archive, UCLA Library Special Collections.*

breath as operas like *Tristan* and *Pelléas*, and frequently held up as superior to every Puccini opera? Were scholars like Grout, and many critics, right to see *L'amore dei tre re* extending the line of *Aida* and *Otello* and to judge it a masterpiece and work of consummate genius? Given that *L'amore dei tre re* is now performed much less often, how, when, and why did the powerful allure of this opera diminish? And what of Montemezzi's career as a

4 INTRODUCTION

whole? Is *L'amore dei tre re* really so immensely superior to his other music? What, in particular, is its relation to *La nave*, the opera Montemezzi himself considered his masterpiece? Why, in the 1920s, did many years pass in which Montemezzi made no new music public, thus effectively losing his chance to establish himself as, definitively, Puccini's heir? Our study, a combination of biography, musical analysis, and reception study, will address these questions and allow readers to come to their own conclusions regarding Montemezzi's place in operatic history.

Enough critics in the past saw Montemezzi as Verdi's true heir to justify this book being called *Succeeding Verdi: The Life and Work of Italo Montemezzi*. But that would have been unduly provocative given Puccini's deserved critical and popular reputation as the nineteenth-century master's successor. Moreover, Montemezzi's operas, especially *L'amore dei tre re*, were regularly judged according to the standards and conventions of Puccini's. The central questions he had to face in his career were whether he could succeed Puccini, and what exactly "succeeding Puccini" might mean, in cultural, aesthetic, and even political terms. The first half of Montemezzi's career shadowed Puccini's to a quite uncanny extent, the younger composer always twenty years behind. Consider that Puccini graduated with a diploma from the Pacini Institute, Lucca, in 1880, Montemezzi with a diploma from the Royal Conservatory, Milan, in 1900. Puccini entered a one-act opera into a competition sponsored by Casa Sonzogno in 1883, Montemezzi in 1903: both failed. Revised and expanded versions of those competition operas proved very successful, however, and laid the foundation for both composers' careers: *Le Villi* for Puccini in December 1884, *Giovanni Gallurese* for Montemezzi in January 1905. These operas led to both composers being signed to Casa Ricordi, Italy's leading music publisher: Puccini in 1884, Montemezzi in 1905. Both composers then spent several years working on an opera which turned out to be nearly a complete failure: Puccini's *Edgar*, premiered in April 1889; Montemezzi's *Héllera*, premiered in March 1909. After this disappointment, they then rebounded with a stunning success: Puccini's *Manon Lescaut*, premiered in February 1893, and Montemezzi's *L'amore dei tre re*, premiered in April 1913, both operas rapidly going on to achieve international popularity. Whether *Le Villi*, *Edgar*, and *Manon Lescaut* represent a more promising career trajectory than *Giovanni Gallurese*, *Héllera*, and *L'amore dei tre re* is worth debating.

At this point, however, the two careers significantly and instructively diverged. Puccini went on to compose those canonical staples *La Bohème*

(1896) and *Tosca* (1900), whereas, in the equivalent period, Montemezzi produced *La nave* (1918), which despite a prestigious launch at La Scala failed to enter the repertoire and ultimately brought the curtain down on his career as an important opera composer. Things could have been very different, with the pattern of correspondences restored. In 1900, Puccini's imagination had traveled eastward, as he was inspired to compose an opera based on David Belasco's play *Madame Butterfly*. In 1920, Montemezzi's imagination similarly traveled eastward, when he was inspired to compose an opera based on Jacques-Henri Bernardin de Saint-Pierre's novella *Paul et Virginie*, set in Mauritius. But while Puccini produced another repertoire staple in *Madama Butterfly* (1904), Montemezzi was unable to complete his *Paul et Virginie* opera, and at this point his operatic career became increasingly the story of one opera: *L'amore dei tre re*.

Montemezzi's career before *La nave* did not simply follow the pattern of Puccini's. *L'amore dei tre re* represents just the sort of advance in Italian opera that *La fanciulla del West*, Puccini's opera of 1910, had anticipated. Critics (and there are an increasing number) who consider *La fanciulla* the older composer's finest achievement are those most likely to be sympathetic to Montemezzi's aesthetic; conversely, opera lovers who regard *La fanciulla* as an unfortunate decline from Puccini's more overtly melodic and popular earlier operas are unlikely to approve Montemezzi's attempt to lead Italian opera further in the direction of the integrated music drama. But in terms of leaving a definite mark on operatic history, Montemezzi claimed a position of leadership only during the long break in Puccini's career in the 1910s. Discussing an earlier era, Jay Nicolaisen has memorably written: "Nineteenth-century exponents of the view that great events call forth great men might have taken satisfaction in the circumstance that the successful portion of Ponchielli's career [1872–1885] fitted so neatly into the period of Verdi's temporary retirement."[6] The situation is rather similar with Montemezzi and Puccini: the former's two most significant operas, *L'amore dei tre re* and *La nave*, fitted neatly into the gap in the latter's career between *La fanciulla del West* and *Il trittico* (Puccini did compose *La rondine* in the intervening period, but this was, until recently, regarded as a minor, problematic work). Had Montemezzi been able to produce an opera of comparable commercial and artistic validity to *L'amore dei tre re* in the 1920s, as

---

[6] Jay Nicolaisen, *Italian Opera in Transition, 1871–1893* (Ann Arbor, MI: UMI Research Press, 1980), p. 73.

6 INTRODUCTION

he fully intended to do, his status as Puccini's successor could have been cemented; as it was, the older composer managed to have the last word with *Turandot* (premiered 1926).

The critical culture that has gathered around *Turandot* has been very damaging, not just to Montemezzi, but to other contemporary Italian opera composers, including his closest rivals, Franco Alfano (1875–1954) and Riccardo Zandonai (1883–1944). *Turandot* came to be mythologized as the end of a tradition, and Puccini is therefore understood as the culminating figure in that tradition—leaving little or no room for younger composers who wrote their finest operas before 1926. At worst, this leads to very pat judgments about how Italian music developed in these years. Alexandra Wilson, for example, has written:

> Puccini was a national composer with no obvious successor. His status as heir to Verdi remained unchallenged; the generation that followed was for the most part more interested in founding a new school of Italian instrumental music than in writing operas with wide popular appeal.[7]

This is remarkably misleading. Grout's emphatic assertion concerning *L'amore dei tre re* being "without doubt the greatest Italian tragic opera since Verdi's *Otello*" very much *does* challenge Puccini's "status as heir to Verdi," and many other such challenges will be encountered in the course of this book. Nor did Montemezzi, as an alternative "heir to Verdi," show any interest in "founding a new school of Italian instrumental music" or abandoning the composition of "operas with wide popular appeal." Though less invested than Puccini in being immediately and widely successful (and remunerated accordingly), he clearly wanted his operas to resonate with a large audience. But Montemezzi, like many of the younger Italian composers, was effectively wrong-footed by an overall sea change in critical attitudes toward popular culture. Grout and many pro-Montemezzi writers regarded him as superior to Puccini in large part because he aimed higher, and if *L'amore dei tre re* was less popular with the "ordinary" opera-goer than *La Bohème* or *Tosca*, that was set down to his credit. But as, from the 1920s onward, popular culture became academically respectable, and art became interesting as much for

---

[7] Alexandra Wilson, *The Puccini Problem: Opera, Nationalism, and Modernity* (Cambridge: Cambridge University Press, 2009), p. 194.

INTRODUCTION 7

what it did, socially, as for what it achieved in itself, so critics gradually made their peace with Puccini's popularity with the middlebrows.

In his lifetime, and especially from about 1910, Puccini's music was consistently controversial and had many detractors. Linda B. Fairtile has documented what she calls "the anti-Puccini movement of the 1910s."[8] In the decade in which Montemezzi composed his finest operas, there was widespread dissatisfaction with Puccini's dominant position in modern Italian music. However, a few years after Puccini's death there was a significant shift, one both reflected in, and encouraged by, Giuseppe Adami's edition of *Giacomo Puccini Epistolario*, published in Italian in 1928 and English in 1931. Adami's book presupposed that Puccini was now worth *studying*, and as Fairtile says, it "laid the groundwork for the systematic study of his creative process."[9] It was soon followed by Richard Specht's *Giacomo Puccini: Das Leben, der Mensch, das Werk* (1931), "generally considered the first serious survey of Puccini's life and works."[10] This newfound belief that Puccini was worth academic attention should be recognized as unfolding in the sort of contexts provided by Gilbert Seldes's epochal study of popular culture, *The Seven Lively Arts* (1924), and Antonio Gramsci's early 1930s reflections on how "Italian artistic 'Democracy'" had taken an operatic rather than literary form, unlike other cultures (Gramsci considered Verdi, Puccini, and Mascagni the best exemplars of this).[11] It is not that Puccini suddenly had more admirers, but that the monumentality and social significance of his achievement could no longer be denied, and the combination of his musical techniques with the "democratic" appeal of his operas (to use Gramsci's loaded term) now seemed worth serious assessment. This has continued to be the case ever since, and as shelves in libraries began filling up with books about Puccini, and as recordings of his operas proliferated, a sort of circular argument was inevitably constructed that he was much more consequential than any of his peers. In the century since, Puccini has become so important to the overall economy of opera that he is, as has been said of certain financial institutions, "too big to fail." As such, much critical energy, and even academic energy, goes into effectively shoring up the status quo.

---

[8] Linda B. Fairtile, *Giacomo Puccini: A Guide to Research* (New York: Garland, 1999), p. 271.
[9] Fairtile, *Giacomo Puccini*, p. 23.
[10] Fairtile, *Giacomo Puccini*, p. 23.
[11] Antonio Gramsci, *Selections from Cultural Writings*, edited by David Forgacs and Geoffrey Nowell-Smith (Cambridge, MA: Harvard University Press, 1985), p. 378.

8   INTRODUCTION

The shift in critical tone in the late 1920s put composers like Montemezzi, Alfano, and Zandonai in a difficult position. Earlier praised for their artistic ambition and high ideals, they now began to find themselves increasingly faulted for lacking the popular touch. Their response, unfortunately, was to set some badly chosen librettos in a rather obvious attempt to demonstrate that they could be "democratic": Alfano's *L'ultimo Lord* (1930), Montemezzi's *La notte di Zoraima* (1931), and Zandonai's *Una partita* (1933) are all good examples. None of these operas fared very well with the public, however, thus only reinforcing Puccini's domination of popular taste and ultimately strengthening the narrative positioning *Turandot* as a terminal point in Italian operatic history. Moreover, the twenty-year gap between Puccini's career and Montemezzi's makes an odd, ironic return here, in a way very much flattering the older composer. *La notte di Zoraima*, set in South America and premiered at La Scala in January 1931, brought the longest gap in Montemezzi's operatic career to an end, but it is his most backward-looking opera. Conversely, Puccini's *La fanciulla del West*, set in North America and premiered at the Metropolitan Opera, New York, in December 1910, brought the longest gap in his operatic career to an end with what is, in many ways, his most forward-looking score. Given these perplexing reversals, champions of Montemezzi, Alfano, and Zandonai necessarily had to appeal to their earlier, more ambitious, operas, and to represent those operas as glorious culminating points in a tradition already in decline before *Turandot*. This is what Grout was doing in describing *L'amore dei tre re* as "the sunset of a long and glorious day," as were the editors of the *Omaggio* volume published in Italy immediately after Montemezzi's death, who described him as "*l'ultimo operista* della grande fioritura italiana" (*the last opera composer* of the great Italian blossoming).[12] An alternative history of Italian opera is gestured at in such claims, and it is a history worth investigating.

Montemezzi never became any sort of brand, or bankable name, like Puccini. *L'amore dei tre re* was never performed because it was by him, and the many opera companies who staged it showed remarkably little interest in staging another Montemezzi opera.[13] Critical interest in his career has been almost nonexistent. He is an obvious victim of today's operatic status quo,

---

[12] "Premessa" in Luigi Tretti and Lionello Fiumi (eds.), *Omaggio a Italo Montemezzi* (Verona: Ghidini and Fiorini, 1952), p. 14.

[13] To the best of our knowledge, in Montemezzi's lifetime only six opera houses, having staged *L'amore dei tre re*, then went on to stage one or more of his other operas: La Scala, the Teatro Filarmonico, Verona, the Teatro Reale, Rome, the Metropolitan Opera, New York, the Chicago Opera, and the Royal Swedish Opera.

INTRODUCTION 9

like several other composers who once seemed to have an assured place in the repertoire. We hope this book will reawaken interest in Montemezzi's music, but even if it does not, our investigation of his career in the context of changes in Italian music, theatre, and society should add substantially to the existing picture of Italian opera in the crucial 1900–1930 period. We hope this study will challenge some of the reader's assumptions about those decades, for the simplified narrative which says that Puccini represents an end point in Italian opera has had such immense cultural and commercial consequences that it is more important than ever to understand how and why that narrative came to be written, what has been lost in consequence, and what might yet be recovered.

1

"A simple man of the land"

The Apprentice Composer, 1875–1900

Italo Montemezzi put Vigasio on the map. He remains a household name there: from every direction the road signs announcing Vigasio, a small town some eight miles from Verona, describe it as the birthplace of the composer. In the middle of the town there is a Via Montemezzi, further to the west, on Via Battisti, the I. Montemezzi Middle School, and in recent years a Hotel Montemezzi has been opened on the road to Verona. Montemezzi's grand tomb is effectively the focal point of the cemetery; electric candles burn before it day and night.

Present-day Vigasio, with a population around 10,000, has the air of a sleepy, affluent backwater, most adult inhabitants being either retired or commuting to work in Verona. By contrast, the Vigasio in which Montemezzi grew up in the 1870s and 1880s was a large, impoverished, agricultural village. In 1881, the population stood at 2,455, with land and wealth concentrated in twenty-six families.[1] The economy was dominated by farming, maize and wheat being the main crops grown, though there was also substantial rice cultivation. A small area of pastureland supported 750 cattle. The only other significant industry was silkworm farming, which had been established in the Po Valley in the tenth century and remained a major employer: in 1893, Vigasio produced 24,600 kilograms (around 54,000 pounds) of silkworm cocoons. There was little secondary industry, with what there was—textile, wine, and pasta production—mostly linked to agriculture. Local affairs were overseen by a mayor and council of representatives of leading families. Until the arrival of the railway in 1877, just after Montemezzi's second birthday, the village was a two-hour coach journey

---

[1] Pierpaolo Brugnoli and Bruno Chiappa (eds.), *Vigasio: Vicende di una comunità e di un territorio* (Vigasio: Comune di Vigasio, 2005), p. 251.

Succeeding Puccini. David Chandler and Raffaele Mellace, Oxford University Press. © Oxford University Press 2025.
DOI: 10.1093/9780197761373.003.0002

from Verona. The industrial revolution bringing the railway also brought increasingly mechanized working practices, which in combination with the agricultural depression of the 1870s and 1880s led to high unemployment and chronic poverty. Montemezzi's boyhood coincided with an economic crisis as centuries-old patterns of existence were overturned: from around 1870, many inhabitants chose to leave in search of a better life overseas, a significant number emigrating to Brazil.[2] Neither picturesque nor prosperous, Vigasio was not a place that received many visitors, apart from seasonal quail shooters. An 1884 "Hunter's Guide" records that in Vigasio "an experienced hunter, accompanied by a good dog, can easily bag about fifty [quail] in one day," and that sportsmen came from as far as Mantua—fifteen miles away—to shoot there.[3]

Montemezzi's father, Bortolo Montemezzi (1836–1922), was born in Sustinenza, a small village some twenty miles southeast of Vigasio, on March 21, 1836, the son of Antonio Montemezzi and his wife Giovanna, née Trojani.[4] In February 1843, the family moved to Vigasio, apparently to join relatives, as there were already Montemezzis established there. A certain Andrea Montemezzi, born in 1783, had established a workshop in Vigasio in the early 1800s.[5] This specialized in the construction of clocks, but also produced all sorts of ratchet mechanisms for agricultural equipment. Bortolo appears to have been apprenticed to this workshop, and to have eventually taken it over, for this became his trade. The work he took most pride in was constructing clocks for churches and other public buildings: a survey published in 1904 described his business as a "factory for tower clocks" (*fabbrica di orologi da torre*).[6] But clockmaking could not provide full-time employment, and most of his time was spent constructing presses and mills for agricultural and industrial use; Montemezzi would later describe his father as "a maker of agricultural implements."[7] Bortolo was an innovator and entered his work in various shows and competitions, winning awards and commendations, including a bronze medal from the Ministry of Agriculture,

[2] Brugnoli and Chiappa, *Vigasio*, p. 253.
[3] O. A., "Guida del Cacciatore in Italia: Vigasio," *Lo Sport Illustrato* 3 (August 30, 1884), p. 1221.
[4] Bortolo Montemezzi death certificate, Comune di Vigasio.
[5] Brugnoli and Chiappa, *Vigasio*, p. 297.
[6] Brugnoli and Chiappa, *Vigasio*, p. 251.
[7] Herbert F. Peyser, "'Let simplicity be the composer's constant objective,' Abjures Italo Montemezzi," *Musical America*, November 22, 1919, p. 3.

12 SUCCEEDING PUCCINI

Industry, and Commerce for his contribution to an 1889 agricultural competition in the Verona region.[8]

Bortolo's local career had been interrupted by conscription into the Austrian army, following the recruiting law of 1819 which made all men aged between twenty and twenty-seven in Lombardy and Venetia liable for eight years' military service.[9] For most of his years of service, Bortolo would have been outside Italy, according to standard Austrian military policy. Little is known of his military career, for his *Grundbuchblätt*, or military record, is unfortunately missing from the Austrian State Archive. The register of the *Grundbuchblätter* at least confirms that he served in the Second Pioneer Battalion. This is interesting, for most Italians in the Verona region were recruited into the 45th regiment; it shows that Bortolo's engineering skills were recognized, though family tradition maintains that his anti-Austrian political views also had something to do with his being separated from the bulk of his compatriots.[10] Whatever his later interpretation of events, though, such slight evidence as there is suggests he had little anti-Austrian feeling while in the army. He was eligible for discharge in 1864, but stayed on, and was promoted to the rank of *Unteroffizier*.[11] Bortolo's military service probably ended after the bloody conflict of 1866, when Austria finally lost Venetia, and the vast majority of Italians in the Imperial Army were repatriated. No doubt he could have told his son much about the dramatic events surrounding Italian unification, and his stories very likely gave birth to Italo's nationalist feelings.

According to family tradition, as Bortolo was leaving Vigasio to enter the Austrian army in 1856, he visited the Donadellis, one of the village's farming families, to say goodbye. Angelo Donadelli (1823–1895) and his wife Grata (1826–1903), née Guerra, had just given birth to a girl named Elisa. Bortolo joked that one day he would make her his bride, and he kept his word. He married Elisa Donadelli (1856–1935), generally known as Lisa, on January 21, 1875, when she was eighteen.[12] It seems likely that the wedding was hastily arranged when Lisa realized she was pregnant, for the future composer, the

---

[8] The certificate he won on this occasion and other, comparable, certificates survive among the Donadelli family documents.

[9] Lawrence Sondhaus, *In the Service of the Emperor: Italians in the Austrian Armed Forces 1814–1918* (Boulder, CO: East European Monographs, 1990), p. 19.

[10] Information from Renata Donadelli.

[11] "Verzeichnis," *Linzer Tages-Post*, September 23, 1865, p. 5. It seems likely that Bortolo had only just achieved his promotion, for the same paper, for September 12, 1865, describes him as a *Korporal* (p. 2).

[12] Comune di Vigasio records.

THE APPRENTICE COMPOSER, 1875–1900   13

couple's only child, was born less than seven months later, on August 4.[13] He was christened Antonio Italo Montemezzi. The unusual name "Italo" had gained a measure of popularity in the nineteenth century for its patriotic resonance, but as Lisa had a younger brother, Martino Italo Donadelli (1860–1940), known in the family as Italo, there may be no wider significance in its being chosen.

The name Antonio was not only the name of the boy's paternal grandfather, but the name of his godfather, Count Antonio Nogarola (1818–1889), a distinguished patron of Bortolo's who lived in Verona but served as the mayor of nearby Castel d'Azzano. A description of him in 1871, when he became mayor, gives some idea of his local importance and character:

> [He] belongs to the oldest, and one of the most illustrious families in the province of Verona. He is the richest landowner in the municipality and was always the first Municipal Representative prior to 1866. Educated and benevolent, he always managed the municipal interests very well. Perhaps of a slightly weak fibre, he prefers conciliation to resolute actions and is therefore all the more esteemed by the population, whose love for him is total and over whom he exerts all his influence. He is a religious man, yet patriotic at the same time.[14]

If Montemezzi was born with any particular advantage, it was this family connection with Nogarola, who made clocks as a hobby and through this route came to know Bortolo. On occasion, the two men worked together. The good relationship did not long survive the birth of the future composer, though. According to family tradition, when, in 1876, a clock largely built by Bortolo was erected in the Piazzetta Monte, Verona, with a plaque stating it had been "constructed and donated" by Nogarola, Bortolo took grave offense and a rift was created, never to be properly repaired. Lisa, inclined to be conciliatory with such a powerful patron, was very upset.[15] Another possible

[13] There has been a good deal of confusion regarding Montemezzi's date of birth. Giuseppe Silvestri, in what appears to have been a simple slip, gives it as September 4: see Silvestri, "Vita e opera: vocazione e volontà," in *Omaggio a Italo Montemezzi*, edited by Piergiorgio Rossetti (Vigasio: Amministrazione Comunale di Vigasio, 2002), p. 18. Other sources, more puzzlingly, have given it as May 31, and remarkably it is this date which appears on the plaque placed on Villa Montemezzi in 1955. Piergiorgio Rossetti explains the confusion in Rossetti, *Omaggio*, p. 142.

[14] Quoted in Gianfranco and Carla Frinzi, *Castel d'Azzano: Storia e Vita* (Castel d'Azzano: n.p., 1993), pp. 147–48.

[15] Information from Renata Donadelli. The clock and plaque in question can still be seen in the Piazzetta Monte. The plaque reads: "Il Conte Antonio Nogarola Questo Orologio Costruiva e Donava MDCCCLXXVI."

14 SUCCEEDING PUCCINI

explanation for the falling out, or its subsequent intensification, is that in 1879 Bortolo became mayor of Vigasio at a time when a bitter dispute was going on with neighboring Castel d'Azzano about boundaries, thus putting himself in direct (and perhaps deliberate) opposition to Nogarola.[16] This may have contributed to the name Antonio soon being dropped for all but a few official purposes, and the future composer becoming generally known as Italo, like his uncle. Nevertheless, there is evidence that Italo continued to benefit from his connection with the Nogarola family, as discussed later.

Angelo Donadelli gave Bortolo and Lisa a house as a wedding present: this was an annex joined perpendicularly to his own house, previously used for storage, but now fitted up to make a separate home. Later photographs of the Montemezzi house (now Villa Montemezzi) give the impression of a rather grand building and thus of the family's affluence (Figure 1.1). This is misleading. First, as just noted, they never owned the whole building; and second, the castellated tower part, incorporating a *colombara*, or dovecote, was only added in the early twentieth century, after Montemezzi had become a successful composer. The house was a good size, and certainly much above the Vigasio average, but it incorporated Bortolo's workshop and was in no sense a genteel residence. Montemezzi later described it as a "Vigasio farmhouse" with "white stone walls."[17] Tullio Serafin evocatively recalled "very much a country house. The furniture was simple, the decor plain, the entire home inelegant in every way. But it was a home, and you felt at home when you walked through the door."[18] The young Italo grew up in what was effectively an extended family of parents, grandparents, and youthful aunts and uncles, just a minute's walk from the center of Vigasio, then known simply as the Piazza (now the Piazza Vittorio Emanuele II). He must have been strongly aware of the practical realities of both his father's workshop and his grandfather's farm. In later years, Montemezzi tended to emphasize the comparatively humble nature of his early life. In 1919 a report stated, on his authority, that Bortolo's "earnings were not considerable in the years of Italo's boyhood but they sufficed to the support of the household."[19]

After Montemezzi's death, Serafin described him, with considerable resonance, as "a simple man of the land" who "never outgrew his background."[20]

---

[16] Frinzi, *Castel d'Azzano*, pp. 163–67.
[17] Enid A. Haupt, "Enchanting Fabric," *Philadelphia Inquirer*, November 14, 1943, p. 4.
[18] Tullio Serafin, "Italo Montemezzi—An Appreciation," *Opera News*, January 19, 1953, p. 31.
[19] Peyser, "'Let simplicity..,'" p. 3.
[20] Serafin, "Italo Montemezzi," p. 31.

Figure 1.1 Villa Montemezzi, Vigasio, mid-1900s. *Donadelli family documents.*

There was a sturdy provincialism about him, at odds with the more cosmopolitan reaches of his music and his later lifestyle. In some respects, his father's influence appears to have been strong. Bortolo's working life was devoted to patiently constructing clocks and other mechanical devices in much the same way that his son would, in time, carefully construct his scores in the same house. Indeed, one of Montemezzi's most remarkable preferences as a composer—as Serafin must have known—was to work on a makeshift table consisting of two planks supported on two sawhorses.[21] But Bortolo was also socially ambitious and inclined to align his interests with the landowning classes and the churches and public bodies for which he worked: tellingly, his becoming mayor of Vigasio was part of a conservative backlash against the previous mayor, Patrizio Ottolini, who had attempted to implement socialist ideas by increasing taxes on the landowners to fund welfare schemes.[22] On the other hand, Bortolo's willingness to break with a powerful patron like Nogarola suggests a proud artisan with strict limits to his deference to social superiors. Such attitudes would help shape Montemezzi's own career.

---

[21] A photograph of the table in question, as it stood in Villa Montemezzi at the end of Montemezzi's life, is reproduced in Rossetti, *Omaggio*, p. 20. It remained there until the 1980s.

[22] Brugnoli and Chiappa, *Vigasio*, p. 252.

16   SUCCEEDING PUCCINI

Montemezzi entered the Vigasio elementary school at the age of six. His education there coincided with a massive enlargement of the school as a result of primary education being made compulsory, in an effort to combat illiteracy: from one teacher in 1870, there were six by 1890.[23] At the school, Montemezzi was presumably known as the mayor's son, and one can reasonably wonder how this affected his relationships with poorer children whose parents felt better represented by Bortolo's predecessor. For his secondary education, he was sent to the Scuola Tecnica Reale (Royal Technical School) in Verona, renamed the Scuola Tecnica Paolo Caliari in 1888 (Caliari being the celebrated sixteenth-century painter generally known as Paolo Veronese).[24] The school had, a few years earlier, been attended by Emilio Salgari (1862–1911), the famous popular novelist. The Scuola Tecnica placed a heavy emphasis on mathematics and science, and Bortolo chose it for that reason: he wanted his son to be an engineer of some sort. This was a sensible wish based on his own sphere of expertise, the abilities he saw in Italo, and his understanding of the way the Italian economy was developing. Unfortunately, although Montemezzi was good at mathematics, he found the subject uncongenial. During his secondary school years, he felt "he was a square peg in a round hole"[25]—ironically, it was his own son, Marco, who would later discover a passion for mathematics and go on to become a university lecturer in the subject. Montemezzi also studied French at secondary school and gained a reasonable proficiency in the language that served him well in later life.

Bortolo enjoyed music and had considerable executive ability. He liked to relax with his flute or violin, and this was probably the first music the future composer heard. In the Austrian army, Bortolo had played in a military band. Late in life, Montemezzi suggested his father had indeed been the leader of the band.[26] When at the Scuola Tecnica, Montemezzi expressed a wish to learn to play music himself and asked for a piano. Bortolo bought a simple upright model for ninety lire, a major financial outlay for the family.[27] Decades later, Montemezzi told Enid A. Haupt that:

> he [Montemezzi] showed such flair for music that his mother provided him with lessons. She paid a young student ten lira a month to teach her son—a

---

[23] Brugnoli and Chiappa, *Vigasio*, p. 286.
[24] Montemezzi's graduation certificate is preserved among the Donadelli family documents.
[25] Verna Arvey, "Visits to the Homes of Famous Composers No. XIV: Italo Montemezzi," *Opera and Concert*, November 1948, p. 15.
[26] Arvey, "Visits to the Homes," p. 15.
[27] Peyser, "'Let simplicity..,'" p. 3.

THE APPRENTICE COMPOSER, 1875–1900   17

rate of about twenty-five cents per lesson.[28] To win over his father, Italo composed a polka; and, despite the teacher's objection that the technique was all wrong, the elder Montemezzi was pleased.[29]

No date is attached to the story, but it presumably occurred after the family's acquisition of the piano and when the question of how seriously Italo was to play it was under discussion. The polka referred to is Montemezzi's first known composition. Montemezzi told Giuseppe Silvestri that his "first [piano] teachers" had been "Lonardi and Tanara,"[30] identifiable as Gaetano Lonardi and Giulio Tanara, both of whom taught piano and singing in Verona.[31] Perhaps one of these was the "young student" of Haupt's anecdote. It is difficult to assess how serious the future composer was about music in the second decade of his life. A brief official biography published by Casa Ricordi in 1933 stated that: "from a very early age, Montemezzi revealed his musical temperament by studying the piano passionately."[32] On other occasions, though, Montemezzi painted a different picture. He told Silvestri he had turned to the piano as a relief from "the burden and the boredom" of mathematics, but had, initially at least, put little effort into the instrument, because the only things he really enjoyed were "playing billiards and going hunting."[33] One can perhaps understand that when requested for a biography by his publisher, Montemezzi wanted to emphasize his efforts to improve himself musically, while as an old man reminiscing by the hearth in his childhood home, he preferred to evoke a truant spirit.

Apart from the business of the piano and the music lessons, just one specific story from Montemezzi's childhood seems to have been preserved. One day, when around fourteen, he heard his father playing a piece of music, learned that it was from an opera, and commented that writing "music for the theatre" was clearly not difficult. "Oh yes? You try then, try and see!" his father replied.[34] Thus Silvestri tells the story. Montemezzi gave a slightly more dramatic version to Verna Arvey, claiming that he said: "I think it wouldn't be very difficult to write an opera!"[35] Whatever the exact words, it is a good

---

[28] In the late 1800s, the lira traded at around five lire to the U.S. dollar (a rate that became fixed between 1900 and 1914), suggesting the young Montemezzi had two lessons a week.

[29] Haupt, "Enchanting Fabric," p. 4.

[30] Silvestri, "Vita e opera," p. 18.

[31] *Annuario d'Italia. Calendario Generale del Regno per l'anno 1892* (Rome, 1892), p. 1282.

[32] *Italo Montemezzi* (Milan: Ricordi, 1933), p. 1.

[33] Silvestri, "Vita e opera," pp. 18–19.

[34] Silvestri, "Vita e opera," p. 19.

[35] Arvey, "Visits to the Homes," p. 15.

18 SUCCEEDING PUCCINI

example of the kind of anecdote which gets recalled and repeated when it starts to appear prophetic, and that has been a standard part of biographies since ancient times. In itself it is trivial, but the story does indirectly illuminate the musical culture of the family. The suggestion surely is that the future composer had not seen an opera at this juncture. Although Verona offered plenty of opportunities to experience opera, it is difficult to imagine the reported incident coming to seem so significant if the Montemezzis were in the habit of even infrequent attendance.

Overall, Montemezzi's performance at the Scuola Tecnica was far from distinguished. Students needed an average score of six out of ten to graduate, and after retaking some exams in the 1889 autumn semester, he was able to graduate on November 13 with a score of 6.4. After this, there is a gap in the biographical record that lasts until 1894. Bortolo believed Italo should pursue the social status which "only a degree and stable profession could grant,"[36] and wanted him to enter the Politecnico in Milan, a university founded in 1863 specifically for the teaching of engineering and architecture. Montemezzi was able to pass the Politecnico's entrance exam in 1894, and it is reasonable to suppose that the intervening years had been devoted to some sort of private study that would equip him with the necessary knowledge. It is difficult to say how much father and son came into conflict in this period. Rather than commenting directly, Silvestri devotes two pages to an account of the Veronese poet Aleardo Aleardi (1812–1878) and the relationship he had with *his* father, which Silvestri guesses to be analogous to the Montemezzi case.[37] Aleardi confessed to a feeling of guilt at the way he repeatedly broke his promises to his father that he would concentrate on the study of law. Silvestri expressly says that Montemezzi revealed no comparable guilt feeling in later life, though it is clear he had no idea whether Montemezzi actually made comparable promises—indeed whether the future composer had even declared an independent ambition to devote his life to music. It is perfectly possible he had not, for he seems outwardly to have gone along with the Politecnico plan until the last minute.

Having passed the entrance exam to the Politecnico, and having just turned nineteen, in autumn 1894 Montemezzi prepared to leave home. But things did not go according to plan, and apart from his later operatic triumphs, the next event in Montemezzi's life has assumed the greatest

---

[36] Silvestri, "Vita e opera," p. 18.
[37] Silvestri, "Vita e opera," pp. 16–18.

THE APPRENTICE COMPOSER, 1875–1900   19

prominence in such brief biographical accounts as exist. This speaks of a relatively uneventful biography no doubt, but it was clearly an important, self-defining moment. Having reached Milan on the train, Montemezzi did not go to the Politecnico. Instead, in a desperate bid to escape the life his father had mapped out for him, he went to the Royal Conservatory of Music and applied to take the admission test for the ten-year composition course. Silvestri states, "I do not know whether it was a sudden or premeditated decision,"[38] but to Arvey, Montemezzi stressed it was the former:

> On the train, he suddenly changed his mind. He felt that it would be a disaster to go ahead in engineering. "What can I do with mathematics?" he asked himself, and realized at that moment that he would prefer anything *but* mathematics! His father's remark about his writing an opera recurred to him and became a challenge. . . . he went to the Conservatory, determined to change a whim into a life-work.[39]

The Royal Conservatory was Italy's leading music school, and Montemezzi's audacity in assuming he could change direction so easily inevitably met with disappointment:

> His youthful confidence received a severe setback at the Conservatory. He was asked immediately just what he wanted to do: play, sing or compose? On the instant he said, "I want to compose!" Then they told him the requirements. It would take nine [*sic*] years of intense work. He was taken aback, picturing himself as being old and grey-haired at the finish of his study, but determined to go through with it nevertheless. Part of the entrance examination was to improvise on the piano. Badly prepared as he was, he tried it and couldn't succeed. So they "threw him out," to use his own words.[40]

The episode begs several questions of an economic nature, though one can only speculate as to the answers. Most importantly, perhaps, did Montemezzi really believe his family would be willing and able to fund him through a decade of musical study? Passing the examination may have put him in a strong position to negotiate; failing it did not, and when he returned to Vigasio with his tail between his legs he found his father "furious at this turn

---

[38] Silvestri, "Vita e opera," p. 19.
[39] Arvey, "Visits to the Homes," p. 15.
[40] Arvey, "Visits to the Homes," p. 15.

20 SUCCEEDING PUCCINI

of events."[41] There was no easy route to reconciliation, for whatever his musical future, Montemezzi had decided he would not enter the Politecnico.

At this juncture, Montemezzi apparently made a trip to France to visit the Exposition universelle, internationale et coloniale at Lyon, as well as Paris. The Exposition attracted nearly four million visitors before its closure on November 11, 1894, and as, like all the great nineteenth-century exhibitions of this nature, it was designed first and foremost to showcase industrial progress, it is possible Bortolo sent his son there in a last bid to convince him that his future lay in the world of engineering. Or perhaps Montemezzi just needed to get away to think things out, or to give his father time to adjust to the situation. From Paris, he sent Bortolo a postcard of the recently built Eiffel tower, expressing a wish for reconciliation and understanding.[42] Bortolo eventually gave in, having little room for maneuver if he wanted to maintain a good relationship with his only child. Silvestri writes, incidentally and curiously, that "[i]t was probably the good Count Nogarola who placated the paternal ire."[43] This cannot refer to Montemezzi's godfather, who had died in 1889. The reference, then, is presumably to Count Lodovico Violini Nogarola (1838–1917), his godfather's nephew and heir, who lived in Verona most of the time.[44] In 1892, he was said to be worth 500,000 lire.[45] The tantalizing suggestion is thus that the wealthy Nogarola family continued to take an interest in the aspirant composer, and in the next chapter we present evidence that in 1904 Count Violini Nogarola assisted Montemezzi's campaign to raise money for the first production of *Giovanni Gallurese*. Whether or not the Count intervened in 1894, there is no doubt that Montemezzi continued to live with his parents and was allowed to pursue his musical studies with a view to taking the Conservatory test again the following year.

Unfortunately, when Montemezzi retook the entrance test in 1895, presumably in a rather more formal fashion, he failed again. Montemezzi told Silvestri that while his first failure left him "disheartened," the second left him "desperate."[46] Such a feeling was fully justified, for at twenty he had, in a worldly point of view, achieved almost nothing. Montemezzi was far behind other talented musicians of his generation. Of his future rivals, Franco Alfano, an exact contemporary, had already completed three years at the

---

[41] Arvey, "Visits to the Homes," p. 15.
[42] Information from Renata Donadelli, who recalled seeing the postcard in question.
[43] Silvestri, "Vita e opera," p. 20.
[44] For details of Count Violini Nogarola, see Frinzi, *Castel d'Azzano*, pp. 173–75.
[45] Frinzi, *Castel d'Azzano*, p. 174.
[46] Silvestri, "Vita e opera," p. 19.

THE APPRENTICE COMPOSER, 1875–1900   21

San Pietro a Majella Conservatory, and was now setting off to Germany to continue his studies at the world-famous Leipzig Conservatory. Riccardo Zandonai, eight years Montemezzi's junior, affords an even more damaging comparison: he had commenced his studies at the Scuola Musicale, Rovereto, in 1894. Despite his being much younger, Zandonai's future career would develop in close parallel with Montemezzi's.

Montemezzi later recognized his second failure as a turning point in his life:

> For the second time he went home, and there came to a major realization. At last he understood that "to do something in this life one *must* work!" He promised his father he would work and kept his word.[47]

This makes it sound comparatively easy, but presumably there were more difficult scenes with Bortolo to negotiate. Possibly Montemezzi's promises to do better were remarkably affecting, or perhaps his father had, despite the double failure, come to see real musical promise in his son; whatever the case, Bortolo and Lisa now made a remarkable investment in Italo's future by sending him to Milan to be privately tutored by Alberto D'Erasmo (1874–1941). There is no record of any talk of Montemezzi simply applying to a lower-level music school; perhaps family pride had now become involved in the matter of getting him into the Royal Conservatory.

D'Erasmo proved an excellent tutor. Although only just over a year Montemezzi's senior, he was far ahead musically and had already graduated from the Royal Conservatory, first in piano (1892) and subsequently in composition (1894),[48] and was now established as a piano teacher. Montemezzi flourished under his tutoring, and so rapid was his progress that D'Erasmo was soon teaching him material far beyond the requirements of the Conservatory entrance test. The result of these months of intense study exceeded all expectations. The composition course at the Conservatory, set up in 1878, was a ten-year program divided into three distinct "schools." Students first took three years of harmony, then three years of counterpoint and fugue, and finally four years of "composition proper" (*composizione propriamente detta*).[49] In practice, though, few students took the full

---

[47] Arvey, "Visits to the Homes," p. 15.

[48] Milan Conservatory records.

[49] Nicholas Baragwanath, *The Italian Traditions and Puccini: Compositional Theory and Practice in Nineteenth-Century Opera* (Bloomington: Indiana University Press, 2011), p. 62.

program, which could be tailored to individual requirements. Puccini, for example, who had already graduated from the Pacini Institute, went straight into the school of "composition proper" in 1880, and was able to compress the four-year course into three years. When Montemezzi took the entrance examination for the third time, in 1896, he so impressed his examiners that he was told he could skip the school of harmony entirely and proceed directly to counterpoint and fugue. This was the first major triumph of his life and must have gone a long way toward compensating for the disappointments and frustrations of the previous two years: he could report with pride that he was now actually further ahead than he would have been if he had simply begun the ten-year program in 1894. Montemezzi would later recall how he met, at the Conservatory, "a young man who had passed that very first [1894] examination when he [Montemezzi] had failed. The young man boasted that by dint of hard work, he had crammed three years of harmony into two."[50] D'Erasmo obviously deserves a good deal of credit for ensuring that Montemezzi was now on level terms.

Montemezzi carried his newfound energy into the Conservatory, which he entered on October 10, 1896.[51] His first teacher there was Michele Saladino (1835–1912), the professor of harmony and counterpoint since 1876, whose widespread fame is gauchely attested to by the young Mascagni: "he is the greatest teacher there is today in Italy for teaching counterpoint and fugue."[52] Saladino was the strict-but-kind type of teacher who expected and rewarded hard work, and Montemezzi was exactly the kind of student he liked: "he [Saladino] immediately took a liking to him [Montemezzi] and the hard work he demonstrated in his studies."[53] Montemezzi later told Arvey that Saladino had "loved [him] very much."[54] The young composer was now extremely ambitious and far from the lazy teenager of a few years earlier. He begged "for four lessons a week instead of two," and Saladino, who prided himself on the toughness of the curriculum, demanded to know why:

Mr. Montemezzi said he'd tell him later, meanwhile growing thinner and thinner. (He had fallen victim to malaria under the strain of so much work.) His teacher [Saladino] noted this condition and sternly reprimanded him

[50] Arvey, "Visits to the Homes," p. 15.
[51] Milan Conservatory records.
[52] David Stivender (ed. and trans.), *Mascagni: An Autobiography Compiled, Edited and Translated from Original Sources* (White Plains, NY: Pro/Am Music Resources, 1988), p. 10.
[53] Silvestri, "Vita e opera," p. 20.
[54] Arvey, "Visits to the Homes," p. 15.

THE APPRENTICE COMPOSER, 1875–1900   23

that he could not be responsible for his health, again asking why he wanted to undertake so much. This time Mr. Montemezzi told him that he intended to go into high composition [*composizione propriamente detta*] the next year. He was told that it was impossible, whereupon he said he *would* do it, with or without help.[55]

Montemezzi's desire to move through the program as quickly as possible doubtless reflects both his awareness that he was behind his contemporaries (he would have been surrounded by younger students) and knowledge of the financial sacrifice his parents were making to allow him to study. His determination carried all before it, and after a year of intense work he was able to pass the exams necessary to enter the school of composition proper.

The statement just quoted is the only reference we have found to Montemezzi's having contracted malaria in 1896. Malaria was "widely regarded as the 'Italian national disease,'" and in the late 1800s, "two million [Italians] were infected, reinfected, or superinfected annually": tens of thousands died.[56] Although it did not, initially, slow Montemezzi down, it may explain why, after working exceptionally hard in his early twenties, he subsequently chose to live at a much less hurried pace—he almost certainly had a fear of reinfection, which was popularly associated with stress. He was not a man of robust health, and this early malaria infection may explain too why he was always remarkably slim, apparently never gaining weight.

Nicholas Baragwanath has published an exhaustive study of the sort of musical training Montemezzi would have obtained from Saladino, and the reader needing a detailed, technical account should refer to that.[57] The aspirant composer would have encountered both traditional "pratico" methods involving the learning of counterpoint through singing and harmony through playing, as well as "teorico" methods, imported into the Italian system from France and Germany, that involved the study of textbooks and writing out of exercises. Montemezzi remembered Saladino above all for the solidly conservative nature of his ideas:

He believed in the sanctity of the three fundamental chords. And as long as his pupils could say their say in these, according to his judgment, he

---

[55] Arvey, "Visits to the Homes," p. 28.

[56] Frank M. Snowden, *The Conquest of Malaria: Italy, 1900–1962* (New Haven, CT: Yale University Press, 2006), pp. 3, 15.

[57] Baragwanath, *The Italian Traditions*, especially pp. 140–87.

24 SUCCEEDING PUCCINI

discountenanced any others. They were to be the immovable ground-work on which they built the structure of their compositions. Harmonic sophistries he refused sternly to tolerate.[58]

Institutional changes were on the side of the impatient student. There was a feeling at the Conservatory that the composition course was too long, and in 1898 it was reduced to six years, with three three-year programs that could be taken concurrently.[59] This change affected Montemezzi, ensuring that he could graduate after three years of composition proper, something he possibly wanted to do in any case. His teacher in these years was Vincenzo Ferroni (1858–1934), who, unusually for an Italian composer of his generation, had studied at the Paris Conservatoire under Massenet and Augustin Savard, while also teaching harmony there.[60] In 1888, he became Professor of Composition at the Milan Conservatory, where he remained for the rest of his career. Ferroni was an active and talented composer with three substantial achievements behind him. In 1885, his *Hymne d'un pâtre Lydien* won an international music competition organized by the French newspaper, *Le Figaro*, which had attracted over 600 entries. In 1890, his opera *Rudello* came in third in the Casa Sonzogno competition famously won by *Cavalleria rusticana* and was published and performed. And his second opera, *Ettore Fieramosca* to his own libretto, brought out at the Teatro Sociale, Como, on January 25, 1896, was again a considerable success. At this stage, it appeared that Ferroni could become a leading light in the larger cultural movement concerned with assimilating modern French influences, especially Massenet, into Italian music, though his career as a composer subsequently declined to the point where, at the time of his death, he was remembered almost entirely as a teacher. In his teaching, he was heavily influenced by his French training; his successful *Corso di Contrappunto e Fuga*, giving some insight into his teaching methods, was published after his death by Ettore Pozzoli.

Montemezzi's relationship with Ferroni is something of a mystery. According to Serafin, "[h]e was a favorite of his composition teacher, Ferroni, who recognized his genius, I believe."[61] But this high appreciation of Montemezzi's merits clearly took time to develop, and if it was expressed

---

[58] Peyser, "'Let simplicity..,'" p. 3.

[59] Baragwanath, *Italian Traditions*, p. 320, n. 51.

[60] The fullest account of Ferroni and his music is Marco Ranaldi, *Vincenzo Ferroni* (Potenza: Edizioni Ermes, 1994).

[61] Serafin, "Italo Montemezzi," p. 10.

THE APPRENTICE COMPOSER, 1875–1900   25

at all, was probably with the benefit of hindsight. Whereas Montemezzi had consistently received very high scores from Saladino, 9.5, 9.5, 9, for his first three terms at the Conservatory, under Ferroni his scores immediately dropped to 8.5, 8.75, 8.75, slightly rising in 1898–1899 to 9, 8.5, 9.25, before plummeting in 1899–1900 to 6.25, 7, 7.5, giving an average of just 6.91 for his final year.[62] Ferroni was a strict assessor and gave other students comparable or lower scores; nevertheless, it is difficult to believe he was recognizing genius. His report at the end of this final year stated: "Clear and musical ideas although not very manly. Study does not kill him. Student with a very modest character."[63] Not surprisingly, perhaps, Montemezzi spoke more, and more fondly, of Saladino than Ferroni in later life.

Montemezzi would subsequently insist that he was largely self-taught in the area of orchestration; given that he was judged a modest man, these claims need to be taken seriously. The fullest statement of the case we have found occurs in Herbert F. Peyser's report of 1919:

[Peyser asks:] Instrumentation? Of whom acquired? Under whose guidance had developed that faultless calculation and combinative skill that effected the woven gold, the glistening fabric of the "Three Kings"?

[Montemezzi answers:] "Of nobody! Under no guidance. Or, rather, under the teachings of my observation alone, and the intuition of my judgment. And in the theater, not the class-room. It is true I had a textbook—a little pocket treatise that I bought for a few cents and that, consequently, gave me very little of what I wanted. But my real lessons in orchestration I got at the Scala, up in the gallery, where I climbed night after night, perching directly over the orchestra, listening and watching. That gallery was my schoolroom; I had no other."[64]

In what appears to have been another interview given in America, Montemezzi remarked similarly:

most of what I know I learned in the gallery at La Scala, as with my very good eyesight I was able to watch the orchestra in the pit from a distance, while hearing at the same time the effects that it produced. Perhaps you will

---

[62] Milan Conservatory records.
[63] "Idee chiare e musicali sebbene poco virili. Non l'uccide lo studio. Allievo modestissimo di carattere." Milan Conservatory records.
[64] Peyser, "'Let simplicity...'," p. 3.

26 SUCCEEDING PUCCINI

be surprised by this, but the truth is I have never read the famous treatise by Berlioz, nor any other.[65]

Given this repeated emphasis on his Scala education, it is useful to catalog what Montemezzi could have seen there. In the 1896–1897 season: *Götterdämmerung, Andrea Chénier, Don Carlo, I puritani, La sonnambula, La Bohème*, and a new opera by Alberto Franchetti, *Il signor di Pourceaugnac*. In the 1898–1899 season (there was no 1897–1898 season): *The Master Singers of Nuremberg*, Mascagni's *Iris*, Meyerbeer's *The Huguenots, Falstaff*, Massenet's *Le roi de Lahore*, and *William Tell*. In 1899–1900: *Siegfried, Otello, Lohengrin*, a new opera by Cesare Galeotti, *Anton, Tosca*, and *Eugene Onegin*. And in 1900–1901: *La Bohème, Tristan und Isolde*, Mascagni's *Le maschere*, Goldmark's *Queen of Sheba, L'elisir d'amore, Mefistofele*, and *Messaline* by the English composer Isidore de Lara. In the last three of these seasons, all the operas were conducted by La Scala's new artistic director, Arturo Toscanini. Montemezzi was particularly impressed by Wagner's operas, which became a lifelong passion.

Montemezzi's visits to La Scala were closely linked to the most important friendship he established in his student years: that with Tullio Serafin (1878–1968). They presumably met soon after Montemezzi's admission to the Conservatory, for they took some of the same classes, and quickly became close friends. The friendship lasted until Montemezzi's death, after which Serafin wrote movingly: "Italo Montemezzi was to me an intimate friend, an associate in music for over half a century, and a real brother."[66] Serafin, almost exactly three years younger than Montemezzi, was born into a family of modest means in the small village of Rottanova near Venice, today a subdivision of Cavarzere.[67] In 1889, just turned eleven, he was able to enter the Royal Conservatory to study the violin, viola, and composition. After two years there, he realized his family was finding it difficult to fund his studies, and consequently made a brave decision to try to support himself. As a talented teenager, he sought out and obtained a wide variety of musical employment in Milan, playing the piano at dancing parties and theatres, working as

[65] This statement appears (in Italian) in the unsigned biographical note on Montemezzi included in the program of the 1938 Teatro Reale dell'Opera revival of *La nave* (n.p.). It is there said to be taken from "an American music magazine," but we have been unable to identify the source and the text given here is thus, necessarily, a translation from the Italian.

[66] Serafin, "Italo Montemezzi," p. 10.

[67] Biographical details about Serafin are from Teodoro Celli and Giuseppe Pugliese, *Tullio Serafin: il patriarca del melodramma* (Venice: Corbo e Fiore, 1985).

a church organist, making up chamber groups with amateur musicians, and accompanying the singers in the vocal school. He was more extroverted and worldly-wise than Montemezzi, and the latter must, one assumes, have been impressed by the sheer range of Serafin's musical activities and his ability to support himself through them. Most significant for Serafin's future career was his work for the vocal school, which involved accompanying extracts from operas, and gave him access to the library of vocal scores. This led him to develop, at a very early age, an ambition to conduct operas, and it is not fanciful to imagine him discussing his career plans with Montemezzi: conversations doubtless recalled by both men when, in later life, Serafin conducted a whole series of Montemezzi premieres and important revivals. Having graduated with a diploma in the viola in 1898, Serafin was offered a contract as the principal viola in the La Scala orchestra, now under Toscanini. He worked there for three years, during which time he also completed his composition diploma. When Montemezzi "perch[ed] directly over the orchestra, listening and watching," he could see his friend down in the pit.

Serafin probably introduced Montemezzi to some of the practical realities of opera production, too. In the first half of 1898, before his graduation, under the anagrammatic alias Alfio Sulterni, he conducted an amateur performance of *L'elisir d'amore*. It is very likely that Montemezzi attended, and quite possible that he was more deeply involved. While playing under Toscanini, Serafin conducted a second amateur performance as Alfio Sulterni, this time of *Don Pasquale*.

A number of Montemezzi's earliest compositions have survived, all related to his Conservatory studies, mostly among the Donadelli family documents. Either he was scrupulous about preserving some of his juvenilia, or this music was simply left behind, and perhaps forgotten, in Vigasio. There are even a couple of fugue exercises, one of which explicitly records its occasion as "Esame di fuga a porte chiuse. Milano, 3 luglio 1898" (Examination in fugue behind closed doors. Milan, July 3, 1898), and his success in this Conservatory examination earned Montemezzi a second-grade award and the corresponding copper medal.[68] More interestingly, there is also a possible single attempt in piano music: a C-major, two-part *Scherzo* (*Allegro*), based on a playful pattern of five quaver notes completed by a Trio, surprisingly in A major. However, since two other piano scores are actually sketches for symphonic movements (of the *Sinfonia in E minor*, discussed below), it is

---

[68] The certificate is preserved among the Donadelli family documents.

28 SUCCEEDING PUCCINI

possible this *Scherzo* was also conceived as preparatory material for a more ambitious symphonic work. The Milan Conservatory archive preserves the first movement, *Allegro*, of an A-major *Sonata per piano e violino*, the title tellingly indicating that the piano is the dominant partner. The sonata rests on a passionate, animated theme of a Romantic character, consistent with Mendelssohn's model, immediately revealed by the violin. Before the recapitulation, it incorporates a fairly extensive intermezzo in C major, the whole work revealing a very fine, spontaneous, melodic inspiration.

The Conservatory archive also contains an intriguing F-major, four-voice spiritual madrigal, opening with the line "Mi soccorri, o madre" (Succor me, O Mother), imploring the Virgin's Mary protection against Satan. The text is the Italian version of Pope Leo XIII's Latin prayer "Ardet pugna ferox, Lucifer ipse viden." Published as early as 1886, this popular prayer was reprinted on several occasions, at least until 1905. Montemezzi's setting does not respect the sequence and ignores two of the fourteen lines of this *sonetto* with Dantesque echoes; indeed, the young composer decided to start with the direct (and therefore overtly dramatic) plea to the Virgin Mary commencing in the middle of the fourth line. Incomplete and scattered with corrections, the manuscript reveals its educational purpose through such explicit comments as "7ª di dominante senza preparazione" (unprepared dominant seventh). Another F-major madrigal, among the Donadelli family documents, "Ornando, come suole" (Adorning, as it usually does), is apparently a four-voice setting of the text composed by Orlando di Lasso as a six-voice madrigal and that appears in his collection *Madrigali: a quattro, cinque et sei voci* published in Nuremberg in 1587.

Another, more noteworthy group of the young Montemezzi's compositions are a few songs for voice and piano designed to test the composer's attitude to setting a text—part of the standard training of a composer-to-be at the Conservatory. Two of the lyrics are by Antonio Ghislanzoni (1824–1893), the poet mainly remembered as the librettist of *Aida*. Not by coincidence, the young Puccini had also set, in 1881–1882, four lyrics from the same collection of Ghislanzoni's *Melodie per canto* (1881; second revised and enlarged edition, 1882) in which Montemezzi found his texts. The first lyric Montemezzi chose, *Il canto di Mignon*, starting "Vedeste mai quel paese gentile" (Have you ever seen that gentle country), had been inspired by Goethe's celebrated "Kennst du das Land" sung by Mignon in *Wilhelm Meisters Lehrjahre* (Example 1.1). Goethe's song expresses the character's longing for the beautiful country (Italy)

Music Example 1.1 *Il canto di Mignon*, bars 1–19.

in which she had grown up. Ghislanzoni's Italian version has been set by several composers, including Pietro Bianchini, Francesco Paolo Frontini, Luigi Malferrari, Alberto Sarti, and, in 1888, by Toscanini. Montemezzi's composition, explicitly for a soprano, is very different from both Frontini's melancholic setting and Toscanini's more dramatic conception. He offers a limpid, G-major version in 6/8 (Bianchini and Frontini chose 9/8), suggestive of light-hearted innocence. The voice flows naturally, discretely supported by two chords per bar, until the mention of babbling water and a gentle breeze activates a rocking piano accompaniment, maintained for

30 SUCCEEDING PUCCINI

the second and third stanzas. The other Ghislanzoni setting, *Una croce in camposanto* (A cross in the cemetery), a lyric first published in 1877, had been previously set by Enrico Loschi, Ponchielli, and Mascagni. It is a much more concentrated, dramatic study of a funereal subject (a night visit to a dead lover's tomb), and Montemezzi succeeds in exploiting, through a limited range of musical gestures (frequently repeated tones), his feeling for harmony, anticipating what would emerge as one of the main concerns and qualities of his music. A third song, "Se un giorno mi vedrai, angelo pio" (If you see me one day, pious angel), takes a text from *Le mie canzoni: Poesie per musica* (1886) by Angelo Bignotti (1863–1923), a journalist, theatre critic, and librettist. This pathetic outburst of a poet venting his spleen on some unspecified girl is set by Montemezzi as a G-minor, *Lento* movement, again based on a limited expressive range, often employing repeated notes, and with ostinato patterns in the accompaniment.

A definite step toward opera can be seen in the three dramatic scenes, or monologues, the young Montemezzi set, one of which survives as both a vocal and full orchestral score. Again, this was a contemporary praxis exemplified by Puccini's *Mentìa l'avviso*, his setting of an extract from an old libretto by Felice Romani as a final exam for the composition class in 1883. Montemezzi resorted to an equally old-fashioned text for his tenor piece, "Qui attenderla in segreto" (Secretly waiting for her here), from *Leonora* by the Neapolitan librettist Marco D'Arienzo (1811–1877), composed by Saverio Mercadante in 1844. Montemezzi set Oscar Muller's jealous monologue (the Scena and Cavatina from Act 3, Scene 4), sung as he waits for an important meeting with Leonora, whom he is going to marry against her will, fearing she loves another man. Montemezzi provides a plain, predictable, but inspired and effective setting as a D-minor *Andante*, introduced by a fluent accompaniment (doubtless to be entrusted to the strings) and raising the tension (*Mosso*, then *accelerando* and *crescendo*) as doubts surface in Oscar's mind. The Cavatina itself displays a regular *Moderato* movement, with a somewhat solemn line for the voice, consistent with the character's attempted confidence.

Another scene for tenor voice is preserved in the Milan Conservatory archives as a working sketch followed by a fair copy of the vocal score: doubtless an examination paper, since the student excuses himself on the cover for the hasty instrumentation caused by the hurry and specifies that the string quartet should come in at a certain point. This is taken from a much more modern libretto, *I Burgravi* by the Sicilian playwright Stefano Interdonato

(1845–1896), which had been composed by Carlo Podestà and first performed in 1881. Montemezzi's text, "Fosco ... ei chiamommi ... io lo credeva ignoto" (Fosco ... he called me ... I thought it unknown), is taken from the opening scene of Act 4, set in an ominous cellar at night. Magno il maledetto ("the cursed"), the defeated burgrave of Heppenheff, is haunted by the thought of Fosco, the brother he killed, whose name Emperor Frederick mysteriously brought up at the end of the previous act. Montemezzi's setting of this overtly Romantic ghost scene (one might think of the young Verdi's *I masnadieri* from 1847) opens with a haunting *Lento* introduction providing an appropriate tension for the *Mosso* entrance of Magno's voice, boisterously performing the lines Montemezzi decided to start with (eight lines of general considerations regarding Magno's situation are omitted) to an ominous, *pianissimo* orchestral accompaniment. The pace goes back to *Lento* (but now 3/4) at "Oh, rimorso," to a syncopated strings accompaniment, while an expressive melody on the clarinet is called up to evoke Fosco's "larva funesta" (menacing ghost). Interestingly, Montemezzi does not strictly distinguish between the Scena and the ensuing Cavatina, "O mio fratel, dal gelido" (O my brother, from the cold), freely setting the lines sometimes in a more lyrical and sometimes in a more recitativo-like manner. He does, though, follow the stage direction detailing Magno's behavior in front of the ghost, culminating in the plea for Fosco's forgiveness and concluding with the dramatic dialogue with the inner voice accusing him of fratricide.

A third scene, entitled *Gelosia*, this time for soprano voice, is Montemezzi's earliest dated original composition, presumably contemporary with his examination fugue from July 1898, for it is dated to the academic year 1897–1898, and almost certainly represents the final essay of that year. Both a vocal and full orchestral score have been preserved (Figure 1.2). Although labeled a "Scena," it does not appear to derive from a libretto, but is rather a poem of unknown origin, made up of eight stanzas of six-syllable quatrains, though somewhat irregular, at least as Montemezzi set it. The female speaker laments her jealous suspicions as she awaits her lover on a balcony on a snowy winter night, a situation oddly anticipating features of both *L'amore dei tre re* and *L'incantesimo*. The text is more lyrical than dramatic, but its melodramatic language is not far from that of opera librettos. The orchestral score reveals something of Montemezzi's ambitions at this early stage of his career. He exploits the full symphony orchestra by emphasizing contrasting sound worlds, such as the grand, boisterous E-flat-major full orchestral opening, the sudden shrinking to the bare chords of the strings just for the second

32 SUCCEEDING PUCCINI

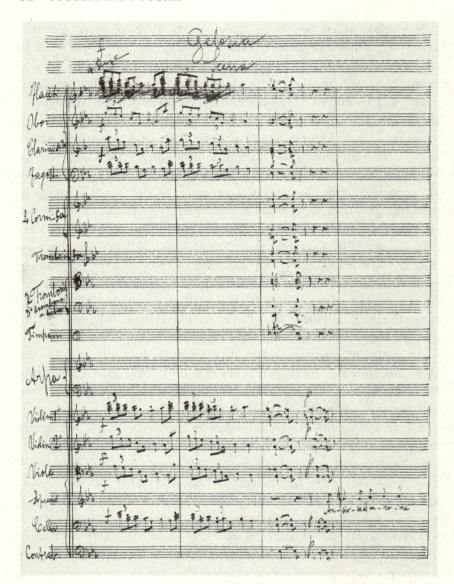

Figure 1.2 The dramatic scene *Gelosia*, 1898. *Donadelli family documents.*

stanza, and the clarinet solo introducing the third stanza, evoking the lateness and the snow, with all the strings muted, and first violins divided. Mutes are lifted for the more dramatic fourth stanza concerning the lady's sorrow, with clarinet and viola introducing the voice, and the orchestral activity

THE APPRENTICE COMPOSER, 1875–1900   33

becoming more and more hectic, reaching an expressive climax at the end of the fifth stanza. The soprano (and the orchestra with her) then rests for a moment, as if stunned by her grief. The overall soundscape is pulled back to *piano* until the harp and a solo violin on the background of divided violins and clarinet announce, *pianissimo* and *leggerissimo*, the happy conclusion to this anxious wait. Tellingly, the young Montemezzi exploited the dramatic potential of a basically lyrical text, relying heavily on the resources of the symphony orchestra.

In his second year under Ferroni, 1898–1899, Montemezzi composed a substantial three-movement *Sinfonia in E minor*. The composition of a symphony had become standard practice for French composers in the 1870s and 1880s, and it is noteworthy that Ferroni himself composed a Symphony in E-flat in 1887, at the end of his Parisian period, and that D'Erasmo, who had studied under Ferroni a few years earlier, composed a *Sinfonia in E minor* as his graduation work. Montemezzi's *Sinfonia* is in three movements, rather than the traditional four—César Franck's Symphony in D minor was one model he could have cited for the aberration—and comprises a 74-page 6/8 *Allegro*, a 28-page G-major *Adagio* in common tempo, and a 30-page (not including the recapitulation of the *Scherzo*) D-major *Allegretto vivo*, also titled *Scherzo* in blue pencil. Overall, it is sound in its construction, carefully crafted, and a convincing demonstration of the young composer's ability to handle the symphony orchestra. Stylistically, though, it is quite uneven. The opening *Allegro*, propelled by an impassioned, relentless drive, is probably the most indebted to Romantic and late Romantic models, from Mendelssohn's *Scottish Symphony* to Dvořák's *New World Symphony*, the latter, unmistakably echoed, also in E minor. Although not totally free from the influence of *Lohengrin*, the *Adagio* displays much more originality in its effective, personal rendering of a contemplative mood. The *Allegretto vivo*, concentrating on the exploitation of a single pervading rhythm introduced right away, displays a modern flavor typical of French symphonic music after 1870 that was immediately recognized at the first performance.

Montemezzi himself conducted the *Adagio* and *Allegretto vivo* at a Conservatory concert on June 12, 1899, the first known performance of any of his music. It is not clear why just these two movements were played: perhaps the young composer had not yet completed the *Allegro*, or perhaps he was allowed only so much space in the program. Whatever the reason, it was an auspicious debut. Giovanni Anfossi (1864–1946), himself a composer, reviewed the concert for Casa Ricordi's *Gazzetta Musicale di Milano*

34 SUCCEEDING PUCCINI

and reported that it was well attended and well received. His review contains what appears to be Montemezzi's first published critical notice:

> Italo Montemezzi limited himself to the orchestral field only. . . . He made us hear the *Adagio* and the *Scherzo* from his *Sinfonia in E minor* for orchestra. The *Adagio* is neat and correct, with a slightly aristocratic (*piuttosto aristocratica*) pace. It succeeds very happily with the well-arranged and balanced string quartet. Perhaps the exaggerated and prolix central development is detrimental to the elegant simplicity, the fluency, and the refinement of its form. However, the flaw, if it exists, can be easily remedied and the many merits [of the work] make it excusable. The *Scherzo* is lively and eccentric. In it, the rhythm, perhaps slightly overused by modern symphony composers, finds a way to become interesting for its originality in the *Trio*.
>
> The composer conducted his own work remarkably well.[69]

Montemezzi's graduation work was a cantata entitled *Frammento del Cantico dei Cantici di Salomone* (Fragment of The Song of Songs of Solomon). Scored for soprano, mezzo, female chorus, and orchestra, it sets a passage from the poetic version of the biblical Song of Songs (Song of Solomon) by Carmelite friar Evasio Leone (1765–1821). First published in 1787, Leone's dramatized presentation of the most mysterious book in the Old Testament, in the form of a dialogue between the Bridegroom and the Bride, with various choral parts, had proved very popular, and was also available in anthologies such as the *Poesie bibliche tradotte da celebri italiani* (1834). Montemezzi chose a short section corresponding to Song of Songs 8:5–7, commencing with a chorus of maidens, already arranged by Leone as *Cantata decima*, the last of ten dramatic units.[70] This involves the Bride, the Bridegroom, a chorus of maidens, and the Bridegroom's friends—though the last named, being silent, could be ignored. Montemezzi's setting omits no less than thirty-two lines of recitative before "Basta non più. Que' teneri trasporti" (No more. Those tender transports), but the main structure is preserved, consisting of a choral opening, a lengthy dialogue in recitative, and two arias for the Bride, the second of which Montemezzi divided into

---

[69] Giovanni Anfossi, "R. Conservatorio di Musica di Milano," *Gazzetta Musicale* 54/24 (June 15, 1899): p. 297.

[70] For the text Montemezzi set, see Evasio Leone, *Il Cantico dei Cantici* (Milan, 1818), pp. 151–63.

Music Example 1.2 *Frammento del Cantico dei Cantici di Salomone*, bars 457–473.

an aria and a concluding duet for the couple. The woodwinds establish a rocking, pastoral opening setting (3/4, *Moderato*, G major) introducing the four-voice (two sopranos, two altos) female chorus, a plain setting of the two stanzas, sparingly employing imitation and counterpoint. An E-major pastoral orchestral interlude involving woodwinds and strings creates the setting for the Bride (soprano) and the Bridegroom (mezzo) to intertwine their dialogue. The soprano moves to D-flat major on a sophisticated muted strings accompaniment, then to A major, until the concepts of "death" and "jealousy" introduce the brass, silent until then, leading to a noisy episode pervaded by an obsessive dactylic rhythm. The first soprano aria is sumptuously orchestrated, whereas the second, limited to a single stanza, is a much simpler F-major aria. The cantata culminates in a mainly homophonic two-voice *Largo*, fading in the *pianissimo* postlude (Example 1.2).

In 1899, Giuseppe Gallignani, director of the Conservatory, had persuaded Toscanini, then at the end of his first Scala season, to sit on the Conservatory's examination board for students graduating in composition. Having presumably found the experience satisfactory, in 1900 Toscanini not only sat on the examination board but volunteered to conduct two concerts of works by graduating students, on June 21 and 28.[71] In the first of these, an orchestra of Conservatory students, supplemented by a few professionals,

---

[71] Harvey Sachs, *Toscanini* (London: Weidenfeld and Nicolson, 1978), p. 73.

36 SUCCEEDING PUCCINI

played the *Frammento* under Toscanini's baton. The concerts were again reviewed by Anfossi, who was notably less enthusiastic about the *Frammento* than he had been about the previous year's *Sinfonia*:

> The *Frammento* . . . has some picturesque and delicate episodes, some lyrical fits overflowing with passion, but it doesn't have a very solid structure, nor is there much connection between text and music. A greater literary culture in particular, and artistic culture in general, could allow Montemezzi's talent to compose better thought out and also more heartfelt works. The orchestral part, sometimes deafening, is not up to the melodic inspiration, which at certain moments is precious and seductive.[72]

The opening chorus was published as *Coro di donzelle* by the Fantuzzi company of Milan, becoming, it would seem, Montemezzi's first published music.

Having obtained his diploma, Montemezzi was uncertain what to do next. According to Silvestri, he found himself asking "what did it [the diploma] serve him for? To teach, to conduct, or to compose?" and experienced "more than one hesitation" before finding "the right track" (*la via giusta*).[73] The "right track" turned out to be composing operas, and by the end of the summer of 1900, it appears Montemezzi had made at least a provisional decision to take a cautious step in this direction.

---

[72] Giovanni Anfossi, "R. Conservatorio di Musica di Milano. I saggi finali," *Gazzetta Musicale di Milano* 55/26 (June 28, 1900): pp. 356–57.

[73] Silvestri, "Vita e opera," p. 21.

2

"The temperament of a born
opera composer"

Bianca and *Giovanni Gallurese*, 1901–1905

In 1865, Vincenzo Bonetti of Bologna left a legacy to fund an opera competition at the Royal Conservatory, Milan. Falling victim to the political convulsions of the time, this was not given royal approval until 1870; then, after further mind-numbing delays, it was ratified as funding for a competition in 1879. An annual prize of 500 lire was offered for "the most beautiful opera in the genre of our Rossinian, Bellinian, and Donizettian traditions" (*la più bella opera nel genere delle nostre tradizioni Rossiniane, Belliniane, Donizettiane*) written by a "young composer."[1] Submissions were judged by a committee of five, selected from the teaching staff. Initially, the Conservatory stipulated that only current students were eligible, and, emphatically, that any student who had completed the composition course could not enter, even if still taking other classes.[2] However, by the 1890s the rules had been relaxed, and former students were allowed to submit an entry in the year after their graduation. Alberto D'Erasmo, Montemezzi's tutor, had taken advantage of this and won the prize in 1895, and it may well be that he first alerted Montemezzi to the possibilities of the competition. For the academic year 1900–1901, Montemezzi took a position as a teacher of harmony at the Conservatory and set about composing an opera for the competition. He must have completed *Bianca* by May 30, 1901, the submission deadline; his manuscript full score survives, along with a separate libretto.[3]

The libretto of *Bianca* is by Giuseppe Zuppone Strani (1858–1940), a well-established poet, translator, and journalist, and notable friend of Giovanni

---

[1] *Raccolta Ufficiale delle Leggi e dei Decreti del regno d'Italia. Anno 1870. Dal N° 5444 al 6206* (Florence: Stamperia Reale, [1871]), p. 944. The decree is dated May 15, 1870.
[2] *Raccolta Ufficiale delle Leggi e dei Decreti del regno d'Italia. Anno 1879. Dal N° 4685 al 5217* (Rome: Stamperia Reale, [1880]), p. 1349.
[3] Donadelli family documents.

Succeeding Puccini. David Chandler and Raffaele Mellace, Oxford University Press. © Oxford University Press 2025.
DOI: 10.1093/9780197761373.003.0003

38 SUCCEEDING PUCCINI

Pascoli. It tells the story of how Bianca, daughter of the Duke of Ferrara, and the pageboy Balduino pledged their love for each other ten years before the represented action; he planted a small linden tree as a symbol of that commitment. After ten years of exile, Balduino now returns as the Marquis of Monferrato to claim his bride, but Bianca no longer recognizes the gentle pageboy in the cruel Marquis, mostly interested in his own glory. When Balduino proves persistent, Bianca orders a forester to fell the linden tree. The blows of his axe produce moans from the tree, echoed by the surrounding forest, and have a palpable physical effect on Bianca; when the tree dies, so does she. The flimsy plot is obviously a pretext for this final *mise-en-scène*, apparently derived, rather oddly, from Tasso's story of Tancredi and Clorinda in *La Gerusalemme liberata*, itself with a source in Virgil's story of Polydorus. It is not clear how much, if any, influence Montemezzi had on the choice of subject, so the possibility can be advanced only with caution that this is the first evidence of his desire to break with the dominant veristic and bourgeois traditions of opera around 1900 in favor of the medieval, aristocratic, and poetic. Nevertheless, it is perfectly possible that the young composer first fell in love with the libretto, then decided to enter the competition.

Montemezzi would have known that Alfredo Catalani and Antonio Smareglia especially, in the previous generation of Italian opera composers, had been attracted to this sort of subject, more akin to German Romanticism, and the former's *Loreley* (1890) was a particularly obvious model. The direct influence of German Romanticism seems almost certain, in fact. Zuppone Strani clearly knew Carl Maria von Weber's epochal operas *Der Freischütz* (1821) and *Euryanthe* (1823), for he had published a short story in which Weber's music plays a central role.[4] Moreover, his near-contemporary libretto *Ondina*, set by Gianni Bucceri (1872–1953) in 1902, treats the same favorite Romantic myth of water nymphs as E. T. A. Hoffmann's seminal *Undine* (1816).[5] From such Romantic traditions, Zuppone Strani took his folk atmosphere, magic associated with nature (nodding back to Tasso), love in its different shades, and hunting as a general frame for a drama which, apart from the tragedy, can be defined as a forest idyll. While some features of the libretto are quite plainly backward-looking, it is worth noting that the intimate, somehow magical belonging of humans to the comprehensive life

---

[4] Giuseppe Zuppone Strani, "Coro di Cacciatori nell'"Euryanthe,"" *Gazzetta Letteraria* 15/40 (October 3, 1891): pp. 314–16.

[5] Bucceri's *Ondina* was finally staged at the Teatro di San Carlo, Naples, on March 29, 1917.

of nature was a feature of contemporary symbolist culture, found, for example, in Dvořák's opera *Rusalka* (1901) and Gabriele D'Annunzio's *Alcyone* (1903), the breakthrough collection of nature idylls that includes the celebrated "La Pioggia nel Pineto."

The libretto of *Bianca* aims at conciseness and is effectively organized through distinct numbers (the corresponding scenes given here in parentheses):

1. Bianca's aria (1)
2. Offstage bridal chorus
3. Bianca and Ricciarda's dialogue (2)
4. Balduino's arrival with his hunting party (3)
5. Bianca's aria (4)
6. Ricciarda and Balduino's dialogue (5)
7. Balduino's aria (6)
8. Interplay between the Wedding Party, Bianca, and Balduino (7–9)
9. Bianca and Balduino's Duet (10)
10. Appearance of the Wedding Party (11)
11. Epilogue: Bianca, Balduino, the Forester, and the felling of the linden tree (12)

Bianca, involved in six of the eleven numbers, is clearly the pivotal character, strategically controlling the entire development of the opera. In her opening monologue, she establishes the whole dramatic situation, leaving us in no doubt about Balduino's past and present moral character long before he appears. She is nearly always on stage, leaving briefly only to let Balduino introduce himself, both on his own (no. 4) and with Ricciarda (no. 6), Bianca's sister, who is represented as her rival (though as Bianca has lost interest in Balduino, the rivalry goes nowhere). Both the main characters introduce themselves in the first portion of the opera (nos. 1–4); their current situation is set out more deeply in the central area featuring their principal arias (nos. 5–7); the climax is reached as they eventually interplay (nos. 8–9) until the fleeting reappearance of the bridal party (no. 10) leads to the tragic epilogue (no. 11).

Bianca, Balduino, and Ricciarda have the naïveté and rigidity of stock fairy-tale types—Zuppone Strani was clearly very attracted to the style of fairy tales—and there is no actual character development, nor, until the very end, any *coup de théâtre*. Despite these limitations, Montemezzi was

40 SUCCEEDING PUCCINI

able to create a remarkable small-sized opera, approximately forty minutes long, in which music gives dramatic life and plausibility to Zuppone Strani's situations and elementary characters. He achieved this goal with three basic strategies: the invention of a small but effective number of leitmotifs; a vivid dramatic use of instrumental color; and the organization of the score through dramatic areas of contrasting atmosphere.

The leitmotifs and orchestral color are closely connected and strongly influence the entire organization of the opera, offering a very early demonstration of Montemezzi's care and taste for orchestral writing, which he regarded as central to the performance of dramatic values. This was a predilection to which he would remain loyal for the rest of his career, and arguably his most personal signature on contemporary Italian opera. Montemezzi's discriminating taste for orchestral color is displayed immediately in *Bianca*'s short but effective prelude. The straightforward exposition of the main theme of the opera, connected with Bianca's love, is entrusted to first and second violins and violas "singing" on octaves an inspired lyrical phrase in *lento*, C-sharp minor, to the harp's lofty accompaniment (Example 2.1). The exact meaning of the theme is revealed as Bianca addresses the tree in the crucial Scene 4 with the words "O sacro tiglio, ahimè!" (O sacred linden tree, alas!), announcing her tragic awareness that she and the tree are bound by fate, and "qui moriranno insieme" (here they will die together) if Balduino betrays her love. The theme resonates again in the confrontation between the two lovers, and at the end of the opera, as the forester fells the tree and we hear the laments of an offstage female chorus (following the stage direction: "Each blow to the tree is reflected not only in the hearts of the two young people, but elicits moans from the tree itself, as if from a living organism. The forest replies with all its echoes. As the linden tree falls, a crash of desperation explodes in the forest, expressing with its many voices the death of the tree"[6]).

Returning to the prelude, an evocative 2-bar bridge performed by the horns leads to a second significant theme, accompanying the curtain rise: this explicit hunting signal in *Allegro*, performed by two horns offstage, establishes the forest setting and, at the same time, evokes Balduino's character. It ushers in a dramatic G-minor, full-orchestral page, based on insistent

---

[6] "Ogni colpo dato all'albero non solo si ripercuote nel cuore dei due giovani, ma strappa all'albero stesso lamenti come a cosa viva. La foresta risponde con tutti i suoi echi. Allorché il tiglio cade, uno schianto di disperazione scoppia nella foresta che piange colle sue molte voci sulla morte dell'albero."

Music Example 2.1 *Bianca*, bars 1–10.

42 SUCCEEDING PUCCINI

triplets and dotted triplets, accompanying Bianca's entry (Example 2.2). Though not quoting any specific motif from the *Ring*, the motivic invention has a strong Wagnerian tinge, exploiting patterns that recall the youthful vitality of Siegfried's Horn and the tension of the Mime-as-Smith motif. A third instrumental color is soon supplied by the oboe and English horn, and this becomes the most significant timbre in the score, occasionally recruiting the bassoon as well. It is associated with the tender, sorrowful character of Bianca, accompanying her presentation aria (Example 2.3) and introducing her G-minor lament, "Il dì ch'ei volse ai sogni miei le terga" (The day he turned his back on my dreams), in Scene 4. Balduino's soliloquy addressing the linden in Scene 6 is similarly introduced by an oboe–English horn duet. The oboe theme from Bianca's presentation aria resonates again in the lengthy, quiet, pathetic introduction to Scene 8 as she gently offers the bride (an undeveloped character, outside the main action) a bracelet, bidding her pray for her, Bianca, who will never know the happiness of marriage. The oboe surfaces again in the dramatic duet in Scene 10, where Bianca states that her only joy lies in the past, when a youth pure as a lily was her lord.

Bianca makes her initial appearance with a bipartite aria ("Sacra foresta"). The first, more complex part, recalling the entire story of her relationship to Balduino, has a central *Poco agitato* section referring to his present violent habits and proposing a new theme connected with Balduino's cruelty to deer and fawns, metaphorically pointing to his unworthiness (Example 2.4). The second part—*Andante moderato* in an enthusiastic G major—celebrates the past joy of their shared childhood as an ascending line in *crescendo* translates the intense longing for the forest, the "genitrice onnipossente e buona" (mother, omnipotent and good), and the "singing" (*cantando*) violins exalt the memory of their promise to live as though in a romantic dream. Bianca's most important contribution comes, however, after her effective confrontation with Ricciarda, in the grand scene and aria in Scene 4, when she directly addresses the linden tree in a beautiful lyrical melody enhanced by sensitive orchestration.

Balduino's aria in Scene 6, concentrating on the emptiness of a life without love, addresses the linden tree in an atmosphere (created by oboe and English horn, as noted above) recalling Bianca's affinity with nature. Before the actual aria, "Chiama, o verde tiglio" (Call, O green linden tree), starts, its restrained but effective lyricism accompanied by muted strings, Balduino evokes the tree's vast shadow and foliage. Here the orchestra performs an apparently explicit reference to the Forest Murmurs (*Waldweben*) motif in

Music Example 2.2 *Bianca*, bars 28–37.

Siegfried; this is supported by a hard-to-read pencil comment which appears to be "Wald*" (Example 2.5). The motif which opened the opera introduces both Scenes 9 and 10, in which we reach the tense confrontation between the two principal characters, both passionate, albeit not sharing the same object. Bianca sublimates her impossible love in the linden tree, and all dialogue ends with her abrupt question, "Chi ti conosce?" (Who knows you?), on a *fortissimo* orchestral chord.

The chorus has a role both dramatically and musically significant. It stands for the happiness promised by conjugal love, inaccessible to Bianca. Moreover, it contributes to establishing the dramatic rhythm, shifting

44 SUCCEEDING PUCCINI

Music Example 2.3 *Bianca*, bars 40–55.

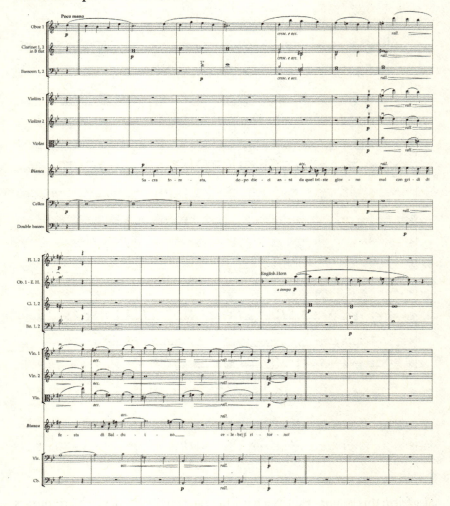

Music Example 2.4 *Bianca*, bars 74–81.

Music Example 2.5 *Bianca*, bars 400–445.

the action from Bianca's first soliloquy to her dialogue with Ricciarda; interplaying with Bianca and Balduino; and in its brief, dreamlike, final appearance, poignantly restating the joy of love, it provides a bridge to the epilogue. Musically, the mostly euphoric tone of the chorus provides welcome variety, contrasting with the dramatic moods of the solo episodes, which are accordingly sharpened by the juxtaposition. The most significant choral episode is certainly the Wedding Party's joyful appearance in Scene 7, when a brief, beautiful symphonic interlude introduces a chorus of peasants that recalls, in its fresh, pastoral, G-major *Allegretto*, famous scenes from *Le nozze di Figaro* and *Der Freischütz*. The peasants dance around the linden tree and throw bouquets, setting the scene for the crucial confrontation between Bianca and Balduino.

46 SUCCEEDING PUCCINI

Montemezzi would have been justified in feeling he had achieved something substantial, and circumstances were propitious, for according to Arthur Pougin, who quizzed him about his career in 1914:

> There were only two competitors, but his [Montemezzi's] rival quit at the last minute. Great joy! Our man naturally thought he would be the winner, and that he would pocket the 500 francs. But it did not happen quite like this: in the end, the prize was not awarded, and he received only 400 francs as an encouragement.[7]

Conservatory records confirm that the amount of 400 lire was awarded, as does Giuseppe Silvestri, who adds, probably on Montemezzi's authority, that in 1900 this was enough to live on for six months.[8] Given the absence of any competition, it was hardly an encouraging start to Montemezzi's operatic career, and his failure to win the full prize is somewhat puzzling—unless *Bianca* was simply judged too remote from the Italian tradition that the competition was designed to promote.

The composition of *Bianca* apart, the only anecdote from Montemezzi's year as a teacher of harmony concerns his paying his respects to Verdi, whose death on January 27, 1901, seemed to symbolize the end of an era. The great composer, having died at the Grand Hotel in Milan, was laid out there for three days before the funeral on January 30. At some point in those three days, Montemezzi, who had wanted to meet Verdi but never managed to do so, "begged" the lawyer in charge of the funeral arrangements for a "glimpse of the body." "[T]he lawyer agreed. He sent the young man in and allowed him to stay for five minutes, alone."[9]

At the end of the academic year 1900–1901, Montemezzi's employment terminated. There is nothing in the Conservatory records to suggest this was anything but a voluntary relinquishing of the position—a conclusion supported by the fact that he appears to have made no further attempts to obtain teaching work, unlike most of his contemporaries. Montemezzi found teaching either uncongenial or incompatible with his ambitions to compose. From this date, in any case, he adopted the mostly relaxed life devoted

---

[7] Arthur Pougin, "Semaine théâtrale," *Le Ménestrel*, May 2, 1914, p. 139. The Latin Monetary Union of 1865 meant that the franc and lira traded at parity.

[8] Giuseppe Silvestri, "Vita e opera: vocazione e volontà," in *Omaggio a Italo Montemezzi*, edited by Piergiorgio Rossetti (Vigasio: Amministrazione Comunale di Vigasio, 2002), p. 21.

[9] Verna Arvey, "Visits to the Homes of Famous Composers No. XIV: Italo Montemezzi," *Opera and Concert*, November 1948, p. 28.

to music which he maintained, with slight interruptions, for the next five decades; as suggested in the previous chapter, his experience of malaria in 1896 may have affected the decision. A 1905 report said Montemezzi had "retired to Vigasio . . . to study in the tranquility of the countryside."[10] He later told David Ewen that he had "lived in semi-seclusion, working hard on his compositions."[11] Much of 1902 was to be devoted to the composing of a new opera for submission to a competition organized by Casa Sonzogno, the second of Italy's music publishers, but at the time of his "retirement" it is not clear whether Montemezzi knew there would be such a competition.[12] Not that it matters very much: if he were contemplating a full-time career as a serious composer, there was no alternative to writing a successful opera.

Sonzogno announced their competition in December 1901: for a one-act opera by a composer who had not had an opera professionally produced. It was the fourth such competition. The first (announced 1883, concluded 1884) is remembered almost entirely because Puccini's *Le Villi* failed to obtain even an honorable mention. By contrast, the second competition (announced 1888, concluded 1890) changed operatic history, for the winner was *Cavalleria rusticana*, with Ferroni's *Rudello* one of the runners-up, as noted in the previous chapter. The immediate and enduring success of Mascagni's opera obviously encouraged further competitions. However, the third competition (announced 1890, concluded 1893) added no new work to the operatic repertoire, and after the experiment had been pursued for a decade, it was glaringly apparent that *Cavalleria rusticana* was the only opera vindicating the expense and trouble incurred by the publisher. Discouraged, Sonzogno announced no further competitions in the nineteenth century, and when they relaunched the idea in 1901 the format was different: an international competition with the grand title "Concorso melodrammatico internazionale." Massenet was appointed president of the judging committee, and a mouthwatering 50,000 lire was offered as prize money (a decade earlier, Mascagni had won just 3,000 lire). The deadline for submissions was January 31, 1903.[13]

---

[10] "Notizie liriche e drammatiche," *La Sera: Giornale politico, finanziario, illustrato*, November 13, 1905, p. 3.

[11] David Ewen, *European Composers Today: A Bibliographical and Critical Guide* (New York: H. W. Wilson, 1954), p. 104.

[12] If Montemezzi had heard of the forthcoming competition it was perhaps through Ferroni who, as a former prizewinner and Sonzogno composer, may have known of the company's intentions.

[13] A useful article on the fourth competition drawn on here is the unsigned "Concorso Internazionale Sonzogno," *Musica e Musicisti* 58/12 (December 1903): pp. 1054–56.

48 SUCCEEDING PUCCINI

There are two quite different accounts of how Montemezzi found his librettist, Francesco D'Angelantonio. The 1905 *Sera* report says that Montemezzi turned for help to "Count Tommaso [*sic*] Castelbarco Pindemonte, who had properties and relations in Vigasio, and always had a keen liking for the young maestro."[14] Though not stated directly, the implication is that the Count's efforts brought about Montemezzi's connection with D'Angelantonio. According to Silvestri, on the other hand, Montemezzi approached Giannino Antona-Traversi (1860–1939), a popular writer of light, satirical comedies, perhaps hoping that the dramatist could be persuaded to write a libretto; Antona-Traversi then put him in contact with D'Angelantonio.[15] If there is some truth to both accounts, it might be concluded that the Count introduced Montemezzi to Antona-Traversi. Montemezzi's aristocratic connection was the Milanese Tomaso Castelbarco Visconti Simonetta (1847–1925), who had married Maria Luisa Pindemonte Rezzonico of Verona in 1880.

Almost nothing is known of D'Angelantonio, an obscure figure from Palermo whose only claim to a footnote in operatic history is that he collaborated with Montemezzi. A subsequent short profile in *Musica e Musicisti* describes him as a "letterato," or scholar, and the accompanying photograph suggests a man in his thirties, or possibly late twenties.[16] No details concerning his background are given, and the main emphasis of the brief article is that he had assisted Montemezzi in the "difficult first step" of the latter's career. The statement that the librettist had "devoted himself to the theatre with great faith" is significant mainly in the sense that the claim was presumably based on information supplied by D'Angelantonio himself. The only physical proof of such devotion at the time of the Sonzogno competition appears to have been a four-act libretto, *Il regno delle ballerine*, which D'Angelantonio had published in 1901, effectively advertising his willingness to collaborate with composers. Subsequent to his work with Montemezzi, he wrote at least three more librettos: *Istoan* (1906), set by Enrico Mineo (1870–1960); *Radda* (1911), set by Alfredo Cuscinà (1881–1955); and *Michette*, an operetta, also for Cuscinà, but never published or performed.

In 1902, Montemezzi made a contract with D'Angelantonio, agreeing to pay 500 lire and five percent of any future profits for a one-act libretto.[17]

---

[14] "Notizie liriche e drammatiche," p. 3.
[15] Silvestri, "Vita e opera," p. 21.
[16] "Francesco D'Angelantonio," *Musica e Musicisti* 60/11 (November 1905): p. 728.
[17] D'Angelantonio to Giulio Ricordi, May 25, 1905. Archivio Storico Ricordi.

These terms, drawn up by two naïve young men, would cause problems later when their opera showed signs of actually being profitable. Silvestri suggests that the libretto D'Angelantonio prepared for the competition was an adaptation of *Il regno delle ballerine*.[18] This is not the case: D'Angelantonio regarded the two librettos as quite distinct and hoped, for some time, that Montemezzi would set both. Nevertheless, the clear parallels between them reveal something of the tenor of his operatic imagination. *Il regno delle ballerine* is a very political libretto, set at the time of the Milanese insurrection in 1848, with Fanny, the prima ballerina at La Scala, competed for by Attilio Bruschini, an Italian poet and political activist, and the Austrian prince Edgardo Pattly, a villainous army officer. *Giovanni Gallurese*, the libretto D'Angelantonio produced for Montemezzi, tells a comparable story, with the heroine fought over by a valorous Italian outlaw and a treacherous Spanish army officer in 1660s Sardinia. D'Angelantonio was clearly a patriot who enjoyed casting Italy's foreign rulers as straightforward villains seeking to ravish Italian women.

It is impossible to say anything for certain about the 1902 *Giovanni Gallurese* except that it was unsuccessful in the Sonzogno competition. It is not even clear what it was called. Assuming that it was very likely in two scenes, following the already classic model of *Cavalleria rusticana*—an assumption supported by the ease with which it was subsequently adapted into a three-act form—it can be conjectured that these scenes roughly corresponded to Acts 1 and 3 of the later full-length opera, a detailed summary of which is given below. Montemezzi spent nine months setting this competition version.[19] In total there were 237 submissions, and the Sonzogno judges initially concentrated on drawing up a short list of twenty operas worth more serious examination. At some point in 1903, and to his intense mortification, Montemezzi was informed that his opera was not on the short list. It is hard to believe he had really staked his career on his ability to win the competition, yet there is no evidence of his composing anything else in these years, and he appears to have genuinely believed that his opera deserved to be successful. He stated repeatedly that the failure was entirely due to D'Angelantonio's libretto. According to Silvestri, Montemezzi "used to say ... that the jury had not even read the score, having already rejected the libretto."[20] As early as 1905, the *Sera* report, clearly drawing on information from Montemezzi

[18] Silvestri, "Vita e opera," p. 21.
[19] Pougin, "Semaine théâtrale," p. 139.
[20] Silvestri, "Vita e opera," p. 21.

50   SUCCEEDING PUCCINI

himself, states: "the Committee of the Sonzogno Competition which had to judge the librettos rejected D'Angelantonio's, so Montemezzi's music was not even submitted to judgement."[21] Montemezzi repeated the claim to Pougin in 1914. He was not a man to make such accusations if unsure of his facts, so it is reasonable to conclude that he had reliable information on the subject. Entries to the competition had to include a separate libretto as well as piano-vocal and orchestral scores, and faced with such a huge pile of manuscripts the judges needed to employ some reasonably quick filtering. Casa Sonzogno was looking for the next *Cavalleria rusticana* and knew that very few operas succeed without a good libretto.

It is worth quoting Pougin's account of what happened next, for though confused, it highlights what appears an odd decision on Montemezzi's part. According to Pougin, the libretto of the competition opera was written by an "unknown poet" of Palermo—politeness, it appears, does not allow him to be named—and:

> Anybody in such a position [as Montemezzi's] may have been tempted to go and strangle the author of such an unfortunate libretto. But Mr. Montemezzi still had faith in its subject. Instead, he contacted a proper librettist, Mr. D'Angelantonio, and urged him to read it. D'Angelantonio agreed to fix this monstrosity, which effectively meant rewriting it from scratch. He prodded the text without compassion, extended it considerably, changing it from one to three acts, and called the transformed result *Giovanni Gallurese*.

Obviously, this is garbled, probably as a result of Montemezzi's imperfect French, but it is easy to see why Pougin was confused. If the one-act libretto was a "monstrosity," why did Montemezzi entrust its author with the task of expanding it? Aside from his "faith in its subject," which may reveal something of his political feelings, there was probably an element of sheer desperation. D'Angelantonio offered to rework the libretto for a very modest 100 lire, and it is most unlikely that Montemezzi could have obtained a three-act libretto from anyone else without a much greater, and very likely unaffordable, financial outlay.[22] He invited D'Angelantonio to come and stay in Vigasio and had him expand and revise the libretto, "according to his [Montemezzi's] plans."[23] The librettist was apparently impressed by Montemezzi's music,

[21] "Notizie liriche e drammatiche," p. 3.
[22] D'Angelantonio to Giulio Ricordi, May 25, 1905.
[23] Silvestri, "Vita e opera," p. 22.

or just by having a composer to work with, and attempted to interest Montemezzi in setting *Il regno delle ballerine* as well. Montemezzi delayed making a decision, but eventually said no, leaving D'Angelantonio with hurt feelings.[24]

The three-act *Giovanni Gallurese* is set in Sardinia in 1662. Giovanni Gallurese is a notable outlaw, having killed a Spanish nobleman who insulted him. He is secretly in love with Maria, the daughter of Nuvis, a miller, whom he has often watched at her work. Rivegas, a Spanish officer, has designs on Maria, and attempts to carry her off with two of his cronies, only to be foiled by Giovanni. The latter, discovering that Maria and her father believe the abductors to have been Giovanni Gallurese and his men, gives them a false name and pretends to be a shepherd (Figure 2.1). When he hears Maria singing of her love for him—she has seen him watching her in the past—he reveals his own love, and Act 1 ends on a note of rapturous mutual understanding. Act 2 begins with a festive scene outside a makeshift inn. Giovanni arrives and he and Maria are ecstatically reunited, but then he hears Rivegas denouncing Giovanni Gallurese the outlaw, and telling of how he, Rivegas,

Figure 2.1 Stage picture of Act 1 of *Giovanni Gallurese*, Teatro Dal Verme, Milan, 1905. *Chandler collection.*

---

[24] D'Angelantonio to Montemezzi, March 20, 1905. Archivio Storico Ricordi.

52   SUCCEEDING PUCCINI

had saved Maria from an attempted abduction. Giovanni's friend Bastiano reveals the truth and Rivegas, publicly humiliated, and realizing Giovanni is there, hurries off to get soldiers to arrest him. There is a fierce battle between Giovanni's men and the Spaniards, watched by an amazed Maria; the Spaniards lose, and Rivegas is captured, but he reveals Giovanni's true identity to Maria, who flees in horror. In Act 3, the outlaws taunt the captured Rivegas before Giovanni describes the ideal of "Liberty" that inspires his actions. The other outlaws want to kill Rivegas, but Giovanni insists he be allowed to go free. Maria, who has watched all this, now declares her continuing, unconditional love for Giovanni, and the ecstatic lovers plan to emigrate. Rivegas, however, having obtained a gun, shoots Giovanni from behind before attempting to rape Maria. Maria, following Giovanni's instruction, manages to sound his horn three times: this summons his followers, who kill the Spaniard. Giovanni dies, his final words expressing love for Maria and lamenting Sardinia's lost liberty.

As Lara Sonja Uras has argued, *Giovanni Gallurese* is an intriguingly hybrid libretto, partly veristic, partly a restoration of the Verdian historical costume drama. Sardinia, an impoverished, backward part of Italy, with a colorful folklore, was becoming a popular setting for operas, probably above all because of the influence of *Cavalleria rusticana* and its Sicilian context: Uras counts at least seventeen librettos with a Sardinian setting between 1892 and 1934, six of them from the 1890s.[25] She shows that D'Angelantonio took the essence of his story—that an outlaw opposed to the Spaniards called Giovanni il Gallurese loved a miller's daughter in the 1660s—from Enrico Costa's historical chronicle *Sassari* (1885), itself based on the *Historia cronológica* (1672/1673) by the Capuchin monk Jorge Aleo.[26] She also suggests the influence of Marco Falgheri's opera *Maricca*, which has a Sicilian setting, but as *Maricca* was only premiered on October 8, 1902, the chronology is complicated: there may just be a coincidence of ideas here.[27]

Despite his inexperience, D'Angelantonio organized his libretto effectively. Act 1 neatly, if conventionally, introduces the three main characters, with the proper action starting only when the presentation is complete. Acts 2 and 3 are unified in time, taking place during the festival and its immediate

---

[25] Lara Sonja Uras, "Un personaggio per Italo Montemezzi. Giovanni Gallurese tra storia e mito," in *Scapigliatura e Fin de Siècle: Libretti d'opera Italiani dall'Unità al primo Novecento*, edited by Johannes Streicher et al. (Rome: ISMEZ, 2006), p. 558.

[26] Uras, "Un personaggio," pp. 561–62.

[27] Uras, "Un personaggio," p. 558.

aftermath. They are, however, set in different locations: the opera ends with the same setting as Act 1, giving the action an additional sense of compactness, a possible legacy of its original one-act form. The overall atmosphere is of ongoing warfare—announced immediately in the brass fanfare of the prelude—as in Verdi's *Trovatore*, and in this *Giovanni Gallurese* anticipates *L'amore dei tre re*. Apart from Nuvis, all the male characters carry weapons, and are always eager to fight. The cast itself is all male, apart from Maria, and Montemezzi provides an immediate and explicit symbolic characterization, with the young and heroic Sardinians, Giovanni and Bastiano, both tenors, while the Spanish roles are entrusted to three baritones and two basses (the only exception to the scheme is the bass Nuvis, on account of his age). However, despite the action-packed plot, the opera does not actually rest on action. Notwithstanding the physical threats to Maria, and the continuous conflict between the Spaniards and Sardinians, a large part of the drama is devoted to contemplative solos and lyrical duets, stimulating Montemezzi's congenial inspiration. It is easy to agree with Alan Mallach that "the character of the work is more lyrical than dramatic."[28]

The setting, the barren Sardinian landscape, is no neutral background, for it plays a major role in the drama. The Sardinian characters partake of the authenticity of a beautiful, peaceful, rural world. As the curtain rises after the brief prelude (Act 1, no. 1), the orchestra conveys a sense of stillness and tranquility, a sophisticated combination of muted strings, oboes, and clarinets producing immobile patterns (repeated notes, regular, syncopated rhythms) which linger as Giovanni enters, forming a background to his solo, which promptly mentions the eternal calm of the Tuffudesu mountain region in northern Sardinia. The drama will return to this "calma eterna," free of human suffering, at the very end of the opera.[29] D'Angelantonio and Montemezzi borrow from the opening of Act 3 of *Tosca* the touch of *couleur locale* provided by a folk song sung offstage by a boy's voice, replacing the Roman stornello with a "nenia sarda" immediately associated with the real-life atmosphere of bells ringing, progressively magnified by winds and strings, in a very interesting symphonic amplification of a folk tune. The soundscape here plunges the action into an enchanted, timeless, almost fairy-tale atmosphere (not that distant from *Bianca*'s), not really belonging to history. Though this might sound incongruous given the realistic subject,

---

[28] Alan Mallach, *The Autumn of Italian Opera: From Verismo to Modernism, 1890–1915* (Boston: Northeastern University Press, 2007), pp. 431–32.

[29] Montemezzi, *Giovanni Gallurese* (vocal score) (Milan: Ricordi, 1905), p. 308.

54 SUCCEEDING PUCCINI

it is worth recalling that *Cavalleria rusticana* itself significantly displayed much less realism than its literary source.

Giovanni Gallurese is centered on a typical operatic love triangle, not unlike that of *Tosca*. The pivotal character is undoubtedly the title role. Giovanni is the type of the melancholic outlaw with Romantic period roots, a sort of depressive Ernani. At the outset, he contrasts nature's peace with his own inner turmoil in a vast, complex, five-part monologue, finally attaining a lyrical, inspired, soaring melodic idea corresponding to the contemplation of Maria's home. He bids a painful farewell to her, intertwined by the voices of oboe and clarinet, and passionately supported by the triplets in the strings (Example 2.6). Overall, the monologue displays a remarkable amount of negativity: contemplating the dawn, Giovanni calls Sardinia the "terra del dolore" (land of grief) and describes his own life as "miseranda" and "angosciosa" (anguished).[30] He utters excessively romantic and gloomy reflections later in Act 1, and we even hear his voice offstage considering suicide, "Sì, vo' morir" (Yes, I wish to die) (Act 1, no. 17),[31] as he resumes the depressive, descending syncopated motif, later taken up *forte* by the strings, first stated in his pessimistic reflections on life—"la vita che val?" (what's life worth?) (Act 1, no. 6).[32] Act 3 offers more room for politics: Giovanni, facing Rivegas, devotes a warm peroration to the cause of liberty, his charges against the Spanish exemplified in a procession of Sardinian refugees crossing the stage. Like Cavaradossi in *Tosca*, Giovanni exalts liberty against tyranny in a rhetorical outburst, made more comprehensible by the withdrawal of orchestral accompaniment (Act 3, nos. 10–11). The libretto was modified to make this more dramatic: the refugees whom Giovanni describes as dispersing in "estranie contrade" (foreign lands) in the libretto,[33] more tragically "si dissolve nel nulla" (dissolve into nothing) in the score.[34] The chorus, solemnly supported by the trombones, responds to Giovanni's aggressive defiance with a hymn to liberty that is missing in the libretto, "Libertà, il sogno inebriante de la vita" (Liberty, the intoxicating dream of life).[35] Giovanni's very last thoughts and words concern not Maria, but Sardinian liberty—"la sarda . . . libertà!!!"—and he dies lamenting that liberty will die with him.[36]

[30] Montemezzi, *Giovanni Gallurese*, pp. 5, 9.
[31] Montemezzi, *Giovanni Gallurese*, p. 37.
[32] Montemezzi, *Giovanni Gallurese*, p. 13.
[33] Francesco D'Angelantonio, *Giovanni Gallurese* (libretto) (Milan: Ricordi, 1905), p. 36.
[34] Montemezzi, *Giovanni Gallurese*, p. 260.
[35] Montemezzi, *Giovanni Gallurese*, pp. 269–70.
[36] Montemezzi, *Giovanni Gallurese*, p. 311.

Music Example 2.6 *Giovanni Gallurese*, Act 1, no. 7, bars 1–8.

Giovanni's rival, Rivegas, is a descendant of the Count of Luna and Scarpia in his unequivocal display of lust. In his very first solo, roughly organized like Giovanni's, and mainly expressing exaltation, he imagines Maria sleeping in her bed, "nudo l'eburneo seno" (naked her ivory breast), then experiences a

Music Example 2.7 *Giovanni Gallurese*, Act 1, no. 9, bars 1–3.

feeling of "frenesìa" when she appears.[37] He is given a specific military connotation in Montemezzi's music, his arrival announced by a wind fanfare, soon extended to the strings, describing the movement of the Spanish troops. This important rhythmic pattern (Example 2.7) unifies the entire scene, still resounding twenty pages later when Rivegas's solo is over, closing this warlike episode before dramatic interest shifts to Maria.

Maria is first heard singing from the garden in front of her humble house, like a distant siren. Her fascination derives from her innocence, notwithstanding the incongruously high literary register—somewhere between Giacomo Leopardi's *Canti* and D'Annunzio's *Poema paradisiaco*—that D'Angelantonio lends this presumably illiterate daughter of a miller in her hymn to the dawn and sun, and later in her Act 1 duet with Giovanni. The much more appropriate musical motif Montemezzi conceived for her is introduced by the clarinet, immediately taken up *piano ed espressivo* by the violas, then by Maria in her tribute to the virgin goddess Aurora, and later, significantly, repeated by the oboe (so much associated with the heroine of Montemezzi's earlier opera), aptly expressing the character's delicate but passionate character (Example 2.8). The final scene of Act 1, culminating in Maria's duet with Giovanni after he has saved her from Rivegas, abounds with expressive motifs in the orchestra: the evocative melody of the English

---

[37] Montemezzi, *Giovanni Gallurese*, pp. 22, 26.

Music Example 2.8 *Giovanni Gallurese*, Act 1, no. 13, bars 2–4.

Music Example 2.9 *Giovanni Gallurese*, Act 1, no. 34, bars 1–9.

horn as Giovanni encourages the half-fainting Nuvis to get up (Act 1, no. 20); the broad oboe melody supporting the dialogue between Nuvis and Maria (Act 1, no. 21); the dramatic unison motif which could be labeled "fear of Gallurese" (Act 1, no. 22); the intense chromatic motif connected to the couple's love resounding in the orchestra as Maria momentarily bids farewell to Giovanni and enters the house (Act 1, no. 28); and Giovanni's desperation motif immediately following (Act 1, no. 29). The final confrontation between the lovers includes Giovanni's bright and confident G-flat romance, "M'era gioia mirar l'amato viso" (It was my joy to gaze at the beloved face) (Example 2.9), followed by a further lyrical moment prior to the very end of the act, "Ne l'occhio tuo nerissimo, profondo" (In your eyes, dark, profound), no. 38, a quiet, C-major melody which Lawrence Gilman later judged, somewhat harshly, as "of incredible triteness and commonness."[38]

Act 2 demonstrates Montemezzi's ability to manage simultaneous actions in different places. It combines two settings, crucial in conveying the characteristic Mediterranean atmosphere so successfully exploited in *Cavalleria rusticana*: the tavern and the church (Figure 2.2). The goal of picturesque realism, later given physical form in the acclaimed sets by Vincenzo Rota

---

[38] Montemezzi, *Giovanni Gallurese*, pp. 73, 82; Lawrence Gilman, "A New Opera at the Metropolitan: Montemezzi's 'Giovanni Gallurese,' for the First Time Here," *New York Herald Tribune*, February 20, 1925, p. 13.

Figure 2.2 Set design for Act 2 of *Giovanni Gallurese*, Teatro Dal Verme, Milan, 1905. *Archivio Storico Ricordi*.

and Mario Sala and costumes by Giuseppe Palanti,[39] is highlighted by the inclusion of the choral song to the moon in Sardinian dialect. As ever, the orchestra plays a vital role from the very opening of the act, accompanying the young people's dance with a *tarantella* rhythm entrusted to the strings, opposed by the military dotted-rhythm in the winds. A tambourine adds to the folk flavor.[40] Montemezzi frames this opening scene, combining sung dialogue, dance, and choral singing, with a varied reprise of the opening tavern conversation, not envisioned by the librettist. As Giovanni enters, his dialogue with Maria is then combined, in an even more virtuosic way, with the hymn to St. Anthony coming from the church, the conversation between Rivegas and his men—Rivegas slandering Giovanni and boasting of saving Maria and being rewarded by her—and Nuvis's and Bastiano's

---

[39] "Il successo del 'Giovanni Gallurese' del M.° Italo Montemezzi," *L'Arena*, January 30–31, 1905, p. 2.

[40] A 1923 article in *L'Unione Sarda* praised the authenticity of the musical setting: "the orchestra skillfully recreates the typical Sardinian country dance accompanied by an accordion." Quoted in Uras, "Un personaggio," p. 558.

Music Example 2.10 *Giovanni Gallurese*, Act 2, no. 8, bars 8–13.

minor, worried interventions from the tavern. The complexity of this grand, three-level action, contrasting the sacred and secular, meant that the printed libretto had first to divide the page into two columns and then change its orientation to render the simultaneity of the action more easily comprehensible.

The two lovers indulge in a long, warm, exuberant duet, opened by Maria's broad, lyrical melody "Or ti guardo e mi sento" (Now I look at you and feel)—Montemezzi notably omitting the "Ma" (but) opening the line (Example 2.10).[41] The melody is later taken up by Giovanni in his "Tu sei l'almo riposo" (You are the wonderful peace), Act 2, no. 9,[42] before culminating in a two-voice section, harp and timpani enhancing a *crescendo* leading into a modulation to G-flat major (Act 2, no. 10). Montemezzi's clever orchestration in the ensuing passage is worth remark, ranging as it does from the rise in tension provided by the full orchestra, to the effective imitation of laughter, to the very sparse instrumentation designed to make the dialogue as comprehensible as possible. After a reprise of the choral hymn combined with José's comments on Giovanni's appearance—Montemezzi's interest in the interaction between crowd and individual possibly influenced by *Boris Godunov*[43]—the procession leaves the church, singing a pseudo-liturgical four-voice hymn. In this context of contrasting sounds, Giovanni bursts out with a passionate, lyrical melody, trying to inspire confidence in Maria, "Sovra il mio sen la fronte tua" (On my chest your brow) (Example 2.11).[44]

If the first part of Act 2, much admired by contemporary critics, is complex spatially, the second is scarcely less so, offering the interesting stage situation in which Maria and Nuvis observe and comment on the offstage fight

---

[41] Montemezzi, *Giovanni Gallurese*, p. 124.

[42] Montemezzi, *Giovanni Gallurese*, p. 128.

[43] Later in his career, many critics discerned the influence of Mussorgsky on Montemezzi's music, especially in Act 3 of *L'amore dei tre re*. *Boris Godunov* received its Italian premiere at La Scala in 1909, but Montemezzi may well have become acquainted with the score earlier.

[44] Montemezzi, *Giovanni Gallurese*, p. 196.

Music Example 2.11 *Giovanni Gallurese*, Act 2, no. 23, bars 16–19.

between Giovanni's men and the Spaniards, followed by Giovanni's proclamation of liberty from the top of the hill (an iconic moment responded to enthusiastically by the first audiences) before the final *coup de théâtre*, as Rivegas reveals Giovanni's true identity to Maria, who immediately lets go of her lover with a scream of terror. The fight is effectively translated into a vast, hectic, E-minor *Allegro molto animato* symphonic page (Act 2, no. 31) which paints the scene Maria is observing for the audience. Giovanni's proclamation of liberty when the fight is over offers a strong contrast with its lyrical, full-voice hymn sustained only by woodwinds and horns, a combination Montemezzi often exploits in this score. After the increasing tension animating the dialogue between Maria and Giovanni, a novel Elsa anxiously inquiring about the identity of her Lohengrin, the very end of the act is undoubtedly less effective, Rivegas revealing Giovanni's true identity amidst laughter before a D-minor *Largo* leads to the fall of the curtain.

Dusk is falling on an eventful day as Act 3 starts immediately afterward, with no extended prelude. Maria's sorrowful feelings are expressed through a desolate, step-by-step, F-minor melody performed by the English horn. The motivic invention keeps close to her theme from Act 1 in her dialogue with Nuvis (Example 2.8) until the lyrical outburst on "Care viole, sola or mi vedete" (Dear violets, you see me alone): conversation with nature allows her to express herself freely, through a plain, repeated-note melody with an idyllic counterpoint of oboe and English horn.[45] The core of the act, however, is the big reconciliation duet between the lovers, suggestively on the verge of inescapable tragedy. Both text and music echo the exchange between Aida and Radamès in Act 3 of *Aida*, but with the dramatic situation reversed: here it is Giovanni who proposes flight from a dangerous situation, and Maria yields only after some hesitation. The encounter opens with Maria's "O luce! O gloria" to an enthusiastic *Allegro con molto slancio* played by the full orchestra, and culminates in the F-sharp major melody of "Un giardin di viole pur t'aspetta" (A garden of violets awaits you), with which Giovanni convinces Maria to flee, supported by the discreet counterpoint of oboe and clarinet.[46] It was presumably Montemezzi's idea to combine this with the offstage farewells of the refugee convoy, for there is no trace of this stereophonic complexity in the libretto. From here the emotional temperature continuously increases, shaping a last, remarkable lyrical sanctuary parallel to those of Act 1 and 2, establishing Montemezzi's habit of granting his lovers a duet in each act. This last duet culminates in the hymn "Esuli andremo" (We go as exiles), sung homorhythmically at the distance of an octave by the lovers, who have now attained a perfect coincidence of goals.[47] Here the *a due* singing of text and music from the central part of the duet resumes with settled determination and enthusiastic orchestral support, crowned by a B-major section, and attaining a final, emphatic high B at the distance of an octave on "Fuggiamo i perigli" (Flee the perils) (Example 2.12).[48]

After the duet, the epilogue arrives suddenly, bringing possibly excessive, somewhat confused action. Rivegas shoots Giovanni (as happened to the Marquis of Posa in *Don Carlo*); Maria blows Giovanni's horn (an echo of *Ernani*?); Rivegas, after a struggle, abducts Maria; she is freed by Giovanni's men; and Rivegas is killed offstage. Only in the theatre, presumably, would the mortally wounded Giovanni wait until the conclusion of this in order to die. He desperately clings to the loyal Bastiano and admits the hopelessness of his situation in an A-minor *Lento*, both strings and woodwinds performing grieving, descending gestures. A beautiful episode with an intimate, chamber atmosphere anticipates his decease: solo cello and oboe start a sorrowful dialogue on a repeated pattern until the English horn introduces Giovanni's "Tutto finì!," opening his final speech with near sacred solemnity.[49] The calm

[45] Montemezzi, *Giovanni Gallurese*, p. 237.
[46] Montemezzi, *Giovanni Gallurese*, pp. 280, 290.
[47] Montemezzi, *Giovanni Gallurese*, p. 295.
[48] Montemezzi, *Giovanni Gallurese*, pp. 299–300.
[49] Montemezzi, *Giovanni Gallurese*, p. 308.

62 SUCCEEDING PUCCINI

Music Example 2.12 *Giovanni Gallurese*, Act 3, no. 32, bars 1–5.

pace of his last, disillusioned thoughts, deprived of real melodic appeal, is animated by the obsessive lament of the violins continuously playing at the distance of an octave, supported by a constant, melancholic strain provided by flutes and clarinets, the whole string section muted (Example 2.13). The libretto ends with an excessively lengthy stage direction commenting on the natural setting against which Giovanni has died, presenting Leopardi-influenced considerations on how the fascinating stillness of Nature betrays a tragic indifference to the woes suffered by humankind.

The autograph full score of *Giovanni Gallurese* in the Archivio Storico Ricordi notably offers, after the final bar, an alternative finale. After Giovanni dies, Maria embraces her father, tells him she is determined to follow her lover, and throws herself off a cliff. The curtain falls as Nuvis mechanically, and in vain, tries to restrain her. We have found no evidence of this alternative ending actually being used.

As he worked on expanding *Giovanni Gallurese*, Montemezzi no doubt retained an embittered interest in the Sonzogno competition. In January 1904, the three finalists were announced: Franco da Venezia's *Il Domino azzurro*, Gabriel Dupont's *La cabrera*, and Lorenzo Filiasi's *Manuel Menendez*. All three were staged at the Teatro Lirico, Milan, and Dupont's opera was judged the overall winner. Montemezzi may have been more struck by Da Venezia (1876–1937) claiming the third prize, for they had been contemporaries at the Royal Conservatory, Da Venezia had been the joint winner of the Bonetti prize in 1899, and for the Sonzogno competition he set

Music Example 2.13 *Giovanni Gallurese*, Act 3, no. 37, bars 8–13.

a libretto by Zuppone Strani. Although Montemezzi cannot have known it at the time, a number of other composers destined for future fame had failed, including Zandonai, Pizzetti, and Delius. It was no disgrace to have lost in such company. What he would have known is that Puccini was the ultimate beneficiary of the first Sonzogno competition, even if he was not the winner. There are some very suggestive correspondences between the fates of *Le Villi* and *Giovanni Gallurese* that suggest Montemezzi may have been deliberately trying to follow in Puccini's footsteps. Indeed, perhaps the biggest difference between the two stories is that while Puccini was largely borne along by events, Montemezzi had to shape his own destiny, with the older composer's experiences to guide him.

In March 1884, Puccini learned that *Le Villi* (then called *Le Willis*) had been unsuccessful in the Sonzogno competition. Early the following month,

64 SUCCEEDING PUCCINI

his librettist, Ferdinando Fontana, organized a select musical party, including journalists, to hear Puccini play through the score at the piano. Those present, including Arrigo Boito, were so impressed that a collection was immediately begun to allow the opera to be staged—the estimated cost being 450 lire. This allowed a performance to be mounted at the Teatro Dal Verme, Milan, on May 31, and on June 8 it was announced that Casa Ricordi had bought all the rights to *Le Villi* and had commissioned a further opera from the young composer.[50] The publisher then persuaded Puccini and Fontana to expand their opera into its two-act form.

An obvious difference in Montemezzi's case is that he undertook the hard work of expanding his opera before making any attempts to publicize it. By early 1904, *Giovanni Gallurese* was complete, at least in short score, and in mid-February—the month after the competition winners were announced—he organized a small private concert in Verona at which he played through his opera on a piano. The reception was very positive. Music critics from the leading Verona newspapers, *L'Adige* and *L'Arena*, were invited, and both gave the concert excited reviews, the latter writing that the audience "listened to his [Montemezzi's] fluent, fresh, spontaneous, often touching and sentimental music, at first with curiosity, then with interest, and finally with enthusiasm."[51] A week later, it was announced that "friends and admirers" of the composer had raised "a considerable sum" to mount a performance of the opera at the Teatro Ristori, Verona, and that Montemezzi would be offering another private performance of the score, perhaps in an effort to find more support, though in the end this seems to have been delayed until November.[52] The distinguished singer Emma Carelli (1877–1928) was said to have accepted the role of Maria.

At this point, the fortunes of *Giovanni Gallurese* seemed to be closely following those of *Le Villi*, but here, apparently, Montemezzi hesitated, probably wondering, with good reason, whether the sort of Verona performance envisaged was really the best way to launch the opera. He decided to turn to Serafin for advice. Having learned what he could under Toscanini, Serafin had commenced his extraordinary six-decade career as one of Italy's leading conductors in 1902, and Montemezzi doubtless assumed his friend knew a

[50] Michele Girardi, *Puccini: His International Art*, trans. Laura Basini (Chicago: University of Chicago Press, 2000), pp. 22–23.
[51] Fox, "Il M.° Italo Montemezzi," *L'Arena*, February 19–20, 1904, p. 3. See also Siegmund, "Giovanni Gallurese," *L'Adige*, February 16, 1904, p. 3.
[52] "Il Melodramma del Maestro Montemezzi al Ristori," *L'Arena*, February 26–27, 1904, p. 3.

BIANCA AND GIOVANNI GALLURESE, 1901–1905   65

good deal more than himself about the practicalities of launching operas. Serafin later recalled:

> I had already started to conduct and was under the wing of [Luigi] Piontelli, a noted impresario, when Italo Montemezzi hunted me out of the music world of Milan and asked my opinion of his *Gallurese*. In the name of our friendship, would I give him a frank estimate of it? Reading it, I was pleased with its value, which was apparent; and I listened carefully while he played the score through on the piano, singing all the parts. I spoke to Piontelli right away. "We'll put it on," he told me, "but you and Montemezzi have to get 7,000 *lire* to cover preliminary expenses." Now, 7,000 *lire* . . . wasn't impossible, but Montemezzi was distressed when he heard how much was needed.[53]

Silvestri's account, derived from Montemezzi, emphasizes a detail that Serafin modestly omits: Piontelli agreed to produce the opera on the basis of Serafin's judgment concerning its value.[54] Silvestri describes Montemezzi as "surprised and scared" by the demand for an advance payment, which he again specifies as 7,000 lire. If this was Piontelli's original demand, however, Montemezzi and Serafin were able to negotiate it down, or at least adjust the terms, so that in the end 6,000 lire (in 1904 equivalent to roughly $1,200) was paid in three installments, but the composer was also liable for the supply of 600 librettos. Montemezzi later reported that he "recognized the justice" of Piontelli's conditions while still finding them "rather unusual."[55] Providing a subsidy to an impresario had been relatively common in the past,[56] but the only other major composer of Montemezzi's generation who commenced his career in this particular self-financing way appears to have been the wealthy Ermanno Wolf-Ferrari (1876–1948), who paid 10,000 lire to have his first opera, *Cenerentola*, performed at the Teatro La Fenice, Venice, in 1900.

Jutta Toelle's study of the Italian impresario system in the late 1800s concludes that Piontelli (died 1908) was "by far the most successful impresario in the last twenty years of the nineteenth century."[57] The 1890s saw

[53] Tullio Serafin, "Italo Montemezzi—An Appreciation," *Opera News*, January 19, 1953, p. 10.
[54] Silvestri, "Vita e opera," p. 22.
[55] Quoted in Maurice Halperson, "How 'Gallurese' Saved an Impresario from Bankruptcy," *Musical America*, February 21, 1925, p. 3.
[56] Mallach, *The Autumn of Italian Opera*, p. 81.
[57] Jutta Toelle, *Oper als Geschäft: Impresari an italienischen Opernhäusern 1860–1900* (Kassel: Bärenreiter, 2007), p. 97.

66   SUCCEEDING PUCCINI

him at the peak of his career. He had developed a close working relationship with Casa Ricordi, where he was regarded as the best in the business and was entrusted with such important premieres as *Falstaff* and *La Bohème*. Around 1900, Piontelli began edging toward retirement, and Montemezzi encountered him at the very end of his career, for the 1904–1905 season proved his last. He treated Montemezzi in a friendly, fostering way and was a very important figure in the young composer's life for several months.[58] The short, handwritten contract he drew up and signed on September 19, 1904, mainly concerned with specifying the financial terms, undertook to stage the opera "during the next season at the Teatro Vittorio Emanuele in Turin with artists to be chosen from among those engaged for the other operas to be staged at the same opera house—same orchestra and identical chorus," and also reserved the right to stage the work at two further opera houses should it prove successful.[59] Serafin would conduct. Although this would be far more expensive than organizing a single performance in Verona, the advantages were clear: *Giovanni Gallurese* could potentially have a long run in a major theatre under the management of a well-connected impresario.

How Montemezzi raised the necessary funds is unclear. Two decades later, he told Maurice Halperson that he had succeeded only with "great difficulty."[60] Silvestri says that Montemezzi approached the music critics of *L'Adige* and *L'Arena* and persuaded them to mount an appeal.[61] We have found no evidence of a printed appeal as such, though, and the critics seem to have confined their public support to very positive notices of the February concert and subsequent events; privately, of course, they may have done much more. Clearly Montemezzi had found a number of financial backers as early as February 1904, and presumably some of these, at least, continued to support him and his opera. The 1905 *Sera* report adds that Montemezzi found in "Count Castelbarco Pindemonte an affectionate ally who, with the friendship and high connections of other generous people, managed to obtain for him the means that allowed *Giovanni Gallurese* to be staged in Turin."[62] This suggests that the Count may have been the biggest single supporter. Count Violini Nogarola, the nephew and heir of Montemezzi's

---

[58] There are several letters between Montemezzi and Piontelli among the Donadelli family documents.

[59] Montemezzi's copy of the contract is reproduced in Piergiorgio Rossetti (ed.), *Omaggio a Italo Montemezzi* (Vigasio: Amministrazione Comunale di Vigasio, 2002), pp. 95–96.

[60] Halperson, "How 'Gallurese' Saved an Impresario," p. 3.

[61] Silvestri, "Vita e opera," p. 22.

[62] "Notizie liriche e drammatiche," p. 3.

godfather, who may have intervened in the composer's career in 1894, was also involved. He organized a second private performance of the score at his home in Castel D'Azzano in late November, collecting together "a large group of kind vacationers and connoisseurs of art."[63] A later report in *L'Arena*, concerning the support given the opera, claims a good deal of credit for the newspaper and names, in particular, Albano Franchini (1852–1915), the owner of the paper and a man with various business interests in Verona, along with Ottorino Cometti and Gedeone Rinaldi, businessmen prominent in local affairs.[64] Altogether, then, it appears that Montemezzi had been able to bring together a wide range of sponsors, from family and friends to aristocratic connections and local businessmen with an interest in promoting Verona.

Montemezzi seems to have been actively involved in the preparation of *Giovanni Gallurese* between the agreement of terms in September and the premiere in January 1905. These involved a great deal of anxiety, for, as he later reported to Halperson, Piontelli's Turin season started badly, and the impresario finally decided to put on Leoncavallo's *La Bohème* as a "last resort": its failure would mean a premature end to the season. Montemezzi believed

> that not even Leoncavallo prayed more fervently in those trying days for the success of "Bohème" than did the humble maëstrino of "Giovanni Gallurese"!
>
> Then matters suddenly changed one day. Piontelli declared he would completely sidetrack "La Bohème" and give my opera instead. "Gallurese" was taken in hand, prepared hurriedly. It is well known that theatrical people are generally superstitious, so my impresario told me that his decision was due to a presentiment which he had that my opera would bring him good luck.[65]

Montemezzi's anxieties were by no means over. The final preparation of *Giovanni Gallurese* was very rushed, and though the principals were ready, the chorus was not. The premiere was scheduled for January 28, a Saturday, and at the dress rehearsal on January 26, Montemezzi was appalled to find

---

[63] "Cronaca Teatrale," *L'Adige*, December 2, 1904, p. 3.

[64] "Il successo del 'Giovanni Gallurese' di Montemezzi a Torino," *L'Arena*, January 29–30, 1905, p. 2.

[65] Halperson, "How 'Gallurese' Saved an Impresario," p. 3.

68   SUCCEEDING PUCCINI

the chorus "singing with the manuscript in their hands."[66] What happened next is recounted by Serafin:

> Frankly, I did not want to conduct a group of singers who obviously did not know their parts. Montemezzi felt the same, but we were young and did not really know what to do. The director of the theatre [Piontelli] told us "Tomorrow, or never," and we became very upset. To go on with it, or not? Worried, we got in touch with Giulio Ricordi, the dean of music publishers. We took the train to Milan at three o'clock in the morning to ask Ricordi's advice. "There is no greater disgrace," he told us, "than to postpone a premiere of a new opera. If it is any way possible, perform it; for if you do not, the public will think the very worst."[67]

The young composer and conductor hurried back to Turin, where they found the chorus had been very proactive about the situation. As Montemezzi reported to Halperson:

> I experienced one of the greatest joys of my life! The chorus sent a delegation to me to say that they were "fire and flame" for my work and that they would study day and night in order to be ready for the first performance. In fact, these good people studied under my guidance faithfully all day Friday, until I could say the saving word: "all is well."[68]

Ugo Tansini (1874–1944), Serafin's deputy on this occasion (and who later conducted *Giovanni Gallurese* himself), subsequently claimed a good deal of credit for convincing Montemezzi and Serafin to go ahead with the premiere.[69]

It was presumably a very drained and anxious Montemezzi who took his place in the Teatro Vittorio Emanuele the following day. If *Giovanni Gallurese* failed, it is hard to see how he could continue justifying his existence as a full-time composer supported by his parents, especially with his father nearing seventy. Serafin was probably hardly less anxious, well aware of the impact that success or failure would have on his friend. Augusto Balboni created the

---

[66] Halperson, "How 'Gallurese' Saved an Impresario," p. 3.
[67] Serafin, "Italo Montemezzi," p. 11.
[68] Halperson, "How 'Gallurese' Saved an Impresario," p. 3.
[69] Nino Alberti, "Giovanni Gallurese di Italo Montemezzi," *Radiocorriere*, November 14–21, 1931, p. 11.

title role, Bice Corsini sang Maria, and Mario Roussel was Rivegas; it was not a particularly distinguished cast.

Fortunately, *Giovanni Gallurese* was an emphatic success. As reported in the *Gazzetta del Popolo*, the events of the evening unfolded thus:

At 8.55 pm, when Maestro Serafin beat on his music stand for the traditional call to order, the audience concentrated silently. However, the silence was soon broken by applause for *Giovanni*'s aria that, well sung by the tenor Balboni, resulted in two curtain calls for the maestro.

The whole act was listened to very attentively and closed with three curtain calls for the artists and the composer, who dragged Maestro Serafin with him on stage. Before this, though, the audience asked for and obtained from Signora Bice Corsini—very good throughout her role—an *encore* of the melody *Profumi a voi non chiedo*, which led to two more curtain calls for the author.

In total, seven curtain calls in Act 1. As a start, it is not bad.

. . . the silence with which the whole Act [2] was listened to is easily explained, because it flows so rapidly and tightly that it does not leave space for interruptions. However, when the curtain fell on this act, four rounds of lively and unanimous applause greeted Maestro Montemezzi and his interpreters on stage, among whom Serafin stood out. In fact, on one occasion the audience called out the two maestros on their own.

The first curtain call in the final act was prompted by Signora Corsini with her nice phrase *Ah padre!*, of which the audience requested an encore, not given. There was further warm applause, with a related curtain call, for the episode of the emigrants. One more interruption of applause was prompted by Balboni when, with his anathema, he strikes *Rivegas*. More applause greeted the ending of the love duet.

When the opera was over, very insistent and warm acclamations called out four times the author, the artists, and maestro Serafin.[70]

Clearly the audience, finding the opera eminently accessible and tuneful, responded very positively to the incorporation of the political and patriotic elements into the tragic love story. After the performance, part of the audience carried Montemezzi in triumph to where he was staying in the Piazza

---

[70] [Ernesto Ferrettini],"La prima di 'Giovanni Gallurese' del M° Montemezzi al Vittorio Emanuele," *Gazzetta del Popolo*, January 29, 1905, p. 5.

70 SUCCEEDING PUCCINI

Castello.[71] The popular acclaim continued and, if anything, strengthened, and Piontelli let the opera run for an impressive fifteen nights. After one of the performances, Montemezzi was presented with an enormous wreath by the artists involved in the production. A testament to how much his success meant to him is that he transported the wreath back to Vigasio and had a special glass-fronted case constructed for it.[72] After the eighth performance, Montemezzi recounted to Halperson, even greater honors came his way:

> [A]bout two thousand people assembled before the theater and gave me an unforgettable ovation. . . . When they saw me leaving the theater in the company of two good friends they started to sing! You know that musical appreciation and a good ear are characteristics of the Italian people, and so I was not surprised to hear the masses sing melodies from my opera. . . . I was overwhelmed and I could not tell you whether I was more elated or perturbed. I tried to hide my emotion by jumping into a passing cab, but the enthusiasts untied the horse and drew the carriage up to the hotel where I stopped, coupling my name with that of the noble hero of Sardinia, Giovanni Gallurese.[73]

Montemezzi was also invited to court by Princess Maria Letizia Bonaparte, the Duchess of Aosta (1866–1926).[74] Reports of Montemezzi's Turinese success appeared in newspapers all over Italy, and the Verona newspapers treated it as a major event, deserving detailed attention. Not since *Pagliacci* (1892), over a decade earlier, had an unknown Italian composer scored such a triumph with his first produced opera.

Ernesto Ferrettini (1860–1937), the highly regarded critic of Turin's *Gazzetta del Popolo*, was as enthusiastic as the public, clearly considering the premiere of *Giovanni Gallurese* akin to the legendary first performance of *Cavalleria rusticana* in Rome:

> Praise be to God! Here at last we are in front of a young maestro who founds all his work as an artist upon a dogma as simple as neglected: to make an opera with music it takes music. . . . Italo Montemezzi, coming forward as modest and enthusiastic as he is, states his faith, his conviction, proclaims

---

[71] Alberti, "Giovanni Gallurese," p. 11.
[72] The wreath in its case is still hanging in Villa Montemezzi.
[73] Halperson, "How 'Gallurese' Saved an Impresario," p. 3.
[74] Alberti, "Giovanni Gallurese," p. 11.

that being able to write is not enough, but that, above all, ideas are needed, and every effort converges to nurture his work on real substance, shunning that awful and arid void, masked with smattering and pinchbeck, that often makes up all the essence and substance of some very modern operas.

Nowadays, operas are usually composed with very few ideas, maybe good ones, but too few and we have also seen cases of half a dozen ideas being sufficient for several operas by the same composer. How different is the route taken—luckily for him—by Montemezzi![75]

Ferrettini regarded Montemezzi above all as a natural melodist, a composer whose dramatic thoughts fell instinctively into a melodic line, but also as a musician with "an uncommon technical skillfulness, conferring on his work a solid and consistent substance." The review is wholly positive and presumably thrilled Montemezzi.

Pier Attilio Omodei, in the more upmarket *La Stampa*, sounded a more cautious note, but the great length of his review was an eloquent demonstration of how seriously he took Montemezzi's arrival on the operatic scene. To Omodei, Montemezzi's talents were undeniable, but he had not yet achieved a clearly individual style:

Montemezzi's music, at least judging from *Giovanni Gallurese*, does not have those characteristic stamps that reveal in its author a distinct musical temperament, a personality as they say. Nor does it have an abundance of ideas, nor an excessive wealth of images, of patterns, of really new or precious attitudes. Yet it is a music free from commonplaces, averse to vulgarity, made on the contrary with a constant clearness of views, nobility of intentions, and skilled mastery of form. In short, it is such as to show in its composer marked qualities as an opera composer and uncommon gifts as a symphonic composer.[76]

Omodei's review is farsighted in the sense that critics unenthused by Montemezzi's music would continue to discuss it in these terms for the rest of his career. Like many subsequent critics, too, Omodei struggled to express his feelings on the matter of originality: *Giovanni Gallurese* did not sound wholly new, yet it did not sound obviously like any other opera either. And

---

[75] [Ferrettini], "La prima di 'Giovanni Gallurese,'" p. 5.
[76] Pier Attilio Omodei, "'Giovanni Gallurese,'" *La Stampa*, January 29, 1905, p. 3.

72 SUCCEEDING PUCCINI

somewhat paradoxically, he faulted Montemezzi for attempting to sound too modern, with frequent changes of key and rhythm, and referred him to the nineteenth-century Italian tradition ("Bellini, Donizetti, Rossini, Verdi . . . the models they left always amaze exactly because they are not outdated"[77]).

Much later in the year, *Musica e Musicisti* published a review of the Turin *Giovanni Gallurese*, effectively as publicity for the opera's first appearance in Milan. The anonymous reviewer, possibly Giulio Ricordi himself, was hardly impartial, for the opera had now become the property of Casa Ricordi and much was expected from it. There was a heavy emphasis on the "colossal" success the work had achieved, but there was analysis, too. In answer, perhaps, to Omodei, whose strictures are ironically referred to, the critic emphasized that a process of maturation and individualization could be seen in the opera: "a flash of bold, youthful, radiant life spreads through the first act, in the second the temperament of a born opera composer takes form and establishes a definitive attitude, in the third this temperament materializes into a true personality and this personality definitely, irresistibly attracts everyone's admiration."[78] The critic then considered what was special about Montemezzi's style:

> in *Gallurese*, the lively, varied, tense, sometimes excitedly eventful drama demanded a music characterized first of all by that so-called rhythmic quickness (*prontezza ritmica*), which is not easy to achieve, which few achieve, and which distinctly characterizes Montemezzi's musical temperament; this is a very important talent because it's the source of life in music (*fonte di vita in musica*), because it's this blessed rhythmic quickness that is the main supporting fulcrum, the ethereal spirit that gives life to the whole musical structure. . . . clarity, simplicity, rapidity full of thought and passion, all these are among Montemezzi's many talents. . . . he is always the poet, a poet in turn picturesque, elegant, passionate, and incisive.[79]

After the breakthrough success of *Giovanni Gallurese*, Montemezzi had the attention of his country, and the future development of his career was a matter of public interest. Photographs of him began appearing in newspapers and magazines, and postcards were printed. Indeed, it is at this juncture that the photographic record begins. Montemezzi looks very slim in these early photographs, serious, and intelligent looking (Figure 2.3). Now and later, he

---

[77] Omodei, "'Giovanni Gallurese,'" p. 4.
[78] "La nostra musica," *Musica e musicisti* 60/10 (October 1905), p. 658.
[79] "La nostra musica," p. 659.

Figure 2.3 Montemezzi (*R*) and Tullio Serafin, 1905. *Donadelli family documents.*

74   SUCCEEDING PUCCINI

would always appear immaculately groomed and dressed, exuding a professional respectability. Tito Gobbi, later admitting the composer's "impressive figure," stressed that Montemezzi looked "rather more like a successful business or professional man than an artist."[80] This was already the case in 1905.

Most importantly, Giulio Ricordi (1840–1912), the man who had quickly moved to purchase *Le Villi* in 1884, traveled to Turin the day after the premiere to offer to buy *Giovanni Gallurese*, no doubt fearing that if he did not move fast, Montemezzi would be signed up by Casa Sonzogno, Casa Ricordi's great rival.[81] Terms were quickly agreed and a contract was duly signed on February 7, 1905. The parallel fates of the two operas meant that the twenty-nine-year-old Montemezzi was now in just the same position as the twenty-five-year-old Puccini had been two decades earlier. Though a few years older, he at least had a more substantial operatic achievement behind him as a foundation on which to build his future career.

[80] Tito Gobbi, *Tito Gobbi on His World of Italian Opera* (London: Hamish Hamilton, 1984), p. 242.
[81] Alberti, "Giovanni Gallurese," p. 11.

3

"How many times I wept"

Héllera and Illica, 1905–1909

Giulio Ricordi was the most powerful man in the world of Italian opera, the owner and director of the music publishing firm he had inherited from his father in 1888. Casa Ricordi had been founded by Giulio's grandfather, Giovanni (1785–1853), in 1808, and by steadily expanding and taking over rival firms had achieved a dominance unprecedented in the history of music publishing. Its history and catalog were coextensive with the rise of modern Italian opera, starting with Rossini. Casa Ricordi, with heavy vested interests, promoted a dynastic, "great man" history of opera in which Rossini was followed by Bellini, Bellini by Donizetti, Donizetti by Verdi, and Verdi by Puccini. However, it had been caught unawares by the rapid rise of the rival Casa Sonzogno in the 1890s and was now eager to sign up promising young composers, hoping to find someone who could, in the fullness of time, succeed Puccini as the next great composer in the tradition, and the catalog. Franco Alfano (1875–1954), Montemezzi's exact contemporary and most immediate rival, had been contracted for an opera as early as 1897, but his *La fonte d'Enscir* (premiered 1898) had been a disappointment, and his *Resurrezione* (premiered 1904), though it would later (after revision) prove one of the most durable Italian operas of this period, had not been particularly successful when first produced. As 1905 commenced, there was still no obvious heir apparent, and the matter of dynasty had become more urgent than Giulio recognized. With *Madama Butterfly* (1904), Puccini, now forty-five, had composed the last in his main series of repertoire staples, and subsequently entered a very unsettled period in his career. There was an obvious opportunity for younger, fresher talent to make its mark.

The contract Giulio agreed with Montemezzi in February 1905 specified that the composer was to be paid 14,000 lire for *Giovanni Gallurese*, 2,000 of which he would receive upon his surrender of the autograph score, and the remaining 12,000 in the form of monthly payments of 500 lire, the first to be paid on March 1, 1905. This regular payment was equivalent to the 200 lire

Succeeding Puccini. David Chandler and Raffaele Mellace, Oxford University Press. © Oxford University Press 2025.
DOI: 10.1093/9780197761373.003.0004

76   SUCCEEDING PUCCINI

monthly stipend Puccini had been placed on two decades earlier, in 1886, and that had been increased to 600 lire after the great success of *Manon Lescaut* in 1893.[1] These were generous terms, and even more generous, potentially, was the thirty-five percent of rental fees that Montemezzi was granted for a term of twenty-five years. The composer was further commissioned to produce a new three- or four-act opera, the libretto of which would be decided beforehand between him and Casa Ricordi and paid for by the firm. Casa Ricordi also reserved the right to commission a second new opera from Montemezzi, the terms to be agreed at a later date. Montemezzi undertook to enter into no agreements with other publishers or impresarios for the following six years.

The contract also specified that Montemezzi should provide Casa Ricordi with a vocal score adaptation of *Giovanni Gallurese*, to be submitted to the publisher within twenty days of the contract being signed. Montemezzi was unable to prepare this in a form suitable for publication, however, and in the end the experienced Ugo Solazzi (1875–1953) was brought in to help, though his name does not appear in the published score, which appeared in November 1905 before being reissued the following year.[2] It contains a strange, almost unrecognizable, frontispiece photograph in which Montemezzi appears to have been attempting to look as much like Puccini as possible (Figure 3.1). Ricordi also issued some extracts from the opera designed for domestic and concert performance—never again would a Montemezzi opera lend itself so readily to this sort of extraction.

Montemezzi was now a wealthy man, with a high upper-middle-class income at a time when the vast majority of Italian workers earned somewhere between 400 and 1,500 lire a year.[3] He could have chosen to live anywhere, but decided to stay in Vigasio with his parents. With two wage earners in the little family, the Montemezzis were part of the small segment of the population with significant surplus income, and one notable consequence was the decision to expand the house with a castellated tower, incorporating a *colombara*, or dovecote, giving it, at least on the outside, an almost aristocratic dignity

[1] Miguel-Ángel Galindo-Martín, María-Teresa Méndez-Picazo, and Thomas Baumert, "Giacomo Puccini and Richard Strauss: The Economics of Music Up to the Dawn of Fascism," in *On Music, Money and Markets: Comparing the Finances of Great Composers*, edited by Thomas Baumert and Francisco Cabrillo (Cham: Springer, 2023), p. 215.

[2] For Solazzi's involvement, see "I. Montemezzi," *Ars et labor* 61/6 (June 1906): p. 556.

[3] This generalization is derived from the figures in P. Scholliers and V. Zamagni (eds.), *Labour's Reward: Real Wages and Economic Change in 19th- and 20th-Century Europe* (Aldershot, UK: Edward Elgar, 1995), pp. 231, 233, and the examples in Emanuela Scarpellini, *Material Nation: A Consumer's History of Modern Italy*, trans. Daphne Hughes and Andrew Newton (Oxford: Oxford University Press, 2011), pp. 8–9, 14.

Figure 3.1 Frontispiece to *Giovanni Gallurese*, 1905.

(Figure 1.1). Montemezzi used to say that *Giovanni Gallurese* paid for the tower.[4] In the course of time, Montemezzi also purchased around ten acres of land by Vigasio's Tartaro River as an investment,[5] and a number of properties,

---

[4] Information from Renata Donadelli.
[5] Montemezzi to Francesco Donadelli, November 19, 1946. Donadelli family documents.

78   SUCCEEDING PUCCINI

again, it would seem, in the Vigasio area. The land was rented to local farmers and the properties to tenants.[6] The evidence suggests, then, that Montemezzi was committed to Vigasio, and eager to have local consequence—an ambition perhaps inherited from his father, the former mayor—while also prudently seeking to diversify his income. He did not want too provincial an existence, however, and in 1908 began renting an apartment in central Milan at Via Petrarca 16, presumably because he was visiting the city sufficiently often to warrant having a regular address there.[7]

Meanwhile, Giulio Ricordi had decided to team Montemezzi with his leading librettist, Luigi Illica, the famous coauthor of *Manon Lescaut*, *La Bohème*, *Tosca*, and *Madama Butterfly*. This was standard practice: Illica had written *La fonte d'Enscir* for Alfano. Giulio's initial proposal, apparently made to the librettist in the course of *Giovanni Gallurese*'s opening run, was that Montemezzi might be able to set the *Maria Antonietta* libretto Illica had been talking about since 1897. Illica had originally hoped that Puccini would be interested in this, but when the composer repeatedly prioritized other projects, *Maria Antonietta* was offered to Mascagni in 1902, though this too eventually led nowhere.[8] Illica, convinced that *Maria Antonietta* could be a masterpiece, was clearly rather appalled by the suggestion that the much less established Montemezzi might compose it. He wrote to Giulio on February 10, 1905, to insist that he still hoped to persuade Puccini to accept the project, adding "for Montemezzi we'll have to find something else."[9] Ironically, had Giulio's proposal been accepted, *Maria Antonietta* would very likely have gotten written and composed; Puccini, though he did start showing serious interest later in 1905, never made a definite commitment. Illica had clearly not suggested "something else" for Montemezzi by April 28, when Giulio wrote again: "Remember that we also have to think about Montemezzi. Let's see if we can make a Wholemountain [*Monteintero*] of him...."[10] (Giulio plays on the literal reading of "Montemezzi" as "mountain

---

[6] Montemezzi's Italian accounts for the years 1939 to 1948 (when he was resident in America) are preserved among the Donadelli family documents and mainly list rental income and tax payments.

[7] The Via Petrarca address is recorded in the files of the *Copialettere* in the Archivio Storico Ricordi for the period 1908 to 1914. We have found no evidence that Montemezzi ever spent much time there, however.

[8] For a complete history of the *Maria Antonietta* project, see Marcello Conati, "*Maria Antonietta* ovvero *L'Austriaca*: Un soggetto abbandonato da Puccini," *Rivista Italiana di Musicologia* 33 (1998): pp. 89–181.

[9] Conati, "*Maria Antonietta*," p. 96.

[10] Mario Morini, "Carteggi inediti di Montemezzi, Illica e Giulio Ricordi per *Héllera*," *Ricordiana*, new series 2/5 (May 1956): p. 234.

halves.") Librettist and composer finally met in May to discuss possible subjects.

For some reason, not specified in the surviving correspondence, Illica and Montemezzi were determined to adapt a French novel, and initially wanted to tackle a recent one. They discussed the possibilities of *La Luciole* (1904) by J.-H. Rosny (a pseudonym of Joseph Henri Honoré Boex and his younger brother Séraphin Justin François Boex) and *Le Serpent noir* (1905) by Paul Adam. In the end, though, they provisionally settled on Pierre Loti's *Ramuntcho* (1897). On June 2 a hopeful Giulio wrote to Illica: "With all my heart I recommend to you the young Montemezzi: I'm convinced that he really can perform, and much, therefore I hope he can find in you that friend I wish for him."[11] But there were tensions almost immediately. Montemezzi, having gone away and read Loti's novel, found he had very justified misgivings, which he expressed to Illica in no uncertain terms on June 9.[12] The story's most obvious attraction, from an operatic point of view, was its setting in the French Basque country, with evocative descriptions of landscapes and local customs. The simplicity of the action and the natural two-act form of the story were also well suited to operatic development. But the ending, in which Gracieuse, the heroine, chooses life in a convent over her love for Ramuntcho, was hardly suitable for an opera unless—as Montemezzi strongly hinted to Illica—it was completely reconceived. There was also the problem that any operatic adaptation was bound to put most of the burden of singing on two singers meant to be teenagers, thus creating formidable casting difficulties—an issue Montemezzi would face again, much later, with his aborted *Paolo e Virginia*.

Perhaps Illica did produce the "outline" of *Ramuntcho* that Montemezzi was requesting, but in either case the composer's doubts hardened into rejection. This did not endear him to Illica, who, still convinced of the value of the subject, now offered it to Puccini, who briskly refused it with reasoning comparable to Montemezzi's.[13] Puccini's refusal appears to have extinguished Illica's hopes of producing an adaptation.[14]

---

[11] Morini, "Carteggi," p. 234.

[12] Morini, "Carteggi," pp. 234–35.

[13] Puccini's reasoning is set out in a letter to Illica of November 11, 1905. See *Carteggi pucciniani*, edited by Eugenio Gara (Milan: Ricordi, 1958), p. 302.

[14] Two operas derived from Loti's novel were subsequently written: one by Stefano Donaudy (1921), with a libretto by his brother, and one by Montemezzi's later American champion Deems Taylor (1942), who wrote the libretto himself. Neither was successful.

80 SUCCEEDING PUCCINI

Meanwhile, after several months of delay, Montemezzi and Illica still needed to agree on a subject. In September the librettist proposed an adaptation of a rather older French novella, Benjamin Constant's *Adolphe* (1816), that he appears to have been contemplating for several years, and that had briefly interested Puccini.[15] This time Montemezzi accepted enthusiastically. Despite the European fame of Constant's novella, this would be the first attempt to adapt it as an opera. The title page of *Adolphe* modestly calls it an "Anecdote," and Constant described it, in his important preface to the third edition, as a

> story . . . written with the sole purpose of proving to one or two friends staying in the country that it was possible to infuse a kind of interest into a novel with characters numbering only two and a situation remaining the same throughout.[16]

Adolphe is a profoundly psychological story told in the first person by the eponymous hero, an embittered, socially awkward, young intellectual, son of a German government minister. Eager to have a romantic experience, he courts the Polish Ellénore, a woman ten years his senior, the established mistress of Count P—. She initially refuses him, but this makes Adolphe more determined, and eventually she falls deeply in love. He is happy for a while, but soon is overwhelmed by the superior strength of her love and her almost fanatic need for him, and he feels trapped. Most of the novel is taken up with Adolphe's agonizing over this situation, longing to escape, but feeling that he has become so responsible for Ellénore's happiness that he must stay in the relationship. In the end, Adolphe is persuaded by a friend of his father's that he should leave Ellénore. He writes a letter promising that he will, but in the event is unable to make the decisive break. His father's friend then intervenes by sending Adolphe's letter to Ellénore. The shock makes her seriously ill and she dies a few days later. Adolphe is no happier after Ellénore's death than he was before.

The very quality which makes *Adolphe* so brilliant as a novel, its intense interiority, presents a huge obstacle to its successful dramatization. Other characters, even Ellénore, hardly seem to exist outside Adolphe's perception

---

[15] For an early reference to a possible *Adolphe* opera, see Giulio Ricordi to Illica, November 27, 1900. Archivio Storico Ricordi.

[16] Benjamin Constant, *Adolphe*, trans. Leonard Tancock (Harmondsworth, UK: Penguin Books, 1964), p. 30.

of them, and though the reader's fascination with Constant's forensic examination of Adolphe outweighs the hero's basic unattractiveness, he hardly seems the stuff of operatic heroes. Nevertheless, the novel answers some of the objections Montemezzi had to *Ramuntcho*: it offered a big, passionate female role and an impressively tragic conclusion. Moreover, as an interiorized, first-person narrative, there was no question that any stage adaptation would have to make drastic alterations, and this is what Illica did. The first two acts of his three-act libretto roughly correspond to the first third of the novel. It is only in the final and shortest act that Adolphe finds himself in the emotional and moral dilemma central to Constant's story.

Even after a decision had been reached on *Adolphe*, Illica was reluctant to start work and apparently was unconvinced by Montemezzi's talents—perhaps annoyed by his attitude, too. At some point in October, he must have written something to Giulio Ricordi to the effect that he wanted to work with the proven genius of Puccini rather than the young composer from Vigasio: *Maria Antonietta* was still his favorite project. Giulio replied on October 30, acknowledging that "the first prize is due to we know whom [Puccini]," but nevertheless reasserting in strong terms his belief in Montemezzi's talents:

> I tell you, after simply listening to the first two run-throughs of *Gallurese* with the orchestra, I am very, very impressed! ... Am I running the risk of making a tremendous blunder? Yet from these hearings it seems to me that we are in the presence of a *Maestro*, and one who perhaps will be able to become a *great Maestro*! I'd like to ask you to pay a short visit to Milan.... I would take you *incognito* to a rehearsal at the Dal Verme, persuaded of the impression you'll have of him [Montemezzi] and that he'll be a *deus ex machina* for us.[17]

Whether or not Illica made the suggested visit, he did get on and write the libretto for Montemezzi over the winter of 1905–1906. Not a modest man, he eventually decided that *Héllera* was one of his best efforts. In a letter to Giulio in 1906, he emphasized how much work he had put into the libretto in terms of structure, characterization, and historical research: "I read everything I could put my hands on from that time [of the action]. And I could say I've done again the work of the good days of *Bohème*." He changed both place

---

[17] Morini, "Carteggi," p. 234.

82 SUCCEEDING PUCCINI

and period, setting the first act in Paris in 1823, the second in Baden-Baden in 1824–1825, and the third, undated, in Poland. He had read numerous authors of the period, he claimed, and by immersing himself in the era had found a way to give inner life to the characters:

> It seems to me I've found the way to a new libretto, very new, in concept as well as in form. By recreating that era (with the lively character of the female protagonist and her drama above all, and also with the figure of the other character, the baritone, the doctor, who is certainly more interesting than the tenor), I was able to live in it. And I found myself fully immersed in the literary romanticism (*romanticismo letterario*).

Such a libretto, Illica reasoned, deserved a congruous setting: "To the passionate, very strong drama, Montemezzi will have to be, at most, a robust, adequate drum. Yet as he did for Sardinia (in Gallurese), I believe he'll be able to do for 1820s France."[18]

Meanwhile, the second production of *Giovanni Gallurese*, now a Casa Ricordi opera, opened at the Teatro Dal Verme, Milan, on November 12, 1905, this time with the well-known husband-and-wife team of Edoardo Garbin and Adelina Stehle singing Giovanni and Maria. It was a success with the public, with four curtain calls after the first act, six after the second, and another four or five at the end.[19] There were nine performances in all. The Milanese critics found plenty to praise, but also spent a good deal of time highlighting what they considered weaknesses. To Giovanni Pozza (1852–1914) in the *Corriere della Sera*, it was "a sincere opera that shuns conventional formulas and facile effects, constantly trying to elevate itself, to be noble and beautiful." However, Pozza found the score weakened by "sentimentalità" and lacking in dramatic contrast, even though it was "already more than very promising."[20] According to the critic for *La Perseveranza*, almost certainly Giovanni Battista Nappi (1857–1932), Montemezzi was a "learned composer who handles the orchestral polyphony in a way which could not be better, with a good variety of colors and a great clarity in lines, with subtle and exquisite skills, [and] who uses the voices effectively, with respect for the singers' throats." On the other hand, though, it was a "mediocre libretto" and

---

[18] Morini, "Carteggi," p. 235. Further evidence of Illica's careful work on the libretto is the small booklet of corrections in the Archivio Storico Ricordi, LIBR00262.

[19] Giovanni Pozza, "Dal Verme: *Giovanni Gallurese*," *Corriere della Sera*, November 13, 1905, p. 4.

[20] Pozza, "Dal Verme," p. 4.

the characters "mechanical puppets rather than men in the flesh."[21] The general consensus was that, as a first opera, it held out much hope for the future, further confirming that Montemezzi had established himself, in Italy, as the most promising opera composer of the younger generation.

Many more productions followed. By June 1906, it had already reached Brescia, Novara, Venice, Trieste, Verona, Rovereto, and Genoa.[22] In 1925, Montemezzi estimated that after the Turin and Milan productions, "about fifty other Italian opera houses" staged the work.[23] It is a striking comment on the dramatic nature of the opera that there were no international productions apart from the one in Italian-speaking Trieste (and, much later, that in New York in 1925, discussed in Chapter 7). As early as June 1905, the Teatro Municipal, in Santiago, Chile, was announcing a plan to stage the opera, but in the end no production materialized.[24] It is also striking that most of the Italian productions took place before World War I. After the war, *Giovanni Gallurese* became a comparative rarity on the stage. This change in the opera's fortunes no doubt has something to do with the impact of the far more sophisticated *L'amore dei tre re* in 1913, and the larger cultural shifts it represented, but it is also the case that cinema had, in the interim, emerged strongly as a more popular medium for action-packed historical drama. And politics surely played a part, too. The simple black-and-white patriotism of *Giovanni Gallurese* worked well in the early 1900s, but after the ghastly carnage and complicated realignments of the war years, the cartoon unreality of D'Angelantonio's libretto stood exposed as an inadequate response to the wounds of history.

Montemezzi composed *Héllera* in Vigasio between the spring of 1906 and the summer of 1908. On October 12, 1906, he wrote to Giulio Ricordi to assure him that the difficulties he had been reported as experiencing (presumably by Illica) were part of the normal routine of composition: "When I work, I always meet with many difficulties, it was the same with Gallurese. However, none of them makes me retreat: rack my brains, yes, tire myself a lot, but I don't care about fatigue. Music is what matters to me, and for it I overcome any obstacle."[25] As a letter to a concerned employer, this was not entirely ingenuous. Difficulties would continue to plague the compositional

---

[21] "'Giovanni Gallurese' del maestro Montemezzi al Verme," *La Perseveranza*, November 13, 1905, p. 3.

[22] "I. Montemezzi," *Ars et labor* 61/6 (June 1906): p. 556.

[23] Halperson, "How 'Gallurese' Saved an Impresario," p. 3.

[24] *Chile Ilustrado* 4/6 (June 1905): n.p. The theatre has no record of any production taking place.

[25] Morini, "Carteggi," p. 236.

84 SUCCEEDING PUCCINI

process, and they had much to do with disagreements between Montemezzi and Illica over certain details. It was these, perhaps, which led to everything taking longer than Montemezzi expected, with a first draft not submitted to Casa Ricordi until November 1907. But Giulio Ricordi was happy with the way things were going, and having seen the draft he wrote very positively to Illica: "I think the work will make a big impression on you, first of all because it's Montemezzi's music, with no aping (*scimmiottature*), and because the most difficult points of the libretto are—at least in my opinion—the best-done ones."[26] Yet when Montemezzi visited Illica at his house in Castell'Arquato in February 1908—combining this with a visit to Modena for a new production of *Giovanni Gallurese*—and played through part of the score, further dissent followed. Although Illica seems to have approved the general character of the score, the conclusion to Act 1 proved a major sticking point. Montemezzi wanted a dramatic climax, a "crescendo of musical interest . . . [of the kind] that leads to enthusiasm."[27] Illica had not written such a scene and did not want to make changes, emphasizing, somewhat ironically, the principle of fidelity to Constant's story. It appears the librettist wanted to end the act with Héllera alone, agonizing over what she should do; Montemezzi wanted a big romantic duet with the lovers pledging themselves to each other. On March 31, Montemezzi wrote Illica a very cajoling letter—"let's talk as good friends, since I realize I'm really a friend to you"—urging a "sacrifice of relative logic" in favor of giving "life" to Act 1.[28] Illica eventually relented, mainly, it appears, because Giulio Ricordi supported Montemezzi; but he remained bitter about the whole affair.

Around the beginning of March 1909, shortly before the premiere of *Héllera*, Montemezzi gave a long interview to "L. C.," a critic for *La Gazzetta del Popolo*. As far as we are aware, this is the most detailed commentary he gave on any of his operas, and it is worth quoting at length for its account of the story and what it reveals of Montemezzi's approach to composition and understanding of his dramatic materials:

> The maestro, slightly suffering from influenza, welcomed me with genuine warmth.
>
> I observed him closely. His genial, artistic figure has not changed at all and maintains the youthful appearance of his sparkling eyes, his rapid

---

[26] Morini, "Carteggi," pp. 236–37.
[27] Morini, "Carteggi," p. 148.
[28] Morini, "Carteggi," p. 237.

and expressive movements; only his physiognomy has been slightly transformed due to his shaving off his moustache, according to the new fashion. [...]

— So, maestro, finally we got to the trial.

— To the coveted trial and I yearn for its taking place. After four years of indefatigable work, I'd like a new baptism from the intelligent and cultured Turinese audience who first applauded "Giovanni Gallurese."

— You are always very kind. And has this new subject of "Hellera" [*sic*] completely satisfied you?

— I am enthusiastic about it; I consider it one of the best of Illica's librettos. Just think that at the reading of it that he did for Ricordi and me, we were moved to tears.

— Therefore it is a great drama of love and passion.

— It is all passion, all, all. I am sorry I cannot offer you a few more detailed hints before the librettos arrive and we send them to the newspapers.

— I perfectly understand; yet does this drama of passion perhaps start with some scene setting (*pittura d'ambiente*)?

— There is nothing decorative, nothing, absolutely nothing. The spectator is immediately drawn into the great whirl of the drama.

The first scene takes place in Hellera's drawing room. She is a lady of the Parisian aristocracy, mother of two angelic little girls, and appears to us anguished over a great, sublime love, an unbounded passion for Adolfo, a young man full of life and idealism who returns her love with equal ardor. The thought of her family makes her feel daunted at the idea of taking flight, but the imperiousness, the fascination of passion and love make her repeat:—"Either love or death!"

— Wonderful, suggestive, continue.

— Nor does the Carnival help to distract her; with lively and cheerful orchestral episodes, we hear the echo of the festive racket.

However, the doctor, a family friend, comes to rouse her. He precedes the little girls by a few moments, and when Hellera sees them she regains control over herself and hugs them while weeping. A sweet and passionate phrase from the strings describes the moving situation.

The doctor pours in a glass, as medicine for a family member, a few drops of a certain poison of which he always has a small vial. Notice this little detail of the vial that will be of capital importance in the last act. Immediately after this, he leaves with the little girls.

86 SUCCEEDING PUCCINI

Hellera left alone, her passion for Adolfo dominates her. She has decided to flee and sings a simple song as an old motif that serves as a call for her lover: she is inviting him to meet her. Adolfo enters, yearning, and from his lips pour the words of love. Then the duet follows, in a very new form, rapid and concise, that ends with an allegro vivace concluding for the singers on a high B flat, after which, with a simple, strong stroke in the orchestra, the curtain quickly falls. Here the first act ends.

* * *

The second act then takes place in Baden-Baden at the Kursaal,[29] the favorite place of Parisian aristocratic society. Here we see again all the characters of the first act [. . .]. The first scene is on a large terrace shaped like a grand salon from which it is possible to make out the city. Some elegant young men, bored, think up a ball for that night and, knowing about the arrival of Hellera and Adolfo, send them an invitation and then retire to organize the evening. The two lovers arrive, wrapped in the sweet charm of continuous love. Adolfo invites Hellera to stop in order to bring her flowers, of which she is a passionate cultivator and lover.

During this brief stop, the doctor passes by, silent and serious. Hellera, in a voice choked by emotion, asks him for information about her daughters. The doctor hides, and Adolfo returns laden with flowers, bringing the invitation to the ball. Here the music becomes more scintillating and bright: from the musical comedy, with which the act started, we pass to broad and passionate phrases, the love theme merges with the descriptive allegro and a spring-like freshness drifts through the orchestra. Hellera and Adolfo withdraw to get ready for the ball. The night falls. The big, festively-lit city appears and an offstage chorus sings a song to the spring interspersed, from a distance, with Hellera's phrase and then with Adolfo's. The violins linger on swift and descriptive movements, in sweet rhythms rocking in the suave melody of an immense musical passion and repeat the hymn to love, youth, and life.

— And does the second act end here?

— Bravo! Here is the artist! That is how it should be, but unfortunately the drama has its own demands. After this suggestive scene, another one that is all lights follows. The salon is sumptuously lit up and the ball begins.

---

[29] The libretto calls this the "Conversationhalle." Illica was clearly thinking of the Conversationshaus, designed by Friedrich Weinbrenner, that was primarily intended as a promenade for spa guests in bad weather. This had opened in 1824, so it appears Illica's desire to incorporate it into the opera led to his 1820s setting for the action.

HÉLLERA AND ILLICA, 1905–1909   87

A slow phrase of a cadenced waltz abruptly broken off invites people to dance. However, the ladies are plotting an offense to Hellera and when she appears they leave the salon, in high disdain. Adolfo is offended by the insult and challenges the gentlemen.

But Hellera embraces him and drags him away, while the orchestra with quick movements describes the stirring of the individual passions. Here the second act ends.

* * *

The final act takes place in a castle in Poland, where the protagonists of the drama have retreated. A big glass door separates the room from a large garden rich in fragrant flowers. Adolfo, tired of this love, lingers over less than happy reflections. Hellera, who has for a long time sensed the increasing coldness or, better, the habitual indifference of her lover, asks him whether he still loves her. An evasive yes by Adolfo reveals, instead, the opposite.

Left alone, Hellera bursts into a flood of tears; she no longer has a family, her little girls, her love, she is alone. . . . The doctor arrives and, while she asks him for the last comfort of being allowed to see her daughters, who are by now young ladies, she informs him of Adolfo's abandoning her. The doctor loses his temper and, while asking Hellera to leave, demands to meet her lover.

And here, a new dramatic episode takes place. Adolfo, offended, asks the doctor with what right he is insulting him. The doctor, making an effort, answers:—"Because I love Hellera; I've always loved her in silence, followed her with a silent and immense ardor. It is with the right of an honest love that I judge your cowardly act." Adolfo, surprised, runs away, and Hellera, who has heard everything from behind the curtains, runs toward the doctor who points out the young girls in the park to her. Hellera, trembling, moved, looks at them and, in an anguished prayer, asks for permission to hug them. This is impossible, for the orders are explicit: for her daughters, their mother is dead. However, the doctor opens a panel in the door, through which Hellera will be able to hear their voices. Here a most moving scene occurs. Hellera hears her children talk, senses their tones, would like to . . . she can't . . . deeply touched, convulsive, almost mad, desperate, in a flood of tears she cries:—"To die . . . to die. . . ."

The young ladies, unaware, move away in the park. Hellera, at the height of agitation, embraces the doctor nervously, exclaiming:—"You, who really loved me, give me the medicine of peace, of oblivion, the vial. . . ." Her friend is devastated, but after a tragic scene with Hellera's delirious prayers,

88 SUCCEEDING PUCCINI

being upset, mad—and saying that he too will soon disappear for good—he gives the vial with the poison to the woman he loves and leaves hurriedly.

Hellera, exulting in the delirium that is absorbing her, orders her servants to pick all the flowers from the garden and arrange them on the armchairs. She writes a note for Adolfo and leaves it together with a small bunch of forget-me-nots. Then, lying down amid the flowers, she drinks the poison.

Adolfo enters, with a quick glance senses the tragedy, runs to Hellera who is still smiling at him, reads the note and drops overwhelmed by sorrow. Here the opera ends.

Touched in the highest degree, I look at the maestro who is crying. He becomes aware of this and says:

— If you only knew how many times I wept while composing my "Hellera...."[30]

It is important to keep in mind that Doctor Souwalki, his love for Héllera, the poison, and the suicide were all additions to Constant's story. Illica considered such elements to be essential for an opera, and Montemezzi was clearly in agreement. Both men judged the *Héllera* libretto first rate, though it would be severely attacked by the critics. It is, notably, the only typically turn-of-the-century bourgeois drama that Montemezzi treated, and in its concern with high society in sumptuous historical and international settings, beautifully conjured up in the set designs by Angelo Parravicini (1868–1925), it follows in the line of such operas as Giordano's *Andrea Chénier* and *Fedora*, and Cilea's *Adriana Lecouvreur* (Figure 3.2). Nowhere else did Montemezzi attempt to depict fashionable parties or such distinctively light-weight characters as Count and Countess D'Auvray and their sophisticated friends, who provide the social context in which the story unfolds.

When *Héllera* was eventually premiered on March 17, 1909, it was a failure. In later life, Montemezzi would explain this with reference to the Messina earthquake of December 28, 1908, the most powerful recorded earthquake in European history.[31] Estimates of the number of dead vary wildly, but most scholars agree that over 100,000 people were killed, while tens of thousands more suffered injury and the loss of homes and livelihoods.

---

[30] L. C., "'Hellera' del Mº Montemezzi: Un'intervista coll'autore," *La Gazzetta del Popolo*, March 2, 1909, p. 5.

[31] Giuseppe Silvestri, "Vita e opera: vocazione e volontà," in *Omaggio a Italo Montemezzi*, edited by Piergiorgio Rossetti (Vigasio: Amministrazione Comunale di Vigasio), p. 24; Verna Arvey, "Visits to the Homes of Famous Composers No. XIV: Italo Montemezzi," *Opera and Concert*, November 1948, p. 29.

Figure 3.2 Set design for Act 3 of *Héllera*, 1909. *Archivio Storico Ricordi*.

The earthquake and its aftermath dominated Italian headlines for weeks, leaving people with a diminished appetite for entertainments of any kind, and, initially, a reluctance to go into large public buildings that might prove vulnerable to aftershocks. Theatres briefly closed completely and then, as they started reopening, often chose to put on charitable events to raise funds to assist the relief efforts. This break in the season played havoc with regular programs and artists' commitments, but other aggravating factors must be taken into account as well.

By 1908, opera in Italy was in a mood of crisis. The country's rapid industrialization from around 1880, and especially after 1896, was affecting every aspect of society, and had given birth to a new mass culture. Imported operettas had been making steady inroads into Italian theatres since the 1860s, but the astonishing success of *The Merry Widow* (*La vedova allegra*) at the Teatro Dal Verme, Milan, where it was brought out on April 27, 1907, less then eighteen months after *Giovanni Gallurese* was staged there, was quite unprecedented. Lehár's operetta played for over 500 performances, setting a commercial standard with which no native opera composer could possibly compete; it "took Milan and subsequently the entire peninsula by

90 SUCCEEDING PUCCINI

storm."[32] As late as 1918, Mascagni was lamenting: "I have a feeling that in the tastes of our audience, the *merry widows* have remained fixed like a big nail."[33] The rapid development of the Italian film industry from 1903 onward was also threatening to steal much of the popular audience away from opera. The sense that a new age had arrived, needing new forms of art, was also being registered in more elite art forms, as famously represented in Filippo Tommaso Marinetti's *Manifesto of Futurism*, published on February 5, 1909, less than six weeks before the premiere of *Héllera*. When Francesco Balilla Pratella got around to issuing *The Manifesto of Futurist Musicians* in October 1910, he was scathing about what he represented as the vulgar, old-fashioned, commercial melodramas on which composers like Puccini had built their reputations. And if opera, in the new century, often seemed to be bleeding support on both sides, losing out to more popular forms of entertainment, while also failing to please the intellectuals, it faced enormous economic and logistical challenges of its own. Large-scale emigration to the Americas in the late 1800s had seen the growth of Italian communities in the New World that were hungry for opera (and, increasingly, operetta), and the emergence of transatlantic steamship services had made it increasingly easy for Italian companies to undertake potentially lucrative American tours. A good number of singers and musicians found themselves better off in America and never came back. It was increasingly difficult for impresarios in Italy to secure the singers they needed, and according to the rules of supply and demand, singers' fees were rising, thus putting pressure on ticket prices.

The creation of the Società Teatrale Internazionale (STIn) in Rome in July 1908, with the Società Teatrale Italo-Argentina (STIA), founded the previous year, as the biggest shareholder, and effectively a partner, was an extraordinarily ambitious project to solve some of these problems by consolidating control of as much of Italy's theatrical industry as possible, then running it according to integrated business models.[34] Its first major, attention-grabbing act was to buy the Teatro Costanzi in Rome outright, on July 29. This, however, took so much of the STIn's starting capital that the grand plans to control Italy's entire theatre world had to be scaled back; the STIn did try to

---

[32] Valeria De Lucca, "Operetta in Italy," in *The Cambridge Companion to Operetta*, edited by Anastasia Belina-Johnson and Derek B. Scott (Cambridge: Cambridge University Press, 2019), p. 221.

[33] Quoted in De Lucca, "Operetta in Italy," p. 227.

[34] For a full, fascinating history of the STIn, see Matteo Paoletti, *Mascagni, Mocchi, Sonzogno: La Società Teatrale Internazionale (1908–1931) e i suoi protagonist* (Bologna: Alma Mater Studiorum, 2015).

monopolize theatrical entertainment in Rome, but outside the capital chose to concentrate on major opera houses and to take over existing concessions, hoping to ensure an efficient circulation of artists and productions. Casa Ricordi, notably, was not part of the STIn, though Casa Sonzogno was a shareholder and closely involved from the outset. If the STIn achieved its goals, Ricordi would eventually have no choice but to join; in the meantime, as the biggest business entity in Italian opera, with potentially much to lose, a cautious wait-and-see policy was wise, and was vindicated by the result.

Héllera was one of several operas affected by what Matteo Paoletti has called the "bulimic enthusiasm" with which the STIn sought to expand its reach in 1908, though it was only belatedly clear this would be the case.[35] By the summer, Montemezzi had finished the score, and Ricordi made a decision to have it premiered at the prestigious Teatro Regio, Turin, where Temistocle Pozzali had been the impresario since 1905 and Serafin was contracted as the principal conductor. In July, Pozzali and Serafin, along with Montemezzi, were accordingly invited to the Ricordi offices in Milan, and the score was played through. On July 19, the composer wrote to Illica that he was "very satisfied . . . because of the impression it [the opera] caused. I'll whisper it in your ear: extraordinary success, for libretto and music."[36] Pozzali agreed to bring out the opera in the following season. But the Regio was one of the theatres the STIn wanted to control, and on October 28 they signed a contract with Pozzali, making him an STIn employee.[37] How much this itself affected *Héllera* is difficult to assess, but it meant that Pozzali's loyalty was now to the STIn rather than Ricordi, and with a guaranteed salary, he had appreciably less interest in securing the success of the new opera. On top of this came the many difficulties and disappointments of the season itself, opening belatedly on December 22, just six days before the earthquake. The effects of the earthquake, the illness of several singers, the difficulty securing replacements, and the problems singers and the STIn had juggling contracts elsewhere then played havoc with the advertised schedule. By mid-February, the local press and public were increasingly angry and inclined to blame the STIn for their disappointments.[38] The constant delays affected *Héllera* badly, because Giannina Russ (1873–1951) had been cast in the title role; Montemezzi considered her "an ideal protagonist," with a "really splendid

[35] Paoletti, *Mascagni, Mocchi, Sonzogno*, p. 53.
[36] Morini, "Carteggi," pp. 237–38.
[37] The entire contract is reproduced in Paoletti, *Mascagni, Mocchi, Sonzogno*, pp. 441–42.
[38] Paoletti, *Mascagni, Mocchi, Sonzogno*, pp. 126–30.

92   SUCCEEDING PUCCINI

voice."[39] Russ, however, was also scheduled to sing Norma at the Teatro Carlo Felice, Genoa, another theatre taken over by the STIn. Delays there meant that *Norma* did not open until January 21, with the last performance taking place on February 10. This delayed the rehearsals of Montemezzi's opera in Turin, and Pozzali was left with no option but to push it back to the very end of the truncated season. This in turn led to Russ being unable to appear at the Casinò Municipale di Sanremo and Pozzali facing a lawsuit.[40]

Although Montemezzi tried to strike an optimistic note in his interview at the start of March, he must have known the Turin audience was in no mood to be generous. There was, though, considerable interest in the new opera. The premiere on March 17, with Russ as Héllera, Edoardo Garbin (1865–1943) as Adolfo, and Oreste Benedetti (1872–1917) as Doctor Souwalki, was attended by Princess Maria Letizia, who had invited Montemezzi to court after the success of *Giovanni Gallurese*, and the theatre was reported as crowded. The most objective comment on the public response is that of Giovanni Pozza, the theatre critic of the *Corriere della Sera*, who had traveled to Turin for the dress rehearsal and premiere, apparently on the strength of the promise shown by *Giovanni Gallurese*. The rehearsal had seemed to go well: Pozza had seen several members of the audience in tears at the end. But the premiere itself was received with an indifference that baffled Pozza, who was perhaps not fully aware of the season's many postponements:

> The large and elegant audience which flocked to the theatre opposed this new music of a young maestro with coldness and resistance, the reasons for which I cannot understand. Was the opera badly listened to or was it badly understood? I do not know. It certainly deserved a less severe judgment.
>
> . . . not all the judges of *Hellera* [*sic*] had the same opinion tonight. Not a few liked the opera: many, though acknowledging its faults, were able to distinguish its merits. Yet, unfortunately, the majority, by judging it perfunctorily after listening absent-mindedly, turned against it. They did not really like any but the first act, the most agile in its forms and the most rapid. In fact, when the curtain was dropped [after Act 1], the applause was very warm, incessant, and general. Then I do not know whether tiredness or hostility began. Some isolated clapping during the second act did not find an echo in the audience. The burst of applause at the end was met with

[39] L. C., "'Hellera' del Mº Montemezzi," p. 5.
[40] Paoletti, *Mascagni, Mocchi, Sonzogno*, p. 128.

HÉLLERA AND ILLICA, 1905–1909   93

some hushing and even some catcalls. The third act was listened to entirely in silence. After the last bar, many applauded very warmly, while others reacted with hissing. Then the applause spread and became more intense. The composer was called two or three times on stage but the audience's resipiscence was too tardy; success had been missed.[41]

The sort of excitement that accompanied the premiere of *Giovanni Gallurese* was not present. Nevertheless, from what Pozza says, Montemezzi may have carried some hopes away from the premiere. But the next day brought further disillusionment. The Turin newspapers were united in their condemnation of the opera. The review in the *Gazzetta del Popolo* was particularly negative. The anonymous reviewer sharply criticized the choice of subject and Illica's treatment of the story—the libretto "was bad in all respects"—before suggesting that the music was disappointing too:

"Hellera" [*sic*] seemed poor, lacking in interest and musical content because the matter Montemezzi was setting to music was poor. It seems that the composer, here and there, became well aware of this, yet he settled for giving us a semblance of emotion rather than real emotion, forgetting Horace's precept: "If you wish me to weep, you must first weep yourself."[42]

This review must have come as a body blow to Montemezzi, for the *Popolo*, which had enthused about *Giovanni Gallurese* four years earlier, had also just published the lengthy interview with him in which his weeping over his subject had been strongly emphasized. It appears he was first the beneficiary, then the victim, of some internal disagreement going on at the paper, and it was perhaps this seeming betrayal he had in mind when, in reporting *Héllera*'s fate to Illica on March 23, he referred to "the hostilities of a shameful and grotesque campaign [against the opera]."[43] Nevertheless, the more prestigious *La Stampa* was not much more positive, though at least inclined to lay the blame for failure squarely on Illica: "the young composer is simply the victim of a mirage, and this mirage, that led other musicians to perdition, has a name and all the charms of deceitful visions: its name is Luigi Illica."[44]

---

[41] Giovanni Pozza, "*Hellera* [*sic*]: opera del maestro I. Montemezzi al Regio di Torino," *Corriere della Sera*, March 18, 1909, p. 3.

[42] "La prima dell'Héllera' al teatro Regio," *Gazzetta del Popolo*, March 18, 1909, p. 5.

[43] Morini, "Carteggi," p. 238.

[44] "La prima di 'Héllera' in Italia," *La Stampa*, March 18, 1909, p. 6.

94 SUCCEEDING PUCCINI

Ars et Labor, Ricordi's own journal, rather desperately claimed, "Although the Turin critics were very sour and unjust, it [*Héllera*] should be considered a sincere and serious success," but even this brief review declared the opera had lost its way in the second act, dragging because of "unnecessary and uninteresting details"—a clear hint that revision was needed.[45] After attending the first three performances, on March 17, 18, and 20, Montemezzi's rather belated report to Illica stated: "I'm happy to announce to you that the 2nd and 3rd nights of *Héllera* mark a growing success as to applause and audience."[46] He was expecting a fourth and final performance the following night, but this was canceled.

The STIn had lost money in theatre after theatre and could ill afford new operas like *Héllera* that were expensive to produce and unlikely to return a profit. The report of Carlo Körner, the financial administrator of the Regio, to the STIn administration brutally summarized the situation, highlighting the always challenging economics of opera production:

> *Héllera* . . . cost us approximately more than 25,000.- lire and did not correspond both artistically and financially to the hopes rightly placed on it. It was a mistake to have accepted a new opera that of royalties alone cost L. 4,350.- L. 4,500 of costumes L. 500.- of footwear – L. 1,000 of props, L. 1,000 of other small expenses – L. 9,000 for the tenor, who was assured six performances! Without taking into account the other artists, the chorus, etc.[47]

It is worth emphasizing again how Montemezzi's career was almost uncannily paralleling Puccini's at a distance of twenty years. Puccini's *Edgar*, his first opera specifically commissioned by Casa Ricordi, and his one great failure, had premiered on April 21, 1889, and played for just three performances. Ferdinando Fontana's libretto took much of the blame for the debacle. Careers develop in a competitive relationship with other careers, of course, and while Puccini's main rival in 1889 had been the consumptive Alfredo Catalani, who would die in 1893, Montemezzi faced rather stiffer competition in 1909. Ricordi now had three composers vying to succeed Puccini as the company's biggest artistic asset, for Alfano and Montemezzi

---

[45] *Ars et Labor* 64/4 (April 1909): p. 318.
[46] Morini, "Carteggi," p. 238.
[47] Quoted in Paoletti, *Mascagni, Mocchi, Sonzogno*, p. 132.

had been joined by the younger Riccardo Zandonai (1883–1944). Zandonai was offered the chance to compose *Il grillo del focolare* (*The Cricket on the Hearth*) in 1906, thus ensuring that all three rivals had operas coming out in the unique 1908–1909 season. Their different fates are worth remark. *Il grillo del focolare*, with a libretto by Cesare Hanau, was brought out under the auspices of Ricordi, and premiered at the Teatro Chiarella, Turin, on November 28, 1908, well before the earthquake, and without the involvement of the STIn. It proved very popular, Zandonai was promoted as a new *Wunderkind*, the press reporting his age as just twenty-three (he was actually twenty-five), and the opera was soon being quite widely produced in Italy as well as showing promising signs of being able to enter the international market. Alfano's *Il Principe Zilah*, with a libretto by Illica, premiered at the Teatro Carlo Felice, Genoa, on February 3, 1909, under the STIn umbrella, was much less successful, managing just four performances and making a loss of 29,000 lire, the biggest of the season.[48] Critics pointed out that one reason for the failure was the immense popularity of *Florodora* (1899), an operetta by the British composer Leslie Stuart, in Genoa at this time.[49] *Il Principe Zilah* was at least brought out early enough in the season to be moved on to the Teatro Costanzi, Rome, for three more performances in April, though these proved no more successful. Zandonai was thus the clear winner of the season. Further evidence that everything was going his way was that Tito Ricordi (1865–1933), now increasingly dominant in the family firm, favored the younger composer. Through his efforts, in May 1909 the firm made an unprecedented gesture of faith in Zandonai's future by sending him on an expenses-paid trip to Spain to undertake field research for his next opera, *Conchita*, which was to have a Spanish setting. No comparable gestures of support were made to Montemezzi or Alfano, and they both experienced significant crises in their careers at this juncture. Alfano fell into a severe depression;[50] it is difficult to assess how the events of the year affected Montemezzi, on the basis of surviving correspondence, but he must, at the least, have been deeply disappointed and concerned for his future as a salaried composer.

Héllera and *Il Principe Zilah* acquired an aura of failure, probably exacerbated by the larger failure of the STIn's first season, that proved

---

[48] Paoletti, *Mascagni, Mocchi, Sonzogno*, p. 142, n. 475.

[49] Paoletti, *Mascagni, Mocchi, Sonzogno*, p. 20.

[50] Konrad Dryden, *Franco Alfano: Transcending "Turandot"* (Lanham, MD: Scarecrow Press, 2010), p. 29.

96 SUCCEEDING PUCCINI

impossible to shake off. But whereas Alfano, by November 1909, was resigned to the fact that, as he wrote, "*Zilah* is dead," and from then on largely disowned the work,[51] Montemezzi never lost faith in *Héllera* and to the very end of his life dreamed of seeing it return to the stage, as subsequent chapters document. He did accept that it needed revision, and soon after the Turin performances started work on a thorough reconsideration of the work with a reluctant Illica, following the advice of Tito Ricordi. Much of the revision was done in the summer of 1909. The main goal was to substantially shorten the opera and make the main dramatic action stand out more clearly. Yet Montemezzi was unsure how best to do this, or at least how to please all the parties with a stake in the work. *Héllera* has by far the most complex textual history of any of his operas. There are, remarkably, four different editions of the vocal score extant: the original 1909 edition (273 pages); a "New Edition 1910," issued no later than April 1910 (218 pages); a second "New Edition 1910," this time in a more structured form, with Act 2 for the first time divided into two parts (238 pages); and a "New Edition 1937" incorporating revisions that Montemezzi had made in May 1935 (239 pages). A second edition of the libretto was published in 1936. While drawing attention to the main differences between the four versions, we concentrate here on the second 1910 score, in which the opera reached something like its definitive form.

The score, as Montemezzi claimed, immediately throws the audience "into the great whirl of the drama," evoking the worldly life of high society with a bright, urgent, bustling, C-major theme entrusted to vociferous woodwinds and strings (Example 3.1). This high society, to which Héllera and Adolfo both belong, acts as a powerful dramatic pole, opposing the former's restless condition to the careless attitude of her social environment, a conflict focused in the short monologue introducing the song she plays on the piano (Act 1, no. 38) (Example 3.2). The insincerity of high society life is emphasized at the outset by Jean, the servant, in a plaintive tirade not that different from Gérard's in *Andrea Chénier* or Michonnet's in *Adriana Lecouvreur*. Montemezzi appropriately set this as an *Allegretto* in minuet rhythm with a regular quaver-note accompaniment by *pizzicato* strings: a clear parody of an *ancien régime* soundscape, anachronistic but not inappropriate for the Second Bourbon Restoration (Act 1, no. 1). The contrast between Héllera's anxiety and the world's careless enjoyment is further highlighted by the Parisian carnival songs heard through

---

[51] Dryden, *Franco Alfano*, p. 28.

Music Example 3.1 *Héllera*, Act 1, bars 1–12.

the window: a device famously used in *La traviata*, and therefore functioning as a sort of dramatic allusion to Verdi's masterpiece.

The double introduction comprising the servant's complaint and the carnival songs, almost totally cut in the first 1910 version,[52] leads to a vast and complex scene, heavily revised in 1910, which introduces Héllera. Very much the central character in the opera, her characterization fully justifies this shift in focus away from Constant's novel, which, as noted above, had centered on Adolphe. Illica's stage directions clarify that he conceived Héllera as an attractive and elegant lady, as in Giovanni Boldini's celebrated portraits, and this image was powerfully supported with the costume designs by Luigi Sapelli (1865–1936), the celebrated designer known as Caramba (Figure 3.3). The

---

[52] The first 1910 edition starts with Maria's "Jean, presto!... in movimento!" (Jean, quick!... get moving!).

Music Example 3.2 *Héllera*, Act 1, no. 38, bars 1–16.

Figure 3.3 Caramba, costume design for *Héllera*, Act 2, 1909. *Archivio Storico Ricordi*.

100   SUCCEEDING PUCCINI

libretto repeatedly refers to the symbolic meaning of Héllera's name, a Tuscan and poetical variant (used, for example, by Politian) for ivy, which "dove avvinghia muore" (will die where it clings).[53] She enters to a beautiful, noble, D-flat-major motif that portrays her melancholic nature (Act 1, no. 13), the orchestra revealing her growing unrest, which culminates in the cry "È uno strazio dell'anima!" (It's the torment of the soul!).[54] Gloomy thoughts about her intolerable life give way to the romanza-like, F-major lyrical invocation to Adolfo, supported by the *piano espressivo* solo violin and oboe (Act 1, no. 17). Héllera's melancholy is suspended by the timely appearance of the Doctor— his lengthy, introductory monologue in the 1909 score subsequently cut, as part of his general reduction in importance—followed by her daughters, and then the noisy party turning up for dinner. The episode with the Count and Countess D'Auvray offers, with its bright, shrill sounds (including a remarkable chatty, three-voice ladies chorus, Act 1, no. 30), a welcome change of mood before Héllera resumes her depressive attitude. She comments on the careless immorality of her friends with a broad melody featuring painful minor-6th ascending (and descending) leaps, "La mia, tortura e spasima" (My soul, tortured and suffering, Act 1, no. 38) (Example 3.2).[55] Both text and music here were modified in the revisions.

Act 1 ends more brightly, however. After the orchestra has depicted the falling snow, seen through the open window, Héllera sits at the piano (actually playing offstage) and sings her song "Il richiamo" ("The Call," Act 1, no. 43), a remarkable case of diegetic music (although not that brilliant in melodic invention) devised by Illica so that the opera can subsequently keep referring back to it. The ensuing duet crowning the act then celebrates the lovers' erotic bliss in what Montemezzi proudly described, in his 1909 interview, as a "very new form, rapid and concise." Adolfo breaks in with a long, E-major, 6/8 *Andante* passionate solo, "Tu che conosci l'idiomi muti" (You who know the mute languages, Act 1, no. 50) (Example 3.3),[56] obtaining a not less passionate reply from Héllera, whom he keeps pressing. The two lovers first share a dreamy atmosphere, then sing together at the distance of an octave, "Il nuovo palpito io sento" (I feel a new throbbing, Act 1, no. 62).[57]

---

[53]   Luigi Illica, *Héllera* (Milan: Ricordi, 1909), p. 21. This is the last line of Act 1.

[54]   Montemezzi, *Héllera* (vocal score) (Milan: Ricordi, 1910), p. 19. This is the second of the 1910 editions.

[55]   Montemezzi, *Héllera*, pp. 51–52.

[56]   Montemezzi, *Héllera*, p. 61.

[57]   Montemezzi, *Héllera*, p. 75. The libretto, notably, did not imagine the lovers sharing the same words here: Illica, *Héllera*, p. 21.

Music Example 3.3 *Héllera*, Act 1, no. 50, bars 1–19.

This final duet, unaltered in all versions of the score, was the main cause of Montemezzi's great quarrel with Illica, who had neither envisioned nor written it,[58] and who found the situation deeply illogical, offending dramatic truth, since this passionate and noisy exchange would take place near the little girls' bedroom in Héllera's family home.

---

[58] It is not clear who wrote the words, but in a passionate letter to Montemezzi of March 30, 1908, Illica seems to suggest that Giulio Ricordi was the author. Archivio Storico Ricordi.

102   SUCCEEDING PUCCINI

Act 2, now in fashionable Baden-Baden, again opens with an evocation of somewhat frenzied frivolity, the assertive symphonic introduction entrusted once more to strings and woodwinds. It is temporarily suspended by the ladies' chatting, but then exploited to support the conversation, before changing into a comical semiquavers "yawning" theme, symbolizing the underlying boredom of the elegant party. This scene was drastically cut, a lengthy part for the Doctor being completely excised; a witty handwritten comment on a working libretto reads: "Doctor's part: make it less . . . socialist!"[59] Héllera and Adolfo suddenly appear, singing a supple, warm melodic invention shared with the orchestra (Act 2, no. 14), establishing a remarkable distance from the music heard so far in this act. As Héllera whispers to Adolfo that she does not dare pronounce the sweet word "happy" (Act 2, no. 20), to a rocking 6/8 meter, a crucial theme expressing the character's intoxicating passion echoes on a solo violin accompanied by the other strings *pizzicato* (Example 3.4). This theme then serves as the postlude to the duet, as Héllera stares "as if inebriated" (*come inebriata*) after the departing Adolfo,[60] before entering into dialogue with the Doctor, to whom she admits, exploiting the same metaphor, that life has been dangerously intoxicating, and will eventually kill her. This encounter with the Doctor reveals all Héllera's unhappiness, well expressed in the depressive *Lento molto*, F-sharp-minor lament on the destiny to which she has condemned her daughters (Act 2, no. 30). Adolfo appears again and hushes Héllera away to the aforementioned passion-theme, when an unexpected E-major evening song from offstage (Act 2, no. 3) ends Part 1 of Act 2 with a remarkable, mostly (though not wholly) homophonic choral intermezzo with which the lovers' voices intertwine (Example 3.5). The dramatic and musical conclusion here, marked in Illica's correction to the printed libretto,[61] represents a significant rethinking of Act 2, with a whole scene omitted that connected the chorus with the subsequent ball; as noted previously, it was not until the second 1910 score that the act was divided into two parts.

The symphonic introduction to Act 2 returns to open Part 2, before turning into a sentimental waltz performed by just the strings, the melody allocated to the first violins (Act 2, no. 46). The waltz is immediately danced onstage, then the melody is sung by the chorus. The waltz rhythm is maintained, hosting the conversation and becoming most lively

---

[59] "Brano Dottore: renderlo meno . . . socialista!" Archivio Storico Ricordi, LIBR00265.
[60] Montemezzi, *Héllera*, p. 119.
[61] Archivio Storico Ricordi, LIBR00266.

Music Example 3.4. *Héllera*, Act 2, no. 20, bars 1–9.

(*animatissimo*) as Héllera and Adolfo appear (Act 2, no. 50). The party abruptly ends with a general exodus, intended to affront Héllera, and Adolfo "challenges the gentlemen." Although actually sung, Adolfo's yelling contains very little music (Act 2, no. 51). Héllera then draws him back into song as she sings *Lento* on a 12/8 meter, while the orchestra plays the passion motif (Example 3.6). Montemezzi again struggled with the finale of the act, though for rather different reasons, as there is no suggestion that he and Illica were in disagreement here. From the final moments of the waltz onward, the various scores offer different solutions to the problem of winding the action up, with

Music Example 3.5 *Héllera*, Act 2, no. 35, bars 4–9.

Adolfo originally entering into a dialogue with Count D'Auvray, a solution Montemezzi surprisingly reverted to in 1935, although otherwise retaining the finale in its revised form. In a letter to Tito Ricordi of July 29, 1909, reporting much progress on the score, Montemezzi described the revised finale in detail, expressing great satisfaction with the more compact, poetical ending that had been achieved, with Héllera soothing Adolfo's anger and the couple disappearing as the curtain falls.[62]

---

[62] Archivio Storico Ricordi.

Music Example 3.6 *Héllera*, Act 2, no. 52, bar 7–no. 53, bar 12.

106 SUCCEEDING PUCCINI

Music Example 3.6 Continued

Act 3, opened by a short orchestral prelude that anticipates Héllera's decision to die, was much less revised than the other acts, despite its cool reception at the premiere. The early confrontation between the two lovers displays an appropriate, irregular development, expressing the couple's struggle to communicate, their emotions articulated mainly by the orchestra as the conversation lapses into silence. They are both, later, given the chance to express extreme passions: Adolfo reveals a deeper, more complex nature than in the previous acts in a solo scene where he even empathizes with the Doctor (Act 3, no. 22), while Héllera displays her desperate longing for her daughters, her last defense, before plunging into the abyss of despair as day falls into night. After the interesting stage situation in which Héllera and the Doctor gaze at her daughters from a distance with a sympathetic solo violin supporting Héllera (Act 3, no. 26), their dialogue brings out their opposite natures, with the Doctor's passionate speech unable to prevent Héllera's obsession with the vial of poison, clearly expressed by the orchestra's chromatic *fortissimo* gesture (Act 3, no. 43). This gesture anticipates the frenetic symphonic outburst as the Doctor exits to the music of the prelude, symbolizing Héllera's longing for death (Act 3, no. 45) (Example 3.7). From the following C-sharp minor *Moderatamente lento* (Act 3, no. 46) onward, the soundscape is dominated by the evening bells from a distant church: a two-note, descending minor-third ostinato performed by two offstage bells with the rarefied counterpoint of an oboe, single woodwinds, and muted horns.[63] The effective, though perhaps too extended, final scene has Adolfo reading the letter the now dead Héllera has left behind. In the 1909 opera, he sings the text on a fixed tone, a repeated E, but in both the 1910 versions, he simply reads the letter with no pitch indication. Montemezzi eventually changed his mind again, however, and in the 1937 score Adolfo reverts to singing, but on different pitches.

The existence of the two 1910 editions of *Héllera* suggests that the revision process was protracted, probably contentious, and for Casa Ricordi, expensive. It is likely that for some time the publisher largely held off promoting the opera while its final form was being settled, and by the time it was settled, Casa Ricordi's publicity operation was largely focused on Puccini's *La fanciulla del West*, the older composer's first new opera in nearly seven years, premiered with great fanfare at the Metropolitan Opera, New York, on December 10, 1910. Nevertheless, it is astonishing that no theatre stepped

---

[63] Montemezzi was notably fascinated by bells, and concluded his last known composition, the symphonic poem *Italia mia! Nulla fermerà il tuo canto!*, with them, as discussed in Chapter 10.

Music Example 3.7 *Héllera*, Act 3, no. 45, bars 1–12.

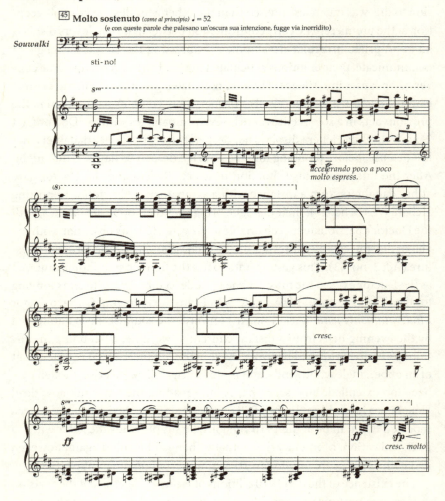

forward to produce the revised *Héllera*, then or later, and that Montemezzi never again saw the opera staged. When Italy's music critics finally had the chance to hear the revised opera broadcast on the radio in 1937, they expressed bafflement at the fact that it had not been heard since 1909, as discussed in Chapter 9, and it is a bafflement the modern scholar can only share, especially given the international prominence Montemezzi achieved with his next opera, *L'amore dei tre re*. Whatever the reason, Casa Ricordi lost out heavily with *Héllera*, and Tito Ricordi, at least, was left with a sense of annoyance that would cast a shadow over the next stage of Montemezzi's career.

If Montemezzi and Alfano both emerged as heavy losers, arguably victims, of the unique 1908–1909 season, there was another significant loser, too: Illica. The veteran librettist saw three of his operas premiered this season, for he had also authored *La Perugina* by the much older Edoardo Mascheroni (1852–1941), brought out at the Teatro San Carlo, Naples, on April 24. All three operas were published by Ricordi, and none of them made any profit. Whether Illica's work really had declined into formula, as critics maintained, or whether audiences had simply tired of his long series of melodramatic love plots, it is difficult to say, but Montemezzi and Alfano were clearly victims of a significant shift in taste. Konrad Dryden concludes that the failure of *Il Principe Zilah* was almost entirely Illica's fault, and he is scathing about the libretto: "Illica's glaringly incompetent hackwork . . . allows little, if any, room for character development."[64] It is impossible to be so dismissive of the *Héllera* libretto, and Montemezzi was mostly very happy with it; nevertheless, it was the end of the Illica era and increasingly obvious that Italian opera needed a new kind of libretto for a new age.[65]

[64] Dryden, *Franco Alfano*, p. 26.
[65] Illica stopped working for Casa Ricordi at this juncture. He was the librettist for Mascagni's *Isabeau*, premiered in 1911, and published by Sonzogno. Illica wrote this libretto in 1904, then revised it under Mascagni's direction in 1908–1909; 1909 was thus the last year in which Illica was able actively to shape modern Italian opera.

4

"A real Italian music drama"

The Making of *L'amore dei tre re*, 1909–1912

In later life, Montemezzi often told the story of how he came to compose *L'amore dei tre re*, the masterpiece which proved the climactic point of his career. These accounts differ slightly, but there are no serious contradictions; putting them together, a reasonably full narrative emerges.

It starts in Milan, in 1909, soon after the premiere of *Héllera*. While attending a horse race, probably at the Parco Trotter, Montemezzi heard talk of the great success of a new play. Sem Benelli's *La cena delle beffe* (The Supper of the Jests) had received its sensational premiere at the Teatro Argentina, Rome, on April 16, and was staged at the Teatro Lirico, Milan, on June 1. The dates suggest that it was talk of the Milanese premiere that Montemezzi heard. Excited by what was being reported, he bought a newspaper containing an extensive review of Benelli's play and devoured the criticism, quickly concluding "that this tragedy had many elements of great importance for the construction of an opera."[1] Without delay, Montemezzi sent a telegram to Benelli, asking if he could obtain the rights to an operatic adaptation. There was no reply. However, "[t]wo weeks later"[2] he had a "chance meeting" with Benelli in Milan,[3] and the latter explained that he had been so short of money at the time of *La cena*'s premiere that the following day he rashly sold the operatic rights to "a musical dilettante."[4] The dilettante in question was the obscure Tommaso Montefiore (1855–1933), who did nothing with his purchase and years later sold the rights on to Giordano. Montemezzi thus missed the chance to base an opera on a sensational new play with a compellingly theatrical plot. He expressed deep disappointment, and Benelli, apparently touched, and having taken a liking to the composer,

---

[1] Quoted in Herbert F. Peyser, "For Deeper Enjoyment of *L'Amore dei tre Re*," *Opera News*, January 10, 1949, p. 4.
[2] Peyser, "For Deeper Enjoyment," p. 4.
[3] Enid A. Haupt, "Enchanting Fabric," *Philadelphia Inquirer*, November 14, 1943, p. 4.
[4] Peyser, "For Deeper Enjoyment," p. 4.

Succeeding Puccini. David Chandler and Raffaele Mellace, Oxford University Press. © Oxford University Press 2025.
DOI: 10.1093/9780197761373.003.0005

hastened to explain that he was at an advanced stage of planning a new tragedy which he thought particularly suited for development as an opera. Montemezzi asked for more details, and then, as he later told the story, "arm in arm we walked through the least crowded part of the city for two hours. He [Benelli] expressed his every idea of all elements which would form his tragedy. I was completely won over!"[5] Benelli already had a working title: *Gli amori dei tre re* (The Loves of Three Kings).[6] In another report of their walk, Montemezzi stated: "Benelli . . . quoted passages which were already simmering in his head. The title itself conveyed a strange significance to me. Its very syllables spelled success."[7]

Montemezzi was so "won over" that at the end of the walk he took Benelli to the Casa Ricordi offices and arranged a provisional contract for an operatic adaptation of the yet unwritten tragedy on the spot. Giulio Ricordi, aware of the huge success of *La cena delle beffe*, and knowing Benelli had produced three successful plays in fifteen months, apparently needed little persuasion. A more formal contract was then drawn up and signed on July 6. This refers to a "private contract dated June 21," which would thus seem to have been the date of Montemezzi and Benelli's walk.[8]

The walk with Benelli would prove the central, defining moment of Montemezzi's artistic career: his future fame and most subsequent events in his life can be related to the imaginative commitment he made that day. Benelli, born on August 10, 1877, in the village of Filettole in Prato, Tuscany, was almost exactly two years younger than Montemezzi (Figure 4.1). His family worked in the local wool and textile industry and their economic difficulties meant that Benelli's schooling had been severely interrupted: he did not complete his secondary education until 1897. From that time, he struggled to support himself through journalism and writing for literary magazines, though his larger ambition was to write for the theatre, an institution which Benelli idealistically viewed as a potent force for social change. His first plays to be performed, *Ferdinando Lassalle* (1902) and *La Terra* (1903), were not successful, and *Vita Gaia* (1904) only very moderately so, so by 1905 Benelli was experiencing an acute sense of career crisis. However, the partly autobiographical bourgeois prose comedy *Tignola*, worked on for several years, was finally premiered in Genoa on February 10, 1908,

---

[5] Peyser, "For Deeper Enjoyment," p. 4.

[6] This title appears on the contract, dated July 6, 1909, in the Archivio Storico Ricordi.

[7] Montemezzi, "Reminiscences of *L'Amore dei Tre Re*," *Opera News*, February 10, 1941, p. 16.

[8] "private scrittura in data 21 Giugno." Archivio Storico Ricordi.

Figure 4.1 (*L to R*) Montemezzi, Sem Benelli, and Franco Alfano, ca. 1913. *Archivio Storico Ricordi.*

and proved a popular and critical success, quickly being taken up by other theatres. Benelli was immediately able to consolidate and build on this breakthrough: *Maschera di Bruto*, premiered in Milan on May 16, 1908, was again successful, and *La cena delle beffe*, the play which had excited Montemezzi, was an overwhelming triumph the following year, elevating Benelli to the first rank of Italian dramatists. It made Benelli a rich man and allowed his aristocratic inclinations to express themselves: in 1910 he began building his famous clifftop castle in Zoagli.

A good idea of how Benelli would have pitched his idea for *Gli amori dei tre re* to Montemezzi can be gleaned from an interview he gave L. R. Montecchi just before the premiere of what had, in the interim, become *L'amore dei tre re*

THE MAKING OF *L'AMORE DEI TRE RE*, 1909–1912   113

(The Love of Three Kings). Benelli was enthusing about his work to someone who had not yet been able to read or see it, and Montecchi clearly noted the plot description down from Benelli's conversation, often, it seems, capturing his exact phrases; the result is fascinating in its concern as much with the concept of the play as the action. The essence of the plot is that the aging Archibaldo was among the leaders of an army of barbarians who invaded Italy forty years earlier. Now ruling part of Italy from his large castle, he has become blind. In an effort to placate the local population, still inclined to rebel, he has married his son, Manfredo, to Fiora, a high-born Italian woman. She, however, was formerly betrothed to her cousin, Avito, an Italian prince, and still loves him. When Manfredo is away fighting the rebels, Avito makes clandestine visits to the castle to see Fiora, assisted by Flaminio, Archibaldo's Italian servant. Archibaldo is suspicious of Fiora, but being blind, he is unable to obtain proof of her infidelity; one day, however, he discovers her with Avito, and though the latter is able to slip away, he captures Fiora and strangles her when she refuses to name her lover. Fiora's body is placed in the castle crypt and Archibaldo puts a powerful poison on her dead lips, hoping her lover will come to give her a final kiss. The plan works, but Manfredo also enters the crypt, meets the dying Avito, feels sorry for him, and then himself kisses his dead wife's still poisoned lips. Thus, at the end, three of the four main protagonists are dead, and Archibaldo faces a terrible loneliness in "endless darkness and sorrow," having lost everything he cared about.[9]

"Perhaps it has never been more true to say of any work that evoking the mists of time is relevant," Benelli told Montecchi.[10] Though loosely set in the Dark Ages, *L'amore dei tre re* is notably unspecific concerning place and time, the vagueness creating an aura of myth. Benelli explained: "The region is not clearly defined, just as the type of the Barbarian invaders is not clearly defined. They may be Franks, or they may be Normans, perhaps more likely the latter, given the Nordic mysticism with which the soul of the young protagonist is woven."[11] Benelli's reference to the Franks and Normans would suggest a period of action between the eighth and twelfth centuries, and this can be further narrowed down with his assertion that the story takes place "well before the year 1000."[12] Montemezzi may have been particularly

---

[9] L. R. Montecchi, "'L'amore dei tre re': Conversando con l'Autore alla vigilia d'armi," *La Maschera* 6/16 (April 17, 1910): p. 3.

[10] Montecchi, "'L'amore dei tre re,'" p. 1.

[11] Montecchi, "'L'amore dei tre re,'" p. 2.

[12] Montecchi, "'L'amore dei tre re,'" p. 1. Benelli refers to "normanni," but given his comment on the date cannot have been thinking of the Norman invasion of southern Italy that commenced in 999.

114   SUCCEEDING PUCCINI

impressed by mention of the Franks, given that Charlemagne's son Pepin, king of Italy (777–810), had resided at Verona and was long believed to have been buried there, at the Basilica of San Zeno. Many subsequent critics, interestingly, assumed the action was set much earlier, in the period of the Germanic invasions of Italy, and this is a legitimate interpretation, albeit one not sanctioned by Benelli.[13]

The most revealing aspect of Benelli's interview is that he regarded the central character to be Manfredo:

> *Manfredo* is the supreme type of goodness, of that goodness which the Gospel has infused in his soul, strong and gentle at the same time. He is a mystic and an enthusiast; he possesses his woman but he adores her as if she were still a virgin, as if she were the source of purity itself, and, in the impetuous outlet of his soul, he struggles between his desire to loosen the coldness that seems to envelop *Fiora* and his fear of breaking the enchantment of that reserve which he attributes to the supreme and holy guilelessness (*ingenuità*) of the woman.[14]

Jole Tragella Monaro's interpretation, that the play's underlying theme is Italy's power to assimilate and transform barbarians from elsewhere, softening and civilizing them into adoration of her distinctive majesty, would appear to be correct, according to Benelli's own understanding of his story.[15] In this sense, the play is built around a fundamental contrast between the characters of the pagan Archibaldo and his Christian son.

The spoken play clarifies a few details not clear in Benelli's summary or the opera. Most importantly, Archibaldo became blind around the time Manfredo was born; Avito was away on a sea voyage when Fiora was married to Manfredo; and the marriage is very recent as the represented action begins. It appears that Benelli imagined Manfredo and Fiora as about twenty, with Avito perhaps slightly older. As a matter of custom and expedience, in

---

In earlier times, "normanni" could be equally understood as Danes or Vikings, these being loosely interchangeable terms for "Northmen."

[13] It is an interpretation that may well have appealed to Montemezzi, given his love of Wagner and the fact that Theodoric the Great, king of the Ostrogoths, had settled in Verona in the late 400s and built a castle on the site of the present Castel San Pietro, which the young composer had probably looked up at hundreds of times.

[14] Montecchi, "'L'amore dei tre re,'" p. 2.

[15] Jole Tragella Monaro, *Sem Benelli, l'uomo e il poeta* (Milan: La Prora, 1953), pp. 64–65.

THE MAKING OF *L'AMORE DEI TRE RE,* 1909–1912   115

the theatre they have generally been played by rather older actors: the roles of Manfredo and Fiora were created by Amedeo Chiantoni and Edvige Reinach (née Guglielmetti), born in 1871 and 1873, respectively. In the opera house, too, these roles have generally been sung by somewhat older singers: Mary Garden, indeed, was still regularly singing Fiora in her mid-fifties. The appearance of older performers in the parts has affected (and perhaps distorted) critical interpretations, giving the impression, in particular, that Manfredo and Fiora have been married for years.

The title of the opera, and the play from which it is derived, has often proved a puzzle. It can seem that Fiora is beloved of two kings (or princes) rather than three. Robert Lawrence put this question to Montemezzi in 1941, when the composer was in New York to conduct *L'amore dei tre re*:

> "It is clear," I proposed, "that Avito and Manfredo are in love with Fiora, but what about Archibaldo? The old man is blind, proud, implacable. Fiora has been faithless to his son, and as the father of Manfredo he strangles her to avenge his family honor."
>
> It was then that Montemezzi contradicted: "When the old king catches Fiora on the terrace after her night with Avito and questions her, she denies everything. He lays hands on her and demands, 'Perchè tremi, se dici il vero?' ('Why do you tremble, if you are telling the truth?'), to which she answers boldly, 'Ed anche voi tremate ... e non mentite' ('You're trembling, too ... and you're not lying'). In short, Archibaldo has a repressed, gnawing love for his daughter-in-law, and she knows it."[16]

Archibaldo's intense interest in Fiora's thoughts and movements can well suggest "repressed" desire. In Benelli's play, though, the passage Montemezzi draws attention to is rather more extended and can be interpreted in more than one way. Fiora implies that there is something sordid in Archibaldo's desire to hold her (allegedly to check whether she is telling the truth), and he backs away shocked, accusing her of sullying a love which, he implies, is pure and paternal. If anything, Benelli suggests that Fiora's actions here are simply self-serving, and that Archibaldo is justified in protesting his innocence. However the passage is interpreted, though—and Montemezzi's own understanding of it may have developed over the years, as Freudian ideas

---

[16] Robert Lawrence, "Figures on the Battlements," *Opera News,* January 4, 1964, pp. 6–7.

116   SUCCEEDING PUCCINI

about sexuality and repression became part of the basic twentieth-century worldview—*L'amore dei tre re* is clearly an apt title.

Having made the decision, in June 1909, that *L'amore dei tre re* would be his next opera, Montemezzi was apparently content to wait for Benelli to write the play; in the meantime, he had the revision of *Héllera* on which to work. Given that Benelli had provided a fairly full account of the planned tragedy, though, it is likely that Montemezzi began thinking in general terms about the sort of music he would need to compose for his new subject, different in tone from anything he had written before. When Benelli had finished his play, in late 1909 or early 1910, he invited Montemezzi to Zoagli and read it through to him. The composer was extremely impressed, later explaining his feelings on this occasion to Giuseppe Adami:

> The poem's passionate and tragic atmosphere, even more than its keen dramatic interest, immediately seemed to me such as to offer broad scope for musical inspiration. Whether the spoken play was successful or not didn't matter much to me, so confident I felt about my choice, and myself. I'm not saying this out of arrogance. The way I see it, even a work that's wrong from a dramatic point of view, and this is not our case, can be, or become, a well-made lyric work. The important thing is that the composer experiences it and feels it the way I was feeling "*L'amore dei tre re*" and experiencing the complex souls of its complex characters. Then it also seemed to me that Benelli's poetry, so incisive, so limpid, and genuine, offered me scope to realize what in my opinion is the true formula of the modern musical drama: the perfect correspondence of words with music.[17]

To Olin Downes, Montemezzi later stated more simply: "The instant I heard Benelli's poem I saw my opera on the stage and felt it in my heart. That is why I was able to evolve it in music."[18]

Benelli's play received its premiere at the Teatro Argentina, Rome, on April 16, 1910, exactly a year after that of *La cena delle beffe*. Montemezzi went to Rome to attend the rehearsals and stayed for the first twelve performances. This intense experience of the play in the theatre left him even more convinced, if that were possible, that he had found the ideal subject. But the play

---

[17] Quoted in Giuseppe Adami, "In attesa de 'L'Amore dei tre re' di Italo Montemezzi," *La Sera: Giornale politico, finanziario, illustrato*, April 7, 1913, p. 2.
[18] Quoted in Olin Downes, "The Quest of a Drama to Sing—Montemezzi and 'Three Kings,'" *New York Times*, March 9, 1924, p. X6.

THE MAKING OF *L'AMORE DEI TRE RE*, 1909–1912   117

was only modestly successful; the audience responded positively to the triangular Archibaldo-Fiora-Avito plot but failed to grasp Benelli's deeper conception of Manfredo as the hero of the play. To them, Manfredo was a somewhat ridiculous, high-minded cuckold, and the lack of sympathy he generated meant that Act 3 fell rather flat, the murder of Fiora largely extinguishing interest in the story. Writing enthusiastically to Tito Ricordi after the first performance, Montemezzi blamed the play's lukewarm success firmly on the inadequate acting of Chiantoni as Manfredo, "misrepresenting the character from beginning to end."[19]

Tito, now effectively head of Casa Ricordi, was disappointed when he heard of the tragedy's reception and was dismayed when he read the play. He believed it was not suitable for an opera and encouraged Montemezzi to break his contract with Benelli. "He [Tito] made every effort to discourage me," Montemezzi told Downes. Montemezzi then turned to friends in an effort to vindicate his project but could find no support. "My friends to whom I described my purpose were equally antagonistic [as Tito]. Every one, except myself, seemed to think it madness to attempt to make an opera from such material."[20] An urgent meeting had to be arranged back in Milan, recollected by Montemezzi as follows:

At last we three—Benelli, [Tito] Ricordi and I—had a meeting. Ricordi became excited. Slapping the manuscript with his palm, he cried, "Who will understand such a libretto! It means this and this and this. It is completely incomprehensible to the public, as has already been shown. And your Fiora! What does she mean to an audience? What is she, this Fiora?"

Benelli replied, "She is a woman. If you cannot understand her, it is useless for me to try to explain. I understand her, and I think he"—indicating me—"also understands. And that is the main thing. I acknowledge that it is not simple to describe what one understands. For example, I understand you, but I could not describe you very easily!"

Ricordi, in desperation, turned to me. "And are you still of the same mind?"

I looked at him in some astonishment. "My friend," I said, "what opinion would you have of my character if I changed overnight a conviction I have

---

[19] "svisando dal principio alla fine il personaggio." Montemezzi to Tito Ricordi, April 18, 1910. Archivio Storico Ricordi.

[20] Downes, "The Quest of a Drama to Sing," p. X6.

118   SUCCEEDING PUCCINI

held from the beginning against all of you? Certainly I have not changed. This drama, to me, is ideal for my needs."

Benelli rejoiced. "I will add something, Mr. Ricordi. If 'L'Amore' is set to music, it shall be by Montemezzi and by none other. If he chooses not to do this I give you my word, without condition, without contract, that my drama shall never become an opera."

Ricordi looked at us as if he thought we had gone quite insane, then said to me, "Very well: you have decided it; you are responsible for the consequences."[21]

It was an audacious stand for Montemezzi to take, with *Héllera* still doing nothing for Casa Ricordi's prosperity. And while he won the immediate battle, it was a stand which seems to have deepened a simmering feud with Tito that was only resolved when *L'amore dei tre re* turned out to be an enormous success.

Much of the opposition Montemezzi encountered must have stemmed from his radical, but ultimately epochal, desire to set a shortened version of Benelli's play without adapting it into a conventional opera libretto. It is a measure of the newness of the idea that the term *Literaturoper* did not yet exist: it was coined by Edgar Istel, a German musicologist, in 1914 to describe "the Strauss-Debussy procedure" (*Verfahren Strauß-Debussy*): that is to say, the "procedure" by which Strauss and Debussy had circumvented the ordinary requirement of an opera composer for a specially prepared libretto by directly setting to music existing spoken plays in *Salome* and *Pelléas et Mélisande*.[22] The general concept can be found in London as early as the 1750s, when John Christopher Smith (1712–1795) experimented, albeit unsuccessfully, with setting shortened versions of Shakespeare's plays to music. But the modern *Literaturoper* began with Alexander Dargomïzhsky (1813–1869), and for several decades it was a wholly Russian phenomenon; it was the premiere of *Pelléas et Mélisande* at the Opéra-Comique, Paris, on April 30, 1902, which brought this new form of opera to international attention and inspired a considerable number of composers across Western Europe to attempt something similar. Italy, though, already had its own limited tradition

[21] Downes, "The Quest of a Drama to Sing," p. X6.
[22] Edgar Istel, *Das Libretto* (Berlin: Schuster and Loeffler, 1914), p. 44. The term *Literaturoper* did not become widely used and standard until the 1970s; before that time, a number of other terms had been used to describe operas that set spoken plays to music. For a useful history of the term, and the theoretical and definitional issues it has raised, see Peter Petersen, "Der Terminus 'Literaturoper'—eine Begriffsbestimmung," *Archiv für Musikwissenschaft* 56 (1999): pp. 52–70.

THE MAKING OF *L'AMORE DEI TRE RE*, 1909–1912   119

of *Literaturopern*. As early as the 1880s, Mascagni had started work on the first Italian example, Heinrich Heine's *Wilhelm Ratcliff*, set in translation. *Guglielmo Ratcliff* was finally completed in 1894 and premiered at La Scala the following year, but it was a short-lived success mainly because of dramatic weaknesses in the Heine play, which had never been staged as a spoken drama. No major Italian composer was tempted to follow Mascagni's lead, but Giacomo Orefice (1865–1922) composed two operas setting shortened versions of plays by Pietro Cossa (1830–1880): *Il Gladiatore* (1898) and *Cecilia* (1902). Much more attention was given to the passing success of Alberto Franchetti's *La figlia di Iorio* (1906), in large part because it set a text by Gabriele D'Annunzio, Italy's most famous living writer, and the play was adapted by D'Annunzio himself. Mascagni, Orefice, and Franchetti had not shown themselves willing to let the text dictate the music to the extent Dargomïzhsky or Debussy had, so the possibilities of an Italian *Literaturoper* were still largely unrealized.[23]

Between 1906 and 1910, there appear to have been no further Italian *Literaturopern*, and Tito Ricordi's position was very likely that the experiment had failed. Montemezzi's refusal to abandon his project in the face of such discouragement reveals not only the strength of his convictions but also a certain prescience, for a brief golden era for the Italian *Literaturoper* was about to commence, inaugurated by *L'amore dei tre re*. Montemezzi's opera was quickly followed by Mascagni's *Parisina*, Zandonai's *Francesca da Rimini*, and Pizzetti's *Fedra*—all three derived from D'Annunzio plays. *L'amore dei tre re* and *Francesca da Rimini* were two of the most successful Italian operas of the decade, while *Fedra*, though never a popular work, laid the foundations of Pizzetti's long and distinguished career as an opera composer. All this was in the future as Montemezzi argued with Tito, and the latter had the past on his side, but if the composer ever had a moment of farsighted artistic vision, this was it. It was a vision inspired not only by Benelli's play but also, surely, by *Pelléas et Mélisande*. It is not that Montemezzi wanted to write a Debussian opera, but that he wanted to write something analogous to it, distinctively Italian instead of distinctively French. Philip Hale, a great champion of Debussy, would note admiringly, after hearing *L'amore*

---

[23] For a fuller account of the emergence of the *Literaturoper* in Italy, though one that omits mention of Orefice's modest, bridging role, see Jürgen Maehder, "The Origins of Italian *Literaturoper*: *Guglielmo Ratcliff*, *La figlia di Iorio*, *Parisina*, and *Francesca da Rimini*," in *Reading Opera*, edited by Arthur Groos and Roger Parker (Princeton, NJ: Princeton University Press, 1988), pp. 92–128.

120 SUCCEEDING PUCCINI

dei tre re: "Montemezzi has done in an Italian way for an Italian drama what Debussy in an ultra-modern French way did for the Belgian Maeterlinck." Nevertheless, "[t]o say . . . that Montemezzi imitated the methods of Debussy would be absurd"; *Pelléas et Mélisande*, Hale explained, was essentially dreamlike and mysterious, while *L'amore dei tre re* was full of "glowing and ecstatic" passion.[24]

The beginning of the compositional process was later recalled by Montemezzi:

> I returned to Vigasio . . . to the quiet of my studio. Gripped by the beauty of this Benellian tragedy I knew that I had embarked on a work of great importance. The tragedy responded absolutely to my conception which was to construct an art work, different from anything that had been done before—a real Italian music drama, with dynamism, drama, poetry—all of it bathed in an atmosphere of musical rapture.
>
> For many days I lived in close contact with the tragedy, scrutinizing profoundly, cutting certain parts and studying its proportions so as to obtain a perfect musical equilibrium. During this work the characters of the various personages entered my blood, awakening the musical expression which illustrated them; and little by little the structures of the new creation appeared to me in their general outline. I became more and more fascinated. I felt myself fully able to realize this dream which was taking shape with so much beauty. And so, with this vision firmly fixed in my mind, I retired to my solitude.[25]

Earlier, Montemezzi had explained to Adami: "Not one verse was changed. I didn't want the words to be a complement to music; instead, I wanted the music to be the winged comment to the words. I limited myself to asking the poet for some cuts where the music could replace the exuberance of the poetry, or where the situation would have become long beyond measure, with serious damage."[26] The libretto that Montemezzi developed, with Benelli's permission, faithfully followed the structure and imaginative movement of the original play. The only significant change came at the start of Act 3, where some conversations about the dead Fiora between ordinary people, not otherwise appearing in the drama, were replaced by a series of mourning

---

[24] Philip Hale, "L'Amore Dei Tre Re" Again Performed," *Boston Herald*, February 15, 1914, p. 7.

[25] Quoted in Peyser, "For Deeper Enjoyment," pp. 4–5.

[26] Quoted in Adami, "In attesa de 'L'Amore dei tre re,'" p. 2.

THE MAKING OF *L'AMORE DEI TRE RE,* 1909–1912   121

choruses which Benelli wrote at Montemezzi's request. In these, the composer told Adami, "Benelli took inspiration from the ancient Sacred Hymns."

Montemezzi was fully aware of the conventions of Italian romantic opera and their evolution, and he was able to exploit them. His libretto has a careful, subtle architecture combining effectiveness and variety. Although the score is not divided by numbers, and resists closed forms, there are places where lyrical singing emerges more prominently, which can be termed *arioso* and *duet*:

Act 1
1. Prelude
2. Scene (Archibaldo, Flaminio)—Arioso (Archibaldo)
3. Interlude
4. Duet (Avito, Fiora)
5. Scene (Archibaldo, Fiora)—Arioso (Archibaldo)
6. Interlude
7. Scene (Manfredo, Archibaldo, Fiora)—Arioso (Manfredo)

Act 2
8. Prelude
9. Scene (Manfredo, Fiora)—Arioso (Manfredo)
10. Interlude
11. Duet (Avito, Fiora)
    a. Duet (Avito, Fiora)
    b. Scene (Ancella, Fiora)
    c. Interlude
    d. Duet (Avito, Fiora)
12. Scene (Archibaldo, Fiora, Flaminio)
13. Scene (Manfredo, Archibaldo, Fiora)—Arioso (Manfredo)
14. Postlude

Act 3
15. Prelude (*Introduzione*)
16. Chorus with solos (Men and Women, a Girl, a Boy, an Old Woman)
17. Interlude
18. Arioso (Avito)
19. Scene (Manfredo, Avito)—Arioso (Manfredo)
20. Scene (Archibaldo, Manfredo)

122 SUCCEEDING PUCCINI

Balance, variety, and the positioning of effective dramatic turns can be recognized as the main principles of the overall architecture. For a *Literaturoper*, *L'amore dei tre re* exhibits a remarkable amount of symmetry, comparable to that in Berg's *Wozzeck* (1925), a later masterpiece of this operatic subgenre. Montemezzi's Acts 1 and 2, both centered on a triple confrontation between Fiora and the three kings, share a symmetrical construction. The core of both is an extended duet between Fiora and Avito (nos. 4 and 11, in both cases introduced by a significant symphonic interlude), surrounded each time by two lyrical statements (*ariosi*), by Archibaldo in Act 1 (nos. 1 and 5) and Manfredo in Act 2 (nos. 9 and 13), usually connected to shorter confrontations with Fiora, the last of which leads to her death. The juxtapositions between her different confrontations with her lover, husband, and father-in-law illuminate her personality and the complex web of her relationships. The long duet with Avito (no. 11), the lyrical core and perfect barycenter of the opera—interrupted by the scene with the servant bringing Manfredo's veil to prolong the dramatic tension—best expresses Fiora's internal conflict. The magnificent Act 2 is particularly effective in organizing a range of emotional situations according to the criterion of greatest contrast. This is true for Act 3 as well: lacking the dead Fiora's voice, it allows the audience to listen to the lyrical singing of the two younger kings immediately before their respective deaths. These *ariosi* effectively contrast with the somber atmosphere established by the mourning *a cappella* chorus at the outset of the act, which provides a solid, vital, Verdian sense of theatre and incorporates, for the sake of variety, the Girl's moving lament, sounding almost like an anticipation of Puccini's Liu. The entire Act 3 is built on a series of remarkable contrasts between symphonic writing, lyrical solo singing, and choral chant. The voice of the choir offstage creeps even into the dialogue between the dying Avito and Manfredo: after Avito's bold invitation "vendicati, uccidimi" (take revenge, kill me), the chorus sings lines unlike anything in Benelli's original play: "L'amore nascerà come fontana / il dì che il Creatore darà / la luce alla sua creatura" (Love will be born like a fountain / on the day the creator gives / light to His creatures).[27]

Montemezzi, perhaps influenced by the public response to Benelli's play, significantly reduced the emphasis on Manfredo as the Christian hero. For example, in the final scene between Avito and Manfredo, the former asks, in

---

[27] Montemezzi, *L'amore dei tre re* (vocal score) (Milan: Ricordi, 1913), pp. 185–87. It is worth noting that the effect here is anticipated by the use of an organ heard "from above" in the final scene of Benelli's play. See Sem Benelli, *L'amore dei tre re* (Milan: Treves, 1910), p. 107.

THE MAKING OF *L'AMORE DEI TRE RE,* 1909–1912   123

the original play: "Questo facesti, tu, che sei chiamato / il santo?" (Have you done this [placed poison on Fiora's lips], you who are called / the saint?).[28] In Montemezzi's abridgement, this becomes simply: "Questo facesti, tu?"[29] Instead, as the structural analysis suggests, Fiora emerges as the central, pivotal character; even in the final act, she dominates the stage, a corpse dressed in white on a bed of flowers. Montemezzi later stated that "[t]he essential drama lies in the struggle between Fiora and Archibaldo"[30]—a tense battle of wits, well captured in a photograph of Lina Scavizzi and Fernando Autori in the roles (Figure 4.2). Fiora's name can be related to the floral fashion in turn-of-the-century opera,[31] but it points to just one aspect of her complex character. She is, with Basiliola (in *La nave*), the most remarkable of Montemezzi's female characters, and while both respond to the contemporary fascination with the figure of the *femme fatale*, Fiora is, arguably, the more sophisticated version of the type. She leads the men in her life through fascination to ruin, yet until the end maintains features of an innocent creature. "Tu sei come una bimba" (You are like a child), Archibaldo tells her in Act 1, "*la gola quasi stretta da una nascente bontà paterna, senile*" (his throat tightening with nascent kindness, paternal and senescent).[32] Montemezzi aptly symbolizes Fiora's state of innocence in her theme, initially presented very early in the opera, as the curtain rises on Act 1, and then restated, unmistakably, when her name is first mentioned in Flaminio's answer to Archibaldo's question about the owner of the bedroom adjacent to the castle hall: "Fiora! La sposa del figliuolo vostro!" (Fiora! The wife of your son!) (Example 4.1).[33] Montemezzi makes her theme resound in sweet woodwinds: flute and oboe gently unwind a descending melody departing from top E_3 and reaching central B_2 in the aethereal landscape created by the accompaniment of *pianissimo* clarinets, bassoon, muted horns, celesta, and harp. As innocent as Fiora might be, her cruel circumstances have forced her to learn the art of deception. The moral dilemma she struggles with is best exemplified in the central portion of Act 2, where in two quite different duets she faces first her husband, then her lover. In the latter, a symbolic stage prop stands visually for

[28] Benelli, *L'amore dei tre re*, p. 114.
[29] Montemezzi, *L'amore dei tre re*, p. 183.
[30] Montemezzi, "Reminiscences," p. 16.
[31] See, for example, *Parsifal*; Spyridon Samaras's *Flora Mirabilis* (1886); Mascagni's *Iris* (1898); Hans Pfitzner's *Die Rose vom Liebesgarten* (1901); and Francesco Cilea's *Adriana Lecouvreur* (1902) and *Gloria* (1907).
[32] Montemezzi, *L'amore dei tre re*, p. 34.
[33] Montemezzi, *L'amore dei tre re*, p. 5.

Figure 4.2 Fernando Autori and Lina Scavizzi as Archibaldo and Fiora, Teatro La Fenice, 1926. *Chandler collection*.

her inner contradiction. Manfredo has a long white veil delivered to her so she can wave farewell to him from the top of the castle. While she obeys her husband, Avito insists on courting her, until she finally desists, overcome by passion and sympathy for her lover: "Ah, tortura! indicibile contrasto!" (Ah, torture! The indescribable contrast!).[34] It is a perfectly contrived scene with great visual and musical impact, the dramatic stakes clear even to the most inattentive audience.

If Fiora is the central character, Archibaldo is undoubtably the opera's driving force, as he is in the original play. His name, Benelli specifies, means *coraggiosissimo*, the bravest.[35] He has a warrior's values, and Montemezzi's treatment of his narration of his descent on Italy as a young conqueror, forty years earlier, the opera's first major set piece, gives it an appropriate vibrant, predatory energy. Blindness has exacerbated his gloomy vision of life and human relationships, and he shows himself extremely suspicious from the

---

[34] Montemezzi, *L'amore dei tre re*, pp. 107–8.
[35] Benelli, *L'amore dei tre re*, p. 9.

Music Example 4.1 *L'amore dei tre re*, Act 1, no. 4, bars 1–5.

start, his first line, both in the play and opera, being a question about the door of Fiora's bedroom: "Guarda quella porta. / È chiusa bene?" (Look at that door. / Is it closed properly?).[36] Archibaldo's suspicions, and their fearful consequences, frame the entire action, so that in the final scenes of each act, all carefully judged for maximum effect, he is the central character. In Act 1, Manfredo's apparent idyll with Fiora—the couple embrace as they leave—is unequivocally contradicted by four bars of hollow, stunned Wagnerian orchestration, introducing, accompanying, and crowning Archibaldo's last lines, as the old warrior is left alone on stage: "Signore mio, se tu m'hai tolto gli occhi / fa ch'io non veda ... che sia cieco ... cieco!" (My Lord, if you have taken my eyes / let me not see ... let me be blind ... blind!) (Example 4.2).[37]

---

[36] Montemezzi, *L'amore dei tre re*, pp. 3–4.
[37] Montemezzi, *L'amore dei tre re*, p. 58.

Music Example 4.2 *L'amore dei tre re*, Act 1, no. 46, bars 1–12.

This finale is a very good example of Montemezzi's ability to convey dramatic meaning through highly condensed symphonic discourse. The composer struggled with it, as a rare surviving piece of draft score demonstrates (Figure 4.3). In the process of revising this passage, Montemezzi found a way to better stress some crucial semantic hubs in Manfredo's exalted discourse ("padre," "figlio," "luce"), radically changed both the harmonic context and

Figure 4.3 *L'amore dei tre re*, abandoned draft, "il figlio ha trovato il suo bene!" Chandler collection.

128   SUCCEEDING PUCCINI

the orchestral accompaniment, and decided to set a longer stretch of Benelli's text than he had originally planned.[38]

The finale of Act 2 is even more remarkable. After Fiora abruptly and defiantly confesses that she has a lover, though refusing to declare his name, the orchestra accompanies the action of Archibaldo strangling her with a powerful interlude in which *fortissimo aspro* chords are followed by a 2-bar "pausa orrenda," Archibaldo supplying the commentary "Silenzio! Notte fonda" (Silence! Deep night) (Example 4.3).[39] The orchestral accompaniment to Archibaldo's subsequent confession to Fiora's murder is equally condensed and beautifully effective. Manfredo reacts passionately with full orchestral support, but Archibaldo's reply dwells in dark, gloomy orchestral colors supporting the singer as he explores the themes of blindness and vengeance, pointing out "la collana di morte delle mie dita paterne" (the collar of death fashioned by my paternal fingers) on Fiora's neck.[40] The postlude to Act 2 downplays the sonorities, reaching the utmost essentiality, as if to concentrate on the visual spectacle of Archibaldo carrying Fiora's corpse away (the iconic scene in Luigi Emilio Caldanzano's famous poster—see frontispiece), as the orchestra plays a funeral march. On the other hand, the finale to Act 3 takes a different form, providing an emphatic conclusion to the opera. As Avito falls dead, while the chorus sings offstage, Manfredo addresses a highly emotional peroration to the dead Fiora. This culminates in a short—everything happens very quickly in this finale—but powerful, truly Straussian symphonic moment, connecting Manfredo to the love-and-death theme centered on the adulterous lovers. As soon as Archibaldo appears, the orchestra suddenly resumes a minimum profile, kept as low as possible as Manfredo utters his last words. The Straussian *fortissimo* then returns—rapidly prepared by music marked *Più sostenuto* and *crescendo*—supporting Archibaldo's ultimate, bitter comment: "Anche tu, dunque, senza rimedio, sei con me nell'ombra" (You too, therefore, without remedy, are with me in the shadows).[41]

Architectural clarity contributes greatly to the opera's effectiveness. A further, crucial element is Montemezzi's ability to translate Benelli's

---

[38] Compare Figure 4.3 with Montemezzi, *L'amore dei tre re*, pp. 54–55.
[39] Montemezzi, *L'amore dei tre re*, pp. 142–43.
[40] Montemezzi, *L'amore dei tre re*, p. 155.
[41] Montemezzi, *L'amore dei tre re*, p. 190.

Music Example 4.3 *L'amore dei tre re*, Act 2, no. 66, bar 13–no. 68, bar 14.

130 SUCCEEDING PUCCINI

Music Example 4.3 Continued

THE MAKING OF *L'AMORE DEI TRE RE*, 1909–1912   131

dramatic situations into music pregnant with psychological introspection. Archibaldo, a role conceived for a commanding singer-actor with real vocal substance, is evoked by means of the telling contrast between the restless vitality of the music depicting his insatiable, not-so-hidden desire for power and pleasure, and the frustrated inaction he is condemned to by blindness. Psychological insight even permeates the atmosphere surrounding the characters in their lonely mountain landscape. Particularly prominent is the elegy of night, anticipated by *Tristan*. Archibaldo urges Flaminio to "torniamo nella notte" (return into the night) in Act 1, and this is echoed immediately afterward by Avito, who comments "È ancora notte fonda" (It is still deep night), thus inaugurating the first love duet of the opera.[42] The movement from the night of blindness to the very different night of clandestine passion is led by the flute, the beautiful, elegiac solo on the trembling surface of the strings acting as an apt bridge to the love idyll. In the following duet, the flute (offstage) is then given the task of conveying the meaning of the lovers' description of their ecstasy—"Incanto lungo . . . senza fine!" (Abiding enchantment . . . without end!)—before immediately afterward mirroring the situation described by the stage direction: "Si stringono perdutamente e si smarriscono nel bacio" (They embrace passionately and are lost in a kiss) (Example 4.4).[43] The flute lends the whole Avito-Fiora duet in Act 1 an exquisite lyrical color, the quiet but expressive melody suggesting something above and beyond the verbal limits of the lovers' language. Here Avito and Fiora seem to move in a symbolist world slightly reminiscent of *Pelléas et Mélisande*, a kind of suspended atmosphere particularly congenial to Montemezzi. The rapt setting of Fiora's "Dammi le labbra" (Give me your lips) was particularly admired by many critics in the 1910s and 1920s, and it is still perceived as one of the lyrical highlights of the opera (Figure 4.4). There is a tragic irony in the many references to lips and kissing, given the conclusion of the opera, but this is not registered in the music.

Montemezzi uses a number of leitmotifs, two of which he introduces at the outset. The brief prelude to Act 1, framed by overtly Wagnerian gestures of contrasting chords in *fortissimo* and *piano*, introduces an obsessive horse-riding motif, connected with Archibaldo the warrior-lord and his unsatiated

---

[42] Montemezzi, *L'amore dei tre re*, p. 23.
[43] Montemezzi, *L'amore dei tre re*, pp. 29–30.

132 SUCCEEDING PUCCINI

Music Example 4.4 *L'amore dei tre re*, Act 1, no. 21, bars 1–6.

Music Example 4.4 Continued

thirst for power and a secure lineage (Example 4.5). This motif is heard again, very appropriately, as Archibaldo recalls the descent of the barbarian army in shining armor—"e movemmo: masnada scintillante" (and we went: a glittering company)—in Act 1,[44] a moment which successfully exploits the orchestra's powers of painterly representation, as well as in the prelude to Act 2, and elsewhere. Indeed, the obsessive anapestic rhythm of this motif can be recognized as an ostinato pervading the entire score, a musical embodiment of Archibaldo's malign presence.[45] Notably, it exploits the same anapestic rhythm Mendelssohn uses to depict Bottom's donkey aspect in the overture to *A Midsummer Night's Dream*, but instead of the bright B-major key

---

[44] Montemezzi, *L'amore dei tre re*, pp. 15–16.
[45] Some critics have heard in Montemezzi's exploitation of ostinato patterns, as well as his employment of the chorus in Act 3, the influence of *Boris Godunov*, first staged in Italy in 1909. See, for example, Peyser, "For Deeper Enjoyment," pp. 6, 31.

Figure 4.4 *L'amore dei tre re*, autograph full score, "Dammi le labbra." *Archivio Storico Ricordi.*

Music Example 4.5 *L'amore dei tre re*, Act 1, bars 5–14.

crowned by the comic leap imitating the donkey's braying (Example 4.6), Montemezzi's version, in gloomy G minor, heads constantly downward to the tonic G as a symbol of Archibaldo's deepest inclinations: his drive to dominate through violence. As the curtain rises, a further motif appears,

Music Example 4.6 Felix Mendelssohn-Bartholdy, Overture to *A Midsummer Night's Dream*, bars 263–268.

heralded by a solo violin and performed by the woodwinds, which we soon learn stands for Fiora's gentle figure, as already discussed (see Example 4.1).

The use of voices is generally somewhat restrained. Notwithstanding those passages of lyrical singing labeled *arioso* and *duet* in our structural scheme, Montemezzi is much keener to avoid closed numbers than Puccini, and he pursues an aesthetic close to the Wagnerian *Musikdrama*, where everything becomes part of an uninterrupted, all-embracing musical flow. This goes a considerable way toward justifying his claim to have created "a real Italian music drama." As W. J. Henderson put it straightforwardly in 1914:

> [The] score contains no tunes which can be lifted out and sung at the Sunday night concerts, as in the case of "Vissi d'arte" [from *Tosca*], or "Che gelida manina" [from *La Bohème*]. The whole lyric play is carried forward in melodic speech, for every phrase is beautifully singable and musically eloquent; but there is nowhere that marshalling of phrases in stanza form which constitutes a "tune."[46]

Montemezzi's underlying model is Italianate veristic vocal writing, strictly syllabic, exclamatory, and melodramatic, not refraining, when needed, from verging on shouting (as when Archibaldo interrogates Fiora in Act 1, or when he addresses her before strangling her, or when Fiora herself cries "Ah! tortura!"). Overtly lyrical phrases occur rather rarely, such as in Manfredo's final peroration before kissing the dead Fiora's mouth, and it is

---

[46] W. J. Henderson, "Montemezzi's Opera a Success," *Opera Magazine*, February 1914, p. 12.

THE MAKING OF *L'AMORE DEI TRE RE,* 1909–1912   137

obviously significant that in this case the singing is immediately amplified by an orchestral *fortissimo.* Most of the time, the vocal melody convincingly, and exactly, adheres to the prosody of Benelli's text. In this, Montemezzi often pursues a melancholic tone accentuating the sense of restrained nobility that many critics have heard in the score. Even the love duets, such as those between Avito and Fiora in Act 1, or Manfredo and Fiora in Act 2, sound mostly subdued in their expression of passion, emotion entrusted to isolated outbursts, subtle utterances, and the all-pervasive voice of the orchestra.

A stunning exception to this general principle of restraint is the complex Avito-Fiora duet in Act 2, where passion runs high throughout, emerging from the excited atmosphere in which it begins. Before the duet starts, a powerful symphonic interlude accompanies Fiora's climbing onto the castle wall after Manfredo's departure, dominated by the haunting doomed-love motif of her husband's farewell, as it might be called, combining a poignant melody on the woodwinds with a military, dotted rhythm played by the violas (Example 4.7). A few minutes later, the long, somber orchestral interlude that coincides with Fiora's veil waving—threatened by Manfredo's farewell motif, this time played in C minor by the full orchestra as Fiora takes the veil out of the case—makes even more poignant the resumption of the Avito-Fiora duet. It now sounds more lyrical, not that distant from Mascagni's vocal writing in *L'amico Fritz.* Avito starts it as a sort of lament in D-flat major (a prominent *Traviata* key), a mournful farewell aimed at moving his lover. The duet grows more and more sensual, in a complex succession of calmer and more agitated moments, constantly threatened by the anapestic rhythm associated with Archibaldo which had already materialized in the orchestral interlude. Fiora gradually gives in, urging Avito to stay and giving him permission to kiss her dress, the growing excitement leading to a remarkable E-major lyrical outburst in a high register—"Ah! La tua fresca voce" (Ah! Your refreshing voice)—as sexually explicit metaphors proliferate.[47] An agitated symphonic interlude accompanies Fiora's descent to Avito and their kissing "*come fossero moribondi d'amore*" (as if dying of love), calming down to pure Tristanesque ecstasy, introduced by the celesta and dominated by the woodwinds, entrusting the flute part of Example 4.4 to the horn as the lovers embrace in the last ecstatic section of the duet (Example 4.8). They sing *lentamente e come in sogno, tutto dimenticando* (slowly, as in a

---

[47] Montemezzi, *L'amore dei tre re,* p. 117.

Music Example 4.7 *L'amore dei tre re*, Act 2, no. 21, bars 5–15.

dream, leaving everything behind), as a tenor voice offstage—a Verdian feature dating back to *La traviata*—is barely heard uttering an evocative "Ah!," enhancing the couple's complete loss of touch with reality: "*Si baciano e restano avvinti perdutamente aboliti nella loro nube amorosa*" (They kiss and

THE MAKING OF *L'AMORE DEI TRE RE*, 1909–1912   139

Music Example 4.8 *L'amore dei tre re*, Act 2, no. 52, bars 1–18.

Music Example 4.8 Continued

Music Example 4.9 *L'amore dei tre re*, Act 3, no. 7, bars 5–8.

remain entwined, completely lost in a loving trance).[48] Poignantly, the situation immediately precedes Fiora's murder. If she has no more chances for such lyrical expression, Avito exploits one more in his farewell to his dead lover and life itself in Act 3. In the early part of his passionate solo, which becomes increasingly dramatic, supported by the surge of the orchestral *crescendo* corresponding to the character's deadly intoxication with Fiora's lips, Montemezzi invents a magical moment, one of the most intimate and convincing lyrical highlights of the opera, solo violin and oboe intertwining with the tenor's voice in his lonely dialogue with his dead lover's corpse: "siamo soli" (we are alone) (Example 4.9).[49]

The importance of orchestral writing in letting this intimate drama develop and unfold its lyrical flight is equal to, if not greater, than the vocal writing. Otheman Stevens correctly concluded that "every sentiment being sung is often presaged and always expressed in tonal picturing of feeling; even action ... is given form by the orchestra."[50] Thoroughly acquainted with Wagner's *Musikdrama* and the German symphonic repertoire, Montemezzi pursues, more than most of his Italian contemporaries, a densely written,

---

[48] Montemezzi, *L'amore dei tre re*, p. 128.
[49] Montemezzi, *L'amore dei tre re*, p. 171.
[50] Otheman Stevens, "Grand Opera 'Three Kings' an Artistic Triumph," *Los Angeles Examiner*, March 7, 1916, Section 1, p. 7.

agile, translucent, and multifaceted orchestral texture, subtle or massive according to the situation. The orchestra follows the action very closely, lending its illustrative qualities and dramatic power, and exalting the essentially psychological nature of the drama: a feature particularly evident in the symphonic pages that resound when the characters fall silent. There is, in general, an elegiac tone typical of Montemezzi. He exploits harmony to increase the dramatic tension, in a measure certainly exceeding its traditional employment in Italian opera, though his harmony basically rests on late-nineteenth-century habits and is remote from avant-garde explorations (Stravinsky's *Rite of Spring* was premiered in Paris less than forty days after *L'amore dei tre re* made its first appearance in Milan). The result is a rather thick harmonic texture, especially where, in correspondence with the most significant moments of the drama, the orchestra contributes to offering the simple voice line a poignant accompaniment (Example 4.10).

A highly significant aspect of Montemezzi's orchestral writing is his development of an updated version of Wagner's Transformation music (*Verwandlungsmusik*), bridging scenes with different atmospheres. In doing this, Montemezzi was following what in 1913 was a modern aesthetics rooted in the Wagnerian idea of *Musikdrama* that D'Annunzio had actualized on the Italian stage. The end of one action and the link to the next, involving different characters, are indeed one of the principal opportunities the composer seizes to show his ability as an orchestrator. As

Music Example 4.10 *L'amore dei tre re*, Act 2, no. 36, bars 5–10.

THE MAKING OF *L'AMORE DEI TRE RE,* 1909–1912   143

already discussed (Example 4.4), in Act 1 a flute solo beautifully connects Archibaldo's world of blindness and night with the contrasting romantic night of Avito and Fiora. Equally impressive, also in Act 1, is the energetic interlude intervening between Fiora's departure and Manfredo's arrival, introducing the knightly, enthusiastic mood characterizing the encounter between father and son—"Figliuolo mio! Giunge la luce con te!" (My son! You bring the light with you!)[51]—before Fiora is mentioned. A complex canvas of the passions agitating the drama is successfully offered in the fine prelude to Act 2, with contrasting war sounds (horse-riding rhythms, trumpet fanfares) and lyrical bursts in the strings. The warm, full orchestral sound very effectively sustaining Manfredo's first passionate lines in this act is abruptly reduced as Fiora replies, her lines given a minimalist accompaniment of evocative *piano* chords without any melodic element, before being promptly resumed as Manfredo addresses her again. Here and elsewhere, it is the orchestra which ultimately takes care of the psychological characterization.

The importance of symphonic music in *L'amore dei tre re* was later accentuated by the only significant revision Montemezzi made to his score in later years. In 1928 he replaced the brief, 10-bar introduction to Act 3, led by the horns, with a new, longer, passionate lyrical prelude; the slightly longer opera was premiered in Rome on March 20, 1929. Montemezzi explained then how he had

> felt the need, after the thundering (*fragorosa*) and tragic final scene of the second act . . . to lead, little by little, the spectator's heart to a different atmosphere, to the sweet, fantastic, and poetic atmosphere in which we find Fiora's lifeless body. This prelude gathers its substance and life from the more appropriate and significant movements of the opera.[52]

The new prelude is pure sound poetry not needing any action, with darkly beautiful music condensing the sentimental fullness of the opera's passions, crowned by a remote, evocative trumpet solo from a distance, recalling Mahler, and strongly contrasting with the *a cappella* chorus opening Act 3. Though composed much later, the prelude is a thoroughly organic part of the score.

---

[51] Montemezzi, *L'amore dei tre re*, pp. 45–46.
[52] Quoted in r.d.r., "Montemezzi parla delle sue opere," *Il Giornale d'Italia*, March 9, 1929, p. 3.

144 SUCCEEDING PUCCINI

As this analysis should have made clear, *L'amore dei tre re* contains unmistakable Wagnerian elements. Nevertheless, Katherine, Montemezzi's future wife, briskly dismissed any suggestion that it was—as some critics claimed—a Wagnerian opera: "it is Italian, not Wagnerian. There is never a dull moment in it. That's the great part of this opera—it moves on."[53] By 1900, Wagner was at odds with the general tendency of opera to become shorter as its social base of support broadened and post-industrial societies evolved a more regulated sense of time. Orefice wrote in 1918 that in Italian performances of Wagner's operas, it was "customary to *amputate* as vigorously as possible, in order to arrive sooner at those moments that subjugate us with the grandiosity of their structural lines and fascinate us with the spell of their expressive beauty."[54] In *L'amore dei tre re*, Wagnerian influence is blended with the faster-moving Italian tradition, as many critics subsequently insisted. Verdi, along with Wagner, was Montemezzi's most consistent inspiration, and he insisted that *Otello* had been his primary model when composing *L'amore dei tre re*:

> I tried to compose a real Italian musical drama, as it was shown to us by our great maestro in the wonderful recitatives of *Otello*. I endeavored to give importance to the melodic *declamato*, to form a whole [*tutto*] between orchestra and stage, to draw each inspiration from the dramatic moment and from the words.[55]

A mature Verdian conciseness permeates the entire score, and notwithstanding the significant role of symphonic music, the dramatic pace never flags. Act 3, for example, lasts barely twenty minutes. There is actually little proper action apart from Fiora's murder at the end of Act 2—the situation in the opera closer to verismo, with a virtually unprepared and unpredictable outburst of violence—and the double poisoning concluding Act 3. Most of the opera consists of static areas, often evoking episodes from the past. The single scenes sound as vocal isles which the orchestra surrounds and unifies. Most remarkable is the way Montemezzi succeeds in reaching an effective balance between the Tristanesque time suspension dominating the frequent duets and the abrupt, even brutal tension derived from verismo featured in the few more dramatic situations.

---

[53] Quoted in Samuel L. Singer, "Two Operas Staged," *Philadelphia Inquirer*, November 20, 1960, p. 7.

[54] Giacomo Orefice, "Rassegna Musicale [*La Nave*]," *Rivista d'Italia*, November 30, 1918, p. 335.

[55] Adami, "In attesa de 'L'Amore dei tre re,'" p. 2.

THE MAKING OF *L'AMORE DEI TRE RE*, 1909–1912   145

Apart from Wagner, it is Debussy who has most often been referred to as an influence on *L'amore dei tre re*. Critics have doubtless been influenced by both *L'amore dei tre re* and *Pelléas et Mélisande* being *Literaturopern*, both telling comparable stories, with overlapping atmospheres, and the clear imprint of delicate impressionist writing of French origin in Montemezzi's score. To these similarities we can add the informal employment of leitmotifs, not systematically nor undergoing thematic development; the total avoidance of closed vocal numbers; the entrusting of a great number of functions to the orchestra; and the brilliant, beautifully effective orchestration. Is it possible to go further? Montemezzi confessed only to "a modified admiration for Debussy": "In the composer of 'Pelleas' [*sic*] he [Montemezzi] deprecates harmonic monotony and the restricted sphere of expression, but reverences the beauty of his conceptions as such."[56] Indeed, though the suspended atmosphere typical of some scenes of Montemezzi's masterpiece might recall Debussy's impressionist writing, the harmonic context of the two scores differs dramatically. Whereas Montemezzi is firmly grounded in late Romantic (at its greatest extent Wagnerian) harmony, *Pelléas* displays much more progressive and experimental harmonic thought, tinged with modal touches, combining and juxtaposing unexpected chords, and ultimately resorting to what has been described as a sophisticated "bifocal harmony," influenced by Russian models.[57] In addition, the orchestral writing also significantly diverges, even when the orchestra is required to comment on similar stage situations. In this respect, Montemezzi really only takes from *Pelléas et Mélisande* a single musical gesture: the rolling triplets obsessing a great part of Debussy's score and contributing to both Mélisande's and Pélleas's leitmotifs (together with sextuplets, possibly derived from Wagner's "Forest Murmurs" leitmotif). These triplets, often entrusted to woodwind instruments, significantly punctuate one of Montemezzi's most inspired and crucial pages, the entrance of Fiora and Avito in Act 1. Their first love duet is opened by the idyllic melody of the offstage flute, dominated by gentle, rolling triplets, and it is heard again as the duet grows more ecstatic, supported and amplified by the accompaniment in triplets of the upper strings—arguably a Debussyian touch (Example 4.4).

Montemezzi began composing *L'amore dei tre re* in short score in the spring of 1910 and work continued all through the following year, Act 2

---

[56] Herbert F. Peyser, "'Let simplicity be the composer's constant objective,' Abjures Italo Montemezzi," *Musical America*, November 22, 1919, p. 4.

[57] Mark DeVoto, "Debussy's Absolute Pitch: Motivic Harmony and Choice of Keys," in *Debussy's Resonance*, edited by François de Médicis and Steven Huebner (Rochester, NY: University of Rochester Press, 2018), p. 423.

146   SUCCEEDING PUCCINI

alone taking "eight months of arduous if enthusiastic" effort.[58] Montemezzi's later accounts of this period tend to suggest that his struggles were solely with the opera itself, as he imposed a "severity" upon himself, intently pursuing "that unity which justified the title 'music drama.'"[59] In fact, though, his work on the opera was interrupted by two unwelcome distractions, the second of which threatened to derail his career completely.

The first interruption was a commission to compose his first non-operatic work since his student days. According to the brief biography of Montemezzi published by Casa Ricordi in 1933, "he received from the Cremona City Council the honorific assignment of composing a *Cantata* for choir and orchestra, to commemorate the 25th anniversary of Amilcare Ponchielli's death."[60] This was presumably in the winter of 1910–1911. The Committee of Honor appointed by the City Council was presided over by Boito and composed of Puccini, Franchetti, and Toscanini. How Montemezzi came to be involved is not clear; presumably none of the committee members relished the idea of composing something themselves, or considered it appropriate to do so. Serafin conducted the two musical events that were organized, and it was perhaps on his recommendation that Montemezzi was approached for this rather thankless task. On the other hand, Montemezzi was comparatively local—Cremona is less than fifty miles from Vigasio—and had been given a very positive reception when *Giovanni Gallurese* was staged in Cremona in 1907,[61] so Cremonese voices may have been raised in his favor. The short *Cantata* has a fulsome text in five stanzas by Giuseppe Adami, describing Ponchielli as "surrounded with glory, stronger than destiny," and identifying him with his most famous opera, *La Gioconda*:

> Alive, in her sorrow,
> your blonde daughter,
> the tragic Gioconda
> sings her songs.
>
> And she repeats again and always
> how your glory is
> our great glory,
> the eternal Melody! (stanzas 4–5)[62]

---

[58] Peyser, "For Deeper Enjoyment," p. 4.

[59] Peyser, "For Deeper Enjoyment," p. 4.

[60] *Italo Montemezzi* (Milan: Ricordi, 1933), p. 2.

[61] "In Platea," *Ars et labor* 62/2 (February 1907): p. 185.

[62] Montemezzi, *Per le Onoranze ad Amilcare Ponchielli nel 25° Anniversario della sua Morte. Cantata* (vocal score) (Milan: Ricordi, 1911), p. 1.

THE MAKING OF *L'AMORE DEI TRE RE*, 1909–1912   147

The elegant, albeit conventional, lines present the classical theme that he who attains glory never dies. There was little chance of the cantata being performed more than once, but Casa Ricordi published a piano-vocal score prepared by Ugo Solazzi and made the orchestral parts available for hire. The full score and the parts have apparently not survived, which is regrettable given the weight Montemezzi unsurprisingly assigns to orchestral music: a prelude, several interludes, and a postlude comprise nearly a third of the printed, sixteen-page score.

The *Cantata*'s remarkable prelude opens as a solemn funeral march in *fortissimo*, then develops into a more languid, sentimental, expressive melodic invention which reaches the top register, possibly pointing to the transcendence of death, before concluding with a dramatic key change from prevailing D minor to B major on a stunned, heartbroken melody. The voices enter quietly with typically operatic, homophonic writing, counterpointed by a broader melody in the orchestra. After a short interlude, the second stanza proposes the artist-hero as triumphant over death: the blatant melody on the arpeggio, as if imitating a trumpet, aptly matches Adami's lines, no doubt recruiting the brass section in force. The following interlude moves from warlike sounds to a syncopated lullaby that leads to the *piano* entrance of the choir and is preserved as a stable accompaniment to stanza 3. The choir softly urges Ponchielli to sleep ("Dormi!") before a more animated, counterpointed page alludes to the celebrated "Dance of the Hours" from *La Gioconda*, exploiting a five-voice scoring with divided basses. Montemezzi exceptionally superimposes the end of stanza 3 upon the beginning of stanza 4, and after more subtle counterpoint at the mention of Gioconda's sorrow, the brief cantata moves to the conclusive, effective hymn to the Italian tradition of melody (of which Montemezzi felt part), *Ancora più sostenuto*, in a bright, stable D-flat major, on an appropriately inspired melodic invention, the orchestra dynamically supporting the apotheosis of the *fortissimo* finale. The *Cantata* was placed at the beginning of the second of the musical events, on May 23, 1911, and "performed by 200 voices, rehearsed and conducted by maestro Serafin, [it was] warmly applauded."[63] It was followed by extracts from Ponchielli's operas.

A much more troubling distraction appeared at the end of 1911. Although *Giovanni Gallurese* was performing well, Casa Ricordi had lost money on

---

[63] "Concerti," *Ars et Labor* 66/6 (June 1911): p. 478.

148   SUCCEEDING PUCCINI

Héllera and overall, after six years of receiving his monthly stipend and royalty payments, Montemezzi had not proved a good investment. At the beginning of December 1911, he found the stipend had not been paid, and on December 5 wrote to Ricordi to point out what he assumed was a mistake. The reply, dated the following day, made it clear that the nonpayment was no oversight, for Montemezzi had "exceed[ed] the credit limit granted by the regulations of the contracts agreed with him."[64] Setting payments against the profits generated by his works, the composer had a negative balance of 24,421 lire. Though much of the negative balance would be covered by the 22,000 lire Montemezzi was due for the two operas he had been contracted to compose, this would still leave Ricordi with a deficit, and "the Board pointed out to the Director that this is contrary to a good rule of administration." In short, there would be no more monthly stipends, no more "preferential treatment," and Montemezzi was encouraged to complete *L'amore dei tre re* as soon as possible. No doubt the figures were all correct, but the letter further confirmed a change of atmosphere at Casa Ricordi to which Montemezzi can hardly have been insensitive. Giulio Ricordi was ailing; his death on June 6, 1912, would mark the end of an era at the firm, and it had a major impact on the careers of several composers, most of whom, Puccini included, were finding Tito a much more difficult employer. From December 1911, if not before, Montemezzi must have been aware that if *L'amore dei tre re* proved a failure, or perhaps just a moderate success, his career at Casa Ricordi would be over, and the chance of his establishing a comparable relationship with any other publisher was negligible.

Now unsalaried, Montemezzi pressed on with *L'amore dei tre re*, and by the spring of 1912 had completed the first two acts in short score. He was clearly having difficulties with Act 3, so he decided to start orchestrating what he had already written:

> After two weeks of rest I launched upon the orchestration. I worked no less arduously for sixty-four days, ten hours a day.
>
> Summer [1912] arrived and I retired to the mountains of the Tyrol, where I had dear friends. These friends who knew that I had to compose the third act, placed a small villa at my disposal. I installed myself there with my libretto, [and] my piano awaiting inspiration. I do not know why but the inspiration would not come and so I lost fifteen days.

---

[64] This important letter is reproduced in Piergiorgio Rossetti (ed.), *Omaggio a Italo Montemezzi* (Vigasio: Amministrazione Comunale di Vigasio, 2002), pp. 100–101.

THE MAKING OF *L'AMORE DEI TRE RE*, 1909–1912   149

During the time I received numerous letters from Venice, where a number of my friends were enjoying themselves. So I felt that a short visit in that enchanting city might be a help. I had the intention of returning to the Tyrol to continue my composition. Yet on my way back [from Venice] I passed through Verona and went directly to Vigàsio to greet my parents. I spent the night at home and the next morning remained in my studio thinking about my opera. In a few moments it became clear to me that I had found the proper atmosphere for my inspiration. My old studio, where I had composed all my operas, contained something mysterious that seemed to animate me. It exalted and inspired me. I dedicated myself completely to the third act and in twelve days the composition was finished. With alacrity I continued my work and in seventeen days the orchestration, too, was complete. All in all, between periods of intense work and periods of rest the composition and orchestration of the entire opera required two years and three months.[65]

By mid-July 1912 the score was being engraved by Casa Ricordi, but Montemezzi was not allowed to bask in any sense of accomplishment. On July 19 he received a bad-tempered letter from Tito Ricordi, who had lost his father the previous month, complaining first about the difficulty of the piano score, and demanding simplifications, but then, more consequentially, criticizing Act 2 as much too long:

I went through the reduction of Act 2; it's long, long, long!!! and it seems to me that you didn't take any account of the pruning and the cuts that we had decided upon together, all the more given that the libretto you sent is not the one where I had marked all the changes and at a distance of such a long time I am at a loss. However, what is certain is that Act 2, which lasts 55 minutes, is long, long, long!!! I deem it absolutely indispensable that we meet to reach an agreement upon what needs to be done in order to make this second act digestible; otherwise, I declare to you that I suspend any work on L'amore dei tre re because I don't want to uselessly waste time and money on an opera that, when put to the test, will have to be revised as unfortunately happened with Hellera.

Then I notice, to my great sorrow, that all your declarations addressed to my person on more than one occasion are nothing but words, because

---

[65] Quoted in Peyser, "For Deeper Enjoyment," pp. 4–5.

150   SUCCEEDING PUCCINI

so far facts have belied them—with how much advantage to you I don't know—but surely inspiring little or no faith in me about your future.[66]

The letter suggests that the relationship between the two men was now strained to the breaking point, and when, on top of that, Montemezzi could reflect on the publisher's clear partiality for Zandonai, whom Tito was privately referring to as "Richard III" (i.e., the successor to Wagner and Strauss), and Zandonai's major success with *Conchita* (1911), the precariousness of his situation must have been all too clear.[67] He had probably hoped that the more sympathetic Giulio Ricordi would act as a buffer between him and Tito's hectoring suggestions.[68]

By September 20 a compromise had been worked out, Montemezzi claiming he had followed Tito's advice "only in part," and that he believed Act 2 was the best thing he had ever composed.[69] It seems unlikely that Act 2 was ever as long as fifty-five minutes, but the published vocal score does notably include a 42-bar section marked as "suppressed in the theatres," and this music is omitted in the printed full score. A shorter, optional cut is also marked, though in this case it appears in the full score.[70] As conducted by Montemezzi, Act 2 was about forty-six minutes long—considerably longer than the other acts, but also the one that has generally made the strongest impression on audiences and critics. By the end of 1912, *L'amore dei tre re* was ready to perform. Whereas both *Giovanni Gallurese* and *Héllera* had been premiered in Turin, this time Casa Ricordi arranged for the opera to be brought out at La Scala, the opera house where Montemezzi had learned his trade, the one he loved best, and that he would later describe as "this magnificent artistic temple of ours."[71] On this stage, his destiny as a composer was to be decided.

---

[66] The letter is reproduced in Rossetti, *Omaggio*, pp. 103–04.

[67] For Tito's clear preference for Zandonai at this date, and the "Richard III" moniker, see Konrad Dryden, *Franco Alfano: Transcending "Turandot"* (Lanham, MD: Scarecrow Press, 2010), p. 36. Supporting this, it was in connection with *Conchita* that Puccini remarked on Tito's favoritism toward Zandonai. See Mosco Carner, *Puccini: A Critical Biography* (London: Gerald Duckworth, 1958), p. 147.

[68] As late as May 26, 1912, when Montemezzi wrote to Casa Ricordi, he preferred to report progress on his score directly to Giulio Ricordi. Archivio Storico Ricordi.

[69] "solo in parte." Montemezzi to Tito Ricordi, September 20, 1912. Archivio Storico Ricordi.

[70] Montemezzi, *L'amore dei tre re*, pp. 122, 136.

[71] "questo nostro magnifico tempio artistico." Montemezzi to Guido Pesenti, June 25, 1936. Chandler collection.

5

"The name of Montemezzi"

L'amore dei tre re on Four Continents, 1913–1928

The prestigious advantage of having *L'amore dei tre re* premiered at La Scala was, to an extent, offset by its scheduling at the very end of the 1912–1913 season. This gravely concerned Montemezzi, who doubtless had all too vivid memories of how late scheduling had helped doom *Héllera*. He lobbied for a more favorable premiere, and in February 1913 traveled to Milan to make his case in person. However, on February 21 he heard definitively from Uberto Visconti di Modrone, the intendant of La Scala, that no change was possible. Montemezzi responded with a very revealing letter to Modrone from the Grand Hôtel Royal the following day, accepting the situation, but also insisting that the effects of the late scheduling might be severely negative, indeed "completely ruinous!" (*vera rovina*!). The letter, a painful emotional protest, apparently written quickly, and at times quite ungrammatical, goes on:

> From the beginning, I knew I was playing my final card, and for that reason I begged and begged to go on stage soon, and I was assured I would. I even had to give up a series of performances of L'Amore dei tre re during the Fair season in my Verona from March 8 onwards, performances that were subject to the possible success of my opera. However, I didn't regret that, because the big push (*impulso*), the one that would decide me, had to be given by La Scala.
>
> I was convinced that my opera (and I still am, firmly) had the qualities to obtain a real success, so that an extensive series of performances, accompanied by an obvious financial return, would have placed me in that artistic position from which alone I could be certain of reaching my goals.[1]

---

[1] "Fin dal principio sapevo giuocare la mia carta estrema, perciò avevo pregato e pregato di andare in scena presto e ne ottenni l'assicurazione. Ho dovuto rinunciare perfino ad una serie di recite dell'*Amore dei tre re* nella stagione di Fiera nella mia Verona dall'8 marzo in poi, recite che erano subordinate ad un eventuale successo della mia opera. Ma non me ne dolsi, perché il grande impulso, quello che decideva di me, doveva essere dato dalla Scala. / Ero convinto che la mia opera (e lo sono

---

Succeeding Puccini. David Chandler and Raffaele Mellace, Oxford University Press. © Oxford University Press 2025.
DOI: 10.1093/9780197761373.003.0006

152 SUCCEEDING PUCCINI

Montemezzi's belief that he was "playing [his] final card" should be taken seriously: a failure would have ended his relationship with Casa Ricordi and very likely have compelled his aging parents to demand that he finally obtain a teaching job, like so many of his peers. Moreover, having insisted on composing a new kind of opera, or "music drama," against the advice of those around him, Montemezzi's artistic judgment was very much on the line. A great deal was at stake in these early months of 1913.

Perhaps adding to Montemezzi's anxiety, as the premiere of *L'amore dei tre re* approached, it was given little publicity. He himself largely avoided contact with journalists. G. B. Nappi, the veteran critic of *La Perseveranza*, reported that: "the composer did not care to give an account of his artistic purposes in advance, by means of interviews; on the contrary, he almost entirely avoided contact with representatives of the press, in order that indiscretions would not prejudice the outcome of his work."[2] Montemezzi was surely remembering his experience with Turin's *Gazzetta del Popolo* in 1909. The only significant exception to this policy, if policy it was, was the interview Montemezzi gave to Giuseppe Adami on April 6, just four days before the premiere, quoted in the previous chapter. This ended very positively, with Montemezzi saying he was "very happy" with the singers, "full of admiration" for Serafin's conducting, and looking forward to the premiere with "very much" hope.[3] But almost immediately after the interview, disaster threatened when Bernardo de Muro, cast as Avito, fell ill. He was replaced by Edoardo Ferrari-Fontana (1878–1936), who had, astonishingly, just three days to prepare. Ferrari-Fontana was coached intensively by Montemezzi, "night and day," later reporting that he found the composer very easy to work with, for "Signor Montemezzi [is] one of the kindest of men . . . a man who is so simple and sincere. With Signor Montemezzi there is no pose, no affectation, and he is modesty itself."[4] Ferrari-Fontana was ready in time, and in the event critics found nothing to fault in his performance. The first cast also included Luisa Villani (1884–1961) as Fiora, Nazzareno De Angelis

---

sempre fermamente) aveva tali qualità da ottenere un vero successo, di modo che una numerosa serie di repliche accompagnate da un evidente rendimento finanziario, mi avrebbe messo in quella posizione artistica, per la quale solamente potevo essere sicuro di raggiungere i miei scopi." Chandler collection.

[2] G. B. Nappi, "'L'amore dei tre re' di Italo Montemezzi alla Scala," *La Perseveranza*, April 11, 1913, p. 2.

[3] Giuseppe Adami, "In attesa de 'L'Amore dei tre re' di Italo Montemezzi," *La Sera: Giornale politico, finanziario, illustrato*, April 7, 1913, p. 2.

[4] Quoted in "Ferrari-Fontana's Creation of Avito," *New-York Tribune*, January 25, 1914, Part 3, p. 4.

L'AMORE DEI TRE RE ON FOUR CONTINENTS   153

(1881–1962) as Archibaldo, and Carlo Galeffi (1884–1961) as Manfredo. Serafin was conducting his third Montemezzi opera premiere.

Because of the absence of advance publicity, in Nappi's assessment, La Scala was by no means full on April 10. The way the evening played out is vividly evoked in his review:

> There were many empty seats in the stalls and not all the boxes were occupied.
>
> None of the spectators would have imagined that they would have to thank Italo Montemezzi for a night rich in very keen emotions, such as they had not experienced for a long time at La Scala as the result of the merits of a new opera by an Italian maestro.
>
> From the beginning, the powerful sound palette and the breadth of the musical lines of the initial scenes dominated the audience. The latter, all of a sudden won by the magnificent piece, the *Hymn to Italy*, where the orchestra bursts into an ardent and most eloquent heroic peroration upon the *declamato* by the bass (Archibaldo), let itself be carried away into long and enthusiastic applause. From that moment, the audience's interest steadily increased. Murmurs of approval often underlined the development of the inspired love duet, over a delightful orchestral background. The scene between Archibaldo and Fiora, filled with an obscure threat; Manfredo's arrival; the instrumental explosion before the end of Act 1; and the drama of the final bars completed the already vivid impression made on the audience. As the curtain fell, they burst into loud and general applause that turned into a big ovation when Montemezzi, after the two curtain calls for the skillful performers, appeared on stage twice, together with Maestro Serafin.
>
> During the *entr'acte*, in the lobby and the foyer, the comments were—*mirabile dictu*—unanimously favorable. Everybody showed grateful surprise at finally being before a work of art of uncommon value.
>
> During Act 2, about which the most favorable forecasts had been made over the last few days, the success acquired a grandiose dimension.
>
> The passage in which Manfredo expresses to Fiora his sorrow for his imminent departure was greeted with a long applause.
>
> The subsequent symphonic descriptive piece, based on a passionate and sorrowful phrase, the great duet with Avito and Fiora, with pressing (*incalzàre*) phrases full of dramatic impetus and sentiment, Archibaldo's unexpected arrival, the scene of Fiora's murder, Manfredo's return, and the

154 SUCCEEDING PUCCINI

finale make up a grandiose lyric picture, drawn by the powerful hand of an artist. After the curtain fell, the audience sprang to its feet and acclaimed the composer, also applauded by the orchestra, four or five times, with loud cries and enthusiastic ovations.

So, the success was complete, definite, imposing, and, what is more important, sincere. The opera passed.

The lesser success of the very short Act 3 does not diminish the significance of this satisfying, well-deserved victory for Maestro Montemezzi, who counted three more curtain calls before the audience left the house.[5]

In 1919, Montemezzi described the premiere of *L'amore dei tre re* as "the greatest emotional experience of my life."[6] Overwhelmed by the congratulations of friends and well-wishers, he "fled to a little café, where no one knew him."[7]

The initial popular response to *L'amore dei tre re* appears to have been entirely positive. Three more scheduled performances were given before the end of the season, and as the acclaim grew, Montemezzi's fears about the consequences of a late scheduling proved groundless. The critics were generally positive, even enthusiastic, and very willing to discuss the opera at length, though not quite striking the ecstatic note that would be heard the following year in America. Giovanni Pozza, in the *Corriere della Sera*, began with some reflections on how Italian audiences had increasingly come to favor foreign operas, meaning that "the victory of an Italian opera means more than the victory of a maestro: it is a statement of the renewal of our music." He found the influences of Wagner and "the Russian and French impressionists" in the score, but argued that this did not really matter, given its "inner and essential qualities":

What can be said only rarely of the many operas appearing every year on our stages can be said of "*L'Amore dei tre re*." The opera has been composed with a dramatic sense and intense communicative warmth. It enthralls us, compelling us to follow it with the force by which it rapidly and impetuously proceeds from one motion expressing passion to another, without losing energy, without lingering over unnecessary details. . . . The value of

---

[5] Nappi, "'L'amore dei tre re,'" p. 2.

[6] Herbert F. Peyser, "'Let simplicity be the composer's constant objective,' Abjures Italo Montemezzi," *Musical America*, November 22, 1919, p. 3.

[7] "Ferrari-Fontana's Creation of Avito," p. 4.

L'AMORE DEI TRE RE ON FOUR CONTINENTS   155

the opera is in the passion that continuously stirs all of it, that warms it, giving it the motion and the pulse of life.

The orchestration was "clear and masterly, not heavy, but rich and complex," though Pozza felt there were too many "emphatic perorations." Of the characters, Pozza judged Archibaldo the only one who was truly convincing and believable, but concluded that for this, "the poet is to be blamed more than the maestro."[8]

Nappi judged that "the composer fully succeeded in his purpose and ... thanks to his music, Benelli's tragedy gained in vitality, and theatrical effectiveness":

> Italo Montemezzi keeps himself in an upper sphere, where the usual vulgar effects of contemporary opera productions are not allowed. He gave us an opera of remarkable artistic maturity, provided with a strong structure, with powerful features, truly theatrical, healthy, and vital.
>
> A homogeneous and solemn character—if not a great prodigality of invention—dominates the three acts. The unity of the dramatic development is matched by that of the musical development and background that proceeds without a break.
>
> This background almost always emphasizes the nature of the characters' feelings. These characters are also well outlined in their different psychological conditions. The music does not lack the grimness of the environment, nor the delicate notes, the nuances, and the poetic tones.
>
> In the entirety of the work, there is the noble purpose of doing art in earnest.

In Act 1, "the *Hymn to Italy* and the *love duet* between Fiora and Avito are among the most inspired pages of modern musical theatre." Like Pozza, Nappi found a good deal of Wagnerian influence in the score, but he put more emphasis on what he regarded as the influence of Richard Strauss on the orchestration, this leading to a conclusion that anticipates much later Italian criticism: "There is no doubt it would have been preferable if the tragic expression of this production, taking place on Latin soil, had been

---

[8] Giovanni Pozza, "'L'amore dei tre Re' del m. Montemezzi rappresentato ieri sera alla Scala," *Corriere della Sera*, April 11, 1913, p. 2.

156   SUCCEEDING PUCCINI

achieved without resorting to these . . . Teutonic means." Like Pozza, too, Nappi found Archibaldo much more convincing than the other characters.[9]

Adami, who of all the critics was perhaps the closest to Montemezzi personally, emphasized that in the many discussions after the performance there had been "the joy of being able to say: here is someone who convinces us and that we like; here at last is a great victory and a sure hope." He heard the influence of Wagner, Strauss, Debussy, Dukas, and Mussorgsky ("whom the young rightly love, and hold dearest"), yet he judged that "this unavoidable influence has been overcome thanks to the utmost virtue of personal vigor, a dramatic, indeed tragic, profound and intense force, with a broad vision and ample line, with a sound Italian breadth." The opera was constructed with "a very rich and noble melodic naturalness," the orchestration was "masterly varied and limpidly clear," and Montemezzi, a "man of the theatre," "appears magnificent in the framing, and in the cut, given to his acts, and in the perfect sense of their measure." Any dramatic weaknesses were laid at Benelli's door.[10]

Perhaps the most theoretical criticism came from Gino Monaldi (1847–1932), an impresario and composer, as well as a very distinguished scholar and critic. He was the author of *Verdi e Wagner* (1887), as well as many other studies of Verdi, and also published books on Puccini and Mascagni. He placed Montemezzi's "wave of melodious ideas" in the larger context of the evolution of melody from regular, "subjective" forms, to descriptive, "asymmetric," "objective" forms that Verdi had set in motion with *Otello*. Modern melody like Montemezzi's, "starts . . . from a complex sentiment, one that is musical and dramatic at the same time, and goes ahead and proceeds only up to the point where the thought of the character leads it, stopping where the poetic thought stops, deviating when it deviates, and distinguishing its various expressions always in a definite way."[11] In Monaldi's view, Montemezzi had achieved his goal:

He intended to turn into reality the real formula of modern musical drama, that is, the perfect correspondence of words to music. There is no doubt he

[9] Nappi, "'L'amore dei tre re,'" p. 2.
[10] Giuseppe Adami, "'L'Amore dei tre re' di I. Montemezzi: Il successo alla Scala," *La Sera: Giornale politico, finanziario, illustrato,* April 11, 1913, p. 2.
[11] Gino Monaldi, "'L'amore dei tre Re' di Italo Montemezzi," *Nuova Antologia,* series 5, 165 (May 1913): p. 144.

L'AMORE DEI TRE RE ON FOUR CONTINENTS   157

succeeded in this, though the musical concept sometimes had to sustain, and suffer, the shortcomings of the stage play.

Montemezzi was most of all "sincere," and against the critics who considered the score Wagnerian, Monaldi argued that "in the inner structure of the work, in its clear main themes, in its well-balanced ensemble pieces, in its sober development, he [Montemezzi] reveals the best qualities of the Italian school." In creating a truly Italian "musical drama," Montemezzi's career path was in fact toward "the attainment of the goal that the opera of the purely Italian school can wriggle out of all the tentacles of the octopus that, under the specious name and pretext of Wagnerism, is trying to stifle it."[12]

Having seen the opera staged, Montemezzi wanted to make some slight changes to his score, mostly in relation to the dramaturgy of Act 2. These were accepted, with one notable exception. He wanted to specify that just before Fiora's murder, Archibaldo is "Grabbing and throwing her stretched out on the bench."[13] This was not included in the score, but Casa Ricordi's detailed production guide, issued in May 1914, states that Archibaldo "throws her [Fiora] onto the bench,"[14] and later photographs of Montemezzi coaching singers confirm that this is how he wanted the scene played.

More consequentially, it was some time after the first performance that the opera's most iconic stage picture was developed: Archibaldo carrying Fiora's dead body flung over his shoulder. Albert Goldberg later confirmed, on Montemezzi's authority, that "[i]n the original production Archibaldo merely carried off Fiora in his arms. The over-the-shoulder business was an afterthought introduced in later performances."[15] Goldberg's wording leaves it unclear whether La Scala audiences saw the "over-the-shoulder" action in 1913, and it is notable that when the opera went into rehearsal in New York in December 1913, the "over-the-shoulder" strategy was not, at first, employed, but did get adopted later.[16] It seems likely that the stage action evolved to match Luigi Emilio Caldanzano's magnificent poster, which though anatomically implausible, distilled the essence of the story into a

---

[12] Monaldi, "'L'amore dei tre Re,'" p. 145.

[13] "Ghermendola e buttandola distesa sulla panchina." Montemezzi to Carlo Chiusuri (a copyist at Casa Ricordi), May 26, 1913. Chandler collection. These hastily written notes appear to represent Montemezzi's comments on a proof copy of the vocal score.

[14] Carlo Clausetti, *Disposizione Scenica per l'opera "L'amore dei tre re"* (Milan: Ricordi, 1914), p. 39.

[15] Albert Goldberg, "Preview Hints Outstanding Season of Opera for City," *Los Angeles Times*, October 5, 1947, Part 3, p. 5.

[16] See David Chandler (ed.), *Americans on Italo Montemezzi* (Norwich: Durrant Publishing, 2014), pp. 80–81.

158　SUCCEEDING PUCCINI

single, unforgettable image (see frontispiece). The production guide, interestingly, did not insist on the "over-the-shoulder" action, merely specifying that, at precisely the right moment:

> Archibaldo will have to raise the dead woman slightly, pass his left arm under her waist and his right arm over her legs, holding them tightly underneath. In this way, he will lift her from the bench without any visible effort. Fiora will remain with her head turned onto her right shoulder and her right arm hanging loose. In this way, Archibaldo will head toward the left door.[17]

However the lift was done, there is no doubt that some basses struggled with the physical challenge involved. Herbert F. Peyser recounts the fascination audiences had with this moment in the performance, fearing an accident, and details an amusing story about how the first Vienna Archibaldo was unable to make the lift.[18]

The second production of *L'amore dei tre re*, conducted by Rodolfo Ferrari, opened at the Teatro Comunale, Cesena, on August 23, 1913. In connection with this, the celebrated local writer Renato Serra (1884–1915) notably wrote a promotional feature about Benelli's story, specifically identifying the foreign invaders as Germans (*germani*);[19] also noteworthy is the fact that Benedetto Croce attended one of the performances, perhaps because of Serra's involvement.[20] Audiences again responded enthusiastically, but the production is most significant because Tito Ricordi was able to organize a visit by Giulio Gatti-Casazza and Arturo Toscanini, the intendant and conductor, respectively, of the Metropolitan Opera House, New York. They were so impressed that they quickly made arrangements to give the international premiere. Other Italian theatres were also starting to schedule *L'amore dei tre re*, and by the end of the year it had appeared at the Teatro Comunale, Bologna; the Teatro Filarmonico, Verona; the Teatro Municipale, Mantua; and the Teatro Verdi, Padua.[21] In the period before Italy's entrance into World War I, it continued its steady conquest of the Italian peninsula, making

---

[17] Clausetti, *Disposizione Scenica*, p. 42.

[18] Herbert F. Peyser, "An Appreciation of L'Amore dei Tre Re," *Musical America*, February 1949, p. 301.

[19] Marino Biondi (ed.), *Serra a Teatro: Commemorazioni e discorsi nel "Comunale" di Cesena (1912–1915)* (Cesena: Il Ponte Vecchio, 2006), pp. 170–74.

[20] Italo De Feo, *Croce: l'uomo e l'opera* (Milan: Mondadori, 1975), p. 248.

[21] Royalty statement, December 31, 1913. Donadelli family documents.

notable first appearances at the Teatro Carlo Felice, Genoa, and the Teatro Petruzzelli, Bari, both in February 1914, the Teatro di San Carlo, Naples, in March 1914, and the Teatro Regio, Turin, in February 1915.

The international premiere of *L'amore dei tre re* took place at the Metropolitan Opera House on January 2, 1914, and in terms of establishing the opera as a major new work was even more significant than the Milan production. Fiora was sung by Lucrezia Bori (1887–1960), Archibaldo by Adamo Didur (1874–1946), Avito by Ferrari-Fontana, and Manfredo by Pasquale Amato (1878–1942). As many of the American critics observed, there had again been little advance publicity, yet the premiere and four subsequent performances were triumphant successes. Toscanini himself reported on January 26 that: "*L'amore dei tre re* has been dazzlingly successful with the public and press. Like no other opera of any other modern composer. I'm still incredulous over it."[22] The New York critics almost unanimously welcomed the opera as a remarkable masterpiece. Henry E. Krehbiel (1854–1923), their acknowledged dean, led the chorus of acclaim, emphasizing that the greatness of the opera flowed from its libretto, "a drama effective in its appeal to eye, ear and emotions":

> It would be difficult to recall another opera in which there is a more puissant exhibition of the elements of contrast in character, of conflicting motives, of the devastating result of passions at war with each other, all of which, nevertheless, challenge sympathy in almost an equal degree.[23]

After the third performance, Krehbiel was fully convinced that:

> Italy has at last found a genius of whom it may well be proud. Italo Montemezzi owns no allegiance to the Veritists; the idiom of Puccini is not his; if he has drunk it is from the spring opened by the Verdi of "Otello." For Montemezzi is a worshipper of beauty, and never once does he violate its sacred canons.[24]

---

[22] *The Letters of Arturo Toscanini*, ed. and trans. Harvey Sachs (London: Faber and Faber, 2002), p. 86.

[23] Henry E. Krehbiel, "'L'Amore Dei Tre Re' Has Premiere," *New-York Tribune*, January 3, 1914, p. 7.

[24] Henry E. Krehbiel, "'I Tre Re' in Ascension," *New-York Tribune*, January 22, 1914, p. 7.

160 SUCCEEDING PUCCINI

Montemezzi's genius had provided what Krehbiel later called "music of supreme fitness," Benelli and the composer creating "as perfect a wedlock as has been accomplished in the field of art," the result "a sincere, a beautiful, a moving work, which for dramatic power surpasses anything that has come out of Italy since the death of Giuseppe Verdi."[25]

Another major New York critic completely won over by Montemezzi's score was W. J. Henderson (1855–1937), who reviewed it for both the *Sun* and *Opera Magazine*. Henderson judged that:

> the most significant quality of the work is its freedom from the domination of the style now the most popular in Italian opera. Montemezzi has boldly rejected the idol Puccini. He has chosen his own methods and elected to appeal to the world with an art almost aristocratic in its manner, certainly seeking for nobility of line and purity of color, and yet as capable of delineating passion as the classic verse of Euripides.

"The union of the music with the text," argued Henderson, "not only in expression of the moods but also in the almost intangible reproduction of the literary style, is extraordinary":

> The combination of all the elements which go to constitute an opera is effected in this score with consummate mastery. The voice parts flow naturally and with character, the orchestra supports and intensifies the vocal utterances, the chorus sings emotion and has pronounced dramatic personality, and the whole creation throbs from beginning to end with an artistic vitality.[26]

The most enduringly enthusiastic of the New York critics was Herbert F. Peyser (1886–1953), who wrote a lengthy review for *Musical America*. Peyser later became a friend of Montemezzi's and continued to write about him and his music for the rest of his life, ranking *L'amore dei tre re* with *Aida* and *Otello* as one of his three favorite operas. Already in 1914 he found that the opera:

---

[25] Henry E. Krehbiel, "Revival of Leon [sic] Benelli Work at Metropolitan Is Auspicious," *New York Tribune*, March 15, 1918, p. 11.

[26] W. J. Henderson, "Real Composer and New Opera," *Sun*, January 3, 1914, p. 6.

Gently and unostentatiously . . . unfolded itself a creation of the purest, most touching, simplest and most resistless beauty, a pregnant new word in the lexicon of modern Italian opera, in many ways the most gratifying example of musical drama from the higher aesthetic standpoints that has come out of Italy since Verdi.[27]

Montemezzi had not "pandered, Puccini-like, to obvious musical appetites" and Benelli's magnificent text was "unutterably of another world . . . from the concoctions of that clever hack Illica!":

In divining the ideal suitability to operatic purposes of a work of this nature and in adapting it to such in bare-faced defiance of all the tenets of Italian veritism, Italo Montemezzi steps forth without warning into the front rank of contemporary operatic writers, one who if he continues to travel the path which he has trodden in "L'Amore dei Tre Re" will prove himself an untold artistic boon to his country by restoring its opera to the sphere of poetry, nobility and dignity from which "realists" have sought in an evil day to divorce it.[28]

All the New York critics recognized the searing power of Toscanini's conducting, yet it is noteworthy that his reading of the score was not approved by Montemezzi. Wallace Brockway and Herbert Weinstock later reported that "when Montemezzi had Toscanini's interpretation described to him in detail, he was shocked. Evidently, the conductor had sacrificed fidelity to dynamics."[29] Despite this, Montemezzi recognized the value of Toscanini's star power and later encouraged him to conduct the opera in Italy.

The New York reception of *L'amore dei tre re* was closely followed by the Boston reception. The recently founded Boston Opera Company had planned to stage the world premiere of Zandonai's *Francesca da Rimini* early in 1914, but when this prestigious event had to be canceled, Montemezzi's opera was substituted. The first Boston performance took place on February 9, with three of the four principals from the Met production (Bori, Ferrari-Fontana, and Amato, joined by Pavel Ludikar as Archibaldo). The conductor

---

[27] Herbert F. Peyser, "Success Unequivocal Crowns 'L'Amore Dei Tre Re' In Its First American Performance," *Musical America*, January 10, 1914, p. 3.

[28] Peyser, "Success Unequivocal," p. 4.

[29] Wallace Brockway and Herbert Weinstock, *The Opera: A History of Its Creation and Performance: 1600–1941* (New York: Simon and Schuster, 1941), p. 415.

162 SUCCEEDING PUCCINI

was Roberto Moranzoni. Thereafter the two productions ran simultaneously, with the final Boston performance on February 18, a day before the final New York one. The Boston critics were just as enthusiastic as their New York colleagues. To H. T. Parker (1867–1934), Montemezzi was emphatically the heir of Verdi, and *L'amore dei tre re* a direct extension of the nineteenth-century master's legacy, ignoring everything in Italian opera that had intervened:

> Montemezzi has the proportioning, the contrasting and the cumulating sense that is essential to music-drama in the theatre.... and out of them rises the crown of Montemezzi's achievements—the ability to fuse each and all of these faculties into a living musico-dramatic unity that sweeps the hearer into it, that bears him along its course, that leaves him no sensations except those that spring from it. Of such is Verdi's "Otello"; of such is Montemezzi's "L'Amore dei Tre Re." Therein they are akin.[30]

In total, the American critics devoted yards of newsprint to *L'amore dei tre re* in 1914, with the vast majority of their commentary overwhelmingly positive.[31]

The third country to experience *L'amore dei tre re* was France. The Boston company took their production to Paris, where it was staged at the Théâtre des Champs-Élysées, the open dress rehearsal on April 24, 1914, followed by the official premiere the next day. Montemezzi traveled to Paris for the occasion, the first of many on which he would see the opera performed outside Italy. Gabriel Davin de Champclos (1863–1946), the music critic for the popular theatre paper *Comœdia*, devoted an extensive feature to the opera and reported that Montemezzi, in garbled French, had expressed great satisfaction with the performance, attributing its success most of all to Vanni Marcoux's Archibaldo:

> Jamais, s'écrie-t-il dans un jargon fortement mâtiné d'italien, jamais, même à la création, à Boston [*sic*; a mistake for Milan], mon œuvre ne m'avait ému à ce point. Et grâce à vous! Bravo! Bravissimo!

---

[30] H. T. Parker, "Montemezzi's Masterpiece of Opera," *Boston Evening Transcript*, February 10, 1914, p. 13.
[31] For a far more detailed examination of the American reception, see Chandler, *Americans on Italo Montemezzi*. This includes eight of the New York reviews and five of the Boston reviews.

Et le maestro Montemezzi écrase sur sa paupière bistrée une larme éloquente et furtive.

("Never," he cries, in a jargon with a strong Italian accent, "never, not even during its creation, in Boston, has my work moved me so much. And that's thanks to you! Bravo! Bravissimo!"

And the maestro Montemezzi wipes a furtive but eloquent tear from his dark eyelid.)[32]

Vanni Marcoux (1877–1962) had a distinctive way of playing Archibaldo as more akin to a character in classical tragedy; perhaps it was this which moved Montemezzi so much.[33]

The French critics were by no means unanimously in favor of *L'amore dei tre re*, but agreed it was a major, even epochal, work deserving serious critical analysis. They could easily relate it to the more consistently literary tradition of opera in France. Davin de Champclos considered that: "[to the] libretto, with its very Shakespearian feel, M. Italo Montemezzi has composed a score that is alive, vigorous, always eloquent, and utterly dramatic. This young musician possesses a sense of theatre and, at times, achieves very powerful effects with very modest means." To Davin de Champclos, it was an essentially Italian work, "directly influenced by Verdi," yet making use of "des procédés wagnériens" so as "to widen the horizon of Italian music and find new ways of expression": an interpretation with which Montemezzi would have warmly agreed.[34]

The veteran commentator on the French musical scene, Arthur Pougin (1834–1921), editor of *Le Ménestrel*, the country's leading music magazine, was equally convinced of the importance of Montemezzi and his opera. An inveterate collector of biographical information, he assembled a sizable biography of the composer, presumably based on information from Montemezzi himself, and included it in his review. The first important biography of Montemezzi, this remains useful today and has been drawn on in the present study. But despite hailing Montemezzi's arrival, Pougin, like some of the other French critics, felt a basic distaste for Benelli's libretto,

---

[32] Gabriel Davin de Champclos, "Au Théâtre des Champs-Élysées: 'L'Amore dei Tre Re'," *Comœdia*, April 25, 1914, p. 2.

[33] Vanni Marcoux first sang Archibaldo in the last of the Boston performances, on February 18, 1914. For a very full account of his distinctive interpretation of the role, see H. T. Parker, "Moranzoni and Marcoux," *Boston Evening Transcript*, February 19, 1914, p. 12.

[34] Davin de Champclos, "Au Théâtre des Champs-Élysées," pp. 1–2.

164　SUCCEEDING PUCCINI

greatly at odds with the American response: "Not only is its drama dark, savage, and ferocious, but in terms of detail, it's completely impenetrable. Facts and emotions are unexplained, and the play only fills the spectator with horror, terror, and dread." Montemezzi's music, on the other hand, had "managed to avoid the excesses, extravagances, and exaggerations in which the current Italian composers often tend to indulge." Montemezzi was "un musicien solide" with "a feeling for the orchestra, and I would add for the dramatic and not the symphonic orchestra."[35] Albert Bazaillas (1867–1924), the author of *Musique et inconscience* (1908), also had doubts about the play, but agreed that Montemezzi had convincingly moved away from verismo thanks to

> two influences that pull him in opposite directions: the influence of Verdi, of whom he displays the flexibility, the warm sincerity, and the technical skills; and the influence of Wagner, whose vast orchestration widens the horizon and increases the depth of the Italian instrumentation. By combining this double influence with his personal talent, M. Montemezzi manages most of the time to escape the distortion imposed by dramatic realism. He gives us a music that is direct, and just as alive and eloquent as the language of emotions.[36]

The French critics consistently drew approving attention to Montemezzi's refinement and opposition to vulgarity. Louis Schneider (1861–1934), who had published the first book-length study of Massenet, and who knew Debussy, judged that:

> if the composition of M. Montemezzi is distinctly modern, it is no less distinctly Italian, which is to say melodic. But this does not mean it bows to the false gods of today's music; it is soberly orchestrated, avoiding instrumental vulgarity and vulgarity of thought. One can see that M. Montemezzi has a feeling for both the theatrical and the symphonic. He seems to make a point of avoiding banality; he is a composer one will have to take note of from now on.[37]

---

[35] Arthur Pougin, "Semaine théâtrale," *Le Ménestrel*, May 2, 1914, p. 139.

[36] Albert Bazaillas, "La Musique," *La Renaissance: politique, littéraire et artistique*, May 9, 1914, p. 22.

[37] Louis Schneider, "Théâtre des Champs-Elysées: L'Amore dei tre Re," *Le Théâtre*, August 1914, p. 3.

Despite such acclaim, Paris would not hear *L'amore dei tre re* again until 1925, when it was staged by Richard Bonelli's American-Italian-French Grand Opera Company, with Mary Garden as Fiora. Meanwhile, having originally been scheduled there in 1915, it finally reached Monte Carlo in 1920, conducted for the first time by Victor de Sabata (1892–1967) and starring Bori as Fiora, Vanni Marcoux as Archibaldo, and Beniamino Gigli (1890–1957) as Avito. De Sabata was to become one of the opera's most acclaimed interpreters, and though Montemezzi was often critical of the pace at which conductors took the score, he seems to have had nothing but admiration for de Sabata's reading, describing it as "one of his [de Sabata's] most magnificent interpretations."[38] In 1927, the Opéra de Nice staged Montemezzi's opera, and for the first time it was sung in a French translation.

On May 27, 1914, *L'amore dei tre re* arrived in London, again with Didur as Archibaldo, Louise Edvina as Fiora, and Moranzoni conducting. There was "a very large audience," including several European royals, and that audience, though "more or less proverbially cautious, not to say conservative, where a new opera is concerned . . . lost their caution and became greatly enthusiastic at curtain fall."[39] This enthusiasm was not shared by most of the critics, however, who unlike their French counterparts had no native tradition of opera remotely akin to *L'amore dei tre re* to shape their judgments. H. C. Colles (1879–1943), the music critic for *The Times*, made fun of the story and claimed to hear "one pumped-up climax of simulated emotion after another."[40] Francis F. Barrett of the *Musical Times* faulted the opera above all for being too redolent of modern Germany: "instead of attempting to improve on his countryman Puccini, just as that composer improved on Verdi, he [Montemezzi] has endeavoured to copy the methods of Dr. Strauss. Mannerisms are the result. The fact is to be regretted, for he certainly has ideas of his own, conveyed by some original orchestral effects."[41] Benelli's libretto was faulted: "It is strange that, after repeated warnings of the bad effect of a dull book, a rising composer should not have been more careful," one reviewer observed tartly.[42] It is hard to resist the conclusion that many British critics were prejudiced against the opera simply because it had been so

---

[38] "una delle sue più magnifiche interpretazioni." Montemezzi to Guido Pesenti, June 25, 1936. Chandler collection.

[39] "Royal Opera. 'L'Amore Dei Tre Re,'" *Daily Telegraph*, May 28, 1914, p. 12.

[40] H. C. Colles, "A New Opera At Covent Garden," *The Times*, May 28, 1914, p. 11.

[41] Francis F. Barrett, "Royal Opera, Covent Garden: The French and Italian Season," *Musical Times* 55 (1914): p. 460.

[42] "L'Amore Dei Tre Re," *Athenæum*, May 30, 1914, p. 770.

166   SUCCEEDING PUCCINI

warmly praised in the United States, for a contest was going on between the two countries as to which was more receptive to modern opera. London had warmly welcomed Strauss's operas, whereas New York had opposed them;[43] the fact that a good many American critics outspokenly preferred *L'amore dei tre re* to *Der Rosenkavalier* meant that the London critics, by condemning the former, could direct another potshot at their American rivals. The contest continued to play out when Zandonai's *Francesca da Rimini* appeared soon afterward. The British critics generally took the view that *Francesca* was the greatest of recent Italian operas, while American critics judged it much inferior to *L'amore dei tre re*.[44]

Despite the mostly negative refrain in the British reviews, some critics were prepared to break ranks. A long and thoughtful review in the *Daily Telegraph* declared:

> His [Montemezzi's] music throughout is rather subtle than obvious, and in his scoring he has much more in common with Debussy than with, say, Puccini. . . . Not that one can put the finger upon this passage or that and point to the influence of another composer. The music, as a fact, is markedly individual. . . . Like Debussy again, Montemezzi lays no store by the set and separate aria or the organized concerted "number," as in the case of Charpentier or Puccini, so that we are little likely to hear extracts of his opera in the concert-room. . . . And that, surely, is high praise indeed, since it points to a particular and peculiar homogeneity in the music of the opera, and assures the sharpness of its dramatic point, even if the note of passion is often almost too reticent. But this is a fault on the right side in Italian opera to-day.[45]

L'amore dei tre re eventually returned to London in 1930, as Chapter 8 documents.

On July 11, 1914, *L'amore dei tre re* reached a third continent when the Teatro Colón, Buenos Aires, staged the first of three performances, with Serafin conducting, Linda Cannetti as Fiora, De Angelis as Archibaldo,

---

[43] Alan Jefferson, *The Operas of Richard Strauss in Britain 1910–1963* (London: Putnam, 1963), p. 21.

[44] For the very different critical receptions of *Francesca da Rimini* in London and New York, see Konrad Dryden, *Riccardo Zandonai: A Biography* (Frankfurt: Peter Lang, 1999), pp. 156–58, 183–85.

[45] "Royal Opera," p. 12.

L'AMORE DEI TRE RE ON FOUR CONTINENTS   167

Galeffi as Manfredo, and Luca Botta as Avito. There was an enthusiastic response from both audiences and critics, the reviewer for *La Razón* judging:

> The score . . . is, as a whole, sympathetic; it is the work of an artist who simultaneously possesses serious musical and dramatic qualities; of a composer who has a more noble concept of his art than some of his more widely-known compatriots; of a musician who, well-informed about what has been written and is being written outside his land, strives to reconcile the inherent qualities of his race's temperament with all the elements of progress, of richness, that both applauded and unknown artists from the other side of the Alps have brought to the specific language of opera.[46]

L'amore dei tre re made a second appearance in Buenos Aires in 1919, at the Teatro Coliseo, before returning to the Colón in 1925, again with Serafin conducting. There were further revivals at the Colón in 1938, 1944, and 1955.

The matter of the Mexican premiere has been complicated by the fact that in 1949 Virgilio Lazzari (1887–1953), the most celebrated Archibaldo, said he had first sung the role in Mexico City in 1916—a claim repeated in a number of reference works.[47] But Lazzari's memory erred: the Mexican premiere was at the Teatro Arbeu, Mexico City, on November 21, 1917. It was conducted by Giorgio Polacco (1873–1960), who had previously conducted *L'amore dei tre re* for the Metropolitan Opera when they gave a performance in Atlanta on April 30, 1915, their first without Toscanini. Polacco's performances in Mexico seem to represent just the second time he conducted the opera, but in the 1920s he regularly conducted it for the Chicago Opera and became one of its most acclaimed interpreters. On November 20 he organized an event that was part lecture, part press conference, part concert to introduce *L'amore dei tre re* to Mexican reviewers and opera devotees. Here he was judged "sincerely enthusiastic," with a "disciple's devotion," "a herald . . . pleased to sing the excellent features of what is unknown to most people." Altogether, "[i]t was a night of unusual artistic feeling, in which Montemezzi prevailed thanks to his genius and his commentator."[48] But even more significant than Polacco's involvement was Lazzari's first performance of what became his

---

[46] Quoted from Roberto Caamaño, *La historia del Teatro Colón: 1908–1968*, 3 vols. (Buenos Aires: Editorial Cinetea, 1979), vol 3, p. 173.

[47] Jane Phillips, "Ay, Every Inch a King," *Opera News*, January 10, 1949, p. 14.

[48] Ruy de Lugo Viña, "El Maestro Polacco Divulgador de la Música Genial de Montemezzi," *El Universal*, November 21, 1917, p. 10. For a summary of Polacco's talk, see "Teatro," *Confeti*, November 22, 1917, pp. 7–8.

168   SUCCEEDING PUCCINI

signature role. "I was very, very young," he later recalled, "but even then I felt the dramatic intensity of Archibaldo. My heart went with him from the first time I looked at the score. . . . I think I knew at once that he stood absolutely alone in opera."[49] Again there was an enthusiastic critical response. It was "the most beautiful and exciting lyrical tragedy that could be produced," the music offered a "powerful description of characters and moods," and the end of Act 2 was "overwhelming," thanks especially to Lazzari.[50] By 1949, Lazzari had sung the role, his favorite, around eighty times.[51] His interpretation, much admired by Montemezzi, can fortunately still be heard,[52] and there is a rich photographic record (Figure 5.1).

L'amore dei tre re made its first appearance in Brazil on September 12, 1919, at the Municipal Theatre, São Paulo. Here it was conducted by Gino Marinuzzi (1882–1945), who had led the Rome premiere in March that year and would later, like Polacco, conduct it for the Chicago Opera. The Brazilian performances starred Gilda Dalla Rizza (1892–1975), a favorite of Puccini's, as Fiora, while De Angelis again took the role of Archibaldo. By this time, Italian critics were increasingly inclined to fret about the opera's Wagnerian qualities, but the Brazilian critics, who mostly admired the opera, disputed this. "More than the influences of other composers," wrote one, "what we noticed . . . was the originality of its orchestration, managing to produce excellent effects of sonority without the overuse of percussion, and that it's an opera with extraordinary qualities for a work of this nature." In Act 2, the same critic judged, "Montemezzi released the entirety of his inspiration . . . with the score admirably underlining the unfolding of the tragedy."[53] Oscar Guanabarino (1851–1937), emphasizing the increasing eclecticism of Italian music since the time of *Aida* (1871), maintained that "Montemezzi is not, certainly, a 'Wagnerist,' but is more a colorist (*colorista*) of his time and, like Wagner, has taken the Italian form and adapted it to his own processes." Montemezzi's "processes," in Guanabarino's opinion, "represent[ed] a step forward from Zandonai"; "the artistic characters of Zandonai and Montemezzi are very distinct, but both are powerful and possess genius."[54]

---

[49] Phillips, "Ay, Every Inch a King," p. 14.

[50] E. G. H., "'Amore dei tre re' en el Arbeau," *El Nacional*, November 22, 1914, p. 4.

[51] Montemezzi to Sem Benelli, February 22, 1949. Archivio Sem Benelli, Biblioteca della Società Economica di Chiavari.

[52] Generous extracts from the Metropolitan Opera's radio broadcast of January 15, 1949, were released on Edward J. Smith's Golden Age of Opera label in 1962 (EJS 241).

[53] "Theatros," *Correio Paulistano*, October 18, 1919, p. 5.

[54] O. G. (Oscar Guanabarino), "Theatros e Musica," *Jornal do Commercio*, September 13, 1919, p. 9.

Figure 5.1 Virgilio Lazzari and Dorothy Kirsten as Archibaldo and Fiora, 1948. *Julian Grant collection.*

In October 1923, *L'amore dei tre re* was brought out at the Teatro Municipal, Santiago, Chile.

Although it is difficult to assess just how much World War I affected the reception and diffusion of *L'amore dei tre re*, there can be no doubt that its impact was momentous. In practical terms, it put an end, in Europe, to the

170 SUCCEEDING PUCCINI

easy circulation of performers that had been such a feature of the opera's early stage career. It is notable, for example, that the Prague premiere in April 1916, conducted by Bohumír Brzobohatý, had a completely non-Italian cast singing a Czech translation by Josef Horný. Of more enduring significance, the complex geopolitical realignments of the war years influenced critical responses. In the period 1914–1918 the opera consolidated a place in the American repertoire, helped by increasing resistance to German music. Montemezzi's critical and popular standing in the United States during the war years is memorably expressed in Giovanni Viafora's 1916 cartoon of the composer, with its caption "Effery time he hav' three King he draw a fulla house" (Figure 5.2).

In Italy, by contrast, the Germanic elements in Montemezzi's score were leading to growing critical reservations. Pizzetti later summed up the problem by stating that *L'amore dei tre re*, a "very noteworthy opera," had given Montemezzi "the status in Italy of being the most Wagnerian among the most renowned opera composers of his generation."[55] This perceived Wagnerianism meant that *L'amore dei tre re* was increasingly judged, not just as an independent opera, but as a symptom of larger cultural affinities of which Italians were increasingly resentful. Thus, by the 1920s there was a gulf between the American and Italian critics. Italian critics were tending to revise their assessments downward, while the Americans were doing the opposite. A particularly good example of the latter is the influential Lawrence Gilman (1878–1939), for his first essay on the opera, published in 1914, is included in all the standard bibliographies of Montemezzi in unexplained preference to other critical accounts of *L'amore dei tre re*. Admirers of the composer can only shake their heads over this, as Gilman himself would have done, for he took a comparatively low view of the opera in 1914, judging it inferior to Puccini's works. Yet by 1928 he had changed his mind completely, championing *L'amore dei tre re* as "the noblest music drama that has come out of Italy" since *Otello*, an opera in a different league from those of the "facile and shallow Puccini."[56]

One of the most eloquent statements of continuing American faith in the opera was supplied by Parker, whose initial enthusiasm only grew over time. He wrote in 1923:

---

[55] Ildebrando Pizzetti, "La 'Nave' di Montemezzi al Reale," *La Tribuna*, December 16, 1938, p. 6.
[56] Lawrence Gilman, "Music," *New York Herald Tribune*, Late Edition, October 30, 1928, p. 21.

L'AMORE DEI TRE RE ON FOUR CONTINENTS   171

Figure 5.2 Cartoon of Montemezzi by Giovanni Viafora, 1916.

172 SUCCEEDING PUCCINI

Time strips defects bare; familiarity revises admirations; yet to this day un-diminished is the place of "L'Amore dei Tre Re" in modern music-drama. Still it fulfills every prescription, answers large to every desire. . . . Music of character, music of mood and trait, music even of circumstance does full of-fice. It is music of the theatre as well, since within that medium it rains stroke upon stroke. The span and force of invention, the abundance and precision of means, the swiftness, the plasticity, the endless, changing vitality all stress it. To something close to splendor, more than once mingle beauty and power.

Manfredo farewells Fiora in a speech of words and tones—both po-etry and both so exalted that from music-drama of the twentieth cen-tury opens the ancient tragedy. Manfredo speaks his devotion—speaks it as men do when with the love of the spirit they would poultice the ache gnawing at their bodies; when against barriers impassable they drive the ardors that deceive despair. Manfredo's voice lies upon the singing actor's tongue; Manfredo's heart in the orchestra cries and bleeds and all in vain. Tragedy again of pity and of fate, expressed in a music that seals reticence with power. Many pages of Wagner, a few pages of Verdi in "Othello," still fewer in Dukas' "Ariane" or d'Indy's "Saint-Christopher," and where else in modern music-drama is there exaltation to match this exaltation? Is it the folly of emotion still streaming and tingling to call it Sophoclean? The classic strain yet haunts Latin blood and brain.[57]

Italian critics were aware of the great acclaim the opera had won in the United States, and by the 1920s it was common for them to mention this in their reviews. In a review of La Scala's revival of the opera in 1926, with Toscanini conducting, the increasingly influential Adriano Lualdi (1885–1971) put the question: "Could it be that the Americans are indeed more intelligent—in music—than we are? Or that our dealers, despite having first-rate merchandise like this, do not know how to trade it?"[58] Lualdi praised the score as particularly atmospheric— "one can feel the tragedy in the air"—and found it "rich in theatrical and musical merits . . . even if it is guilty of Wagnerism." But the immense gap between his verdict and that of the opera's American champions is clear when his account of Manfredo is compared to Parker's: "Manfredo is . . . the most musically colorless figure of the whole tragedy. The composer did not believe in the truth of his love and did not

[57] H. T. Parker, "Montemezzi and Polacco," *Musical Leader*, February 1, 1923, p. 103.
[58] Adriano Lualdi, *Serate musicali* (Milan: Treves, 1928), p. 242.

L'AMORE DEI TRE RE ON FOUR CONTINENTS   173

penetrate his character's soul. Therefore, everything he [Manfredo] says appears, and is, declamatory and cold."[59]

As with any period of operatic history, there was no precise triangulation between critical verdicts, audience responses, and the willingness of theatre managements to stage *L'amore dei tre re*. Hundreds of reviews stand testament to the fact that, as in London in 1914, the public was often much more enthusiastic than the critics. On the other hand, there are also many reviews by critics who, convinced of the high value of the opera, express frustration at its not being staged more often. Nevertheless, there is certainly some correlation between the critical temperature and the number of performances in Italy and the United States. At La Scala, for example, *L'amore dei tre re* was revived for three performances in 1914, but then did not appear there again until 1926, when it was put on twice, first for three, then for two performances (in the interim it had appeared at Milan's Teatro Dal Verme in 1919, in a production postponed from 1917). It appeared at La Scala again in 1932 (six performances), 1937 (three performances), 1948 (three performances), and 1953 (four performances). In total then, La Scala performed the opera twelve times in the period 1913–1930, and another sixteen times in the period 1931–1953, after which it was not revived again until 2023. Figures can be interpreted in different ways, and a positive interpretation here would be that the only other opera by Montemezzi's immediate rivals that performed so well was Zandonai's *Francesca da Rimini*. Moreover, by Italian standards, La Scala's commitment to the opera was exceptional. A contrast can be made with the Teatro Petruzzelli, Bari, which in 1914 became the first theatre in southern Italy to stage the work. It was put on for five performances, but never revived there. Yet *Francesca da Rimini*, first staged in Bari in 1920, was revived in 1921, 1927, 1928, 1936, and 1942, for a total of twenty-six performances.[60] But even La Scala's performance history pales in comparison with that of the Metropolitan Opera, where *L'amore dei tre re* was staged fifty-three times in the period 1914–1930, and another thirteen times in the period 1931–1949, after which it received no more performances there.

However, this does not tell the whole story, for while *L'amore dei tre re* was widely played across Italy, in a whole series of distinct productions, in the United States it was played by a handful of companies who would also, on occasion, tour it. In 1915 the Met production was taken to Philadelphia and

---

[59] Lualdi, *Serate musicali*, p. 241.

[60] Statistics are from Alfredo Giovine, *L'Opera in Musica in Teatri di Bari* (Bari: Archivio delle tradizioni popolari baresi, 1969), pp. 86, 90.

174 SUCCEEDING PUCCINI

Atlanta, while the newly constituted Boston Grand Opera Company took theirs to Chicago, St. Louis, Louisville, Detroit, New York, Philadelphia, Washington, DC, and Baltimore. The Chicago performances, in October 1915, are particularly important, for the Chicago Opera Association, headed by Cleofonte Campanini, soon afterward mounted their own production of the opera, first performed on December 4, with Ferrari-Fontana again taking the role of Avito, Clarence Whitehill as Archibaldo, Graham Marr as Manfredo, and Louise Edvina as Fiora. In 1916 the Boston Company continued its tour, presenting Montemezzi's opera in Buffalo, Cincinnati, Cleveland, Pittsburgh, Denver, Portland, Los Angeles, San Francisco, Seattle, Kansas City, and Omaha. In the 1920s, the Chicago Opera in turn started touring their production, which by 1929 had been performed in Chicago itself nineteen times. As well as annual New York performances between 1920 and 1922, it was presented in Cleveland in 1920, Denver in 1921, Los Angeles and San Francisco in 1921 and 1922, Baltimore, Milwaukee, and Pittsburgh in 1922, and Boston in 1923, 1925, and 1929. San Francisco having thus seen two touring productions, in 1925 the San Francisco Opera, founded 1923, mounted a production of their own. It was regularly repeated until 1966 and usually was taken to Los Angeles, too. Special mention must also be made of the Ravinia Opera, founded in 1912 to offer summer seasons of opera at an easy distance from Chicago. *L'amore dei tre re* was first given there on August 3, 1918, with Claudia Muzio as Fiora. Such was its success that Montemezzi's opera became a staple of their repertoire, given two or three performances every single season through to 1932 (thirty-four performances in all), when the company collapsed due to economic problems caused by the Depression. Thus, the vast majority of American performances of *L'amore dei tre re* before 1930 were staged by just five companies.

World War I certainly slowed the diffusion of *L'amore dei tre re* through Italy and goes a considerable way toward explaining why it only reached, say, the Teatro Costanzi, Rome, in 1919. On the other hand, the war hardly explains why it was first staged in Trieste, at the Teatro Verdi, in 1921, in Venice, at the Teatro La Fenice, in 1922, or in Palermo, at the Teatro Massimo, as late as 1947. In general, after the initial excitement, Italian opera houses seem to have taken the view that it was an opera they should stage at some point, but not necessarily with any urgency, and leading opera houses across Europe regarded it in a similar light. The extremely rapid diffusion of certain new Italian operas that had been such a feature of the 1890s, rapidly buoying Puccini to international fame, was now a phenomenon of the past, so national or significant regional premieres of *L'amore dei tre re* are often widely staggered. To take the Iberian Peninsula as an example, Montemezzi's opera was brought out at the Teatro Real, Madrid, as early as March 1915, with the celebrated Spanish tenor Antonio Cortis (1891–1952) singing Avito; it reached the Teatro Nacional de São Carlos, Lisbon, in February 1920, with Ferrari-Fontana returning to the role of Avito; but only appeared at the Gran Teatre del Liceu, Barcelona, in 1930.

If World War I had a significant impact on the different fates of *L'amore dei tre re* in Italy and the United States, it affected the opera's fortunes in the German-speaking part of Europe even more. Here the most politicized episode of critical reception eventually unfolded. The first mentions of the opera in the German press, in April 1913, were positive,[61] and it was originally scheduled to appear at the Charlottenburg Opera, Berlin, in the autumn of 1914. When it finally had its German premiere there on September 19, 1919, sung in a German translation by Alfred Brüggemann, Germany was reeling from defeat. In this context, the German critics mostly took the line that Georg Hartmann, the director, was making a generous gesture in staging an Italian opera at all:

> The opera house in Charlottenburg has become the first theatre to re-establish relations with the outside world. By staging the German premiere of Italo Montemezzi's tragic opera "The Love of Three Kings," opera house director Hartmann was aiming to fulfill former commitments while at the same time offering reconciliation and compensation. The question is: will those on the other side of the Alps take the outstretched hand?[62]

Much of the commentary was implicitly, and quite often explicitly, couched in nationalistic terms. Bruno Schrader (1861–1926), for example, judged that the opera's "flawless beauty is breathtaking in both the vocal and orchestral parts, but soon becomes tiring, as it is too monotonous and lacks any personal characteristics." Therefore: "one feels there was no need to travel across the Alps; there are plenty of better, but overlooked, German works of this genre available."[63] Paul Schwers (1874–1939) went further, giving the opera

---

[61] Carolin Krahn, "Schweben zwischen Liebe und Tod: L'amore dei tre re als Klangsynthese der Jahrhundertwende," *Die Liebe der drei Könige* (program) (Lübeck: Theater Lübeck, 2022), pp. 18–19.

[62] G. Sch., "Montemezzi: Die Liebe dreier Könige," *Neue Musik Zeitung* 41 (1920): p. 13.

[63] Bruno Schrader, "Die Liebe dreier Könige," *Neue Zeitschrift für Musik* 86 (September 25, 1919): p. 252.

176   SUCCEEDING PUCCINI

one of the most damning reviews it had yet received. Montemezzi's music, he declared, was "a mix of new French technique and Wagnerian sentiment":

> [Montemezzi] deserves our sympathy for making honest, accomplished music without false pose and because, as an Italian, he does not blindly follow in the footsteps of Puccini. Mind you, he would do well to heed the latter a little. How to tie the knot and consolidate the essentials at an opportune moment he can learn from the Italian masters. As to how to become a *real* dramatist, he may want to listen in on the Germans.[64]

Most of the German critics wanted to find fault with *L'amore dei tre re*, but, like their French counterparts, they concentrated their fire on Benelli's libretto, which they found unconvincing, irrational, historically inaccurate, and "disgusting" in its violence—apparently upset that the playwright seemed to be attacking the Germanic invaders of Italy. By contrast, they nearly all found something to praise in Montemezzi's music, particularly his orchestration and the choral scene in Act 3. And in a few cases this developed into real admiration, as in a review probably by August Spanuth (1857–1920):

> There is much to like about Montemezzi's music. While it certainly lacks any features that might clearly profile the composer, it comes across as entirely honest and warm; it never abuses the listener with any intrusive characteristics, and, for all its sweet melodiousness, also steers clear of any banal aural flattery. Montemezzi has adopted many features of Wagner's tonal language, but without ever once allowing this to obscure the underlying Italian nature of the music. In the end, his style is closer to that of old Verdi—and, thankfully, even further from any veristic eccentricities.[65]

Altogether, enough positives were found in the music to suggest that, at a less sensitive moment, *L'amore dei tre re* may have been able to establish itself in German theatres. As it was, it did not return to Berlin until 1928. On February 16, 1922, meanwhile, it appeared at the Volksoper in Vienna in a production directed by August Markowsky and conducted by Rudolf Weirich.

---

[64] Paul Schwers, "Die Liebe dreier Könige," *Allgemeine Musik-Zeitung* 46 (1919): p. 508.
[65] "Deutsches Opernhaus: 'Die Liebe dreier Könige,'" *Signale für die musikalische Welt* 77 (September 24, 1919): pp. 597–98.

L'AMORE DEI TRE RE ON FOUR CONTINENTS   177

In 1928, Montemezzi's music finally reached a fourth continent when the Melba-Williamson Opera Company in Australia, founded in 1911, performed *L'amore dei tre re* on July 4 at His Majesty's Theatre, Melbourne, before taking it on to Sydney. They had originally hoped to include it in their 1924 tour but were unable to do so for logistical reasons. The performances were conducted by Emilio Rossi, and featured Lina Scavizzi as Fiora, Fernando Autori as Archibaldo, Francesco Merli as Avito, and Apollo Granforte as Manfredo. Dame Nellie Melba was in the audience. The opera proved a huge success with the Australian public, the critics agreeing that "there was more applause at the fall of the final curtain than at any previous performance during the season—not excluding even the opening night, when Verdi's Aida [*sic*] was so triumphantly produced."[66] Much of the criticism struck the enraptured note previously heard mainly in the United States. Thorold Waters (1876–1956), writing for the *Australian Musical News*, declared emphatically:

> Since the intangible tapestries of "Pelleas and Melisande" [*sic*] were woven by Debussy, there has been no opera wearing less trace of artifice than Italo Montemezzi's "L'amore dei tre Re." Its music springs from a deep well of inspiration to rush to the surface with a golden liquidity and broaden tragically. Nothing more spontaneous and molten could be imagined for an orchestra, yet it would be difficult for any analyst of music to point out one superfluous note, and just as difficult for anyone to scent a whiff of Wagner, a hint of Puccini, a faint aroma of Debussy, or anything of that sort. Montemezzi was so genuinely inspired in the composition of "L'amore dei tre Re" that he forgot the other men's music and evolved his own with an almost inconceivable consistency in this imitative age, and a succinctness with few parallels.

The Act 2 duet between Fiora and Avito was "the most passionate thing in opera since Wagner expressed overmastering emotion unsurpassably in 'Tristan and Isolde.'"[67] Other critics produced interesting reflections on the question of how Montemezzi compared to Puccini. Fritz Hart (1874–1949), the English composer of many operas, who was doubtless aware of British reservations about *L'amore dei tre re*, judged: "certainly he [Montemezzi] has

---

[66] Fritz Hart, "Farewell to Grand Opera," *Table Talk*, July 12, 1928, p. 18.
[67] Thorold Waters, "Three Kings Provide a Right Royal Night: How Montemezzi's Lustrous Opera Scored a Triumph," *Australian Musical News*, August 1, 1928, p. 10a.

178 SUCCEEDING PUCCINI

not the genius of a Puccini—though intellectually he would seem to be superiorly gifted. He has a fine sense of design, climax and color. His harmonic powers are sufficiently developed to enable him to express himself with unfailing success, but they are wholly out-of-date."[68] On the other hand, the anonymous reviewer for *The Age*, probably Arthur Ernest Howard Nickson (1876–1964), considered *L'amore dei tre re* a "stupendous work" and insisted: "The popular mind might prefer Puccini with his open realism, but Montemezzi, in The Love of the Three Kings, would be chosen in preference by the connoisseur, who desires a more profound type of operatic expression, and a drama artistically balanced in its main essentials."[69]

Over the years, as *L'amore dei tre re* traveled round the world, it brought Montemezzi hundreds of thousands of lire in royalties, his income from his music peaking in the few years after World War 1. For the twelve months from July 1, 1921, to June 30, 1922, for example, roughly corresponding to his first year of marriage, he earned 36,908 lire in royalties.[70]

In March and April 1914, meanwhile, Fonotipia, the Italian record label established in 1904, invited soprano Elisa Landau, tenor Bettino Cappelli, baritone Enrico Nani, and bass Amleto Galli into their studios to record extracts from *L'amore dei tre re* with orchestra. This was the first attempt at a studio recording of Montemezzi's music and much the most ambitious one before Arturo Basile made the first complete recording of *L'amore dei tre re* in 1950. It immediately established the basic problem: as there were no "numbers" as such in Montemezzi's score, it was difficult to extract sections rounded and coherent enough for release as gramophone records. This is the most likely explanation for the fact that, though several extracts were recorded, only one was released: a double-sided disc of Nani in a moving, beautifully captured rendering of Manfredo's "Suonata è l'ora della partenza" (The hour of departure has sounded) from Act 2.[71] Presumably Montemezzi had a copy of this record, and perhaps of the unreleased recordings, too. It would soon become clear how unusual it was, for despite the popularity of the opera in theatres, it was not until 1921 that a second recording was made, when Adamo Didur recorded Archibaldo's "Son quarant' anni" (It is forty years) for Pathé, and in total there would be only a handful of records in the gramophone era.[72]

---

[68] Hart, "Farewell to Grand Opera," p. 18.

[69] "Grand Opera. L'amore Dei Tre Re," *The Age*, July 5, 1928, p. 15.

[70] Archivio Storico Ricordi, Copialettere.

[71] Società Italiana di Fonotipia 69185/6.

[72] We are aware of only six 78 records of music from *L'amore dei tre re* and none from Montemezzi's other operas.

The period when popular Italian operas supplied a stream of "hits" to the recording industry was largely over.

By the time World War I erupted, it was clear that *L'amore dei tre re* could capture the imagination of audiences and critics around the world. It had given the most convincing answer yet presented to the question of what Italian opera might look like after Puccini. But the person Montemezzi needed to impress most was Tito Ricordi, who, as the previous chapter documented, had little faith in the opera before its premiere. Tito was not a man to question a positive endorsement by the public and critics, however, and by 1914 relations between Montemezzi and Casa Ricordi were much warmer. They were doubtless helped by the fact that Zandonai's *Melenis*, given two productions in the 1912–1913 season, and never revived since, had been a definite flop, while Alfano's *L'ombra di Don Giovanni*, brought out in the 1913–1914 season, had proved a disaster, and led to a complete break between the composer and the publisher. For ten months, Montemezzi was able to regain, with little room for dispute, his position as the leader among the younger Ricordi composers. But on February 19, 1914, at the Teatro Regio, Turin, Zandonai's *Francesca da Rimini* made its first appearance: the opera which would prove *L'amore dei tre re*'s closest, most enduring rival. Zandonai started work on this *Literaturoper*, setting Gabriele D'Annunzio's play of the same title, in 1912, well before the premiere of *L'amore dei tre re*, but almost certainly with the knowledge that Montemezzi had been working on a comparable project for two years. Zandonai's biographer, Konrad Dryden, writes that: "*Francesca da Rimini* is undoubtedly Zandonai's greatest work, in which he reached the apex of his own very personal art, but it should not be forgotten that much of this greatness rests with its superb libretto. D'Annunzio's text inspired Zandonai to a surge of inspiration that overshadowed everything he had written previously."[73] Much the same could be said of *L'amore dei tre re* and Montemezzi's response to Benelli's play.

In winter 1914–1915, Illica, eager to make a comeback, approached Casa Ricordi with a proposal for an opera to be called *Italia*, the libretto for which he proposed to co-write with Renato Simoni. It was, it would appear, to be a sort of corrective, patriotic alternative to *Germania* (1902), the libretto Illica had written for Alberto Franchetti. Tito apparently liked the idea and believed it would be a good subject for Montemezzi; Illica, however, still nurtured a grudge against Montemezzi, and hoped the opera could be

---

[73] Dryden, *Riccardo Zandonai*, p. 111.

180 SUCCEEDING PUCCINI

entrusted to Zandonai (a composer he had not worked with before). This prompted Tito to set out his feeling on the merits of his two leading younger generation composers:

> since the objective is to have "Italia" turn into something quite good, I believe the designated maestro should be Montemezzi, whose foray into the heroic genre has proven victorious.
>
> I have never considered Zandonai, nor do I now; he is a first-rate talent but possibly not one who could relate to such a subject—maybe yes, maybe no....
>
> For me, I'll stick with the name of Montemezzi.[74]

It would be rash to read too much into this, but clearly the somewhat brittle Zandonai was no longer the favorite he had been two or three years earlier. As Italy entered 1915, and moved inexorably toward war, the "heroic genre" and the *Literaturoper* seemed to represent a distinctive new kind of Italian opera, one in which Montemezzi and Zandonai were the leading masters (Mascagni's comparable *Parisina* of 1913, again setting a D'Annunzio text, had, by contrast, proved a notable failure, while Puccini, working on his Viennese commission, *La rondine*, to Tito's intense disapproval, was completely out of contention). Yet the seeming convergence between Montemezzi and Zandonai was short-lived, and from this point their careers diverged widely and instructively. In 1914, Zandonai decided that his next stage work would be a comic opera, *La via della finestra*, with a libretto adapted by Adami from Eugene Scribe's comédie-vaudeville *Une femme qui se jette par la fenêtre* (1847). Zandonai considered this "a light and optimistic work," and though he later expressed doubts as to whether it was really the right opera for the "heroic moment" of the war, by the summer of 1916 "[h]e felt that his only contribution to the war effort was to continue work on the third act of *La via della finestra*, hoping one day to thereby allieve [*sic*] his countrymen's spirits."[75] This left Montemezzi free to dominate the "heroic genre," and though *Italia* would never be written, he found an apt substitute; his "contribution to the war effort" was to be utterly different from Zandonai's.

---

[74] "poiché si tratta di far uscire da 'Italia' qualche cosa di molto buono io credo che il maestro designato sia il Montemezzi il quale—nel genere eroico—ha fatto la sua prova e l'ha vinta. / Non ho mai pensato e non penso allo Zandonai, ingegno di prim'ordine, ma che non so se sentirebbe un tal soggetto—forse sì, forse no.... / Per me rimango fermo nel nome di Montemezzi." Tito Ricordi to Illica, February 22, 1915. Archivio Storico Ricordi.

[75] Dryden, *Riccardo Zandonai*, pp. 174, 180.

6

"Enthusiasm for my Homeland"

La nave and D'Annunzio, 1914–1919

L'amore dei tre re very much put Montemezzi's career back on track, and after he had seen it successfully launched at La Scala there was a pressing need for him to reorganize his finances and choose his next subject. Montemezzi went to Milan in June 1913 to discuss his future with Casa Ricordi and entered into perhaps the most vexed financial negotiations of his life. He had originally agreed to a fee of 8,000 lire for *L'amore dei tre re*, the same as for *Héllera*, but was later able to negotiate a higher fee of 10,000 lire, in exchange for a commitment to compose a further opera as well. This, however, presupposed sufficient income from *Héllera* to maintain his 500 lire monthly stipend. In fact, as noted in the previous chapter, all payments from Casa Ricordi to Montemezzi had been suspended in December 1911. Having been unpaid for eighteen months, and having now delivered a successful opera, Montemezzi clearly believed he deserved more than 10,000 lire for it, and the publisher was willing to pay more, but only if strict conditions were met. A somewhat exasperated letter Montemezzi wrote to Tito Ricordi from the Hôtel Angioli-Simplon, Milan, on June 27, 1913, reveals what these conditions were:

> I felt confident that you were not going to insist with regard to the 50% for the extinction of my debt and, likewise, for the 600 monthly lire instead of the 700 I had requested.
>
> I really thought I wasn't asking for much! However, I don't want to insist any longer. Please have the contract drawn up within the terms expounded to me, if you really don't believe you can do anything more for me.[1]

---

[1] "Mi ritenevo sicuro che Ella non avrebbe insistito riguardo alla percentuale del 50% ad estinzione del mio debito, come pure per le 600 mensili invece delle 700 da me richieste. / Credevo davvero di non domandare molto! Ma non voglio più insistere. Faccia pure stendere il contratto nei sensi espostimi, se Ella proprio non crede di poter fare altro per me." Chandler collection.

Succeeding Puccini. David Chandler and Raffaele Mellace, Oxford University Press. © Oxford University Press 2025.
DOI: 10.1093/9780197761373.003.0007

182 SUCCEEDING PUCCINI

In the end, Montemezzi was paid 15,000 lire for *L'amore dei tre re*, leaving his debt to Casa Ricordi as 9,421 lire, and fifty percent of his royalties was withheld until it was fully repaid. A new contract, signed on June 28, succinctly set out the terms on which he would continue working for Ricordi.[2] Montemezzi undertook to compose two further full-length operas for the company, and to give precedence to these over other compositions. On delivery of the first, he would be paid 10,000 lire; on delivery of the second, 12,000. These prices, comparable to what Zandonai was being paid at this time, fall well short of the 40,000 lire Puccini was getting for his operas, and reflect continuing reservations about Montemezzi's commercial viability.[3] No time limit was set for the operas' completion, but doubtless Montemezzi had strong memories of what had happened in 1911 and understood that he could only extend his credit so far—though the immense profitability of *L'amore dei tre re* prevented this from becoming an issue.

Having secured Casa Ricordi's continuing support, the next step was to choose a new subject. This was no easy matter: after finding *L'amore dei tre re* so perfect for his needs, Montemezzi had become harder to please and less willing to compromise. And at this juncture, one of the greatest frustrations of his career began to manifest itself, for he very much wanted to base an opera on Edmond Rostand's 1895 verse play *La princesse lointaine* (The Faraway Princess). Until at least 1930, this was an important aspiration, but one he was never able to fulfill because of the unwillingness of Rostand (1868–1918), and subsequently Rostand's widow, to sell the rights. Though some reference works state that Montemezzi actually commenced an opera based on *La princesse lointaine*, we have found no evidence that he did so.

Nevertheless, Montemezzi's intense, prolonged, frustrated attraction to Rostand's play is an important part of his artistic career, so it is necessary to get some sense of the subject he longed to treat. Inspired by the legendary story of the twelfth-century troubadour Jaufre Rudel, *La princesse lointaine* is an extraordinary hymn to ideal love. Rudel has fallen in love with Mélissinde, the princess of Tripoli, based purely on reports of her extraordinary beauty, and he has composed songs for her—those songs have reached her ears and have inspired a fondness for him. At the end of his life, Rudel sails from his home in Aquitaine, hoping to see Mélissinde before his death. After great

[2] Archivio Storico Ricordi.
[3] For Zandonai's fees, see Konrad Dryden, *Riccardo Zandonai: A Biography* (Frankfurt: Peter Lang, 1999), p. 209. According to Zandonai, *Francesca da Rimini*, contracted in May 1912, was the first opera for which he was paid 10,000 lire.

sufferings on the voyage, by the time he reaches Tripoli he is a dying man. His young friend Bertrand d'Allamanon, who has been inspired by the romanticism of Rudel's quest, goes ashore in an attempt to persuade the princess to visit Rudel. Here the emotional complications begin, for Mélissinde is deeply attracted to Bertrand and wants him to forget his friend and become her lover. Bertrand eventually succumbs, but when a misunderstood cry from outside seems to signal Rudel's death, he is consumed by guilt and keenly reproaches Mélissinde. At this, she rejects him, and herself feeling guilt, hurriedly prepares to visit Rudel, now known to be still alive. Rudel dies in Mélissinde's arms, his dream come true; Mélissinde pledges never to love another and to spend the rest of her life in a monastery; Bertrand prepares to go and fight in the Crusades. The complex interrelationships between the three principal characters, all expressing themselves in beautiful poetry, are fascinating, as are the disagreements between Rudel's physician and chaplain on the value of his quest (the latter giving it, effectively, a spiritual interpretation). The play has great theatrical—the role of Mélissinde was created for Sarah Bernhardt—and musical possibilities, and there was something epochal about Montemezzi's attraction to its remarkable blend of different elements, for, as the following chapter documents, Alfano and Zandonai later followed him in aspiring to make an opera from it.

By late spring 1914, Montemezzi had made a definite decision that *La princesse lointaine* was his preferred subject, and he wrote to Tito Ricordi on June 2: "I'll be grateful to you if you can tell me when you will go there [Paris] to negotiate with Rostand.... We have been wasting precious time and the <u>Principessa</u>... is stupendous!"[4] There had, clearly, been some earlier agreement that Ricordi would negotiate for the rights. A few days later, however, there was disappointing news from Tito: he would not see Rostand, had not obtained the rights, and wanted Montemezzi to choose a new subject for the time being, even though he did not rule out the possibility of a future opera derived from the play. Montemezzi was left confused and bitterly disappointed:

> I couldn't possibly expect such news, and I really don't know what to attribute this sudden change to. I remember that the negotiations with <u>Rostand</u>, according to what you told me, were advanced to such a point

---

[4] "Le sarò grato se Ella mi dirà quando vi andrà [Parigi] per trattare con Rostand [. . .] Si sta perdendo un tempo prezioso e la <u>Principessa</u>... è stupenda!" Archivio Storico Ricordi.

184 SUCCEEDING PUCCINI

as to give rise to all hopes, although you, being a practical man, stated that until the contract was signed you didn't feel certain.... It is most painful to miss out on the realization of a dream that seemed so close! Because we'll have to accept, unfortunately, that we will never again find a "Principessa lontana."[5]

Whether there was a satisfactory explanation is unclear, but Montemezzi was forced to abandon his "dream" for the time being.

Around this time, rumors that Montemezzi had chosen his new subject reached the press and, in the manner of rumors, grew and grew until in February 1915 the New York *Sun* was declaring: "It is safe to say that the next work by Montemezzi to be made known here (probably in the season after next) will be his setting of Rostand's 'Princesse Lointaine.' It is hoped that the first performance on any stage will be the production at the Metropolitan and that the young composer will be present."[6] Eight years later, H. T. Parker would even state: "upon his study-table he [Montemezzi] holds, never quite finished, 'La Princesse Lointaine.'"[7] Thus, in our reading, commenced the legend that Montemezzi actually started composing an opera entitled *La principessa lontana*.

Montemezzi owned a bound typescript Italian verse translation of Rostand's play by the well-known poet Cosimo Giogieri Contri (1870–1943).[8] Contri's translation was published by Casa Sonzogno in 1920, with a preface dated October 1919. The published translation is substantially the same as Montemezzi's typescript, though numerous small changes establish that the typescript is a draft, presumably obtained by the composer sometime before the published version appeared. How long before, we have been unable to establish: given all the disruption caused by the war, it could have been a matter of years. The typescript suggests that, probably from the beginning, Montemezzi imagined *La principessa lontana* as a second

---

[5] "Non era possibile che io mi aspettassi una simile notizia e non so davvero a che cosa attribuire questo improvviso cambiamento. Ricordo che le trattative con Rostand, a quanto Ella mi disse, erano a tanto, da dar adito ad ogni speranza, sebbene Ella, da uomo pratico, affermasse che finché il contratto non era firmato non si riteneva sicuro.... Vedersi sfuggire la realizzazione di un sogno che sembrava così prossimo! Perché bisognerà purtroppo constatare che una "Principessa lontana" non la troveremo mai più." Montemezzi to Tito Ricordi, June 10, 1914. Archivio Storico Ricordi.

[6] "Montemezzi Opera at Metropolitan," *Sun*, February 12, 1915, p. 7. The writer was probably W. J. Henderson, the paper's music critic.

[7] H. T. Parker, "Montemezzi and Polacco," *Musical Leader*, February 1, 1923, p. 103.

[8] Donadelli family documents.

Literaturoper, its libretto a shortened but fairly literal Italian translation of the play.

Montemezzi may have fought harder for *La princesse lointaine* in 1914 if he had not become interested in another, alternative project. One day in April 1914 he was sitting in a restaurant in Milan, eating a steak, when he suddenly had an "inspiration": "What if I set *La Nave* to music?"[9] *La nave* (1908) was a very long, episodic, nationalistic play by Gabriele D'Annunzio, and apart from its glowing poetry, a radically different work from *La princesse lointaine*. But both would have been *Literaturopern*, and Montemezzi may well have reflected that he was the only major Italian composer of *Literaturopern* who had not set a D'Annunzio play. The fashion had started, as noted in Chapter 4, with Alberto Franchetti's *La figlia di Iorio* of 1906 and was extended by Mascagni's *Parisina* of 1913, Zandonai's *Francesca da Rimini* of 1914, and Pizzetti's *Fedra* of 1915. Moreover, having signed a contract for two operas, Montemezzi's initial thought was perhaps that the Rostand and D'Annunzio plays could make a powerful contrasting pair, the one concerned with ideal, the other with perverted love. He was so excited by his new "inspiration" that "without losing any time, he called a waiter and sent him, immediately, to the nearest bookseller, to buy a copy of the tragedy."[10] In his earliest public account of how he came to compose *La nave*, Montemezzi reported that the initial moment of excitement in the restaurant was almost immediately followed by doubts, as he found himself overwhelmed by "the extent of the picture and the large size of the tragedy."[11] A later account, by contrast, speaks of a long period of study in which he felt alternately encouraged and discouraged: "I spent weeks and weeks prying into its [the play's] proportions, studying its characters in depth . . . those epic figures, stirring in a gigantic picture, were beating at my imagination, not allowing me peace."[12] All reports agree, though, that Montemezzi did not begin composing *La nave* until April 1915, and for much of the intervening period *La princesse lointaine* apparently remained his first choice of subject.

Montemezzi later told Vincenzo Bucci that the final decision to compose *La nave* was made on a visit to "a strip of Trento land" (*un lembo di terra trentina*), seemingly around March 1915.[13] This odd description is loaded

---

[9] Vincenzo Bucci, "'La Nave' nel Cantiere: Un varo alla Scala di Milano," *Emporium* 48 (October 1918): p. 176.

[10] Bucci, "'La Nave,'" p. 176.

[11] Bucci, "'La Nave,'" p. 177.

[12] Montemezzi, "Come scrissi la musica per 'La Nave,'" *Scenario* 7 (April 1938): p. 217.

[13] Bucci, "'La Nave,'" p. 177.

186   SUCCEEDING PUCCINI

with political significance. Trentino was in Austrian hands until the end of World War I, and the suggestion seems to be that Montemezzi had been to the border region. The question whether Italy should enter the war—*the* question in Italy at the time—was closely bound up with the *irredenta*, the lost territories like Trentino that were still, after three wars of independence, in Austrian hands. On his visit, Montemezzi experienced a sense of historical destiny: "The place, the proximity of the event, the significance his opera would assume in the coming hour, revived in him his purpose of setting *La Nave* to music."[14] Years later, he explained: "my wish to make a work of art was fed by the wish to make also a work of propaganda."[15]

Montemezzi went to Milan to discuss the idea with Tito Ricordi, who approved it and declared he would shorten the text (which needed drastic abridgement) himself, and immediately apply to D'Annunzio for permission. Tito was doubtless feeling confident, for his shortened version of *Francesca da Rimini*, prepared for Zandonai, had been praised by D'Annunzio and formed the basis of an opera that was showing encouraging signs of becoming a permanent addition to the repertoire. He was also, perhaps, keen to undertake this task himself, rather than entrusting it to Montemezzi (who had made most of the decisions in regard to *L'amore dei tre re*), for they had rather different views of the project. Montemezzi had a more political, nationalistic, and propagandistic understanding of the planned opera, while Tito was more interested in creating a profitable work of wide appeal. In a revealing letter to D'Annunzio of April 9, 1915, Tito commented on the "good deal" on offer and recommended Montemezzi in the following terms: "the composer I'm proposing to you for the 'Nave' won't be an innovator, won't be able to go back to the pure sources of our ancient music (!!) [an ironic allusion to Pizzetti, who had composed the incidental music for the original play], but he will write good music that will please the audience."[16] D'Annunzio, always needing money and craving glory, promptly made a provisional agreement to sell the rights, replying to Tito on April 14, 1915. In just a week, the latter then prepared a shortened version of the play. Montemezzi told Bucci that "the adapter became so passionate about his work, and identified himself with it to such an extent, that having completed it he telegraphed

[14] Bucci, "'La Nave,'" p. 177.
[15] Montemezzi, "Come scrissi," p. 217.
[16] "il compositore che ti offro per la 'Nave' non sarà un innovatore, non sarà capace di risalire alle fonti pure della nostra antica musica (!!), ma scriverà della buona musica che piacerà al pubblico." Archivio Storico Ricordi.

the composer: 'I've finished *La Nave*.'"[17] Montemezzi then very deliberately wrote the first notes on April 25, a day carefully chosen, for it was St. Mark's Day, the patron saint of Venice. The action was the more significant given that D'Annunzio had not yet approved Tito's abridgement.

D'Annunzio's *Nave* represents a sustained effort to create an epic myth of the foundation of Venice, comparable to that of the founding of Rome in which Romulus kills his brother Remus. The play, taking the form of a Prologue and three Episodes, is set on an island in the Venetian estuary around AD 552. The early Venetians are building their city while fighting for independence from the Byzantine Empire. They have recently revolted against their Tribune, Orso Faledro, who stands accused of extorting property from his fellow Venetians and secret dealings with the Greeks; Orso and four of his sons have been blinded. Marco Gràtico becomes the new Tribune, and his brother Sergio is appointed bishop. Basiliola, the beautiful, demonic daughter of Orso Faledro, takes revenge on the Gràtici by seducing both brothers before provoking them into a duel in which Marco kills Sergio. Marco then explains to the people that he will expiate the sin of fratricide by banishing himself on the great ship of the play's title, setting out on a voyage of discovery and conquest. He orders that Basiliola be fixed to the ship's prow as a figurehead, but she determines her own fate, throwing herself into an altar fire in an act of self-immolation. Subsequent to his interview with Montemezzi on the subject, Bucci described the play as portraying "the battle of the hero against the obscure forces that attempt to thwart the heroic life," and this is the best way to make sense of it.[18] Feminine beauty, rather than being an inspiration, as in *La princesse lointaine*, is here a dangerous distraction. Yet *La nave* is by no means straightforward, for Basiliola distills the complex of love-hatred feelings that D'Annunzio felt toward women, and the play seems to admire as much it condemns her.

The immediate problem facing an operatic adaptation was the sheer length of the tragedy; Tito Ricordi needed to cut more than half the lines, though he was able to maintain the overall proportions. His general desire to push the play toward a more conventional melodrama is revealed in some major changes to the text, carrying significant dramatic and musical implications. First, he made it less consciously intellectual by greatly reducing D'Annunzio's

---

[17] Bucci, "'La Nave,'" p. 178.
[18] Bucci, "'La Nave,'" p. 176.

188 SUCCEEDING PUCCINI

many historical and geographical references. The playwright's antiquarian enthusiasms are still evident in the libretto, but considerably reduced in importance. Second, Tito removed much of the choral material originally set by Pizzetti. D'Annunzio had created a system of contrasting choruses, symbolic of the clash between Christianity and paganism, but so much of this is cut that the theme largely, though not wholly, disappears. Third, he cut Marco's proclamation of Venetian freedom from the end of the Prologue, notably dampening the patriotic potential of the opera, presumably to make it more suitable for the international market. Fourth, Tito deleted Ema, the mother of the Gràtici, completely, leaving Basiliola as the only significant female character and depriving her of a contrast with a thoroughly antithetical antagonist. The main effect of these changes was to reduce the epic aspect of the play, the story of a people, so as to foreground Basiliola and Marco (soprano and tenor) as the only protagonists, with a dramatic and vocal weight much superior to the other roles—even Sergio is a rather undeveloped character in the libretto. On top of all this, Tito's cuts also changed the character of Basiliola. The references to her madness and demonic qualities are largely excised, as are the more daring cues and stage directions highlighting her dangerous sexuality. By the time Tito had finished, Basiliola was much closer to the stereotypical perverse seducer, known to Italian drama since the late nineteenth century. The final significant change comes at the very end: instead of immolating herself, Basiliola is, following Marco's order, crucified on the ship's prow.[19]

Even with all these changes, the abridged play was far from a conventional operatic libretto, both structurally and thematically. Indeed, *La nave* is much the least coherent of the librettos Montemezzi set, and the American critic William L. Hubbard succinctly captured the basic problem: "'The Ship' in libretto form is ambiguous and confusing. There are big holes in the drama which may have been well filled for the minds of Mr. Ricordi and Mr. Montemezzi, but which the person unfamiliar with the original drama of D'Annunzio has no way of leveling up."[20] The best answer to this is to imagine the work, as Adriano Lualdi later suggested, as "akin to a series of large

[19] For a much fuller account of the process of adaptation, see Raffaele Mellace, "Prolegomeni a una lettura della 'Nave': Una collaborazione tra d'Annunzio, Montemezzi e Tito Ricordi," *Chigiana* 47 (2008): pp. 417–53.
[20] William L. Hubbard, "Music and the Musicians," *Chicago Sunday Tribune*, November 23, 1919, Section 8, p. 1.

LA NAVE AND D'ANNUNZIO, 1914–1919   189

frescoes":[21] that is to say, a series of interconnected, detailed "pictures," with the spectator required to make imaginative leaps between them.

Montemezzi's desire not just to tell the story, but to make the opera a "work of propaganda"—propaganda usually relying on clear messaging—compounded the challenges he now faced. In one respect, though, he was arguably fortunate, for the mere fact that D'Annunzio was his librettist gave the opera a propagandistic gravitas that no other Italian writer could have supplied. When Montemezzi first contemplated setting *La nave* in 1914, D'Annunzio was well established as Italy's most famous living man of letters, thanks as much to his womanizing exploits and the extravagance of his private life as his writing.[22] But in the early days of Montemezzi's work on *La nave*, the power of D'Annunzio's name increased exponentially, probably reinforcing the excited composer's feelings that he was engaged on a work of destiny. In the spring of 1915, D'Annunzio returned from self-imposed exile in France (where he had sought to escape his creditors) and immediately became a vocal leader of the pro-war movement, making a series of rabble-rousing, anti-government speeches. When parliament finally passed a vote for war against Austria-Hungary on May 20, many Italians were left, mistakenly, with the impression that it was D'Annunzio, more than anyone else, who had forced the government's hand.[23] Italian democracy had been dealt a crippling blow: this was the month the Fascists would later mythologize when they used "the glorious days of May" as a rallying cry. In this heated, patriotic atmosphere, the operatic *Nave* began to take shape, and while Montemezzi composed, D'Annunzio fought. The poet immediately volunteered for combat duties, served in both the army and air force, and made "deliberate efforts to participate in the most daring and dangerous military actions,"[24] quickly becoming a bona fide war hero. This would have a considerable impact on Montemezzi's own experience of the war years.

---

[21] Adriano Lualdi, " 'La Nave' di d'Annunzio e Montemezzi al Reale," *Il Giornale d'Italia*, December 16, 1938, p. 5.

[22] For a succinct summary of D'Annunzio's reputation and widespread popularity in the years before World War I, see John Robert Woodhouse, *Gabriele D'Annunzio: Defiant Archangel* (Oxford: Clarendon Press, 1998), p. 240. Woodhouse notes: "For almost thirty years not a week had passed without D'Annunzio's name appearing in the newspapers."

[23] In fact, on April 26, 1915, the day after Montemezzi commenced work on *La nave*, Antonio Salandra's government had secretly signed the Treaty of London guaranteeing Italian support for the "Triple Entente" of Britain, France, and Russia.

[24] Alfredo Bonadeo, *D'Annunzio and the Great War* (Madison, NJ: Fairleigh Dickinson University Press, 1995), p. 14.

190   SUCCEEDING PUCCINI

Unlike D'Annunzio, unlike Benelli, and unlike many young Italian artists, Montemezzi had no wish to participate in the war personally. It was probably easy enough to make the argument to himself: How could he, a composer on the verge of forty, with no military training, materially assist Italy at the front? Moreover, *La nave* was to be his war work, a musician's contribution to the national struggle now commencing. The first part of the war seems to have been uneventful for Montemezzi personally as he settled back into the familiar Vigasio routine and set about composing a work of national significance. No doubt he was eagerly reading the newspapers, but the message these conveyed was increasingly discomforting: despite the heroics and idealism of D'Annunzio, Benelli, and thousands of their compatriots, and despite widespread, naïve hopes that the war would be short and triumphant, things were not going Italy's way, the soldiers were disgruntled, and antiwar feeling was spreading. As he worked on his great "work of propaganda," Montemezzi would have been constantly reading and hearing about Italian losses and reversals, something that may explain, in part, why *La nave* does not strike a particularly triumphal note.

Montemezzi had about seventeen months of peace to work on his new opera before, in the autumn of 1916, Italy began conscripting men born in 1874 and 1875. "I'm a soldier" (*sono soldato*) he wrote abruptly to D'Annunzio, with obvious dismay, on October 6.[25] Montemezzi was assigned to the noncombatant army and given duties at the large military hospital in Verona, constructed by the Austrians in the 1850s. It seems likely that around this juncture he rented a riverside apartment on Lungadige Rubele, Verona, a short distance from the hospital. This served as a second home over the next few years, and Montemezzi installed a piano there, clearly expecting to be able to continue work on *La nave*.[26] The poet Lionello Fiumi's memory of sometimes seeing the composer on the streets of Verona, "always in a great hurry," seemingly refers to this period.[27] But Montemezzi found it hard to compose while also working at the hospital, and in the spring of 1917 appealed to D'Annunzio to help him obtain an exemption from military duties. D'Annunzio produced a "precious and marvelous document"

---

[25] Adriano Bassi (ed.), *Caro maestro (D'Annunzio e i musicisti)* (Genoa: De Ferrari, 1997), p. 97. This is the earliest known letter between Montemezzi and D'Annunzio, though it is clear there had been earlier contact.

[26] Lionello Fiumi vividly describes visiting Montemezzi at this apartment on a freezing day in January 1918. See "Montemezzi 'veronese,'" in *Omaggio a Italo Montemezzi*, edited by Piergiorgio Rossetti (Vigasio: Amministrazione Comunale di Vigasio, 2002), pp. 37–39.

[27] Fiumi, "Montemezzi 'veronese,'" p. 37.

LA NAVE AND D'ANNUNZIO, 1914–1919   191

securing Montemezzi a three-month convalescent leave; "I am finally free," the composer wrote gratefully on April 14.[28] Montemezzi now pushed on hard with the opera and completed the composition (but not the orchestration) in early July. He then traveled to Venice, hoping to report his progress directly to D'Annunzio, while also asking for help extending his period of leave; but the poet was not at home, and in the end Montemezzi had to explain these things in a letter of July 8.[29] It is not clear what happened next, but D'Annunzio appears to have obtained a temporary suspension of duties for Montemezzi, while also promising a more substantial intervention in the composer's reluctant military career. On August 13, Montemezzi was predicting that he would complete the opera by March 15, 1918, in time for an expected spring season at La Scala.[30]

In October, however, Montemezzi's creative routines were upset again, as he was conscripted into an office job in the Military Division of Verona, serving under General Giorgio Bompiani (1854–1934). Two desperate letters to D'Annunzio apparently went unanswered, so with "the courage of the madmen," Montemezzi went to the poet's house in Venice and made his case in person. He now got what he wanted:

> He [D'Annunzio] sent me two letters at the Hotel Danieli, one for my Chief of Staff in Verona and one for me. The letter for the Chief was simple and logical. It asked him to grant me reduced office hours ... because my duty could be dealt with by any other soldier and the instrumentation of *La Nave*, it said, could be done only by its composer.[31]

Bompiani was convinced—flattered, probably, to be getting a letter from D'Annunzio—and the composer was given an almost complete exemption from military duties. Assured now that he would not face further interruption, Montemezzi pressed on with the orchestration, which was provisionally complete when he wrote "The end of La Nave. Vigasio 13 June 1918" in his score.[32] However, there was then more work to do, correcting and revising, and finally on July 27, Montemezzi exultantly proclaimed "I've finished!" (*Ho finito!*).[33] His later claim that he worked on the orchestration

---

[28] Bassi, *Caro maestro*, p. 98.
[29] Bassi, *Caro maestro*, pp. 99–100.
[30] Bassi, *Caro maestro*, p. 102.
[31] Montemezzi, "Come scrissi," p. 218.
[32] "Fine della Nave. Vigasio 13 giugno 1918." Autograph score, p. 137. Archivio Storico Ricordi.
[33] Letter to Carlo Clausetti, Archivio Storico Ricordi.

192   SUCCEEDING PUCCINI

"nine hours a day for nine consecutive months" presumably refers to the period from the autumn of 1917 to the summer of 1918.[34] The suggestion of a regular, daily routine again says a good deal about Montemezzi's methodical approach to composition.

From a compositional point of view, a few fundamental choices guided Montemezzi. He relied even more strongly on the approach developed in *L'amore dei tre re*: the creation of an extraordinary variety and mobility of conflicting attitudes and situations, with a marked penchant for transition from one atmosphere to another diametrically opposed, thus holding the audience's attention through mechanisms based on contrast and surprise. To this end, Montemezzi juxtaposed sequences with heterogeneous dramatic hues, trusting this technique to maintain continuous tension in the score. A good place to commence an analysis is the important instrumental interlude which prepares, after an agonizing wait, for the first appearance of Basiliola. This moment is fundamental for the action and the character. As she becomes aware of the blinding of her brothers (Prologue, no. 29), Basiliola: "looks around, hesitating and anxious. She stops before the miserable pile. She drops her father's hand. The horror turns her pale. But her strength, after a dreadful pause, prevails over her trembling."[35] The orchestra subtly takes responsibility for the depiction of her contrasting feelings—emotion, fear, anger, pride—by attacking with a terrifying *fortissimo* played by the full orchestra, this soon leaving space for the more transparent voices of solo violas and basses (*fortepiano*), before being closely followed by a *crescendo* of the tympani leading to the exposition of a homophonic theme played by the upper strings and woodwinds over *fortissimo* brass chords.

In general, it is easy to recognize the prevalence of an attitude that is often grandiose: a musical translation of the magniloquence innate to D'Annunzio's tragedy, and that survived the interventions of Tito Ricordi. The Prologue includes one of the most remarkable examples. As Basiliola leaves the stage, leading her father into the church, a grand musico-dramatic conception, serving as the finale of the Prologue, begins to unfold (Prologue, nos. 42–76). The arrival of the Gràtico fleet with the bodies of the martyrs and the solemn procession to the church is staged as a magnificent, triumphal show, establishing the political and religious power of the Gràtico brothers. Their arrival, preceded by the symphonic depiction of the sea, is announced by

---

[34] Montemezzi, "Come scrissi," p. 218.
[35] Montemezzi, *La nave* (vocal score) (Milan: Ricordi, 1919), p. 57.

eight offstage *buccine* (modern imitations of the ancient brass instruments developed by the Roman army) and the increasingly excited voices of the sailors. This then leads to two brief, consecutive religious choruses, linked by a symphonic movement accompanying the procession with essential but effective orchestral gestures that provide the scene with a remarkable sense of unity. The entrance of Marco and Sergio Gràtico, their official investiture, and the subsequent conflict with Basiliola are thus enhanced by a grand choral frame, with the chorus repeatedly involved in a tight dialogue with Marco, until Basiliola breaks onto the stage. Symmetrically, at the other end of the opera, in the dialogue between Marco, some secondary characters, and the People, who are applauding the launch of the ship in the Third Episode, the *sostenuto* in *fortissimo* acquires more agitation while various characters volunteer to be part of the crew, arousing the enthusiastic reaction of the chorus. While preserving a *fortissimo* dynamic, the passage becomes increasingly animated, then acquires a more composed solemnity for the selection of the sailors under the auspices of the eternal name of Rome, culminating in the people's blessing when the six-part chorus enters loudly, declaiming "Gloria agli eletti!" (Glory to the chosen!), a textual insert added by Montemezzi to crown the episode.[36] The voices sing long notes, the full orchestra plays, the tympani roll, while on stage the eight *buccine* join in to double the vocal melody (Example 6.1).

However, the expression of a grandiose patriotism does not silence the other notable voice in the score, and perhaps that of greatest value: the impressionist evocation of twilit atmospheres. To this end, Montemezzi displays the talent of an expert orchestrator, capable of endless refinements, following an intelligently pursued strategy. Often the clangor of the late Romantic orchestra disappears in very transparent writing, as happens, programmatically, even before the curtain is raised. Indeed, the orchestral prelude to the Prologue proposes a wavy pattern with sextuplets in the first violins playing *piano*, and strings, winds, and harp in the background (Example 6.2). When the curtain is raised, the sextuplet figuration continues, with harp and celesta to add color, while the Voice of the Boatswain is sustained by a discreet little choir of woodwinds. The terrible tragedy of the Gràtici thus appears immersed in a glaucous, luminescent landscape, an evocation of the waves of the Adriatic from which the action emerges. It is remarkable that all this is completely independent of any scenic indication: D'Annunzio, by contrast,

[36] Montemezzi, *La nave*, p. 364.

194 SUCCEEDING PUCCINI

Music Example 6.1 *La nave*, Episode 3, no. 16, bars 6–16.

Music Example 6.1 Continued

had opened his drama by emphasizing the brisk industriousness of a shipyard in an urbanized landscape. Montemezzi obviously knew another opera opening with a similar movement of liquid sextuplets symbolizing the waters from which the story emerges, and the contiguity, whether intentional

Music Example 6.2 *La nave*, Prologue, bars 1–11.

or accidental, with the motif of the waves from the Prelude to *Das Rheingold* reveals his tendency to plan his opera in a way that is partly independent of D'Annunzio's text and allows for purely musical characterization. The color of the beginning is symmetrically proposed again at the opening of the Third Episode, as the substantially identical initial eight bars of the Prologue that suggested the Adriatic = Rhine equation are taken up, starting a delicate symphonic-choral scene with an auroral timbre, where the orchestra replies *alternatim* to the Catechumens' (novices') morning hymn sung by an *a cappella* four-voice choir: a masterful, perfectly achieved blending of contrasting orchestral and pictorial effects and vocal sound poetry, giving way (no. 9) to a dynamic symphonic movement prompted by Marco Gràtico's call on his men. In the first numbers of the Third Episode, the orchestral intervention at no. 2 is especially suggestive (strings, woodwinds, horns, harp, celesta, and a small bell offstage), and has as its phonic contrast the choral strophe "Ut pio Regis [*sic*] pariter canentes" with full orchestra (no. 3) that gives way to a trembling and gentle orchestration (no. 4). The stage direction "L'ammonimento si tace nel cielo che biancheggia" (The warning is lost in the whitening sky),[37] evocative of the lyrical atmosphere of D'Annunzio's *Alcyone* poems, finds a consistent *pendant* in Montemezzi's orchestration and is a perfect comment on the musical scene acting as a frame to the episode of the launch of the ship. Most of the critics subsequently detected Wagnerian features in the score.

It is in such shoals, of which there are many, where the martial uproar of the score is stilled, that the most authentic merits in Montemezzi's music should probably be identified, in line with that lyrical vocation powerfully expressed in *L'amore dei tre re*. Basiliola's scene of seduction in the Third Episode is in this respect exemplary. Coming immediately after the heroic tone prevailing in the passage where the crew is selected, the audience is suddenly exposed to an irruption from the Faledra, who is desperate, yet determined to claim her own dignity: "Gràtico, ricòrdati di me / e di quest'ara!" (Gràtico, remember me / Bound to this altar!).[38] Starting from "Pel tuo bacio / d'amore e d'odio" (By your kiss / of love and hatred) (no. 19), Montemezzi's orchestra begins a noticeable *rallentando molto* (slowing down), accompanying the long monologue of the protagonist always with a *dolce, espressiva, dolcissima* intention (Example 6.3).[39] This sort of subtlety, here and elsewhere, exalts the effective lyricism of the singing line. It is a quality which never fails Basiliola, who in this scene astutely takes advantage of Marco Gràtico's memory of a conflictual yet beguiling erotic relationship, as well as his greed for glory and power (Third Episode, nos. 20–26). Her alluring qualities are even more effective

---

[37] Montemezzi, *La nave*, p. 345.
[38] Montemezzi, *La nave*, p. 368.
[39] Montemezzi, *La nave*, p. 369. There is an intriguing error here. D'Annunzio had written "Pel mio bacio," and this appears in the printed libretto, but Montemezzi set it as "Pel tuo bacio" (autograph score, Third Episode, p. 70).

198 SUCCEEDING PUCCINI

Music Example 6.3 *La nave*, Episode 3, no. 19, bars 5–11.

when coupled with important scenic gestures, as in the acme of sensuality in the First Episode, when Basiliola drops her tunic and remains bare-breasted in an attitude of challenge to the monk Traba and of seduction to Marco. Introduced by the elated laughter of the "temptress," and characterized by a remarkable phonic violence, that gesture is followed by an episode with a very different tone: while Basiliola "takes off her refulgent belt; and starts to bend down . . ." (First Episode, no. 24),[40] the orchestra embroiders a very delicate page, entrusted to a *solo* violin, *dolce espressivo*, then to a viola, accompanied only by the strings.

The orchestration is certainly one of the strong points of the opera, and it was almost unanimously praised by the critics. Surprisingly, however, independent symphonic pages are rare, and largely restricted to the preludes to each episode, despite a number of claims along the lines of: "Montemezzi is scrupulously symphonic in his treatment of the score. To him the singers are only part of his orchestra."[41] Verdi would have appreciated this loyalty to the tradition of nineteenth-century Italian opera. Apart from the preludes, there are only concise symphonic interludes, like those accompanying the entries of Orso Faledro and Basiliola in the Prologue (nos. 19 and 29). The long instrumental page preceding the landing of the Gràtici is more noteworthy (Prologue, no. 41). Toward the end of this interlude, the eight *buccine* that later have a strong presence in the final episode resound from behind the scenes. The *buccine* are the most eccentric aspect of the orchestration, characterizing the magniloquent aspect of the score, just as the cello represents, especially in the First Episode, its lyrical soul, and is entrusted with the exposition of the themes of greater moment: for example in the symphonic prelude to the First Episode, where the cellos propose an *espressivo e forte* melody, the theme of seduction that will prove critical in the whole episode. A few pages later, the cello follows Basiliola's intervention like her shadow (no. 6); a cello solo accompanies the last prayer of the Survivor that the Faledra run him through (no. 17), and it is heard again when Basiliola has fulfilled the dying man's wish (no. 19); and it figures importantly, with the seduction theme, in the very long duet between Marco Gràtico and Basiliola at no. 36 (Example 6.4). A further example of Montemezzi's sophisticated, chamber-like orchestration is heard as Basiliola approaches Marco and invites him to drink from a cup during the banquet, escorted by a solo violin

---

[40] Montemezzi, *La nave*, p. 191.
[41] "Chicago Hears American Premiere of 'La Nave,'" *Musical Courier*, November 20, 1919, p. 6.

set against the insinuating line of muted first violins, then muted horns, before Marco answers to a background of oboes, clarinet, and the strings' *pianissimo tremolo* (Second Episode, no. 23).

Montemezzi makes some use of thematic planning, even if this aspect of the score remains relatively undeveloped. The "seduction" motif expounded by the cellos is the key thematic signature tune of the opera, a musical symbol of Basiliola. First stated by her father, Orso Faledro, in the Prologue, it consists of: (1) two starting notes; (2) a large leap onto a long sustained note; and (3) the descent to a lower grade (Example 6.5). Its pattern corresponds to the intonation of the name "Ba-si-liò-la." By conforming to the name of the seductress as a symbol of her identity, it synthetically records her unbounded ambition, irresistible charm, and uncontrolled, irrational tension, before finally coming to identify itself with the name Aquileia ("A-qui-lè-ia"), her fatal homeland. It is no accident that she will shout "Aquileia" in the last

Music Example 6.4 *La nave*, Episode 1, bars 1–7.

Music Example 6.5 *La nave*, Prologue, no. 24, bars 13–21.

bars of the Second Episode, over the notes of this unmistakable melodic gesture (Example 6.6). This finale of the Second Episode (nos. 48–50), in which Basiliola is captured and tied to the altar while Sergio Gràtico's corpse still lies covered on the ground, sets her cries against a background of an effective combination of choral writing (liturgical chant and offstage alarms) and sea-like orchestral accompaniment. On the lips of the Faledra, as well as on those of the other characters, stated in several versions, the seduction motif returns at every dramatic junction of capital importance: played by the cellos at the opening of the First Episode, as noted above; thrown down with scorn, like a gauntlet, by Basiliola to the monk Traba, "Accòstati, se osi, uomo di Dio" (Come over here, if you dare, man of God) (First Episode, no. 23);[42] and employed obsessively in the course of the dramatic duet between Basiliola and Marco Gràtico in the Third Episode, when it is used both by the Faledra to induce her lover to take her on the Ship, and by Marco himself, who is nearly overwhelmed by her charms (nos. 21–24) (Example 6.7). The passionate lyricism of this leading motif contrasts with the overall orientation of the vocal

---

[42] Montemezzi, *La nave*, p. 189.

style of *La nave*, which has an undoubtedly opposite tendency. Indeed, a vocal style of veristic derivation dominates the score, sometimes tending in the direction of an omnipresent *declamato*, sometimes flaring up in lyrical fervor, sometimes subdued in modest tones. A remarkable example of effective text setting is Basiliola's introduction to, and commentary on, the crucial

Music Example 6.6 *La nave*, Episode 2, no. 49, bars 9–14.

duel between the two brothers (Second Episode, nos. 39–42): we see the bloody fight through her eyes, similar in a way to how we see Cavaradossi's execution through Tosca's. Her brief, excited comments punctuate the action on a continuously changing, essential orchestral support, based on a memorable, haunting motif in the basses.

Music Example 6.7 *La nave*, Episode 3, no. 21, bar 1–no. 24, bar 9.

204 SUCCEEDING PUCCINI

Music Example 6.7 Continued

Music Example 6.7 Continued

Music Example 6.7 Continued

(Duri sono i nodi, con isforzo l'uomo li scioglie e s'indugia, mentre la tentatrice ancora una volta ricerca il sogno celato nel cuore avventuroso del navigatore adriatico e lo volge verso l'Oriente)

Music Example 6.7 Continued

Music Example 6.7 Continued

On the whole, *La nave* represents a significant departure from *L'amore dei tre re*. The two operas obviously share a number of features, most notably the striving toward psychological characterization and the dominating *declamato* writing for the voice. However, *La nave* has a much broader scope, presenting individual destinies against the background of historical turmoil, thus creating a genuinely epic feeling which unites individuals and crowds, comparable to that of Mussorgsky's *Boris Godunov* or *Khovanshchina*. Solemn public gestures contribute to the building of an effective formal frame, with the impressive and dramatic use of the chorus now integral to the opera. Moreover, the refined orchestration of *La nave* represents a further step in Montemezzi's campaign to give Italian opera a truly symphonic nature, a campaign in which few of his contemporaries were invested, though there is a remarkable parallel in this respect with Alfano's most ambitious opera, *La leggenda di Sakùntala*, commenced in 1914 and finally premiered in 1921. The stress on the chorus and orchestra, albeit not overruling individual singing and characterization, makes *La nave* a distinctively new and different project.

After the orchestration was complete, there was a crucial rite of passage to be negotiated: the score had to be introduced to D'Annunzio. The poet-warrior suggested that this should take place at the home of Ugo Levi (1878–1971) in Venice: the fact that he was having an affair with Levi's wife, Olga, presumably factored into this decision, and one wonders what suppressed passions were simmering in the room as the composer played through his long score. In Montemezzi's words:

> The audition took two nights, first because the poor composer, at the piano, didn't have lungs adequate, or rather fit, to support the strain; then because the Poet, interested in the musical development, in the adherence of the words to the music, in the treatment of the crowds, etcetera, lingered over details, commenting extensively, and with his marvelous speech that kept us spellbound![43]

It is noteworthy that neither here, nor in any other account we are aware of, does Montemezzi suggest that D'Annunzio praised the music. The obvious conclusion is that the writer offered, at best, cautious approval, for the composer's modesty did not prevent him, in general, from reporting positive acclaim. It is easy to imagine D'Annunzio's commentary mainly concerning his own contribution to the opera, and he probably knew that his favorite contemporary composer, Pizzetti, who produced the incidental music for the original spoken *Nave*, did not think much of the Montemezzian *Literaturoper*. On the other hand, D'Annunzio cannot have failed to grasp that the opera had a grand, monumental quality, that its propaganda aspect was timely, and that its performance would add something to his own glory. Perhaps thinking most of all of the last aspect, he made Montemezzi a pledge without precedent in operatic history: that on the night of the opera's premiere he would bomb Pula (known in Italian as Pola) in Croatia, a port used as a base by the Austrian navy.

There was never any question that *La nave*, like *L'amore dei tre re*, would receive its premiere at La Scala. Yet the theatre had endured a difficult time

---

[43] Montemezzi, "Come scrissi," p. 218.

210   SUCCEEDING PUCCINI

during the war. After the 1916–1917 season, Uberto Visconti, who had been managing it, terminated his contract, informing the Milanese authorities that it was impossible to stage good productions in wartime conditions.[44] In September 1917 the Artisti Lirici Associati presented a plan to run La Scala if they could get financial support from the city. The disastrous reversals Italy suffered that autumn meant that further discussion was put off until the following year; nevertheless, the Associati made provisional plans for a spring season that would include *La nave* in April or May. Serafin was chosen to conduct, and casting decisions were made.[45] However, when talks between the Associati and the Milanese authorities commenced in April 1918, it was proposed that the planned spring season should be presented in the autumn. It now looked as though the war was finally heading toward an allied victory, and on April 19, Montemezzi wrote to Tito Ricordi: "We shall transform our opera of propaganda into a ritual celebration for our victorious Homeland."[46] La Scala opened again in September, with the organization running it now called the Società Italiana fra Artisti Lirici, or SIFAL. *La nave* was scheduled for November, presumably in recognition of the fact that it would take considerable time to prepare. This delay meant that the premiere on November 3 coincided exactly with the end of the war: it was, remarkably, the very day that Italy signed an armistice with Austria and Italian troops entered Trento and Trieste. D'Annunzio thus lost his excuse to reinforce the opera's message with a bombing raid.

G. B. Nappi, the influential critic of *La Perseveranza*, detailed how Montemezzi appeared in the run-up to the premiere:

> Those who, in the last few days, saw and approached the composer of *La Nave*, must have been impressed by his calmness, his serenity. He was convinced he had given the best of himself to his work, and that he had not taken upon himself a task superior to his powers. He felt that his opera—though discussed as well—would be appreciated.[47]

---

[44] For this and other information in this paragraph, see Carlo Gatti, *Il Teatro alla Scala nella storia e nell'arte (1778–1963)*, 2 vols. (Milan: Ricordi, 1964), vol. 1, pp. 64–66.

[45] Ruby Mercer, *The Tenor of His Time: Edward Johnson of the Met* (Toronto: Clarke, Irwin and Company, 1976), p. 81.

[46] "Noi trasformeremo la nostra opera di propaganda in una celebrazione rituale per la Patria vittoriosa." Archivio Storico Ricordi.

[47] G. B. Nappi, "A proposito di 'La Nave' del maestro Italo Montemezzi," *La Perseveranza*, November 5, 1918, p. 2.

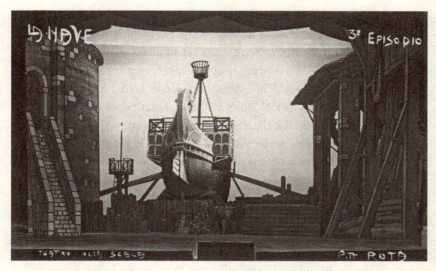

Figure 6.1 Set design for *La nave*, Third Episode, 1918. *Museo Teatrale alla Scala*.

Yet on the night of the premiere, Montemezzi was absent because of illness; "confined to bed," according to one report.[48] It must have been a serious illness for him to miss this long-anticipated occasion (the only premiere of any of his operas he was unable to attend), and there must be some suspicion that stress was involved. Fortunately, he recovered sufficiently to be able to attend the second and most subsequent performances.

Elena Rakowska (1882–1964), Serafin's wife, was cast as Basiliola, Edward Johnson ("Edoardo di Giovanni," 1878–1959) as Marco Gràtico, and Francesco Cigada (1878–1966) as Sergio. The sets and costumes, designed by the notable painter Guido Marussig (1885–1972), were based on a good deal of historical research (Figure 6.1). The premiere took place in an extraordinarily emotional and patriotic atmosphere. The start of the performance was delayed for some forty-five minutes by the full audience insisting on cheering and singing the national anthems of Italy and its allies to express their feelings on the events of the day. Serafin, who was conducting, was very willing to indulge them, and his account of the evening, written long afterward, is worth quoting:

---

[48] Ugo Navarra, *Noterelle critiche sulla tragedia lirica di Gabriele D'Annunzio* La Nave *ridotta da Tito Ricordi per la Musica di Italo Montemezzi* (Milan, 1918), p. 13.

212 SUCCEEDING PUCCINI

One always calls them "historical nights," but that one was "historical" indeed. The house was chock-full. After Act 1 [sic], which received a lot of applause, I had gone down into the orchestra pit to start the second, in fact I was already on the rostrum, when the lights came on again, the curtain opened slightly, and Tito Ricordi appeared, saying loudly: "Italian troops have entered Trento!" Don't ask me to describe what happened in the house. I struck up the Marcia Reale [i.e., the National Anthem], but who heard it, amid that loud noise of clapping, amid those shouts of joy? I managed to perform Act 2 and when, after the interval, I went back on the rostrum, the same scene was repeated. Again the lights, again the curtain slightly opened, and again Tito Ricordi came forward to say: "The Italians have landed at Trieste!" It was a fantastic frenzy, with people hugging each other, waving handkerchiefs, laughing, and crying.

Today, at the distance of such a long time, I think that the history of nations should be judged in centuries, not in years. Yet I can't forget that night of tremendous joy, when a period of anxieties and mourning came to an end for Italy; it was a tragic period, but also a glorious one. And I am moved, picturing myself there on the rostrum again, overwhelmed by that storm of exultancy.[49]

Perhaps the most objective report on the first night is Johnson's. He had little interest in the politics of the occasion, but after rehearsing the role of the hero for months he was eager for a good artistic outcome and felt this had been achieved. He wrote to his daughter after the performance: "*La Nave* was a great success for Babbino [Johnson] and for Signora Rakowska. It was a memorable evening, and there was not a vacant seat in all of La Scala! Your poor Babbino had a cold, but he sang as though there was nothing wrong." Johnson's biographer judges it "one of his most outstanding successes and personal triumphs."[50]

It was difficult, though, to disentangle the success (or not) of the opera from the larger sense of a historical "moment" with which it was, partly by design, partly by accident, bound up. The critics believed that the audience's response to the opera itself had not been wholly positive. The reviewer for the *Corriere della Sera*, probably Renato Simoni, reported that the new work's reception, "though it had all the warmth and grandeur of a sincere

---

[49] Quoted in Teodoro Celli and Giuseppe Pugliese, *Tullio Serafin: Il patriarca del melodramma* (Venice: Corbo e Fiore, 1985), pp. 96–97.
[50] Mercer, *The Tenor of His Time*, p. 83.

success, was only occasionally truly enthusiastic."[51] He and others counted twelve curtain calls, of which four were after the Prologue, three after the First Episode, three after the Second Episode, and two at the final curtain. This suggests that *La nave* was not able to hold the audience's interest to the end; tiredness may well have been a factor, for it was a very long night for all concerned. But Simoni, if he was the *Corriere* reviewer, felt that the "difficult" nature of the music, with no big, regularly shaped melodies for the audience to relax into, had limited the expression of enthusiasm. The ending may also have felt a little anti-climactic, La Scala's engineers having apparently ducked the challenge of having the ship actually move, as the action seems to demand. None of the reviews mentions any movement, and Norman Bel Geddes, who designed the opera for Chicago the following year, was sure that at La Scala "the curtain came down as the ship was about to slide down the ways."[52]

The critics were in no doubt that *La nave* was a major work, and they discussed it at length. Ugo Navarra, indeed, wrote such a long, two-part review for the *Corriere di Milano* that he decided to republish it separately as a fourteen-page pamphlet—the fullest discussion of Montemezzi and his music to this date.[53] None of the critics, however, was prepared to give *La nave* unconditional approval. Though there were, inevitably, a good many differences between their judgments, there was also a striking consensus concerning what was good and what was problematic about the new opera. On the positive side, Montemezzi's treatment of the orchestra and chorus won high praise. On the negative side, D'Annunzio's play was judged unsuitable for operatic setting, this leading to the related problem of long sections of declamatory singing with little lyricism; furthermore, Montemezzi's very obvious debt to German music in an overtly nationalistic Italian tragedy bothered many reviewers. Giannotto Bastianelli (1883–1927), writing in *La Nazione*, acknowledged Montemezzi as "a seeker of his own ways on the very worn-out floorboards of the Italian musical stage," but complained that the opera had not "offered me that new formula which for a long time we have been eagerly looking for from Italian composers. . . . It is always the

---

[51] Renato Simoni, "'La Nave' alla Scala," *Corriere della Sera*, November 4, 1918, p. 2. For the attribution of this review to Simoni, see David Chandler (ed.), *Essays on the Montemezzi-D'Annunzio 'Nave,'* 2nd ed. (Norwich: Durrant Publishing, 2014), pp. 58–59.

[52] Norman Bel Geddes, *Miracle in the Evening: An Autobiography* (New York: Doubleday, 1960), p. 212.

[53] Navarra, *Noterelle critiche sulla tragedia lirica.*

214 SUCCEEDING PUCCINI

now outdated attitude of Wagnerian-Romantic-Germanic derivation, even though, as in the case of Montemezzi, the attitude may have developed in a personal and independent fashion."[54] Bastianelli heard the influence of Richard Strauss, as did Simoni, if he was the reviewer for the *Corriere della Sera*, who judged that "some formulas . . . borrowed from the melodramatic music on the other side of the Alps appear too insistently: in Basiliola's wild passion, the echo of Salome's can be heard too often; in the structure of the ensemble pieces, in the development of the melody, in some details of the harmonization, the reflection of Wagner's art is too evident."[55] The most intriguing criticism along this line came from fellow opera composer Giacomo Orefice (1865–1922), who suggested that Wagnerian influence was appropriate in *L'amore dei tre re*, because of the "Teutonic" characters Archibaldo and Manfredo, but was unsuited to *La nave*, in which D'Annunzio had sought to reveal "the *Italian soul*."[56] Such criticisms were of course all sharpened by the recent experience of war.[57]

There were ten performances of *La nave* in all, and Montemezzi attended the majority of them. He would often claim, in the future, that the audiences had been uniformly enthusiastic, but he must have realized that it was not a straightforward enthusiasm for the opera, and in fact he gradually came around to arguing, albeit tendentiously, that the impact of *La nave* in 1918 had been "swept away, necessarily, by our [Italian] Victory."[58] For audiences, the music was part of a combustible mix that included Italy's victory in the war, D'Annunzio's celebrity as a war hero, and inescapable political considerations. Montemezzi witnessed an incident involving Toscanini at one of the performances:

> At a certain point of the performance, the members of the then Socialist municipality [who had been anti-war] entered, silently and shyly, their box. In the opposite box was Toscanini with his family. As soon as the illustrious artist saw those gentlemen appear, he stood up and swore at them. A moment later, maestro Serafin left his platform, climbed a chair and swore

---

[54] Review of December 23, 1918, in Giannotto Bastianelli, *Il nuovo dio della musica*, ed. Marcello De Angelis (Turin: Einaudi, 1978), pp. 211–12.

[55] Simoni(?), "'La Nave' alla Scala," p. 2.

[56] Giacomo Orefice, "Rassegna Musicale [*La Nave*]," *Rivista d'Italia*, November 30, 1918, p. 335.

[57] Seven of the original reviews, including Navarra's complete pamphlet, are included, in English translation, in Chandler (ed.), *Essays on the Montemezzi–D'Annunzio 'Nave.'*

[58] "travolta, necessariamente, dalla nostra Vittoria." Montemezzi to Angelo Scandiani, August 20, 1926. Chandler collection.

himself. Within a second, the entire imposing crowd joined the two maestros in their violent invective and the unfortunate men were forced to leave, amid derision and dins.[59]

Toscanini, no doubt particularly interested in the new opera after conducting *L'amore dei tre re* to such immense acclaim in the United States, asked to see the score, a moment Montemezzi vividly recalled a year later: "I can see him [Toscanini] even now as he read it for the first time, sweeping the pages of the orchestral score with his eyes—his near-sightedness made him fairly glue his face to the pages, which he brusquely raised and lowered, as if to embrace the full scope of the instrumentation at a glance—and emitting dark growls that, with him, indicate satisfaction."[60] Toscanini, however, would never conduct *La nave*.

There was now the piano-vocal score to prepare, and Montemezzi's particular views on this reveal much about his attitude toward the opera. He wrote to Casa Ricordi on January 29, 1919:

La Nave was composed in the atmosphere of war, with the vision of victory; and it was the enthusiasm for my Homeland which armed me with the courage necessary to be able to take upon myself such a big task. It is precisely to my Homeland that La Nave is dedicated. It [the dedication] should be placed on the first page beside the photograph. It should occupy the whole page. The type (in gold, if possible) should be large and bold and with ornaments. It must be an artistic thing. Like this:

TO

MY

HOMELAND

and nothing else. Then, in my opinion, on the page after the photograph I would deem it appropriate to put: *Performed for the first time at La Scala on the day November 3, 1918.* The date of the capture of Trieste and Trento deserves this.[61]

---

[59] Quoted in r.d.r., "Montemezzi parla delle sue opere," *Il Giornale d'Italia*, March 9, 1929, p. 3.

[60] Herbert F. Peyser, "'Let simplicity be the composer's constant objective,' Abjures Italo Montemezzi," *Musical America*, November 22, 1919, p. 3.

[61] Archivio Storico Ricordi. For the Italian version of this, see Mellace, "Prolegomeni a una lettura," p. 426.

216   SUCCEEDING PUCCINI

Three days earlier, on January 26, 1919, Tito Ricordi had unexpectedly, and somewhat acrimoniously, resigned from the company his great-grandfather had founded. This may well have influenced Casa Ricordi's decision to refuse Montemezzi's requests, thus closing the most politicized chapter of the composer's career. It is difficult to assess just how big an impact Tito's departure had on the future fate of *La nave* more generally, but it was surely a negative one: the new management team of Renzo Valcarenghi and Carlo Clausetti did not have the same strong interest in promoting the opera and may even have been disinclined to support a work which, if it became well known, would inevitably keep their predecessor's name in the public eye.

Montemezzi went into 1919 full of optimism that other Italian productions of *La nave* would soon materialize. He was particularly excited at the prospect of a "grande rappresentazione" of the opera in Venice.[62] Yet neither this nor any other Italian production actually took place, and the only consolation was Cleofonte Campanini stepping forward to claim the international premiere for his Chicago company. The Venice project seems to have been abandoned on economic grounds,[63] and the sheer cost was no doubt a deterrent elsewhere too, as Italy started to rebuild itself. Zandonai's much slighter *La via della finestra*, finally premiered at the Teatro Rossini, Pesaro, on July 27, 1919, though by no means a major success, was cheaper and easier to produce, and saw many more productions. Nevertheless, it is hard to avoid the conclusion that the larger movement of history did the most to ground *La nave*. In January 1919, President Woodrow Wilson and his wife made a triumphal five-day visit to Italy, greeted everywhere by enthusiastic crowds who probably realized that without American support Italy would have lost the war, succumbed to socialist revolution, or both. They arrived in Milan on January 5, where Wilson was inspired to say: "I have never known such a greeting as the people of Milan have given me on the streets. It has brought tears to my eyes, because I know that it comes from their hearts."[64] Montemezzi was on hand to witness a good deal of this, as he was involved with plans to entertain the Wilsons at La Scala in the evening.[65] He may well have shaken hands or exchanged words with the American president, and he almost certainly witnessed the speech Wilson made from the Scala

---

[62] Bassi, *Caro maestro*, p. 105.

[63] Montemezzi to Carlo Clausetti, February 22, 1919. Archivio Storico Ricordi.

[64] Woodrow Wilson, *America and the League of Nations: Addresses in Europe*, compiled by Lyman P. Powell and Fred B. Hodgins (Chicago and New York: Rand McNally, 1919), p. 115.

[65] Montemezzi, "Come scrissi," p. 218.

balcony. The Wilsons ate their dinner at the opera house, in the company of many dignitaries, and were then entertained with an extract from *Aida* conducted by Serafin: the celebration of the triumphant return of Radames with a concluding "picture" in which Amneris held aloft the stars and stripes and Aida (sung by Luisa Villani, the first Fiora) the Italian tricolor.[66]

Italian memories of Wilson soon began to turn bitter, however. The American president never intended to honor the terms of the April 1915 Treaty of London which secured Italy's entry into the war; indeed, he liked to pretend that he knew nothing about it.[67] When the Peace Conference opened in Paris on January 18, it soon became clear that the promises made to Italy were not considered binding, and that the Italians were being offered much less. Particularly galling was the realization that Wilson had reached significant compromises with Britain and France; it was only with Italy that he seemed determined to take a hard line. No one did more to fan the flames of discontent than D'Annunzio, who addressed angry crowds with the message that there should be no compromise on the Italian side. Whereas Wilson wanted Italy to have less than the Treaty of London promised, D'Annunzio wanted more, claiming nothing less than the entire Dalmatian coast for his country. His views on the matter were set out in a stridently nationalistic *Lettera ai Dalmati* (Letter to the Dalmatian People), published in various newspapers in January 1919 and also in the form of a pamphlet. When Montemezzi visited D'Annunzio in Venice, early in 1919, he was given a copy of the pamphlet, with the inscription: *"To Italo Montemezzi, who struck up the cry: 'Give the whole Adriatic to the Venetians!'"*[68] This was something the composer treasured, and there is no reason to suppose that he disagreed with the contents of the *Lettera*, an application of the imaginative idea of *La nave* to the actual political situation.

As 1919 moved on, it was increasingly obvious that there would be a violent collision between D'Annunzio and the ultra-nationalists and Italy's need to compromise, to some extent, with the new European order. This may well have made theatres shy of staging *La nave*; the less specifically nationalistic *L'amore dei tre re*, with its vision of Italy carved up by outsiders, was a safer bet,

---

[66] These details are taken from "Wilson Hailed as 'Liberty Apostle' as He Quits Italy," *New York Tribune*, January 7, 1919, p. 11; and E. Herbert-Cesari, "An English Girl Dances at the Scala," *Musical Times* 60 (1919): pp. 90–91. Many later references to the event inaccurately state that the whole of *Aida* was performed.

[67] Daniela Rossini, *Woodrow Wilson and the American Myth in Italy: Culture, Diplomacy, and War Propaganda*, trans. Antony Shugaar (Cambridge, MA: Harvard University Press, 2008), pp. 139–40.

[68] Montemezzi, "Come scrissi," p. 218.

218 SUCCEEDING PUCCINI

and in March it finally made its first appearance in Rome, with Montemezzi going there for the rehearsals and performances. But such diversions, though doubtless welcome, probably did little to dispel Montemezzi's growing anxiety over the political situation and the way it was likely to affect *La nave*. In the summer, matters came to a head over the issue of Fiume. Fiume, now Rijeka in Croatia, was a city that up to this time was "practically unknown to the average inhabitant, not merely of Great Britain and France, but, what is still more surprising, of even Italy itself."[69] It had not been mentioned in the Treaty of London. However, in 1918 the Italian population there, afraid of being permanently attached to the newly founded Yugoslavia, began to agitate for annexation to Italy. The following spring, when it became clear that Wilson was opposed to the terms of the Treaty of London, and even more to any further Italian claims, "all bonds of restraint were broken by the Annexationist party."[70] By now, Montemezzi would have been paying serious attention, for Sem Benelli, who had established impeccable nationalist credentials in the war, and symbolically made himself a citizen of Fiume, briefly became a key figure in the developing drama. In June, he developed a plan by which Fiume would have its own army, paid for by the issuance of treasury bonds. Benelli's leadership of the planned army was actually announced, but in the end he refused the job, perhaps, as Michael A. Leeden speculates, because he was aware that overtures had already been made to D'Annunzio to lead a coup.[71]

On September 12, 1919, D'Annunzio reached the zenith of his international celebrity when, to the astonishment of the world, he led an armed takeover of Fiume, quietly easing out the Allied soldiers who had been guarding the city while peace negotiations continued. By this juncture it must be imagined that Montemezzi was devouring the newspapers. Not only was the author of *La nave* in charge of Fiume, but the author of *L'amore dei tre re* was there too, as a leading supporter. Moreover, Montemezzi had a personal and family interest in the matter, for his young cousin Renato Donadelli (1898–1967), who had grown up in the adjoining house, had enlisted in D'Annunzio's ragtag army.[72] It is tempting to suppose that Montemezzi's existing connection with D'Annunzio may have had something to do, directly or indirectly,

---

[69] J. N. MacDonald, *A Political Escapade: The Story of Fiume and D'Annunzio* (London: John Murray, 1921), p. 12.

[70] MacDonald, *A Political Escapade*, p. 43.

[71] Michael A. Ledeen, *The First Duce: D'Annunzio at Fiume* (Baltimore, MD, and London: Johns Hopkins University Press, 1977), pp. 50–51.

[72] Pierpaolo Brugnoli and Bruno Chiappa (eds.), *Vigasio: Vicende di una comunità e di un territorio* (Vigasio: Comune di Vigasio, 2005), p. 305.

LA NAVE AND D'ANNUNZIO, 1914–1919   219

with Donadelli's appearance in Fiume. It is also tempting to suppose that Montemezzi would have traveled to Fiume in the autumn of 1919 to show his support for the coup, were it not for the fact that he was preparing to sail to America. As it was, it was not until November 1920, after many of the events narrated in the following chapter, that Montemezzi visited Fiume. He traveled in the company of Toscanini and the La Scala orchestra, which had been invited to perform there by D'Annunzio.[73] Also in the 1920 party was the younger composer Adriano Lualdi (1884–1969), destined to become a figure of enormous power in Italian musical life during the Fascist years, who would later write sympathetic, insightful criticism of Montemezzi's works, some of which is quoted in the present book. D'Annunzio laid on some military exercises to entertain the musicians, presented various medals, and made a flowery speech in praise of Toscanini.[74] But Montemezzi was witnessing the end of D'Annunzio's great adventure. On December 24, 1920, combined action by the Italian army and navy drove the poet and his followers out of Fiume. D'Annunzio returned to Italy, where he quickly faded into political irrelevance. He may have continued to be Montemezzi's hero, but after 1920 he did not offer a credible political alternative to the Fascism he had done much to inspire.

---

[73] Adriano Lualdi, "D'Annunzio e la Musica," *Piazza delle Belle Arti* 5 (1957–58): pp. 144–68.
[74] Harvey Sachs, *Toscanini* (London: Weidenfeld and Nicolson, 1978), pp. 143–44.

7

"Lost in looking for librettos"
America, Marriage, Inertia, 1919–1926

Montemezzi's 1919–1920 visit to the United States, undertaken in response to an invitation to conduct *La nave* in Chicago, represents the zenith of his career in terms of performances, acclaim, and personal celebrity. It was personally transformative, too: he met his future wife, a wealthy American heiress. There is a real sense that, as Montemezzi set sail from Genoa on October 17, 1919, on the *Duca degli Abruzzi* of the Italian Royal Mail line, he was commencing the second act of his life.

Montemezzi arrived in New York on November 2, and having been registered on Ellis Island, where he was recorded as 5 feet 7 inches in height, with brown eyes and a fair complexion,[1] he "was met by friends at the pier at the foot of West Fifty-fifth street" and taken to the spectacular Biltmore Hotel, opened in 1913, where he was to stay.[2] *L'amore dei tre re* was well known in New York, and in the next two days Montemezzi was treated as a celebrity. People were eager to meet him and show him what the city had to offer, and much interest was shown in him personally. Indeed, this brief visit inspired two of the fullest descriptions of the composer, worth quoting at length for the vivid impression they give of Montemezzi at this midpoint in his career. Charles Henry Meltzer and Herbert F. Peyser met Montemezzi in his tenth-floor room at the Biltmore, in a sort of press conference arranged for November 3. Physically speaking, Montemezzi struck Meltzer as:

> Introspective, dreamy, full of his own thoughts. . . . His tall, slight form, crowned by a poetic head, bespoke a man ill-fitted for real, modern life. His sensitive mouth, his aquiline nose, and delicate features, confirmed

---

[1] Ellis Island Records. This estimate of Montemezzi's height erred on the short side. When he entered the United States in 1923, his height was recorded as 5 feet 9 inches, and in 1925 it was recorded as 5 feet 8 inches. He was often described as tall: a perception shaped by his very slim build and upright posture.

[2] J. MacB, "Arrives From Italy," *Washington Times*, November 9, 1919, p. 11.

Succeeding Puccini. David Chandler and Raffaele Mellace, Oxford University Press. © Oxford University Press 2025.
DOI: 10.1093/9780197761373.003.0008

this view of him. The sweep of his already greying hair above his forehead completed the impression. By comparison Puccini, with his bluff *bonhomie*, the late Leoncavallo, with his paunch and his wee legs, Zandonai, who is hard and gaunt of face, and Mascagni, who is worn and wan with nervousness, might have seemed commonplace. I could not say that he suggested greatness. The adjective that perhaps describes him best is the Italian "simpatico."[3]

Peyser, on the other hand, described his subject thus:

His face calls to mind pictures of the early Berlioz. As much as the gauntness of feature and frame, the conand [*sic*] tranquil demeanor suggest [*sic*] an origin other than Latin. The seamed cheeks and brow, the angularity of high cheek bones, the long and sharp-pointed nose, the tight-drawn, thin lips and strong jaw no less than the impressive stature, spare figure and looseness of limb, cunningly counterfeit the New England farmer. A wavy shock of hair, streaked with spreading grayness, terminates the broad forehead. Under shaggy eyebrows burn eyes penetrating without sharpness, eyes that seem now to contemplate remote perspectives and, anon, are blithely alert to the matter of the moment. He is thirty-nine, they say [*sic*; actually forty-four]. He looks more. His life has been, in the superficial sense, uneventful. Yet, his countenance, like one of Gilbert's idealistic personages, "wears sorrow's interesting trace."[4]

Meltzer did not attempt a separate appraisal of Montemezzi's character, but Peyser did, and he was tremendously impressed. While he had found Puccini, in 1910 (in New York for the premiere of *La fanciulla del West*), insufferably pretentious and self-satisfied, he found Montemezzi the very opposite:

Montemezzi has the simplicity of greatness. . . . The man has an easy consciousness of the value of his handiwork and confident trust in his powers. He dominates his genius, he does not flaunt it. His reticence is that of mastery, joined to an acute sense of the fitness of things.

---

[3] Charles Henry Meltzer, "Montemezzi and His Music," *The Review* 1/27 (November 15, 1919): p. 588.

[4] Herbert Peyser, "'Let simplicity be the composer's constant objective,' Abjures Italo Montemezzi," *Musical America*, November 22, 1919, p. 3. The reference is to Gilbert and Sullivan's *Patience*.

222 SUCCEEDING PUCCINI

. . . Naive he decidedly is, almost childlike, or countrified. But by no means shrinking. He speaks with a quiet intensity of enthusiasm, all the more forceful because restrained, and is sparing of gesture or vivid play of features. But one feels in the man the aristocracy of soul, the patrician traits of the antique Roman.[5]

Montemezzi also dilated upon his artistic creed, in what is perhaps his fullest statement of it:

I do not compose for the public, I compose for myself. I do not defer to a collective opinion or strive to forestall a likely popular dissent. I do not admit the artist's pre-required obligation to content the public only in measure as the public wills to be pleased and comprehending. Let the artist lift up the public to the plane of his ideal, so far as he contrives to attain that level. . . . if the artist's ideal is valid and ennobling and his inspiration commensurate he must finally gain the acceptance he sought.

For reasons following upon such aims I have never incorporated in a score of mine passages or effects designed to placate the public for some other scene or effect. I could never construct a piece of symmetrical lyricism not the inescapable outgrowth of the dramatic situation and inevitably arrived at. Melody, of course, melody at all times! But melody only that logically adapts itself to the drama's insistences. For opera, only the poetic subject, be it historic, allegorical or otherwise—so long as it be remote, and hence musically suggestive.

Above all else simplicity! Let simplicity be the composer's never forgotten objective—simplicity not necessarily in execution, but in appearance and in effect. The supreme creations of our art are simple. They contain, to be sure, intricacies of organization almost past belief. But their complexities are chiefly apparent to the specialists. . . . I have striven in my own work for this end. The scores of 'L'Amore' and of 'La Nave' are massed with intricacy of detail. The complete and unified effect conveys the illusion of simplicity. And simplicity is attainable only to those who strive never to lose in their music purity and integrity of the formal line and definable contour.[6]

---

[5] 'Peyser, "'Let simplicity . . ," p. 3.
[6] Quoted in Peyser, "'Let simplicity . . ," p. 4.

AMERICA, MARRIAGE, INERTIA, 1919–1926   223

Asked about his influences, Montemezzi was reluctant to acknowledge specific debts. However, he spoke highly of "the modern Russians," offered qualified praise of Debussy, and owned to a special love of Catalani—apparently giving the impression that Catalani was his favorite Italian composer.[7]

On November 4, Montemezzi traveled to Chicago with George Maxwell, the head of Casa Ricordi's New York office. The lead-up to the international premiere of *La nave* is well documented thanks to Norman Bel Geddes, the set designer, and the Chicago press, which judged the premiere a great honor to the city. *La nave* was to be the most expensive production the Chicago Opera (founded 1910) had ever mounted, and Bel Geddes had spent months working on what he wanted to be an unprecedentedly spectacular experience. He planned a particularly striking ending, with the ship moving toward the audience: "When Rosa Raisa, the star of the performance, is crucified as the figurehead, she will actually be in the auditorium."[8] As Bel Geddes developed his plans, with increasing excitement, he paid scant regard to the photographs of the La Scala production he had been sent as a model. Maxwell was furious when he discovered this, claiming the sets should have been "a facsimile of the La Scala production," and arranging a press conference to denounce Geddes in no uncertain terms: "Think of great artists like D'Annunzio, the master of Fiume who wrote the play, and Montemezzi, master of modern Italian music, being made victims of the artistic creed of a young American, Norman Bel Geddes, who has done the stage pictures!"[9] This ensured an air of controversy around the production, increasing public interest; all the tickets had been sold well in advance, but nevertheless hundreds of people turned up hopefully on the day, and some tickets changed hands for a high premium. Raisa as Basiliola was singing alongside Alessandro Dolci as Marco Gràtico and Giacomo Rimini as Sergio.

The first performance, on November 18, opened the Chicago season. "It was just 8:15," Paul T. Gilbert reported, when "a bashful, delicately featured man with gray hair and slightly hollowed cheeks mounted the director's stand."[10] William L. Hubbard remembered a little differently: "At 8.12 a tall, slender, dark complexioned man appeared at the right of the orchestra pit,

---

[7] Meltzer, "Montemezzi," p. 588; Peyser, "'Let simplicity..'," p. 4.

[8] Norman Bel Geddes, *Miracle in the Evening: An Autobiography* (Garden City, NY: Doubleday, 1960), p. 212.

[9] Quoted in Bel Geddes, *Miracle in the Evening*, pp. 213, 214.

[10] Paul T. Gilbert, "'Wonderful!': That's What All Say of 'La Nave,'" *Chicago Evening Post*, November 19, 1919, p. 9.

224 SUCCEEDING PUCCINI

advanced quietly to the conductor's desk, and picked up the baton."[11] The critics agreed that it was hard to believe this was the first time Montemezzi had conducted an opera. The incisive authority with which he led the huge musical forces won high praise. "[H]e is one of the born conductors, with a well defined idea of what he wants in the performance of his music and a complete certainty of how to go to work to get it," judged Edward C. Moore, who saw in the composer "the manner of an earnest artist without mannerisms."[12] Montemezzi himself felt he had conducted "molto bene" (very well).[13] Altogether, the occasion was a triumph, and after the Prologue and each of the Episodes, Montemezzi and the principals appeared before the curtain to tumultuous applause. At the end, there was a standing ovation.

The Chicago critics found it difficult to separate the success of the opera itself from the great sense of occasion, and the sheer spectacle of it all. They had so much to say about Raisa's greatly admired portrayal of Basiliola, and Bel Geddes's challenge to La Scala, that they did not always leave much room for discussion of the opera itself. The most positive criticism, and that most in tune with Montemezzi's ambitions, came from Karleton Hackett:

> "La Nave" is a tremendous score, far too important a work to attempt to grasp at a first hearing, yet one which leaves an indelible impression of power and sincerity. It is a somber drama and somberly told thru [sic] the music. The music is a great symphonic poem conceived on broad lines and sustained with force to the magnificent climax of the final act.[14]

Hackett was particularly admiring of the "elemental power" of the chorus: "In no modern work for the operatic stage has the chorus played so important a part." Other critics, too, emphasized the symphonic nature of the score and the substantial choral element. Hubbard, perhaps the most respected Chicago critic, wrote:

> Montemezzi fashions melodies which are attractive and which have indi-viduality, but they are short melodies, and he uses them orchestrally and

---

[11] William L. Hubbard, "Composer of 'La Nave' a 'Hit' as Opera Opens," *Chicago Daily Tribune*, November 19, 1919, p. 3.

[12] Edward C. Moore, "Raisa Opens Opera Season," *Chicago Daily Journal*, November 19, 1919, p. 13.

[13] Letter to Casa Ricordi, December 7, 1919. Archivio Storico Ricordi.

[14] Karleton Hackett, "Sig. Montemezzi Scores Triumph in His New Opera," *Chicago Evening Post*, November 19, 1919, p. 9.

AMERICA, MARRIAGE, INERTIA, 1919–1926 **225**

vocally in symphonic manner, interweaving them as does the purely instrumental writer. The result is a constant shifting of shade and line, and the resultant music is less easy of grasp than is the more frankly tuneful. Yet such is the composer's skill in handling his material that he produces tonal waves and masses, the power, color, or sensuous quality of which is such that even the indifferent listener is impressed and moved.[15]

Despite such positive comments, the critics were not convinced by the plot. Like their Italian counterparts, they did not consider D'Annunzio's play a good basis for an opera, and they found, for the most part, the score too symphonic and unmelodic.[16] Perhaps most mortifying for Montemezzi was the fact that every critic who ventured on a comparison declared *L'amore dei tre re* the finer opera.

Astonishingly, after all the preparation, anxiety, and expense, *La nave* played for just two performances. No more were ever planned. This was not a comment on the merits of the work, but a production philosophy of bringing out as many operas as possible each season. But the greatest misfortune befalling *La nave* is that the Chicago Opera's plan to take it to New York, for their short season at the Lexington Theatre, was canceled. As early as February 1919, the *New York Times* was reporting that "Italy's latest operatic sensation" was to mark the opening night of the Chicago company's New York season.[17] The belief that *La nave* was coming to New York apparently prevented any of the city's major critics from making the trip to Chicago to see it there. The decision to cancel was probably above all an economic one: it is surely significant that even without transporting such a costly production, the Chicago company made a reported loss of some $200,000 in the course of their five weeks' tenure of the Lexington.[18] But there may have been lingering discords concerning Bel Geddes's designs, too, and another factor was almost certainly Mary Garden's readiness to sing Fiora, for this offered a Montemezzi "sensation" of something like equivalent value. There remains one of the great what-ifs of Montemezzi's career. How would his leading New York champions have evaluated *La nave*? Would their views, if positive, have encouraged other companies around the world to produce the work?

[15] William L. Hubbard, "Music and the Musicians," *Chicago Sunday Tribune*, November 23, 1919, Section 8, p. 1.
[16] Eight reviews are collected in David Chandler (ed.), *Essays on the Montemezzi-D'Annunzio 'Nave,'* 2nd edition (Norwich: Durrant Publishing, 2014).
[17] "Lexington Opera," *New York Times*, February 16, 1919, p. 6.
[18] "Chicago Opera Company's Losses Here Total $200,000," *New York Clipper*, March 3, 1920, p. 6.

226 SUCCEEDING PUCCINI

After conducting the postponed second performance of *La nave* on December 3, Montemezzi stayed in Chicago for the rest of the year, developing an important friendship with Garden (1874–1967), perhaps the most famous active female opera singer in America. Known for her scandalous private life, indomitable personality, and bluntly opinionated, feisty manner, she was not an easy person to get on with, at least for any length of time, yet Montemezzi retained a close friendship with her for the rest of his life. As with most of his relationships, frustratingly little is known about it, but by 1926 Garden was sufficiently close to the Montemezzis to become godmother to their son. We speculate that she took an adoptive attitude to Montemezzi in the course of his visit to Chicago, speaking to him in French, and freely handing out advice, opinions, and introductions. In a world that must, in many ways, have been alien, he was probably pleased and flattered to have such a powerful ally. But he influenced her, too, and the most important consequence of his visit to Chicago was Garden's being persuaded to undertake the role of Fiora in Italian, a language she had never sung in before. *L'amore dei tre re* was only added to the 1919–1920 Chicago season after Montemezzi's arrival there.

The reports of how Garden (and later Grace Moore) performed Fiora offer valuable insights into how Montemezzi understood his opera and its correct interpretation. He must have been aware, at least in general terms, of how Bori had interpreted Fiora in New York—"the helpless, tragic girl, fighting her love, and dying for it" in Deems Taylor's summary[19]—and how that had significantly influenced American understanding of the opera. This was not the way Benelli and Montemezzi understood the role, however, and working with Garden in the winter of 1919–1920 was a chance to set things right. Bori and Garden agreed that Fiora was a complicated character, but they differed greatly on the nature of the complication. Bori considered that: "Fiora is a complex woman, and she does try, like Isolde, to resist the temptation that Avito represents."[20] In other words, Fiora is naturally pure but is led into "temptation" by sexual passion, just as the New York critics liked to understand the story. By contrast, Garden judged, according to Moore, that "Fiora [was] a magnificent liar and the most complicated woman in the operatic repertoire. 'Neither Fiora nor Mélisande ever tells the truth,' explained Mary to me. 'That is part of their magic, and this weakness is the touchstone in the

[19] Deems Taylor, "At the Metropolitan," *World*, November 17, 1922, p. 11.
[20] Lanfranco Rasponi, *The Last Prima Donnas* (New York: Knopf, 1982), p. 439.

creation of either role.' "[21] There was very little of the "helpless ... girl" about Garden's disingenuous Fiora, long inured to deceit as a defense against the tragedies of her fate. Garden judged *L'amore dei tre re* the greatest opera since *Pelléas et Mélisande* and passionately identified with the heroine: "I didn't *study* Fiora; I *was* Fiora." She felt that the "special quality" of Fiora "was passion and terror, and I put these things in my voice."[22] Her performances were marked by a combination of high theatricality and verisimilitude that astounded many viewers. In the United States, Garden would go on to dominate the role for a decade, generally singing opposite Virgilio Lazzari's commanding Archibaldo—in Chicago, Montemezzi trained Lazzari "to be such an Archibaldo as to conquer the doubts of Mary Garden" (Figure 7.1).[23]

The first of two Chicago performances of *L'amore dei tre re*, on January 9, 1920, proved a dazzling triumph for both Montemezzi and Garden. At the end of Act 2, "there was one of the most enthusiastic demonstrations which this theater has ever witnessed."[24] The reviews the following day enthused about not only how brilliantly Garden had sung in Italian but also the immense achievement of the opera itself. Hubbard stated categorically that it was "the most sincere, most powerful, and most beautiful opera any modern Italian has given the world."[25] Herman Devries went even further:

The great Montemezzi, who wrote it, is, as I said when I first heard the opera, a Shakespeare in music, and, like the great poet and playwright, is of classic outline.

In my opinion, it is one of the best operas ever written.[26]

Montemezzi can hardly have missed the lesson that *La nave* had a lot of catching up to do if it was to compete with its predecessor. The second performance of *L'amore dei tre re* on January 17 was followed, the next day, by a dinner in Montemezzi's honor arranged by the principal artists involved in the productions of his two operas. Afterward there were many speeches,

---

[21] Grace Moore, *You're Only Human Once* (London: Latimer House, 1947), p. 152.

[22] Mary Garden and Louis Biancolli, *Mary Garden's Story* (New York: Simon and Schuster, 1951), pp. 165, 166.

[23] Robert Lawrence, "Figures on the Battlements," *Opera News*, January 4, 1964, p. 6.

[24] Karleton Hackett, "Opera Audience Cheers Artists in 'Three Kings,'" *Chicago Evening Post*, January 10, 1920, p. 7.

[25] William L. Hubbard, "Mary Garden, in Italian Opera, Sings Brilliantly," *Chicago Daily Tribune*, January 10, 1920, p. 13.

[26] Herman Devries, "'L'Amore' One of Greatest Operas," *Chicago Evening American*, January 12, 1920. Cutting among the Donadelli family documents.

Figure 7.1 Mary Garden as Fiora, 1921. *Chandler collection.*

including a short one in Italian by Montemezzi.[27] This dinner appears to have represented his farewell to Chicago, and he left soon afterward for New York, traveling with members of the Chicago company.

The Chicago Opera opened their season at the Lexington Theatre on January 26, the promised "sensation" of *La nave* replaced by the sensation of Garden in *L'amore dei tre re*. To Montemezzi himself, she was now (if not earlier) overwhelming in the role: after one of the New York performances, he felt so "overcome" at the end of Act 2 that he had to be "led to the foyer by kindly friends, trembling with the thrill of fired emotions."[28] The New York critics recognized the power and novelty of Garden's performance, and it won over some former doubters. Henry T. Finck, the only major critic unimpressed by the opera in 1914, was soon stating: "Few things so great have been seen on the operatic stage as her [Garden's] impersonation of Fiora.... Stage art can go no further."[29] But other critics, who had come to love the opera in Bori's interpretation, were less enthused. It all proved good publicity for the opera itself, and the value of giving the public and critics something to debate was further highlighted on February 28, when the Met staged its own production with Claudia Muzio as Fiora and Adamo Didur as Archibaldo. Montemezzi attended the first Met performance and was "called before the curtain and roundly applauded even by the orchestra, which is assumed to be neutral or dormant in its musical leanings."[30]

These were great days for Montemezzi, who at just this juncture met his future wife. This occurred through the agency of D'Annunzio's third son, Ugo Veniero D'Annunzio (1887–1945), the Italian government representative of the Caproni airplane manufacturer in the United States. He traveled to Chicago for the performances of *La nave* and became acquainted with Montemezzi. In New York, subsequently, the two men saw each other a good deal. Ugo was already a "good friend" of a wealthy, unmarried New York woman, Katherine Leith, and decided to introduce her to the composer. The story the Montemezzis later reported to Verna Arvey was that:

> [Ugo] said one day [to Katherine], "You speak four words of Italian; Maestro [Montemezzi] doesn't speak any English." It seemed to him to be as good a

---

[27] "Mary a Kisser, Not a Talker, at Opera Banquet," *Chicago Daily Tribune*, January 19, 1920, p. 1.

[28] Felix Deyo, "Montemezzi's 'L'Amore dei Tre Re' Opens Metropolitan Opera Season," *Standard Union* (Brooklyn), October 30, 1928, p. 19.

[29] Henry T. Finck, "Mary Garden's Fiora," *New York Evening Post*, February 11, 1921, p. 6.

[30] James Gibbons Huneker, "'The Love of Three Kings' Sung," *World*, February 29, 1920, p. 16.

230 SUCCEEDING PUCCINI

reason as any for the foundation of a friendship, so he introduced the composer to the vivacious American girl. They had a good time together, and were staunch friends by the time Mr. Montemezzi left for Europe.[31]

The crucial omitted information is that they could both speak French.

Katherine was not conventionally beautiful—"I would like to be a little beautiful but it is not possible," she wrote plaintively to Montemezzi the following year[32]—but she was cultured, friendly, very sociable, and very wealthy, with a $200,000 trust fund in her name generating an annuity of $10,000 a year, equivalent to approximately 200,000 lire (Figure 7.2).[33] She was born Kate Levy to Jewish parents on May 17, 1885, in Hartford, Connecticut.[34] When still a girl she became known as Katherine rather than Kate,[35] and when World War I broke out, her father, William Levy (1856–1919), changed the family name to Leith. As an adult, she was apparently keen to avoid being identified as Jewish, and her Italian family was not told of her ethnic background, though they suspected it.[36] William Levy had run the Sunny Brook Distillery Company's New York operation. The company was immensely successful, and by the end of 1916 was claiming to have sold approximately 53 million bottles of whiskey, at that time a record for an American distilling company.[37] The family lived in New York much of the year, latterly in an apartment in the Hotel Chatham, Vanderbilt Avenue, but they also had a summer home on Jerome Avenue, in Deal, New Jersey. Levy had business interests in California too and "always spent a part of each winter on the Pacific coast"[38]—hence the likelihood that Katherine knew something of the state where she and Montemezzi would eventually settle. Levy, a Republican, was appointed mayor of Deal in 1909, having previously served as president of the town council.[39] A prominent and much-respected

[31] Verna Arvey, "Visits to the Homes of Famous Composers No. XIV: Italo Montemezzi," *Opera and Concert*, November 1948, p. 14.
[32] "Vorrei essere un poco bella ma non è possibile." Katherine Leith to Montemezzi, April 4, 1921. Donadelli family documents.
[33] Katherine Leith to Montemezzi, letter postmarked December 27, 1920. Donadelli family documents.
[34] Birth certificate, City of Hartford.
[35] *Proceedings of the Sixty-Fifth Annual Meeting of the Hebrew Benevolent and Orphan Asylum Society of the City of New York* (New York, 1888), p. 25.
[36] Information from Renata Donadelli.
[37] "1,760,425 Cases of Sunny Brook Whiskey," *Wine and Spirit Bulletin*, December 1, 1916, p. 30.
[38] "Mayor Leith of Deal Is Dead of Heart Disease," *Asbury Park Evening Press*, May 16, 1919, p. 2.
[39] "Hogencamp Quits as Deal's Mayor," *Asbury Park Evening Press*, January 2, 1909, p. 1.

Figure 7.2 Katherine and Italo Montemezzi, January 1925. *Chandler collection.*

figure in local affairs, he died of heart disease on May 15, 1919, leaving his widow and three daughters immensely rich.

When Montemezzi met Katherine in early 1920, her two younger sisters were already married. Margaret, born 1889, had married Richard Genée Conried, son of Heinrich Conried, the former director of the Metropolitan Opera, as early as 1911, and had two children; Dorothy, nine years Katherine's junior, had married Stanley Allen Brown on April 2, 1919, and would give birth to her first child in 1920. Katherine appears to have worried that she had missed the chance to marry, and almost certainly deceived Montemezzi about her age. The temptation to reduce it had started early; in the 1910 United States census, taken in April 1910, she had given her age as 23, and consistent with that gave it as 33 for the 1920 census. Nevertheless, it is still startling to see her date of birth on her wedding certificate given as May 17, 1891.[40] This was her "official" date of birth from then on, but Katherine sometimes forgot this, and continued to give her age inconsistently.[41] However

---

[40] Donadelli family documents.
[41] For example, when the Montemezzis arrived in the United States together on December 6, 1923, Katherine recorded her age on their arrival documents as 33, when she was really 38, but according to the 1891 fiction, just 32. Ellis Island records.

untruthful about her age, there was no doubt that she was an enthusiastic opera lover. "I had my first Met season ticket when I was 13—I was crazy over opera even then" she told an interviewer years later, adding that *L'amore dei tre re* was her favorite opera even before she met its composer.[42] Katherine's initial attitude toward Montemezzi is thus likely to have been that of an enthusiastic, perhaps even worshipful, admirer.

The Montemezzis gave Arvey a shortened, simplified, sanitized account of their courtship. According to this, by the time Montemezzi sailed from New York on March 28, Katherine was ready to commit herself to a marriage-oriented relationship, but the composer preferred to leave things "at the friendship stage, so that they merely corresponded with each other." However, that summer Montemezzi had something of an epiphany:

> In the summer of 1920, Mr. Montemezzi went to the Tyrol, alone. There, in the high mountains, he would take a walk, alone, every morning at nine o'clock. At noon he would return to the hotel, alone, for his lunch. The first day he was struck by seeing a large number of young couples in love, engrossed in each other and no longer alone. The second day he saw a loving couple with an attractive baby. After a week of feeling the contrast between this and his own aloneness, he was inspired to write a letter to Miss Leith. In it he told her that in eighteen days he would be at his home in Verona and asked her to let him know by telegram "if your idea is the same as mine." When he arrived home, the telegram awaited him. It said, "I have the same idea."[43]

Katherine's letters to Montemezzi, preserved among the Donadelli family documents, tell a more complicated story. On March 31, three days after he sailed, she wrote him a very emotional letter in French. It makes clear that, one evening shortly before his departure, she had made a declaration of love, and possibly of sexual availability: "Maybe it would have been better to have said nothing, but there are times when one loses control in the face of a very serious situation—You will never imagine how much I suffer."[44] Montemezzi had apparently responded with the words "Luckily for you

---

[42] Judy Jennings, "Composer's Widow Here," *Philadelphia Inquirer*, January 7, 1956, p. 8.

[43] Arvey, "Visits to the Homes," p. 14.

[44] "Peut-être il aurait mieux été d'avoir rien dit, mais il y a des moments où on perd le contrôle en face d'une situation très grave—Vous ne pourrez jamais vous imaginer comme je souffre." Donadelli family documents.

AMERICA, MARRIAGE, INERTIA, 1919–1926   233

I am an honest man"—"honest" perhaps a mistake for "honorable"—presumably as a way of saying he would not take advantage of her passion for him, but also making it clear that he did not think a romantic relationship could work.[45] Katherine continued to write regularly, but her fourth letter, on May 5, ruefully noted that there had been no reply. She announced plans to visit France and Italy in the summer, and asked Montemezzi's advice on the matter, though without any specific suggestion that they should meet. Still, it appears, there was no reply, and some time after this Katherine seems to have largely abandoned both romantic hopes and thoughts of Europe, and on June 25 set off on a long tour through Canada, Alaska, Yellowstone Park, and Colorado. Montemezzi, for his part, did visit the Tyrol in August 1920, staying in the Karersee Hotel, Bolzano,[46] and it is clear he did write from there to Katherine. His letter was forwarded to her in Colorado Springs, but it was hardly the decisive breakthrough that the Montemezzis later reported to Arvey. Whether or not Katherine sent a telegram first, her full reply, postmarked September 1, expresses her joy in receiving the letter: "I am truly sensitive to the expressions of your friendship."[47] She hoped Montemezzi would visit New York again in the winter, and that she could see him in Europe the following year. But it is clear that Katherine still wanted much more from the relationship than Montemezzi. Her next surviving communication, a telegram dated November 21, rather desperately urged him to come to New York, but he stayed in Italy.

While Katherine's feelings are clear, Montemezzi's largely have to be inferred, but it is easy enough to guess that, having long assumed he would live in or near Vigasio, and probably marry a Catholic Italian woman, he was disoriented at having apparently won the heart of a wealthy heiress in New York who was not Catholic, knew little Italian, and was used to an extravagant lifestyle remote from his own. What would a future with her involve? There was an additional complication, too: according to family tradition, he had been actively courting the daughter of a noble family in the Verona area prior to his transatlantic voyage.[48] Any conflict was painfully resolved on his return to Vigasio, where he learned that the woman he had been courting had married, or had become engaged, to someone else.

---

[45] "heureusement pour vous je suis un homme honnête."
[46] There are four letters and telegrams Montemezzi sent from the hotel between August 12 and August 23, 1920, in the Archivio Storico Ricordi.
[47] "Io sono veramente sensibile alla espressioni della sua amicizia."
[48] Information from Renata Donadelli.

234 SUCCEEDING PUCCINI

Altogether, 1920 is likely to have been an emotionally complicated year for Montemezzi, both reflecting and exacerbating his professional frustrations.

Just how much a sense of international horizons and changing times affected Montemezzi's creative aspirations is unclear, but it is surely significant that he now abandoned the sort of nationalist themes found in *Giovanni Gallurese*, *L'amore dei tre re*, and above all *La nave*. After completing *La nave*, his thoughts immediately reverted to *La princesse lointaine*, and in 1918–1919 several reports appeared in the Italian and international press to the effect that his next opera would be based on Rostand's play. At least as late as the spring of 1920, Montemezzi hoped this would be the case. On May 24 he wrote to Renzo Valcarenghi, the new joint director of Casa Ricordi:

> During these last days I read and reread Principessa lontana in the French text. It is superb! It is really what is needed. There is everything in that poem: staging, drama, movement, poetry, and an extraordinary musicality. Rostand has died [he had died in 1918] and it may be possible now to conclude negotiations positively if they are conducted with good will. We need to move heaven and earth to obtain it. Also, we would have the advantage of not wasting too much time because the libretto is, we could say, already done.[49]

Cosimo Giorgieri Contri's Italian translation, which Montemezzi had seen in advance, had just been published, possibly giving fresh urgency to the composer's appeal for "negotiations." The Rostand estate continued to be unwilling to relinquish the rights, however, and thus eventually ended any possibility of another Montemezzi *Literaturoper*.

It is not clear when, or if, Montemezzi abandoned all hopes of *La princesse lointaine*, but by the mid-1920s Rostand's widow was more inclined to sell the rights to Alfano, perhaps because he was proposing to set not the play itself, but a libretto adapted from it by Henri Cain. On June 15, 1926, Alfano wrote: "For some time I have been dreaming of an operatic adaptation of *La Princesse Lointaine*. . . . I was able to meet Madame Rostand in Paris and to have . . . eventually, the promise that *Princesse Lointaine* would

---

[49] "Ho letto e riletto in questi giorni la Principessa lontana nel testo francese. È superba! È veramente quello che ci vuole. C'è tutto in quel poema: messa in scena, dramma, movimento, poesia e una musicalità straordinaria. Rostand è morto e può essere probabile ora condurre in porto delle trattative se condotte con buona volontà. Bisogna fare fuoco e fiamma per averla. Avremmo poi il vantaggio di non perdere troppo tempo perché il libretto si può dire che è bello e fatto." Archivio Storico Ricordi.

be mine if my publisher and I provide satisfactory conditions."[50] A letter of Cain's to Madame Rostand, dated June 25, states that he had given Alfano "the Princesse Lointaine libretto you had promised him in my presence," and that the composer had enthusiastically commenced work.[51] In the end, though, Madame Rostand's demands were prohibitive and Cain's libretto was never set (perhaps by way of apology, Alfano and Cain were allowed to adapt *Cyrano de Bergerac* a few years later, the opera finally making its first appearance in 1936). If Montemezzi knew of Alfano's negotiations, they would presumably have upset him a great deal. Next, it was Zandonai's turn to show interest, which he did in 1930: but this again led nowhere.[52] In the end, the rights were obtained by the French composer Georges Martin Witkowski (1867–1943), whose *Princesse lointaine* was premiered in 1934, but made little impact. Meanwhile, the amateur Italian composer Otello Cavara (1877–1928) had written and composed a free operatic adaptation of Rostand's play entitled *La principessa lontana*, presumably without permission; this was posthumously performed in Vicenza, also in 1934.

While still hoping to compose *La princesse lointaine*, Montemezzi had set off on what proved a frustrating, decade-long quest for a satisfactory, purpose-written libretto. In New York, he had complained at great length about the difficulty of finding suitable librettos:

> "Most of my time," said he, "is lost in looking for librettos."
> And then he launched into a lament about the dearth of good librettists nowadays, the difficulty of unearthing a fit theme, the hardships of adapting one's libretto, when at last it had been discovered, to the composer's moods....
> "In Italy to-day we have Adami and Forzano...."
> For ten minutes Montemezzi harped and harped on this matter of librettos.[53]

Giuseppe Adami and Giovacchino Forzano—the writers who had worked with Puccini on *Il trittico* (1918)—were clearly Montemezzi's first choices as literary collaborators, but they were not, initially, available, and sometime

---

[50] Quoted in Konrad Dryden, *Franco Alfano: Transcending "Turandot"* (Lanham, MD: Scarecrow Press, 2010), p. 64.

[51] "le livret de la Princesse Lointaine que vous lui aviez promis en ma présence." Chandler collection.

[52] Konrad Dryden, *Riccardo Zandonai: A Biography* (Frankfurt: Peter Lang, 1999), p. 302.

[53] Meltzer, "Montemezzi," p. 588.

236 SUCCEEDING PUCCINI

after his return from the United States, Montemezzi teamed up instead with Renato Simoni, the playwright and critic from Verona who, it appears, had written the most positive review of *La nave* in 1918. It was a collaboration that Montemezzi soon came to regret. Simoni had shown ominously little interest in writing librettos in the past. He had adapted *La secchia rapita* (1910) from an eighteenth-century libretto for Giulio Ricordi, written *Madame Sans-Gêne* (1915) for Giordano, and then, in the winter of 1919–1920, had been drawn into working with Adami on what would eventually be *Turandot*. The first clear reference to the new project in the incomplete preserved correspondence appears in a letter of February 14, 1921, in which an obviously frustrated Montemezzi exclaims: "Simoni had promised me Act I by Christmas!!!"[54] Soon afterward, announcements of the planned opera began appearing in the press. The chosen subject was the classic French novella, *Paul et Virginie* (1788) by Jacques-Henri Bernardin de Saint-Pierre (1737–1814), set in Mauritius. Here the odd pattern of parallels between Montemezzi and Puccini, at the distance of twenty years, resurfaces, for it was in 1900 that the older composer's imagination had traveled eastward, when he was inspired by David Belasco's play *Madame Butterfly*. But though Puccini had thoroughly vindicated his turn to an exotic subject, *Paul et Virginie* was, in many ways, an odd choice. There had been at least thirteen earlier operatic treatments, but most of these dated back to the late 1700s and early 1800s, when the novella was most in vogue; they include a notable Italian version by Pietro Carlo Guglielmi (1817). However, the only adaptation with any currency in the early twentieth century was the 1876 French version by Victor Massé, with a libretto by the famous partnership of Jules Barbier and Michel Carré. The novella itself was still popular, and Montemezzi and Simoni presumably reasoned that there was scope for a new, modern treatment. In this they were, remarkably but (one must assume) entirely coincidentally, supported by Jean Cocteau and Eric Satie, who commenced work on their *Paul & Virginie* opéra-comique in 1920.[55] Like Montemezzi's, Satie's opera was never completed or performed.

The difficulties of 1920 spilled over into 1921. Between December 22, 1920, and January 25, 1921, Katherine wrote thirteen letters to Montemezzi,

---

[54] "Simoni mi aveva promesso il I° atto per Natale!!!" Montemezzi to Carlo Clausetti, Archivio Storico Ricordi.

[55] Robert Orledge, *Satie the Composer* (Cambridge: Cambridge University Press, 1990), p. 235.

effectively proposing marriage. He seems to have delayed replying until late January or early February, but when she did finally receive a letter from him, she was left very disappointed, and in a "terrible state."[56] Montemezzi must have said something to the effect that he was not ready for such a large commitment. Rather than giving up, though, Katherine, who had been planning to travel to Europe at the end of March, expedited her arrangements and arrived in Le Havre with her mother at the end of February, then traveled to Italy in a leisurely fashion, via Paris and Nice. She clearly wanted to avoid giving the impression that she had come to Europe simply to see Montemezzi. Nevertheless, in April and May she was able to spend a considerable amount of time with him in Italy, including two weeks in Genoa that seem to have been decisive. Seeing Katherine again, and perhaps seeing just how much effort she had put into learning Italian, and that she was willing to live in Italy, seems to have resolved most of Montemezzi's doubts. Toward the end of May, Katherine and her mother returned to Paris, where they took up an extended residence at the luxurious Hôtel de Crillon. At this point, it is clear, she considered Montemezzi and herself unofficially engaged; the remaining question was simply when they would marry. "As for me, I will do it tomorrow morning," she wrote cajolingly on June 6.[57] Katherine clearly considered her wealth a major part of her attraction, and, perhaps surprisingly, worried that it might be insufficient. The same June 6 letter explained that she could obtain an extra $5,000 a year from her mother. Montemezzi can have been in no doubt that an immensely wealthy lifestyle was on offer, potentially making him one of the richest composers to have ever lived, albeit still well behind Puccini in terms of income.[58] In July, he and Katherine met again in the upmarket spa town of Aix-les-Bains and finalized their plans. They were married in Paris on August 24, 1921, "before a few close friends and relatives of the couple."[59] In France, unlike Italy, civil marriage was the cultural norm, and Paris may have been preferred for this reason, in addition

[56] "condizione terribile." Katherine Leith to Montemezzi, letter postmarked February 10, 1921. Donadelli family documents.

[57] "Quant à moi, je le ferais demain matin."

[58] Katherine and Montemezzi's combined annual income in 1921 would have been approximately equal to Puccini's earnings in the years before World War I. After the war, however, Puccini benefited from a great increase in royalty payments, and by 1921 had annual income approaching an astonishing 800,000 lire. For a fascinating study of Puccini's steadily accumulating wealth, see Miguel-Ángel Galindo-Martín, María-Teresa Méndez-Picazo, and Thomas Baumert, "Giacomo Puccini and Richard Strauss: The Economics of Music Up to the Dawn of Fascism," in *On Music, Money and Markets: Comparing the Finances of Great Composers*, edited by Thomas Baumert and Francisco Cabrillo (Cham: Springer, 2023), pp. 209–223.

[59] *Pacific Coast Musical Review*, October 1, 1921, p. 10.

238   SUCCEEDING PUCCINI

to Katherine's having made it her temporary home. Katherine's mother was present, but Montemezzi's parents were unable to attend.[60]

After the wedding ceremony, there was a "lavish lunch at the Ritz Hotel with many guests,"[61] and the bridegroom was understood as saying, in his speech, that he had "written a new opera based on his romance with Miss Leith."[62] We suspect that what he actually said, or meant, was that he was drawing on his "romance with Miss Leith" in *Paolo e Virginia*, on which he was then, stretching a point, working. Initially there was a "brief honeymoon" (*breve luna di miele*) in Belgium,[63] with short stays in Brussels and Ostend, before they headed back to Paris on September 1.[64] However, it is difficult to determine just when the couple's sense of being on honeymoon ended. Soon afterward, the soprano Frances Alda, who happened to consider *L'amore dei tre re* "the finest opera to be written in my time,"[65] and who was married to Giulio Gatti-Casazza, the general manager of the Metropolitan Opera, found herself staying in the next suite to the Montemezzis' in a hotel on the Venice Lido. She believed they were on their honeymoon then, and later recorded: "They were tremendously in love, and quite refreshingly and occasionally embarrassingly frank about it."[66] In October they were in Rome.

U.S. citizenship rules meant that Katherine was now an Italian citizen. She initially registered her residence as Vigasio, but the Montemezzis devoted much of their early married life to travel and appear to have delayed making a decision on where to settle. It is notable that all Montemezzi's 1922 letters in the Archivio Storico Ricordi were sent from hotels: from Monte Carlo, Vienna, Madrid, Mendola, and Venice. At some point the couple decided to live in Milan, and Katherine bought a large, second-floor apartment in a new house at Via Maggiolini 1, designed by the notable architect Alfredo Campanini, for 200,000 lire, or about $10,000—a bargain by New York standards.[67] The Montemezzis moved there in 1923. Photographs taken

---

[60] Montemezzi to his parents, August 24, 1921. Donadelli family documents.
[61] "splendida colazione all'Hotel Ritz con molti invitati." Montemezzi to his parents, August 24, 1921.
[62] "Famous Opera Composer Weds American Pianist," *Pittsburgh Gazette Times*, August 26, 1921, p. 14.
[63] Montemezzi to his parents, August 24, 1921.
[64] Montemezzi to Carlo Clausetti, August 28, 1921. Archivio Storico Ricordi.
[65] Frances Alda, *Men, Women and Tenors* (Boston: Houghton Mifflin, 1937), p. 263.
[66] Alda, *Men, Women and Tenors*, p. 263.
[67] Notary act 9798, July 24, 1923. Agenzia delle Entrate, Servizio di Pubblicità Immobiliare di Milano 3.

Figure 7.3 The Montemezzis' apartment in Milan, 1930s. *Donadelli family documents.*

before they left the apartment in 1939 show a series of elegantly designed rooms, full of antique furniture, paintings, and objets d'art (Figure 7.3). The Montemezzis eventually employed no less than seven staff here,[68] though the number was probably fewer before the birth of their son in 1926, and most of them would have lived elsewhere.

Little is known of the Montemezzis' private life, though they told Arvey of how Katherine, a talented pianist, had quickly given up playing:

> One day, she [Katherine] relates, Mr. Montemezzi was in his studio and she in the other room. She was playing *La Nave* at sight—a difficult score. He listened for an hour, then came in and said very quietly, "When are you going to play a right note?" After that "insult," as she laughingly terms it, she never played again. She felt that one musician in the family was enough.[69]

[68] Information from Renata Donadelli.
[69] Arvey, "Visits to the Homes," p. 14.

240   SUCCEEDING PUCCINI

Another revealing memory, that would appear to apply most of all to the frustrations of the 1920s, was:

> Inside [the apartment] it was music from 9 a.m. to 6 p.m. as Montemezzi labored at the piano on one composition after another.... "I had to keep the house very quiet," she [Katherine] said. Many times he would get disgusted and rewrite; many times he would ask her for her opinion, she said as she recalled how she had to be ready for anything.[70]

Given that he published very little after his marriage, this seems to suggest that Montemezzi spent a good deal of time writing music that was abandoned and, as far as we know, destroyed.

The sense of a new epoch commencing in his life would have been painfully brought home to Montemezzi when his father died on March 5, 1922. His mother, now in her mid-sixties, stayed on in the family home, where Montemezzi and Katherine regularly visited her. There continued to be plenty of traveling, something Katherine clearly expected. There were many visits to luxury resorts, the spa town of Carlsbad (Karlovy Vary) being a regular summer destination, and Venice another favorite vacation place. There were long stays in New York in the winter of 1923–1924 and again in 1925, discussed in more detail later. Most years the Montemezzis received visits from Katherine's mother, and there was plenty of socializing in Milan. Among their friends, they counted Giordano and Mascagni; they considered the latter "the greatest wit they ever knew."[71] There is good reason to suppose that Montemezzi found this very different from his previous lifestyle, and this, with the fact that he no longer had a financial incentive to compose, proved inimical to sustained creative work.

Professionally speaking, Montemezzi was undoubtedly frustrated. Simoni's delays with *Paolo e Virginia* had continued, and eventually he declared that he wanted to complete *Turandot* first. On March 19, 1921, Montemezzi had responded: "I am speechless.... He could have said earlier that he wanted to complete Turandot."[72] Another deadline for the submission of Act I in the summer was missed, and in his early married life

---

[70] Norman Frisch, "Widow Loved Montemezzi and His Operas," *Daily News* (Los Angeles), October 19, 1952, p. 28.

[71] Arvey, "Visits to the Homes," p. 28.

[72] "io non ho più parole da esprimere.... Doveva dirlo prima che voleva finire il Turandot." Montemezzi to Carlo Clausetti, Archivio Storico Ricordi.

AMERICA, MARRIAGE, INERTIA, 1919–1926   241

Montemezzi had no libretto on which to work. In October, the alternative possibility was raised of him collaborating with Arturo Rossato (1882–1942), who had written *Giulietta e Romeo* for Zandonai, and subsequently became Zandonai's regular librettist.[73] By 1922, Montemezzi was casting around, with something like desperation, for another libretto. A letter of February 19 mentions successful negotiations with Tommaso Montefiore, the minor composer who obtained the rights to Benelli's *La cena delle beffe* and did nothing with them;[74] but in the end, Casa Sonzogno obtained the rights and Giordano composed the opera. In March and April, meanwhile, Montemezzi was announcing an interest in *Sly*, the libretto Forzano had written for Puccini in 1920, and that was eventually—after Puccini committed himself to *Turandot*—set by Ermanno Wolf-Ferrari. By August, Montemezzi was keen to embark on yet another project: an operatic adaptation of Louis N. Parker's *The Cardinal* (1901), which had enjoyed some success in Italy, to be made by Claudio Guastalla (1880–1948), who was later to become Respighi's regular librettist. None of these ideas was pursued very far, and it is hard to avoid the conclusion that 1922 was a particularly restless, frustration-filled year for Montemezzi the composer.

At some point in 1922, a decision was made that Simoni would not, or could not, complete *Paolo e Virginia* on his own, and that Adami, who Montemezzi clearly considered a superior librettist, would be a coauthor. As Simoni and Adami were already collaborating on *Turandot*, it may have seemed a natural progression for them to work simultaneously on a second libretto. Adami's involvement brought the stuttering project back to life, and in early 1923 a second round of announcements appeared in the press. In July that year, Montemezzi finally received the complete libretto of *Paolo e Virginia* just before he and Katherine set off for a stay in their beloved Carlsbad:

> I have in my hands the libretto, which is beautiful (Adami brought it to me one hour before I left), although it needs to be reviewed a little and perhaps in some parts discussed further and with more calm than what we have had so far. But it is beautiful, it is beautiful, it is beautiful![75]

[73] Casa Ricordi to Montemezzi, October 21, 1921. Archivio Storico Ricordi, Copialettere.

[74] Montemezzi to Renzo Valcarenghi. Archivio Storico Ricordi.

[75] "Ho in mano il libretto che è bellissimo (Adami me lo ha portato un'ora prima che io partissi) ma va un poco riveduto e forse in qualche parte discusso ancora e con più tranquillità di quella che abbiamo avuto fino ad ora. Ma è bello, è bello, è bello!" Montemezzi to Renzo Valcarenghi, July 16, 1923. Archivio Storico Ricordi.

242 SUCCEEDING PUCCINI

Clearly a good deal of enthusiasm had survived the long delay. But immediately there were some doubts and, Puccini-like, Montemezzi was soon demanding changes. It appears some composition was done in 1923, but not much. And now America brought another major disruption to Montemezzi's regular work routines.

Montemezzi and Katherine made a nearly five-month trip to the United States over the winter of 1923–1924, initially staying with her mother, now resident at the sumptuous Ambassador Hotel, New York (opened 1921). They later described the trip as a time of "travel and rest."[76] In the United States, Montemezzi again found himself treated like a celebrity to a much greater extent than in Italy. As well as telling the press he was at work on *Paolo*, he expressed his views on all sorts of topics, including, notably, the need for greater public support for opera in the United States:

> Signor Montemezzi said that permanent opera companies could be maintained in every American city if the Government carried out the plan in effect in Milan, where the theatres and movie houses were compelled to divert 2 per cent. of their proceeds for the expenses of La Scala.
>
> "In this way good art could be built up at the expense of poor art," he said.[77]

The highlight of the trip for Montemezzi the musician was a special presentation at the Metropolitan Opera House on January 9, 1924. Met records suggest this was the thirty-ninth performance of *L'amore dei tre re* by the company, but somebody miscounted, perhaps deliberately, and decided it was the fortieth performance, as well as the tenth anniversary of the New York premiere: the perfect occasion to honor the composer. After Act I, the U.S. and Italian national anthems were played, and after the second, "Montemezzi was brought on [the stage] and after the audience had enthusiastically brought him back again and again Paul D. Cravath came out with him, as well as a man bearing a silver wreath." Cravath, an influential member of the Met's board, then made a speech reflecting on how the opera: "held an honorable place in our annual repertoire." Montemezzi was hailed as having "earned high rank on the roll of honor of the great masters of opera," and was

[76] "Italo Montemezzi Back Again in U.S. to Witness Production of Early Work," *Musical America*, January 24, 1925, p. 2.
[77] Quoted in "Italian Composer Here," *New York Times*, December 7, 1923, p. 25.

presented with the wreath.[78] After the performance, there was a second, private presentation. Gatti-Casazza gave Montemezzi a gold pen and expressed the wish that he would use it to write another opera. A year earlier, such a gift might have been received with more pain than pleasure, but it is probable that Montemezzi now felt emboldened to stress he was indeed composing again, given all the press reports concerning *Paolo e Virginia*. A month later, the *New York Times* reported: "Recently he began composing the opera 'Paola [*sic*] E Virginia' and said that he expected to finish the composition within two years."[79] A lavish Met premiere was available for the asking.

The Montemezzis attended the season's last performance of *L'amore dei tre re* on February 15, after which they were the guests of honor at a special dinner hosted by the Italian Musical League and the Italian ambassador, Prince Gelasio Caetani.[80] This was initially announced as a farewell dinner, with the Montemezzis about to return to Italy, but they made a late decision to extend their stay, apparently so that Montemezzi could coach Grace Moore (1898–1947), who was hoping to audition at the Metropolitan Opera. Moore's career to this juncture had been in revue and operetta, but she was determined to move into opera, and later described how Montemezzi had "fanned my hopes by saying, 'You know you have definite operatic talent.' He told me that I must learn to concentrate on singing as a natural spontaneous function. 'Singing right,' he said, 'is the easiest thing in the world, and singing wrong the hardest.'"[81] In Moore's account, "I chose an aria from Montemezzi's opera *Giovanni Gallurese* for the audition, and Montemezzi himself coached me at the piano, day after day at the studio."[82] This experience of singing an operatic aria in its composer's presence was a turning point in Moore's career: "Irving [Berlin]'s lovely and simple songs were suddenly not enough—they lacked the soaring notes I wanted...I had only one ambition—Opera."[83]

The audition took place on April 10, 1924, with Montemezzi present. Gatti-Casazza acknowledged that Moore had a "good voice," but said she needed another year of training; in the end she would not make her Met debut until 1928, after which she quickly established herself as one of the leading American singers of her generation.[84] For Montemezzi, the reward

[78] Deems Taylor, "At the Metropolitan," *World*, January 10, 1924, p. 15.
[79] "Italo Montemezzi Sails," *New York Times*, February 17, 1924, p. S8.
[80] "Farewell Dinner to Maestro Montemezzi," *New York Evening Post*, February 11, 1924, p. 5.
[81] Moore, *You're Only Human Once*, pp. 89–90.
[82] Moore, *You're Only Human Once*, p. 91.
[83] Moore, *You're Only Human Once*, pp. 91–92.
[84] John Kobler, *Otto, the Magnificent: The Life of Otto Kahn* (New York: Scribner, 1988), p. 168.

244   SUCCEEDING PUCCINI

for his efforts with the *Gallurese* aria came much sooner. Not only had he established an important friendship with Moore, which continued until her death, but he had strategically drawn Gatti-Casazza's attention to an opera still unheard in the United States. It would be fascinating to know what conversation followed the audition, for less than five weeks later Gatti-Casazza announced that *Giovanni Gallurese* would be staged at the Met the following season.[85] By the time Montemezzi finally left the United States, he presumably had some private assurance that the opera was being looked at favorably.

Whatever efforts had been made earlier, Montemezzi's major creative struggle with *Paolo e Virginia* took place after his return from the United States in 1924. In terms of subject, it was a wholly new departure: a Rousseauist tale of innocent young love thriving on the Île de France (Mauritius) before being destroyed by the long reach of European civilization.[86] And it is an odd, unsatisfactory libretto, with the missionary, who appears only briefly in the novel, developed into the main antagonist—the traditional, villainous baritone role, but a pale shadow of the Monk Traba in *La nave*.[87] It is because of his denunciation of Virginia's "impure desires" in Act 1 that the real nature of the young lovers' feelings becomes clear to them. In Act 2, the missionary appears again, this time with the island's governor, insisting that Virginia go to France to inherit the fortune God has intended for her: eventually, reluctantly, she agrees to go. Act 3 begins with a scene between the missionary and Paolo, the former advising the latter to stop pining over Virginia. They are interrupted by news that a ship bearing Virginia has arrived. The ship is wrecked in a violent storm, and though Paolo successfully brings Virginia ashore, she dies after exchanging final words of hope with him. Simoni and Adami appear to have intended the missionary to represent not so much an individual antagonist as an orthodox attitude somehow spelling the doom of the young lovers, yet the fact that Virginia dies because of a storm contradicts this, as does, to a lesser extent, the libretto's emphasis on Paolo and Virginia's own strong Christian faith, mixed with pantheistic sentiment. The dramatic stakes do not seem very significant until the very end of the story, and this, combined with the extreme youth and naïveté of the adolescent lovers, and

---

[85] W. J. Henderson, "Two New Operas on List for Metropolitan's Next Season," *Sun*, May 17, 1924, p. 4.

[86] A typescript of the libretto, formerly owned by María Isabel Curubeto Godoy, is held by the Instituto Nacional de Musicología Carlos Vega, Buenos Aires.

[87] A revealing contrast can be made with Barbier and Carré's far more exciting adaptation for Victor Massé, in which a brutal plantation owner is the villain: he becomes infatuated with Virginia and even follows her to France.

AMERICA, MARRIAGE, INERTIA, 1919–1926   245

all the suggested sights and sounds of a tropical landscape Montemezzi knew very little about, presented the composer with formidable challenges he ultimately failed to overcome.

Nevertheless, Montemezzi clearly composed a good deal of music for *Paolo e Virginia*, and in late 1924 appears to have felt certain that the opera would be completed. His professional relationship with Casa Ricordi was still largely defined by the contract signed in 1913, discussed in the previous chapter, but this had been massively devalued by the rampant inflation which began affecting the Italian economy from 1915. By 1924, the urban cost of living was over four times what it had been in 1913.[88] In recognition of this, a new contract was drawn up on December 30, 1924, naming *Paolo e Virginia* as Montemezzi's next opera, and stipulating that 40,000 lire would be paid on his surrender of the score; an agreement was also made that Casa Ricordi would reimburse the composer the 16,000 lire he had paid his librettists.[89] This fascinating contract reveals just how much Ricordi saw Montemezzi as an important but unproductive asset, for he was also offered 100,000 lire for a second full-length opera, as well as a chance to extend his copyright on his earlier works. Yet despite such financial inducements, no doubt rendered less than dazzling by Katherine's 300,000 lire a year, momentum on *Paolo e Virginia* quickly ran out in the new year. Montemezzi was still committed to composing it in February 1925, and demanding more revisions to the libretto,[90] and there is a probable further reference to it in a letter of May 25, 1925 (Montemezzi simply asking "Has Adami finished?"), but thereafter the documentary trail goes cold, and it is to be hoped more evidence bearing on the question will emerge somewhere.[91] By June 1926, at the latest, Montemezzi had decided to work such music as he had written into a symphonic poem instead.[92] In a later interview with Nino Alberti, Montemezzi explained that, "having abandoned the idea of an opera, he gathered the core ideas of it in a symphonic poem."[93] But in general it was not

---

[88] P. Scholliers and V. Zamagni (eds.), *Labour's Reward: Real Wages and Economic Change in 19th- and 20th-Century Europe* (Aldershot, UK: Edward Elgar, 1995), pp. 231–32.

[89] Archivio Storico Ricordi, Copialettere.

[90] Montemezzi to Carlo Clausetti and Renzo Valcarenghi, February 4, 1925. Archivio Storico Ricordi.

[91] "Ha finito Adami?" Montemezzi to Carlo Clausetti and Renzo Valcarenghi. Archivio Storico Ricordi.

[92] Arthur Judson to George Engles, December 27, 1927. Morgan Library and Museum, MFC J93.E58 (2). Judson reports meeting Montemezzi in Europe the previous year and finding him working on a symphonic poem. He was in Europe during June 1926 and back in the United States by July 7. Information kindly supplied by Judson's biographer, James Doering.

[93] Nino Alberti, "La Stagione Lirica dell'Eiar," *Radio Corriere*, August 2–8, 1936, p. 6.

246 SUCCEEDING PUCCINI

something he wanted to discuss, and it is easy to infer that he felt somewhat embarrassed and ashamed that so many years had passed without a new opera appearing. The libretto became Casa Ricordi's property, and Guido Valcarenghi, in charge of Ricordi's Buenos Aires office, obtained it for the Argentine composer María Isabel Curubeto Godoy (1898–1959). By 1930 she was translating and setting it. Curubeto Godoy later reported that she was told Montemezzi abandoned the subject as simply too distant from *La nave*—a polite, official reason no doubt, though with a good deal of truth in it.[94] Her *Pablo y Virginia* was finally brought out at the Teatro Colón, Buenos Aires, in 1946.

Montemezzi's creative frustrations in this period must have been exacerbated by the fact that everyone else seemed to be having a better decade than himself. Mascagni and Giordano, whose careers had been flagging for years, enjoyed remarkable comebacks, the former with *Il piccolo Marat* in 1921, the latter with *La cena delle beffe* in 1924. Alfano, after a long break from opera, produced his second masterpiece in the genre, *La leggenda di Sakùntala*, in 1921; Pizzetti his, *Dèbora e Jaéle*, in 1922; while Zandonai scored major successes with *Giulietta e Romeo* (1922) and *I cavalieri di Ekebù* (1924). Then there was Puccini himself, whose nearly complete *Turandot* was being much talked about in operatic circles in 1924. None of the other composers had achieved such consistent success as Puccini, and it was hard to avoid the sense of an era's end when the composer of *La Bohème*, *Tosca*, and *Madama Butterfly* died in Brussels on November 29, 1924. Puccini's body was brought to Milan on December 3, and Montemezzi, Adami, and Simoni were among the pallbearers. The question of who the older composer's successor would be was now truly open. Montemezzi's claim, which had looked so strong a decade earlier, was severely compromised by his failure to produce a successful follow-up to *L'amore dei tre re*. As his faith in *Paolo e Virginia* gradually dissipated, he became increasingly convinced that *La nave* had not received its proper due and needed to be promoted and revived. Slowly but surely, and perhaps fatally for his overall career, Montemezzi began to look backward rather than forward.

In the complex political climate of 1919–1920, no third production of *La nave* had materialized, as discussed in the previous chapter. A plan to re-launch the opera magnificently was started in 1922. Giuseppe Torres, a

---

[94] Julia Ottolenghi, "'Pablo y Virginia': La ópera que por primera vez en el mundo compone una mujer, y era mujer es argentina," *El Hogar*, July 5, 1946, p. 33.

AMERICA, MARRIAGE, INERTIA, 1919–1926   247

Venetian architect, developed the idea of a grand staging of the opera in St. Mark's Square, Venice. In the autumn, a meeting was held at D'Annunzio's new home, the Vittoriale, involving the poet, the composer, Torres himself, and Guido Marussig, who had designed the Scala production. D'Annunzio gave "wise advice" on what they all considered a "grandiose enterprise," but the plan was dropped, apparently because, now heavily involved in developing the Vittoriale, he lost interest.[95] This was the last time Montemezzi saw him. After the failure of this ambitious scheme, guaranteed plentiful publicity, Montemezzi had the modest consolation of seeing the Teatro Filarmonico, Verona, stage *La nave* in their 1922–1923 season. Opening on March 8, 1923, there were eight performances, reusing Marussig's designs. Montemezzi took a very active interest in the production, attending all the rehearsals and advising on the presentation. The Verona *Nave* was a local success, and indeed a strong expression of local feeling, but it received almost no attention in the national press, and Italy's music critics soon forgot that it had taken place.

Montemezzi wanted much more than this, and had there been a conveniently extractable aria from *La nave* for Moore to sing at her audition, his 1920s might have worked out rather differently. As it was, the Metropolitan Opera's 1925 production of *Giovanni Gallurese* assumed considerable importance, and a strong argument can be made that this was the most professionally significant event of the decade: the best chance Montemezzi had to shrug off his strengthening "single opera" reputation. Recognizing the importance of the revival, Montemezzi took the opportunity to make a few small alterations to the score and traveled to New York to assist at the rehearsals and attend the performances. The Montemezzis thus sailed from Genoa again on January 6, 1925, arriving in New York on January 18, and again staying with Katherine's mother at the Ambassador Hotel, an easy walking distance from the Metropolitan Opera House. Montemezzi spent much time with Serafin in the course of this visit, for the latter had been appointed principal conductor at the Met in 1924. The cast, including Giacomo Lauri-Volpi as Gallurese, Maria Mueller (Müller) as Maria, and Giuseppe Danise as Rivegas, worked closely with Montemezzi, Serafin, and Samuel Thewman, the director: a creative environment sufficiently interesting for *Musical America* to devote a special photo feature to it.[96]

---

[95] Montemezzi, "Come scrissi la musica per 'La Nave,'" *Scenario* 7 (April 1938): p. 218.

[96] "When Heroes Sing Lyric Lays in Street Clothes: Rehearsing for a Première at the Metropolitan," *Musical America*, April 4, 1925, p. 3.

248   SUCCEEDING PUCCINI

The New World premiere of *Giovanni Gallurese* on February 19, 1925, was followed by three more performances in New York and a further one in Philadelphia. It was a popular success. An unsigned report in the *New York Evening Post* after three performances gives perhaps the best idea of how the opera was received:

> [H]owever much the cognoscenti may snicker at such an opera as Montemezzi's "Giovanni Gallurese," it continues to be embraced by the Metropolitan audiences with frantic enthusiasm.
>
> . . . there were cheers from the large subscription audience for this rather flimsy story of a Sardinian bandit. . . . Where the critical minded may have found musical bromides of a stale school of Italian opera, an aggressive majority found stirring arias, eminently singable and, it may be added, vigorously sung.[97]

Oscar Thompson reported in *Musical America* that the premiere was another of Montemezzi's great American nights: "Summoned repeatedly before the curtain by a demonstrative audience, and presented with an enormous ornamental wreath, the distinguished Italian bowed and beamed his happiness after each of the three acts. It was a kingly reception which New York thus extended to the composer of its beloved 'L'Amore dei Tre Re.'"[98] But the critics were much less enthused. Lawrence Gilman in the *Herald Tribune* and Ernest Newman acting as guest critic for the *Evening Post* savaged the opera as quite unworthy of production. On the other hand, Deems Taylor, now starting to make his mark as one of the most influential American critics, judged that: "Considered purely as music, it [*Giovanni Gallurese*] is better than much of Puccini, and infinitely above the usual run of contemporary opera music by lesser lights."[99] However he, like the other critics, considered the libretto poor and the opera as a whole far below the level of *L'amore dei tre re*. This appears to have been the last time Montemezzi saw his youthful opus staged.

Back in Italy, Montemezzi resigned himself to his final, doomed battle with the libretto of *Paolo e Virginia*. But another struggle did come to a successful conclusion this year. Though pretending otherwise, Katherine Montemezzi

[97] "'Giovanni Gallurese' at the Metropolitan," *New York Evening Post*, March 10, 1925, p. 13.

[98] Oscar Thompson, "Early Montemezzi Opera Given First American Hearing," *Musical America*, February 28, 1925, p. 1.

[99] Deems Taylor, "At the Metropolitan," *World*, February 20, 1925, p. 11.

was thirty-six at the time of her wedding, and she came from a culture in which women were expected to produce heirs. There can be little doubt that, from an early stage in their marriage, the Montemezzis sought to have a child. As her fortieth birthday approached, Katherine became increasingly anxious and began seeing a gynecologist in Paris, the gynecological capital of Europe.[100] She finally became pregnant in late summer 1925.

Katherine's pregnancy was not the only reason that the spring of 1926 was a particularly significant moment in Montemezzi's biography. On March 27, 1926, Toscanini conducted the first of three performances of *L'amore dei tre re* at La Scala, fulfilling a promise to the composer originally made in 1923.[101] Montemezzi was present and was warmly acclaimed. *Turandot* was originally scheduled for March, too, and had there not been delays with Puccini's posthumous masterpiece, the two operas might have been seen in close juxtaposition. In fact, *Turandot*, again under Toscanini's baton, followed almost exactly four weeks later, on April 25. Montemezzi missed this because of his and Katherine's plans to go to Paris for the birth of their child, and it is hard to resist the thought that he may have been glad of such a good excuse to absent himself from Milan. By April 7, the Montemezzis were installed in an apartment at 5 Square du Trocadéro, Paris, and on May 10, Katherine gave birth to a healthy baby boy.[102] He was christened Marco Antonio, his first name after Marco Gràtico, and was to be the Montemezzis' only child. Soon afterward, Montemezzi made the long journey to Monte Carlo to see Garden, presumably to ask her to be Marco's godmother, for she accepted this role in the family.[103]

The month his son was born, Montemezzi found time to talk with Angelo Scandiani (1872–1930), the general manager of La Scala, to make a case for a revival of *La nave*. A letter he wrote to Scandiani later this year gives a good idea of the arguments he made. First was the quality of D'Annunzio's tragedy, "one of the most beautiful things ever written," and that, far from being dated, it was "more the expression of the post-war period with all its intensity and speed of life." Second were the unsatisfactory circumstances of

---

[100] Information from Renata Donadelli. For the preeminence of Paris in gynecology, see George Weisz, *Divide and Conquer: A Comparative History of Medical Specialization* (New York: Oxford University Press, 2005), p. 208.

[101] Montemezzi to Toscanini, September 26, 1924. Chandler collection.

[102] Having moved into the apartment, Montemezzi immediately wrote to Toscanini (letter in Chandler collection).

[103] For Montemezzi's visit to Garden at this juncture, see Moore, *You're Only Human Once*, p. 108, though Moore does not link it to Marco's birth. For Garden's accepting the role of godmother, see Lawrence, "Figures on the Battlements," p. 6.

250 SUCCEEDING PUCCINI

the original La Scala production, with the audience so distracted by news of the war, and most younger men unable to attend. Finally, there was the fact that the opera was "[t]he realization of . . . my highest aspiration," and the suggestion that Montemezzi had not yet received his due in Italy.[104] Montemezzi had certainly made efforts to get his operas performed before, but this conversation with Scandiani and the subsequent letters appear to represent a new seriousness of approach, and a campaign very specifically designed to get *La nave* back on the stage—a project which increasingly obsessed him from now on. Given the timing, it is hard to avoid the conclusion that this had something to do with Montemezzi's becoming a father, the impact of *Turandot*, Puccini's challenge from beyond the grave, and the realization that *Paolo e Virginia*, written by the very men who had written *Turandot*, was simply not going to work.

[104] "una delle cose più belle che mai sieno state scritte"; "più l'espressione del dopoguerra con tutta la sua intensità e rapidità di vita"; "La realizzazione di . . . mia massima aspirazione." Montemezzi to Scandiani, August 20, 1926. Chandler collection.

8

"A sort of *loisir*"

Paolo e Virginia and *La notte di Zoraima*, 1927–1932

In 1912, Fausto Torrefranca published his notorious polemic, *Puccini e l'opera internazionale*, condemning the commercialism of Italy's most famous living composer while calling for a revival of the country's rich tradition of instrumental music. Plenty of young composers were willing to heed the positive part of Torrefranca's case. The ensuing shift toward the classical forms of instrumental music, gradually strengthening after World War I, is particularly associated with the so-called generation of '80, centered on Pizzetti, Malipiero, Casella, and Respighi. Montemezzi was not much older than these composers and was slightly younger than his friend Alfano, who is frequently linked with them, but he largely stuck to the position he had set out in the United States in 1919: "In Italy music means opera, the present experiments in other forms to the contrary notwithstanding."[1] Such an attitude put him at a serious disadvantage in the 1920s, for it inevitably meant that he was not included in many new musical initiatives. From about 1923, as the Fascists consolidated control over Italy, it also had political ramifications: Mussolini's government wanted to associate itself with a sense of cultural rebirth, so art which could claim to be both classical and modern was much in favor.

Alfano offers the most telling contrast at this juncture. He still regarded himself as primarily an opera composer, but by the 1920s much of his creative effort was going into chamber music, putting him on a different, stronger footing in the altered musical climate of the new decade. He was also far nimbler in negotiating the political realignments, signing Giovanni Gentile's "Manifesto of Fascist Intellectuals" in 1925 and developing strong connections with the younger musicians rising to power in Italy's musical institutions. The way this benefited Alfano is succinctly illustrated by the fact

---

[1] Herbert F. Peyser, "'Let simplicity be the composer's constant objective,' Abjures Italo Montemezzi," *Musical America*, November 22, 1919, p. 4.

Succeeding Puccini. David Chandler and Raffaele Mellace, Oxford University Press. © Oxford University Press 2025.
DOI: 10.1093/9780197761373.003.0009

252   SUCCEEDING PUCCINI

that his Second String Quartet received its premiere in Mussolini's home on March 26, 1927, the composer sitting beside the dictator.[2] This exclusive premiere, widely reported, was one of many events in the early Fascist years highlighting Montemezzi's comparative remoteness from the center of power.

Another episode soon afterward particularly upset Montemezzi and gave a new direction to his grievances. On October 23, 1926, a group of composers led by Adriano Lualdi and Alceo Toni, and including Alfano, had visited Mussolini to set out proposals for a "Mostra del '900 musicale italiano" (Exhibition of twentieth-century Italian music) to be held in Bologna. This group would variously call itself the National Syndicate of Professional Milanese Musicians or, less pompously, the Musicians Syndicate of Milan.[3] A photograph taken with the composers gathered around Mussolini reveals much about the hierarchy even within this "in" group: Alfano and Lualdi appear as the most prominent.[4] The Syndicate was effectively attempting to counter the influence of the more internationalist Corporazione delle Nuove Musiche founded by Casella in 1923, but their plan was grand, patriotic, and allegedly open to all "schools" and "tendencies" in Italian music. Mussolini gave his blessing, and the government contributed 80,000 lire in funding.[5] The "Mostra" took place between March 31 and April 12, 1927, and included works by fifty-seven living composers, some members of the organizing Syndicate, others invited to supply something for the program, and still others required to submit their music to an adjudicating committee. Among the composers still well known today, Alfano, Casella, Malipiero, Pizzetti, Respighi, Wolf-Ferrari, and Zandonai all had works included in the various concerts. Conspicuously absent from the program were Cilea, Giordano, Mascagni, and Montemezzi. As a prominent composer resident in Milan, with personal connections to many of the organizers, Montemezzi had particularly good reasons for feeling excluded. Vittorio Gnecchi (1876–1954), another Milan-based opera composer not included in the scheme, was left with similar hurt feelings.[6] Though most of the program consisted of orchestral and chamber works, choral pieces, and songs, several extracts

---

[2] Franco Sciannameo, "Turandot, Mussolini, and the Second String Quartet: Aspects of Alfano," *Musical Times* 143 (2002): pp. 27–41.

[3] "Notizie," *Musica d'Oggi* 9 (1927): pp. 60, 92.

[4] It is reproduced in Sciannameo, "Turandot," p. 27.

[5] Fiamma Nicolodi, *Musica e musicisti nel ventennio fascista* (Fiesole: Discanto, 1984), p. 163.

[6] Marco Iannelli, *The Cassandra Case: Vittorio Gnecchi, a 20th Century Story* (Milan: Bietti Media, 2007), pp. 162–63, 175. Gnecchi was a great admirer of Montemezzi, as detailed in our Epilogue.

PAOLO E VIRGINIA AND LA NOTTE DI ZORAIMA   253

from operas were included—Alfano was represented by his "*Danza e Finale dell'opera Sakuntala*"—so there was no obvious reason for the exclusion of composers like Montemezzi and Gnecchi.

On this occasion, Montemezzi took his grievance in a rather unexpected direction, lobbying Ernesto Belloni (1883–1938), the mayor of Milan, first in a series of telephone calls, and then in a letter of June 15, 1927: "I can't keep silent to you, my friend, that such an unfair valuation of the artistic forces of Italy from those who, for the most part, have the reins, humiliates me and robs me of my peace."[7] As the "Mostra" was a Milanese initiative, funded by public money, there was some reason for complaining to Belloni, but it is not clear what Montemezzi expected the mayor to do, and it is doubtful whether Belloni, busy with ambitious plans to develop Milan, would have welcomed the composer's lobbying. Nevertheless, although it is almost certain that nothing was achieved, this is a significant episode in Montemezzi's career, directly anticipating his lobbying of the national government, which commenced the following year.

One clear lesson from the "Mostra," and the general development of Italian musical life it highlighted, was that Montemezzi would be increasingly disadvantaged if he had no non-operatic music to offer concert programmers. As noted in the previous chapter, he had, probably in 1926, started adapting some music composed for the abandoned *Paolo e Virginia* opera into a symphonic poem, or "poema musicale per orchestra,"[8] and the events of the spring of 1927 may have given an embittered zest to the project. By December 10, 1927, it was provisionally complete, though some composition continued through much of 1928.[9] If the new *Paolo e Virginia* was, at some level, a response to the modern school of Italian instrumental music, it was nevertheless an odd, even defiant, one, for it is bathed in a luxuriant late Romanticism and stands in an obvious line of descent from Richard Strauss's symphonic poems. Moreover, Montemezzi's initial wish was to have the premiere in the United States, in the 1928–1929 season, conducting the work himself: a plan very likely intended to impress his internationalist

---

[7] "Ma non posso tacere a Lei amico, che una così ingiusta valutazione delle forze artistiche d'Italia da parte di coloro che in gran parte ne hanno le redini, mi umiglia e mi toglie la pace." Chandler collection. The Comune of Milan unfortunately has no records pertaining to Montemezzi's telephone calls to Belloni, nor of the latter's response to the composer.

[8] In the autograph score, the adjective "sinfonico" is crossed out and substituted with "musicale," and the revised form appears in the printed score. In the original autograph sketch of the program, the title is "Poema sinfonico."

[9] In a March 1929 interview, discussed later, Montemezzi reported he had "recently" been working on the score: see r.d.r., "Montemezzi parla delle sue opere," *Il Giornale d'Italia*, March 9, 1929, p. 3.

254 SUCCEEDING PUCCINI

credentials on his Italian contemporaries, few of whom could contemplate New World premieres.[10] In the end, though, for reasons we have been unable to establish, the American premiere, for which Montemezzi wanted a fee of $1,000, fell through, and *Paolo e Virginia* made its first appearance in Italy, but not until 1930.

Casa Ricordi, which had not seen a new Montemezzi composition since 1918, was clearly impressed by *Paolo e Virginia*, judging it a work with potentially broad international appeal. They signed a contract for it in November 1928, originally agreeing to a fee of 4,000 lire, but soon afterward substituting an arrangement by which Montemezzi would receive a generous sixty percent of rental fees.[11] The published pocket-sized full score, which appeared in June 1929, designed mainly as a listening aid, includes a précis of the represented story, as well as notes on the events inserted into the score itself in four languages—Italian, English, French, and German. The précis is close to the Bernardin de Saint-Pierre novella, mercifully omitting the missionary, who had become so prominent in the abandoned libretto, as discussed in the previous chapter. The précis and notes suggest that the music is meant, to an unusual extent, to be *narrative*, and behind this surely lies the fact that Montemezzi was working with musical material connected in his mind with specific events and feelings in the story. Nevertheless, the narrative emphasis is rather contradicted by his contemporary description of the work as "an essentially lyrical musical poem, in which I believe I have lavished all the melodious nature of my soul,"[12] and this, arguably, better describes the result. *Paolo e Virginia* reveals Montemezzi's most intimate and personal inspiration, demonstrating something of the role and importance of orchestral music in his overall concept of musical creation. Indeed, the impression the "poema musicale" gives is that the symphonic form proved the most suitable medium to tell the story with the lyrical and elegiac emphasis that Montemezzi wanted.

An autograph sketch of Montemezzi's detailed program for his symphonic poem survives.[13] It includes excerpts from the Italian translation of the novella by Virginio Soncini, first published in 1822 and often reprinted. The manuscript reveals that Montemezzi originally planned to use more extended quotations, and these are still perfectly readable even

[10] Arthur Judson to George Engles, December 10, 1927. Morgan Library and Museum, New York.
[11] Casa Ricordi to Montemezzi, November 20, 1928. Archivio Storico Ricordi, Copialettere.
[12] r.d.r., "Montemezzi parla delle sue opere," p. 3.
[13] Donadelli family documents.

PAOLO E VIRGINIA AND LA NOTTE DI ZORAIMA   255

though partly crossed out in such a way that the remaining text has, in each case, been reduced to a few lines, and even a single sentence at the beginning. Initially, the quotations are connected by statements added by Montemezzi himself to summarize the story. Sometimes the quotations were altered by the composer, who was not always sure how he should modify Soncini's translation to better serve his purposes. However, after establishing the initial, lyrical situation, the peaceful, loving atmosphere on the island, Montemezzi soon abandoned the idea of quoting from the novella, choosing instead to rely on brief summarizing statements that carry the reader rapidly through the story. These are the notes included in the published score.

The program unfolds in the following stages:

1. Paolo and Virginia's happiness on Mauritius in reciprocal love; they have a simple but joyous life, secluded from the outer world (nos. 1–9).
2. The Governor announces that Virginia's aunt wants her in France. The young people's opposition is useless. Paolo protests, and Virginia tries to comfort him (nos. 10–17).
3. Virginia is far away, but Paolo still feels her presence and aura. Suddenly a ship appears, but a terrible storm erupts, and the ship is wrecked. Virginia is taken to the shore but dies in Paolo's arms. A silent procession carries her to her home; her aura, a symbol of her love for Paolo, remains even then (nos. 18–32).

There are, then, three episodes: a static one, depicting a stable situation; an intermediate and dynamic one, comparable in length, interrupting that situation; and a third, longer and more complex, covering the period from Virginia's departure to her funeral, with the dramatic events of the shipwreck and her death in between.

Paolo e Virginia demonstrates Montemezzi's effectiveness as an orchestrator and gives expression to the descriptive nature of the inspiration which had powerfully surfaced in *La nave*, the aqueous atmosphere of which is aptly exploited by the symphonic poem. Nevertheless, the soundscape incorporates little physical or naturalistic description; from the representation of the serene life of the young couple at the outset, it rather expresses the sentimental atmosphere of the story, the intimate spiritual life of the characters. Montemezzi significantly labels the only natural event in the story, the storm, a "tempesta d'anime e di elementi" (tempest of souls

256   SUCCEEDING PUCCINI

and [natural] elements).[14] His score conveys, in diatonic writing, a serene, idyllic, "prevailing" mood, and this is, arguably, the main weakness of *Paolo e Virginia*, for as Alberto Gasco later commented, "everywhere there is a feeling of slightly monotonous peace. . . . The idyll seems to continue infinitely, despite the dismal passage of Death."[15]

Paolo e Virginia begins with an E-major soundscape marked *piano*, with conjunct motion motifs entrusted to the strings (muted violas and cellos) and woodwinds, establishing the serene, loving atmosphere in which the protagonists dwell. There is a notably lyrical, albeit restrained, expressiveness in the gentle, descending melody that prevails by conjunct motion, proposed *dolce* by clarinet and bassoon, then engaging in an intimate dialogue with the violins and finally the entire orchestra (Example 8.1). The bliss is "delightfully disturbed" (says Montemezzi's textual comment) by love,[16] voiced by the melody—*piano, dolce, nostalgico*—of the muted trumpet in the new *Molto lentamente*, D-major section, immediately taken up *dolce, espressivo* by a solo violin (Example 8.2). Although in the autograph the adjective *nostalgico* has been crossed out, the calm, elegiac melody appropriately expresses the frailty and instability of happiness. It represents Virginia's aura, which will linger over the island after her departure and even after her death. As Montemezzi puts it: "her candor, her goodness, sweetness, and love remain in the island and Paolo feels all their fragrance."[17] As the idyll is interrupted, the music grows more dramatic, without, however, becoming notably clamorous or dissonant. Instead, Montemezzi provides a couple of convincing examples of sound painting: a solemn *recit* by cellos and basses (no. 10) stands for the Governor's inexorable order, and a querulous, agitated prayer—a five-way division of the first violins, *con ansia*—represents Virginia's response. Though the middle section does not offer any really interesting event, Montemezzi recovers expressive power when he depicts Virginia's absence (no. 18). The trumpet tune (later taken up by the cellos) reverts to the earlier elegiac mode, a static, delicate filigree of strings and woodwinds subtly curling the sound surface, even if nothing actually happens. When the (not very frightful) tempest is over, the spectacular shipwreck takes place, the major mode contributing to the epic rather than dramatic tone.

[14] Montemezzi, *Paolo e Virginia* (Milan: Ricordi, 1929), p. 38.
[15] Alberto Gasco, "'Paolo e Virginia' di Montemezzi all'Augusteo," *La Tribuna*, April 1, 1930, p. 3.
[16] Montemezzi, *Paolo e Virginia*, p. 4.
[17] Montemezzi, *Paolo e Virginia*, p. 32.

PAOLO E VIRGINIA AND *LA NOTTE DI ZORAIMA* 257

Music Example 8.1 *Paolo e Virginia*, no. 3, bar 5–no. 4, bar 3.

The last part of the symphonic poem includes some of the subtlest ideas in the score. Montemezzi invests the woodwinds with an almost anthropomorphic role in collecting Virginia's body and grieving over her, directly expressing Paolo's feelings and his final words to his beloved. The textual comment tells us that Paolo calls tenderly on Virginia, a desperate invocation heard first from the trumpet and then, *con dolore e commozione*, from the sorrowful oboe, sounding elegiac and exotic at the same time, backed up by the warm tide of the violins in their upper register (Example 8.3). A bell—one of Montemezzi's favorite ways of adding color—adds to the magical rather than mournful atmosphere as Virginia's body is carried to her grave (no. 31). The restrained, conjunct motion motif with which the symphonic poem had started returns (no. 32, *Lentamente come al principio*), played calmly as at the beginning by violas and cellos, then evolving into a vast, luminous sound surface as it is taken up by the full orchestra. As the violins exploit their upper register, a very euphonic, soft,

Music Example 8.2 *Paolo e Virginia*, no. 4, bar 11–no. 6, bar 11.

Music Example 8.3 *Paolo e Virginia*, no. 29, bars 2–3.

quiet apotheosis develops, suffused more with Mediterranean than tropical light (Example 8.4).

Montemezzi's musical language in *Paolo e Virginia*, strictly tonal, was without any doubt conservative by 1929. Its main reference remains the Wagnerian model, even though it is devoid of any significant chromatism. "The ecstatic finale of [Strauss's] *Death and Transfiguration* must have impressed Montemezzi in a very special way," Gasco observed, not without malice, but nonetheless appropriately.[18] What separates Montemezzi from the Wagner-Strauss model is, however, the typically Italian conciseness, equivalent to the outstanding conciseness of *L'amore dei tre re*. Overall, *Paolo e Virginia* can be judged a remarkable, although by no means innovative, addition to the twentieth-century Italian symphonic repertoire.

Perhaps encouraged by his work on the symphonic poem, it was in 1928 that Montemezzi decided to compose a prelude to Act 3 of *L'amore dei tre re*, as discussed in Chapter 4.

An important interview that Montemezzi gave in March 1929 supplies a useful guide to his feelings about his career at the end of this frustrating decade. He made it clear that however much he had enjoyed composing *Paolo e Virginia*, his overwhelming loyalty was still to opera. He expressed satisfaction with the continuing success of *L'amore dei tre re* and lamented the "injustice" of *La nave* having fallen into oblivion, before being asked about his earlier operas:

– [the interviewer asks] what news can you give us of *Giovanni Gallurese*?
– They have irreparably buried him, after a wonderful tour of very many cities, and it might even be that the cruel sentence is just; but another opera, that one forgotten too, lives all the time at the top of my heart. It is especially dear to me, and I am convinced that it will not be long before it reappears on the stage.

---

[18] Gasco, "'Paolo e Virginia,'" p. 3.

260 SUCCEEDING PUCCINI

Music Example 8.4 *Paolo e Virginia*, no. 32, bar 1–no. 4, bar 3.

PAOLO E VIRGINIA AND LA NOTTE DI ZORAIMA   261

– Which one?

– *Héllera*, with a libretto by Illica, which, after the premiere at the Regio in Turin in 1910 [*sic*], was not granted the right of appeal.

A slight veil of melancholy hovered over Montemezzi's broad forehead.[19]

Montemezzi told the interviewer he had been offered a world premiere at the Metropolitan Opera, sparking the following exchange:

– So, is the new opera already ready? What is it?

– It is ready. . . . In my thoughts and wishes. For some time, I have been cherishing the idea of setting to music *La principessa lontana* by Rostand, but now all my dreams are directed toward a beautiful and fatal woman: *La Dogaressa*. The libretto is by Giuseppe Adami, but the three acts and four scenes are not yet completely in my hands.

The *Dogaressa* project appears to have developed, in a sense, from the failure of *Paolo e Virginia*, for Montemezzi remained eager to work with Adami. In the winter of 1927–1928 he was considering a *Didone abbandonata* libretto by Adami,[20] but by the summer of 1928 had declared in favor of *La Dogaressa*, with Adami proposing to develop a plot very loosely based on the real-life story of Margherita Dalmet, or Dalmaz (1739–1817), the penultimate Dogaressa of Venice. On June 22, Montemezzi informed Casa Ricordi that *La Dogaressa* was now his first choice of subject.[21] Adami set to work more or less straight away, and the following month sent the composer a detailed outline of Act 1. There were discussions and delays, but by March 1929, Montemezzi had clearly seen a good deal of the libretto. Adami completed his work in May and the opera was formally announced the same month.[22]

The real Margherita Dalmet had been a rope dancer in Constantinople before becoming the second wife of Paolo Renier (1710–1789). Given her unsavory past, lack of nobility, and the fact that the marriage had been conducted in secret, when Renier was elected Doge in 1779, she was not officially accepted as the Dogaressa. According to Pompeo Gherardo Molmenti,

[19] r.d.r., "Montemezzi parla delle sue opere," p. 3.
[20] Casa Ricordi to Montemezzi, February 2, 1928. Archivio Storico Ricordi, Copialettere.
[21] Montemezzi to Carlo Clausetti. Archivio Storico Ricordi.
[22] A scanned version of Adami's typescript, dated May 1929, is available on the Internet Culturale website. For the first formal announcement of the forthcoming work, see *Musica d'oggi* 11 (1929): p. 142.

262 SUCCEEDING PUCCINI

Adami's most likely source for the story, things were worked out quite comfortably, however:

> Margherita adapted herself quietly to her new condition. Although Margherita did not appear at the public ceremonies, where the Dogaressa's presence was deemed necessary, and her place beside the Doge was occupied by his niece, Giustina Renier, the young wife of Marcantonio Michiel, yet all within and without the Palace called the quondam rope-dancer "Dogaressa."[23]

This was no good for an opera, so Adami, apparently fascinated by the idea of the Doge's niece sometimes standing in for his wife, devised a plot in which Margherita, jealous of Giustina (here Giustiniana) taking her place, embarks on a sudden affair with Marco Pisani, Giustiniana's lover. An improbable series of events culminates in Margherita's spectacular, public suicide, and Marco's telling the crowd that Venice is responsible for her death by refusing to accept her as the Dogaressa.

Presumably Montemezzi studied this libretto as he had studied the texts of *L'amore dei tre re* and *La nave*, but by the end of the year he had decided he could not compose it.[24] Was this a failure on his part or Adami's? The libretto lacks any sort of emotional logic. The fact that the real Margherita accepted her lot, profited richly from it, and outlived her husband by decades, brings home the very contrived nature of Adami's tragedy. The plot asks us to believe that Margherita is a devoted, selfless wife ready to absent herself when her husband is made Doge but is so piqued by jealousy when she sees his niece accompanying him to his coronation that she recklessly throws herself into an affair with another man. Could such a heroine be convincingly brought to life? Montemezzi was justified in feeling a sense of despair, and in this case it appears the libretto was never set by anyone.

Two full-length Montemezzi operas—*Paolo e Virginia* and *La Dogaressa*—had now been confidently announced to the world, and there had been much talk of a third, *La principessa lontana*, yet none of them would ever appear. The idea that he was the great new hope of Italian opera, made much of after the success of *L'amore dei tre re*, was looking increasingly hollow. This was

---

[23] W. G. Melmonti (actually Pompeo Gherardo Molmenti), *The Dogaressa*, trans. Clare Brune (London: Remington, 1887), p. 277.

[24] On December 28, 1929, Casa Ricordi wrote to Montemezzi to request the return of the libretto, acknowledging that he had opted not to compose it. Archivio Storico Ricordi, Copialettere.

PAOLO E VIRGINIA AND LA NOTTE DI ZORAIMA   263

taking a toll on Montemezzi's confidence, and in late 1928 he made a decision to prioritize the composition of a one-act opera, *La notte di Zoraima*, or, as it was originally known, *La notte di Zoraida* (the name Zoraida is found in *Don Quixote* and, notably, in Donizetti's *Zoraida di Granata*).[25] Intriguingly, Montemezzi made no mention of this opera in his March 1929 interview and appears to have initially kept it secret, perhaps because composing a one-act opera was, technically at least, in violation of his contract with Casa Ricordi. Indeed, in a notable departure from his earlier practice, he signed a contract for the opera with the publisher on December 30, 1930, only a month before its premiere, accepting a largely token fee of 15,000 lire.[26] Single-act operas were no longer fashionable, but Montemezzi may have been tempted to try one by Alfano's *Madonna Imperia*, premiered in Turin in 1927 and staged in New York the following year. Initially, he seemingly considered *La notte di Zoraima* a side project, a warm-up, a confidence-booster before launching into *La Dogaressa*, or some other larger-scale work. Such views began circulating when the new opera became public knowledge in 1930. Andrea Della Corte, at the time of the premiere, stated: "Some people think this work . . . is a sort of *loisir* [relaxation] that the composer wanted to allow himself and should not therefore be taken to represent that much hoped-for opera in which Montemezzi can be judged in his fullest and most flourishing maturity."[27] In other words, *La notte di Zoraima* was to be the prelude to the great work of Montemezzi's maturity, not the great work itself.

La notte di Zoraima has a libretto by Mario Ghisalberti (1902–1980). Born in Venice, the son of a merchant, he obtained his baccalaureate from the Liceo Foscarini, Venice, in 1920, and enrolled in the Faculty of Law at the University of Padua in 1922, though he never graduated. He began publishing poetry and journalism, and his first play, *Due piccole mani*, a one-act sentimental drama set during World War I, was premiered in Bologna on December 19, 1924, and subsequently performed in Milan, Venice, and Florence. A second play, a tragedy called *Erode*, was unsuccessfully premiered in Naples in November 1926.[28] This appears to represent the extent of Ghisalberti's theatrical works to have seen production at the time he

---

[25] The change of name/title was made very late, in October 1930. See Mario Ghisalberti to Carlo Clausetti, October 19, 1930, Archivio Storico Ricordi.

[26] Archivio Storico Ricordi.

[27] Andrea Della Corte, "'La notte di Zoraima' di Italo Montemezzi," *La Stampa*, February 1, 1931, p. 2.

[28] Information concerning Ghisalberti's early life is taken from *Poeti Novecento* (Milan: Mondadori, 1928), p. 75, supplemented with information from the archives of the University of Padua.

264 SUCCEEDING PUCCINI

began working with Montemezzi. By 1928, he had decided that he wanted to write librettos, and according to his own account, he sold a libretto entitled *Guitti* to Casa Sonzogno in December 1928, and then, the following month, was introduced to Ermanno Wolf-Ferrari, with whom he began working regularly, initially on adapting Goldoni's comedy *La vedova scaltra* into a libretto for the opera of the same title that would premiere on March 5, 1931, five weeks after *La notte di Zoraima*.[29] It appears, though, that Ghisalberti had made contact with Montemezzi even before this juncture. Fortuitously, in 2014 a postcard from Ghisalberti to his wife came on the market, in which he writes from Milan on December 2, 1928: "This morning I phoned Mont. but he has to go to church, so I'll see him after lunch. . . . <u>Mont. has already started setting to music</u>."[30] It is almost certain that "Mont." is Montemezzi, and Ghisalberti's excited comment on composition having commenced suggests the composer had only very recently accepted a libretto. Although it is not certain that this libretto was *La notte di Zoraima*, the balance of probability is very much in favor of its being so.

After Montemezzi's projects with such famous writers as Illica, Benelli, and D'Annunzio, attempted collaboration with an expert librettist like Adami, and embrace of the most up-to-date trends in Italian dramaturgy, the collaboration with Ghisalberti is, on the face of it, hard to explain. Later, after interviewing the composer, Nino Alberti reported: "When he [Montemezzi] came across Ghisalberti's libretto, he was taken by it at once and the opera was born in an atmosphere of keen enthusiasm."[31] It thus appears that Ghisalberti wrote the libretto first, then began seeking out potential composers. In an interview with Raymond Hall, Montemezzi sketched the attraction of Ghisalberti as a librettist: "a young poet, at once gifted and pliable, whose sensibilities coincide singularly with his [Montemezzi's] own, and whose conceptions he has been able to mold to his needs."[32]

The Ghisalberti postcard, if it does refer to *La notte di Zoraima*, complicates the opera's chronology, for a report later circulated that Montemezzi had started composing the new opera in the autumn of 1929.[33]

---

[29] Mario Ghisalberti, "Come nacque *La vedova scaltra*," in Ermanno Wolf-Ferrari, *La vedova scaltra* (program) (Venice: Teatro La Fenice, 2007), pp. 35–42.

[30] "Stamani ho telefonato a Mont. ma deve andare in chiesa, quindi lo vedrò dopo pranzo. . . . Mont. ha già cominciato a musicare." Chandler collection.

[31] Nino Alberti, "La Stagione Lirica dell'Eiar," *Radio Corriere*, August 2–8, 1936, p. 6.

[32] Raymond Hall, "Montemezzi's One-Act Opera," *New York Times*, January 25, 1931, p. X8.

[33] Gildo Cioli, " 'Notte di Zoraima' di Italo Montemezzi alla 'Scala,' " *Il Giornale d'Italia*, February 3, 1931, p. 3. Cioli says the opera was composed between autumn 1929 and autumn 1930, which is compatible with the one year that Montemezzi told Alberti he had spent on the score.

It may be the case that Montemezzi was inclined to distinguish preliminary work from the main period of daily composition, especially if, as seems likely, he wanted to downplay the amount of time he had invested in his "*loisir*." More consequentially, it is likely that he wanted to avoid giving the impression that he was working on *La notte di Zoraima* at a time when, officially, he was still committed to *La Dogaressa* and the terms of his 1924 contract with Casa Ricordi. In the end, in any case, however much music was composed in 1928 and 1929, much of the composition appears to have been done quite urgently. In the summer of 1930, perhaps finding conditions at home unconducive to sustained creative work, Montemezzi took off to St. Moritz for several weeks of work on the score, then proceeded to Vigasio for a prolonged stay, where, in October, he came down with sciatica, blaming this on the damp room in which he had worked in Switzerland.[34] At this juncture, Montemezzi had still not completed the opera, even though much of the score had been engraved by Ricordi and arrangements were underway to bring it out at La Scala in the following season. There were still details to sort out with Ghisalberti, too, and the final, much-corrected libretto was only submitted to Ricordi on October 23.[35] The composition appears to have been completed in early November.

La notte di Zoraima is set soon after the Spanish conquest of Peru, amidst the ruins of an Inca palace. Zoraima, the lover and promised bride of the dethroned Inca king, Muscar, lives there and is an active assistant to him in the insurgency he leads against the Spanish. Unfortunately, she is also desired by Pedrito, the captain of the Spanish, who is hunting Muscar, and who has a Spanish wife, Manuela. One day, just as Muscar is organizing an ambitious raid on a Spanish munitions convoy, and looking forward to his imminent wedding to Zoraima, he is shot and wounded by Pedrito. He manages to get to the palace, where he is followed shortly afterward by the Spaniard. Zoraima protects Muscar by offering to become Pedrito's lover if he lets his enemy escape. Pedrito, consumed by lust, agrees, but as soon as a message arrives confirming that Muscar has been safely conveyed away, Zoraima stabs herself and dies, "transfigured in a vision of happiness."[36] The story represents Ghisalberti's first crude engagement with a subject which came to obsess him: the encounter of the European and

---

[34] Montemezzi to Carlo Clausetti, October 28, 1930. Archivio Storico Ricordi.

[35] *Bollettino della Proprietà Intellettuale* (Rome: Istituto Poligrafico dello Stato, 1930), p. 1877, n. 100. The autograph libretto is in the Archivio Storico Ricordi.

[36] Italo Montemezzi, *La notte di Zoraima* (vocal score) (Milan: Ricordi, 1931), p. 149.

266   SUCCEEDING PUCCINI

non-European in the period of European expansion, especially in the Americas.[37] *La notte di Zoraima* was perhaps designed to capitalize on the contemporary fascination with the Incas prompted by Hiram Bingham's sensational discoveries of the "lost" Inca cities of Machu Picchu and Vitcos in 1911. Bingham himself became convinced that Machu Picchu was Vilcabamba, the last stronghold of the Incas, the base from which they maintained a guerrilla war against the Spaniards—a theory which may, loosely, have inspired Ghisalberti.

Montemezzi claimed that his attraction to the story was "because it contains dramatic elements used in operas of every period. These elements are fundamental, clear, obvious and accessible to all."[38] There is an element of preemptive defense about the claim, an *excusatio non petita*. Ghisalberti offered a careful unification of time and place and fluid, swift-moving drama: after the failure of *Paolo e Virginia*, this may have been enough to excite the composer's interest. But the whole concept of the opera is remarkably backward-looking, with dramatic elements comparable to those in *Il trovatore*. Moreover, there is a vulgarity in the libretto that one would hardly expect Montemezzi to endorse: consider the low-level insults—"bagascia" (whore) and "serpe schifosa" (disgusting snake)—with which the Spanish crowd addresses Zoraima. It is possible, though, to understand *La notte di Zoraima* as designed to gently make both artistic and political points. The supposed timelessness of the "dramatic elements" may have been intended as a deliberate riposte to the more experimental tendencies in 1920s opera. And while *Giovanni Gallurese*, *L'amore dei tre re*, and *La nave* all represented Italy as the victim of foreign aggression, *La notte di Zoraima* endorses armed resistance to European colonization. It is difficult to know how far to push the political argument, given that neither Montemezzi nor his critics mentioned any analogies to contemporary concerns. But—to mention just the most obvious—it is worth noting that Omar al-Mukhtar (1858–1931), who had been leading a guerrilla war against the Italian occupation of Libya for years, scored one of his most notable successes on March 28, 1927, ambushing the Italian Seventh Libyan Battalion and killing more than 300 soldiers. Whether or not Ghisalberti or Montemezzi consciously understood their opera as a response to such events, there is no doubt that *La notte di Zoraima*

---

[37] Ghisalberti's three major novels, *Le sette città* (1941), concerning the search for El Dorado, *L'oro e la croce* (1944; published in English as *Christopher Columbus*, 1949), and *I pesci volanti* (1948), all deal with colonial encounters.

[38] Quoted in Hall, "Montemezzi's One-Act Opera," p. X8.

Music Example 8.5 *La notte di Zoraima*, bars 1–4.

is a long way from the heady nationalism of *La nave*, as all Montemezzi's 1920s projects were.

Despite the old-fashioned clumsiness of the libretto, and the limited scope for characterization, Montemezzi, as always, was able to support the action with effective orchestral writing, and it is here that the value of the opera is most apparent. He told Hall that "there are moments of true symphonic treatment in the score."[39] This is evident immediately, the first scene being intelligently constructed through the intertwining of two symphonic motifs. The first (Example 8.5), characterizing the miniature 6-bar prelude before the curtain rises, consists of a galloping motif, sharing the same function as the obsessive horse-riding motif introduced at the beginning of *L'amore dei tre re*, in connection with Archibaldo (Example 4.5). The second, following immediately as an ascending line in 6/8 meter and *più lento*, reveals its meaning as a flight motif in its association with the words "Non potranno inseguirci . . . / Avremo tempo di guadagnar la montagna" (They cannot pursue us . . . / We'll have time to reach the mountains) (Example 8.6).[40] The horse-riding motif takes on a major role as Zoraima hides behind a wall and the Spanish convoy approaches; meanwhile, an offstage tenor voice sings in large note values, doubled by an English horn.

---

[39] Quoted in Hall, "Montemezzi's One-Act Opera," p. X8.
[40] Montemezzi, *La notte di Zoraima*, pp. 2–3.

268 SUCCEEDING PUCCINI

Music Example 8.6 *La notte di Zoraima*, bars 13–17.

PAOLO E VIRGINIA AND LA NOTTE DI ZORAIMA 269

However, Montemezzi's intelligent use of the orchestra is demonstrated best in his plan of punctuating and articulating the action with miniature symphonic interludes. There are no less than seven of these. The first (nos. 6–7) occurs after Zoraima urgently dispatches Lyoval to alert Muscar to Pedrito's plans. She is briefly alone on stage, then is joined by the insurgents, whom she orders to hide. Before her dialogue with them starts, the orchestra simulates a frenetic horse ride with successive waves of *crescendo*. As she hides with the insurgents, the aforementioned tenor voice is heard vocalizing offstage. Just a few minutes into the opera, the orchestra here first creates an atmosphere of high tension, then, combined with the tenor singing a plain, stepwise melody, lyrically intensifies the dreamlike sense of suspense and expectation accompanying the preparation for the attack on the Spanish convoy, Montemezzi carefully varying the orchestral writing.[41] The second symphonic interlude (nos. 10–12) occurs as the insurgents depart to attack the convoy, leaving Zoraima alone in romantic moonlight. This lengthy interlude importantly prepares us for her first reunion with Muscar. A broad melodic sweep grows in the orchestra, led by the *piano espressivo* melody of the violins, translating Zoraima's growing apprehension into the increasingly poignant musical invention immediately preceding Muscar's abrupt appearance.[42] In the third symphonic page (no. 19), just a miniature 7-bar episode, Muscar and Zoraima "gaze into each other's eyes in infinite tenderness, clasped in an embrace," at the zenith of their love duet.[43] Montemezzi prescribes divided second violins and in the full score explicitly states "espressivo il canto delle viole" and "espressivo il canto dei celli": in other words, both violas and cellos should sing rather than play their parts, expressing the color of ecstatic love.[44]

Later, the fifth, brief interlude (no. 31) offers a potent surprise effect. Left alone again, the moon now veiled by cloud, Zoraima worries that Muscar will be killed. The orchestra, heard for the first time in its full capacity, starts a monumental *crescendo* in solemn and heavy *Largamente*, punctuated by constant and frequent accents, making the audience aware of Zoraima's gloomy thoughts, and creating an appropriate atmosphere for the arrival of the badly wounded Muscar.[45] The seventh and final orchestral episode,

[41] Montemezzi, *La notte di Zoraima*, pp. 15–17.
[42] Montemezzi, *La notte di Zoraima*, pp. 25–29.
[43] Montemezzi, *La notte di Zoraima*, p. 43.
[44] Montemezzi, *La notte di Zoraima*, manuscript full score, Archivio Storico Ricordi, p. 120.
[45] Montemezzi, *La notte di Zoraima*, p. 72.

270 SUCCEEDING PUCCINI

occurring much later (no. 55), acts as a crucial divide between the busy, violent scene with the Spanish crowd and the following one, when Pedrito is left alone with Zoraima. The crowd is urging Pedrito to find and kill Muscar (hidden by Zoraima), and as he authoritatively orders them to leave, the orchestra covers their departure. Although clearly ordinary stage music, the creeping of the bassoons, violas, cellos, and basses on the constant, haunting sound of the cymbals effectively conveys the lingering tension, building a bridge between the danger of the bloodthirsty crowd which has just been averted and the approaching climactic confrontation between Pedrito and Zoraima.[46]

Montemezzi is, more generally, very precise in his orchestral commentary. There are many examples, only a few of which need detailing here. At the outset of the cautious meeting between Zoraima and Muscar (no. 12), a sweet oboe melody lingers on the background of muted horns and string tremolo. As Manuela reluctantly approaches the palace, a solo oboe announces her presence with an evocative, triadic melody in the upper register (no. 25), and a varied, longer version of it subsequently accompanies her anguished appeal, thus firmly associating her character with the oboe's melancholic sound. Again, as Manuela recalls a lullaby she sings to her baby, a beautiful, extended viola solo labeled *espressivo amoroso* is heard (no. 29).[47] The best example, though, is possibly the sophisticated thread supporting Zoraima's seductive proposal to Pedrito as she exults in the inebriation caused by her lips and the stupor resulting from her caresses (no. 57). Introduced by flute arabesques, Zoraima's siren song flows on the background of muted strings until cellos and basses start playing *pizzicato* against muted second violins and violas, as Pedrito realizes he is unable to resist Zoraima's appeal. This moment, with its sophisticated timbres, resurrecting the sensual atmosphere of *La nave*, finally moves a significant step forward from the traditional Leonora of *Il trovatore* (Example 8.7). Zoraima enhances her seduction with the promise of taking Pedrito up to the mountains, her caressing voice supported by the lyrical commentary of solo violin and clarinet creating an atmosphere of pure bliss, the "gioia dolcissima" (sweetest joy) she promises.[48] It is possibly only here that Zoraima acquires a convincing stature, briefly allowing her to stand alongside Fiora and, more especially, Basiliola.

---

[46] Montemezzi, *La notte di Zoraima*, pp. 110–112.
[47] Montemezzi, *La notte di Zoraima*, p. 59.
[48] Montemezzi, *La notte di Zoraima*, p. 135.

As we would expect, Montemezzi employs the full orchestra for great emotional tides, for example when Muscar urges Zoraima to assist him in freeing his country, or when she declares that her happiness depends on him. On occasion, Montemezzi plays effectively with the sharp dynamic

Music Example 8.7 *La notte di Zoraima*, no. 57, bars 1–17.

272   SUCCEEDING PUCCINI

Music Example 8.7 Continued

contrast between grand symphonic gestures from the full orchestra and chamber sonorities. This notably happens in the confrontation between Pedrito and Zoraima (no. 46), where the full orchestra mimics *fortissimo* the Spaniard's aggressiveness, while Zoraima's calm self-control is expressed in the dwindling of the orchestra to just strings and horns. However, the most effective employment of dynamic contrast occurs at the very end of the opera (no. 72). As the dying Zoraima utters her last words, beginning "Ah! Gioia suprema!," the full orchestra sustains in *fortissimo* her exalted state, "transfigured in a vision of happiness," but her significant statement "Muscar è in salvo" (Muscar is safe), clarifying her deepest motivation, is accompanied by just a solo violin and strings *piano espressivo* (Example 8.8).[49]

Montemezzi was clearly very happy with the opportunities Ghisalberti afforded him to embed the chorus in the dramatic action, asserting that the choral element was particularly important, and that the librettist, understanding this, had adapted the libretto appropriately.[50] He explained: "In the treatment of the choral parts, I have followed the line of my last opera, 'La Nave,' in which the chorus functions as a personage in the drama and as an integral part of the dramatic economy."[51] The male chorus of insurgents appears at the outset of the opera in dialogue with Zoraima, delivering a series of rapid, lively replies, mostly in quavers. This is actually a rather brief appearance and precedes a long stretch of traditional, solo-centered scenes. The most consequential choral episode comes with the abrupt, violent arrival of the Spanish crowd with their prisoner, a crowd Ghisalberti describes as "the desperate, picturesque crowd that Spain sent to its new colonies, following the *conquistadors*: jailbirds, dubious women, adventurers of all sorts."[52] Here there is totally different writing for a mixed-voice choir: generally homophonic, it nevertheless exploits the different voices responding to Pedrito and makes moderate use of shouting, the notation *gridando* (shouting) used several times to stress the rough character of this disreputable group. This very effective scene includes threats and insults hurled at Zoraima, the questioning of the insurgent prisoner, and finally Zoraima's appeal to Pedrito, superimposed over that of the crowd (Figure 8.1). At this point, the clash between the crowd and Pedrito reaches its climax, the

[49] Montemezzi, *La notte di Zoraima*, p. 149.
[50] "La Musica," *Giovedì: Settimanale di letteratura teatro arte e informazioni mondiali*, October 30, 1930, p. 11.
[51] Hall, "Montemezzi's One-Act Opera," p. X8.
[52] Montemezzi, *La notte di Zoraima*, p. 95.

Music Example 8.8 *La notte di Zoraima*, no. 72, bars 1–8.

Music Example 8.8 Continued

Figure 8.1 The crowd scene in *La notte di Zoraima*, Metropolitan Opera House, 1931. *Metropolitan Opera Archives.*

latter swearing he will personally take responsibility for the prisoner and Zoraima, thus convincing the crowd to leave (Example 8.9). After this dramatic highpoint, one of the most effective and appropriate choral episodes Montemezzi ever composed, the chorus is not heard again until the final scene. As soon as Zoraima stabs herself, the screams of the crowd concerning the forest's having caught fire are heard offstage. The screams get louder as the crowd breaks onto the stage, precipitating a short, final dialogue with

Music Example 8.9 *La notte di Zoraima*, no. 54, bar 9–no. 55, bar 14.

Music Example 8.9 Continued

Pedrito which allows a powerful contrast between the harsh, homophonic cries from the chorus and Zoraima's dying words, addressed to Muscar, as she sings "transfigured." When completing work on the score, Montemezzi claimed: "It's a very effective finale: it ends the opera magnificently."[53]

The vocal score of *La notte di Zoraima*, published in 1931, reproduced a handwritten inscription: "A mio figlio Marco."

While work continued on *La notte di Zoraima*, the premiere of *Paolo e Virginia* took place at the Augusteo Concert Hall, Rome, on March 30, 1930: the first premiere of a wholly new Montemezzi composition since 1918. The conductor was Bernardino Molinari. The critics were reasonably positive, without being enthusiastic. The sweetly lyrical nature of the work and the nobility of its organic symphonic architecture were praised, and critics opposed to modernism welcomed its defiant rejection of the postwar musical developments they disliked. The audience, who also heard works by Paisiello, Schubert, and Lorenzo Perosi on this occasion, was reported as responding with "exceptional warmth."[54] Montemezzi had reasons to feel satisfied, but *Paolo e Virginia* did not establish itself as a standard concert work, and he himself did little to promote it in later years. Its next appearance appears to have been in a concert at the Teatro La Fenice, Venice, on May 9, 1930, and it featured in a La Scala concert on May 13, 1931.

Another 1930 event worth documenting is Montemezzi's first visit to Britain in the summer, to coincide with a revival of *L'amore dei tre re* at Covent Garden. It was one of a series of visits to European capitals to promote interest in his masterwork. In 1925 he and Katherine had been to Paris for the lavish revival with Mary Garden as Fiora, and in 1928 he was in Berlin for a revival that, less successful, still saw him applauded on

---

[53] "È un finale di grande effetto: chiude l'opera magnificamente." Montemezzi to Carlo Clausetti, October 28, 1930. Archivio Storico Ricordi.
[54] Gasco, "'Paolo e Virginia,'" p. 3.

278 SUCCEEDING PUCCINI

a German stage. Over the years, Katherine would later recall, "she and her husband visited practically every capital of Europe to witness performances of 'The Love of Three Kings.'"[55] The London visit is the best documented. Rosa Ponselle, the reigning queen of the Met, was singing Fiora and it was the first time Montemezzi heard her in the role. The critical reaction showed the old transatlantic rivalries still very much in place. "The revival of *L'Amore dei tre re* now would be surprising . . . but for the fact that it has . . . gained some acceptance in America," sniffed *The Times*.[56] Ernest Newman—who had trashed *Giovanni Gallurese* in 1925—was the most distinguished critic to review the production; he judged that "[t]here is hardly a single page of his [Montemezzi's] score that, as music, is fit to line Puccini's or the early Verdi's waste-paper basket; but almost all of it 'comes off' on the stage."[57] But "R. H. I." in the *Daily Telegraph* was more generous: "He [Montemezzi] was much more refined than either Leoncavallo or Mascagni; his music . . . has a sense of poetry which the others lacked, and take it all in all it gives a greater pleasure in the hearing."[58] There was plenty of applause and Montemezzi was emboldened to send a telegram to Mussolini, reporting a "triumphant out-come."[59] A check was made as to whether the composer was accurate in his assessment, and congratulations were then returned. The popular novelist Ida Cook (1904–1986), a great opera-lover, wrote two decades later of how "[t]hat [1930] season ended with what I have always regarded as one of the half-dozen supreme performances I have been privileged to hear: *L'Amore dei Tre Re* with Ponselle and Pinza, absolutely at the top of their form."[60] Cook was so impressed by Montemezzi's opera that she made it a significant plot element in her late novel, *Remembered Serenade* (1975).

The Montemezzis apparently did not attend that second performance on July 4, and this may be because Covent Garden had arranged with the BBC for Act 3 to be given a live broadcast. It is tempting to imagine them sitting by a radio in their hotel, or the home of some acquaintance, listening to the program. They stayed in London for a few weeks and on July 12 were among the guests of honor at a lavish dinner staged by Ponselle at the Savoy Hotel. The courses were all named after one of the diners and included Poularde

[55] Norman Frisch, "Widow Loved Montemezzi and His Operas," *Daily News* (Los Angeles), October 19, 1952, p. 28.
[56] "Covent Garden Opera," *The Times*, July 1, 1930, p. 14.
[57] Ernest Newman, "The Week's Music," *Sunday Times*, July 6, 1930, p. 7.
[58] R. H. I., "Pre-War Opera Revived," *Daily Telegraph*, July 1, 1930, p. 8.
[59] Nicolodi, *Musica e Musicisti*, p. 415.
[60] Ida Cook, *We Followed Our Stars* (London: Hamish Hamilton, 1950), p. 50.

PAOLO E VIRGINIA AND LA NOTTE DI ZORAIMA   279

Montemezzi and Coeur Flottant Ponselle.[61] Undoubtedly the Montemezzis enjoyed many such dinners in expensive restaurants in the presence of operatic dignitaries and titled people, but this one stands out in that we can be sure where they were, who they were with, and what they were eating on a particular evening. Montemezzi almost certainly talked to his host about her singing Zoraima: which she did, the following year, in New York.

La notte di Zoraima received its premiere at La Scala on January 31, 1931— Montemezzi's only opera set in the Americas thus appearing almost exactly twenty years after Puccini's only opera set in the Americas, as noted in our Introduction. The title role was sung by Giuseppina Cobelli (1898–1948), Manuela by the young Maria Caniglia (1905–79), Pedrito by Carmelo Maugeri (1889–1986), and Muscar by Paolo Marion (1895–1962), and the production was directed by Mario Frigerio. De Sabata, appointed principal conductor at La Scala the previous year, was scheduled to conduct, but Montemezzi stepped in at a week's notice and took the opportunity to launch the work.[62] This unexpected change meant programs and librettos had to be corrected with pasted errata slips, but a poster was printed with the composer's name in place (Figure 8.2). Montemezzi "appeared on his rostrum at exactly 9 o'clock [and] was greeted by unanimous applause."[63] The critics agreed that the audience responded very favorably to the new opera. Gaetano Cesari, in the *Corriere della Sera*, recorded that the "success was affirmed by the nine curtain calls that followed the performance of the opera. Montemezzi appeared on stage seven times surrounded by the artists and also together with the librettist Ghisalberti and maestro [Vittore] Veneziani [the chorus master]. However, the loudest ovation was directed to him when he appeared on stage alone."[64] This was doubtless all very gratifying, but certain allowances need to be made: there were many friends of the Montemezzis in the audience; a well-known opera composer was being welcomed back to the stage after over a decade of "silence" (as several critics put it); and at a time when opera seemed set on a course ever more remote from popular culture, *La notte di Zoraima* was, as Montemezzi had predicted, easy to follow and enjoy. Cesari emphasized the accessibility of the work and felt the audience was expressing "the pleasure they derived from listening to the musician's

[61] A copy of the menu, signed by all the diners, is in the Chandler collection.
[62] Raymond Hall, "Latest Montemezzi Opera," *New York Times*, May 3, 1931, p. X8.
[63] Della Corte, "'La notte di Zoraima,'" p. 2.
[64] Gaetano Cesari, "'La notte di Zoraima' di Italo Montemezzi alla Scala," *Corriere della Sera*, February 1, 1931, p. 5.

Figure 8.2 Poster for *La notte di Zoraima*, La Scala, 1931. *Archivio Storico Teatro alla Scala.*

PAOLO E VIRGINIA AND LA NOTTE DI ZORAIMA   281

plain and flowing melodic discourse, without having had the need to impose on themselves any efforts for reflection or comprehension."[65]

The critics were generally friendly. *Il Popolo d'Italia*, the Fascist Party paper, judged that "the lyrical accent of *La notte di Zoraima* has its own particular way of proceeding that impresses a distinct character on the work, to which it gives a pace that's never vulgar, but always interesting and lofty." The critic found "lyrical inspiration" and "pages of keen musical interest."[66] Cesari was notably more positive than he had been about *La nave* in 1918, tracing the influence of *Aida* in the scene between Zoraima and Manuela, though also suggesting that the opera offered nothing new. He found the libretto old-fashioned, as did Della Corte in *La Stampa*, who also found it "dense and entangled" with insufficient characterization and atmosphere. But Della Corte had warm words of praise for the music:

> Montemezzi . . . is a wonderful symphonist, as he proved again tonight. It is well known how Montemezzi's musical conception derives, in some aspects, from Wagner's, and this score is again a proof of the fact. However, the author of *La nave* possesses his own structure and his own personality that come out especially in the *recitativos*. It still means, too, that his melody is inspired, spontaneous, and worthy, although it draws more on feelings than on color.[67]

Adriano Lualdi, in *Emporium*, was still more scathing about the libretto ("a string of rattletraps from the oldest melodramatic arsenal"), and, like other critics, he emphasized that Montemezzi had not changed his style, despite the exotic setting—and he thought the style was old-fashioned. Nevertheless, he was mostly positive about the music:

> the music of this opera has the great merit of clearness and theatricality that manifests itself not only in the variety and frankness of attitudes but also in the sense of economy that avoids all lengthiness and manages to hold the listeners' attention all the time. Other merits are its melodic character with many a fine page which can be pointed out, a few moments of deeply heartfelt and expressed *declamato*, and, above all, the care the composer took all

---

[65] Cesari, "'La notte di Zoraima,'" p. 5.
[66] g. s., "'La Notte di Zoraima' di Italo Montemezzi," *Il Popolo d'Italia*, February 1, 1931, p. 2.
[67] Della Corte, "'La notte di Zoraima,'" p. 2.

282   SUCCEEDING PUCCINI

the time in keeping the orchestral sonorities in the background, this way leaving the stage fully in the foreground. This, if I am not mistaken, is an achievement, compared with previous operas.[68]

Casella summed up the general feeling when he stated that *La notte di Zoraima* "obtained a good success . . . but adds nothing to the *Amore dei tre re* of the same composer."[69] Gildo Cioli agreed, but concluded, more positively, that Montemezzi had "valiantly defended the high place he [had already] conquered."[70]

After the second performance, on February 5, Montemezzi wrote of the "splendid outcome" to Mussolini, representing it as a vindication of his artistic creed, and assuring the dictator he was "doing as much as I can to propagandize the necessity of giving melody the place of honor it deserves."[71] Any assessment of Montemezzi's Italian career is faced with the apparent paradox that *La notte di Zoraima* was greeted more warmly by critics in 1931 than *La nave* had been greeted in 1918; but there was a difference hardly flattering to the composer. The critics had recognized *La nave* as a major work with which they found several faults; *La notte di Zoraima* seemed, by contrast, a comparatively unimportant but (libretto apart) generally praiseworthy opera.

The international premiere of *La notte di Zoraima* took place not in the United States, as might have been expected, but at the Royal Swedish Opera, where five performances were given between October 16, 1931, and January 13, 1932, oddly programmed alongside De Falla's ballet, *The Three-Cornered Hat.* A young Jussi Björling (1911–1960) sang the offstage Voice. Though *L'amore dei tre re* had proved successful in Sweden in 1927, the appearance of *La notte di Zoraima* there is a little hard to explain, and we speculate it may have had something to do with Ghisalberti's wife, Marguerite Pyhlson, being the daughter of a wealthy Swedish businessman, Karl Pyhlson (1860–1933). Ghisalberti was certainly active in promoting performances abroad.[72] The new opera attracted plenty of press attention, but the Swedish critics were

---

[68] Adriano Lualdi, "2 Febbraio: 'La Notte di Zoraima' di I. Montemezzi alla Scala," *Emporium* 73 (May 1931): p. 313.

[69] Alfredo Casella, "La Musica in Italia nel 1931," *L'Almanacco degli Artisti 1932* (Rome: Laziale, 1932), p. 84.

[70] Cioli, "'Notte di Zoraima,'" p. 3.

[71] Nicolodi, *Musica e Musicisti*, p. 417.

[72] See Mario Ghisalberti to Casa Ricordi, August 21, 1931, Archivio Storico Ricordi. This letter, concerning efforts to promote the opera in the German-speaking lands, notes, remarkably, that copies of the libretto and score had been sent to the very young Herbert von Karajan.

PAOLO E VIRGINIA AND LA NOTTE DI ZORAIMA 283

not very positive in their assessments: they condemned the libretto as commonplace, and though they praised the quality of Montemezzi's score, they found the opera so intense and heavily orchestrated that the singers seemed continually struggling to be heard.[73] Montemezzi was very interested in the Swedish response, obtaining copies of some of the reviews and drawing up summaries of two of them.[74]

But it was in New York, not Stockholm, that the fate of *La notte di Zoraima* was decided. The Metropolitan Opera put on four performances in New York and one in Philadelphia between December 2, 1931, and January 12, 1932, with Ponselle in the title role and Serafin conducting. By all accounts, there was nothing wrong with the production itself, and Ponselle was very good: it was the opera that was faulted. Of the major American critics who reviewed the production, only A. Walter Kramer gave the opera a wholly positive notice, even finding praise for the libretto:

> "La Notte di Zoraima," a setting of a well contrived libretto by Mario Ghisalberti, has much to recommend it. It is genuine music of the stage, music that fits the action, that has a true dramatic stripe, that can boast a spontaneous lyricism in a day when younger and less gifted men prefer rather to decry melodic naturalness than to write it,— assuming that they can![75]

Kramer found "an exceptional aristocracy in Montemezzi's musical speech . . . a big sweep in his climaxes, a romantic glamor, a terribly sincere feeling through it all, which ought to give it a place among the few one-act operas that remain in the repertoire."[76]

No other critic of importance came close to such a verdict. Deems Taylor, the next most friendly, heard "flowing, melodious music, direct, almost naive in its appeal, simply harmonized, grateful to the voice, distinguished by a sincerity and intellectual honesty that keeps its simplicity and tunefulness from any suspicion of cheapness. It is well and discreetly orchestrated." But he judged the story "hackneyed" and "old-fashioned," the characters "two-dimensional puppets."[77] Other critics found the libretto hopeless, the score

---

[73] The Royal Swedish Opera Archive contains a collection of press cuttings.

[74] Donadelli family documents.

[75] A. Walter Kramer, "Montemezzi Opera Is Given Premiere at Metropolitan," *Musical America*, December 10, 1931, p. 3.

[76] Kramer, "Montemezzi Opera," p. 5.

[77] Deems Taylor, "Taylor Reviews New Opera at the Metropolitan," *New York American*, December 3, 1931, p. 13 (later editions).

284 SUCCEEDING PUCCINI

a pale imitation of *L'amore dei tre re*. Lawrence Gilman memorably captured the general feeling when he wrote that "Montemezzi has disclosed no fresh enkindlement, from without or from within; he has merely warmed over yesterday's considerably diminished sustenance."[78]

A poignant sense of disappointment breathes through many of the New York reviews. These were critics who, for the most part, considered *L'amore dei tre re* one of the greatest operas of the century and who had waited a long time for a successor, having missed *La nave*. The disappointment may explain why negative judgments seem to have intensified over time. Herbert F. Peyser had missed the performances, as he was in Europe, but on his return heard "appalling things about it [*Zoraima*], uttered with truculence and heat."[79] When Ponselle was, later in life, asked to inscribe her thoughts of various operas on a stack of programs, she simply wrote "No!" on that of *La notte di Zoraima*. Yet she considered *L'amore dei tre re* "unquestionably a masterwork... Fiora was one of my favorite roles."[80]

By the time the American verdict on *La notte di Zoraima* had been delivered, La Scala had made the decision to repeat their production in the 1931–1932 season, and it received four more performances, this time with Vincenzo Guicciardi as Pedrito. But here its stage career in Italy came to an end, though the Teatro Reale in Rome at least talked of the possibility of a production.[81] Given that Montemezzi's American triumphs were well known in Italy, it was doubtless a blow to Italian pride that this opera, acclaimed in Milan, had been so curtly dismissed in New York. After 1931, in any case, *La notte di Zoraima* was neither a new work nor an established classic, and like so many operas in that category it fell by the wayside. It is worth noting, though, that as late as 1978, Maria Caniglia, the first Manuela, and later an admired Fiora, expressed astonishment at this: "Oddly, this opera, which was so enthusiastically received that it was repeated the following season by popular demand, has disappeared, like the other very valid Montemezzi work *Giovanni Gallurese*.... These are the insurmountable mysteries of this world."[82]

---

[78] Lawrence Gilman, "Montemezzi's New Opera, 'La Notte di Zoraima,' Given at the Metropolitan," *New York Herald Tribune*, December 3, 1931, p. 20.

[79] Herbert F. Peyser, "An Appreciation of L'Amore dei Tre Re," *Musical America*, February 1949, p. 14.

[80] Rosa Ponselle and James A. Drake, *Ponselle: A Singer's Life* (New York: Doubleday, 1982), pp. 239, 125.

[81] Nicolodi, *Musica e Musicisti*, p. 419, n. 19.

[82] Quoted in Lanfranco Rasponi, *The Last Prima Donnas* (New York: Knopf, 1982), p. 237.

Katherine made a ten-week trip to the United States to take in the performances of *La notte di Zoraima*. She had a second purpose, too: the law having changed, she now undertook the necessary steps to regain U.S. citizenship. This would have significant consequences for the family later in the decade. Montemezzi, however, stayed in Italy. He had a notable excuse: his cousin Renato Donadelli, who as a young man had served in D'Annunzio's army in Fiume, had become a celebrated aviator. He was part of Italo Balbo's historic flight of twelve seaplanes and fifty men across the Southern Atlantic from Orbetello to Rio de Janeiro between December 17, 1930, and January 15, 1931, which made headlines worldwide. Renato then stayed in Brazil for a year, working for the Italian government, and when he finally returned to Vigasio in January 1932, a special ceremony and presentation were held in which Montemezzi took a prominent role.[83]

Balbo was minister for the Air Force and a leading figure in the Fascist hierarchy, meaning that Renato was not only an embodiment of the "set sail toward the World" spirit of *La nave*, but just two telephone calls away from Mussolini, at a time when proximity to the dictator carried enormous weight. These facts must have given Montemezzi plenty to think about, for he was now cultivating the support of the Fascist authorities. As noted in the previous chapter, he was campaigning for a revival of *La nave* at La Scala in 1926, and the following year lobbying the mayor of Milan about being neglected by those who "hold the reins." The campaign at La Scala continued, and on July 5, 1928, when he was on an extended holiday at Le Touquet, the theatre sent him a somewhat exasperated letter, referring to "the many verbal and written discussions of the previous years" regarding *La nave*.[84] Perhaps recognition that he was getting nowhere in Milan led Montemezzi to shift his goal to the Teatro Reale dell'Opera in Rome, opened on February 28, 1928, as a showpiece national opera house (a grand Fascist project which had seen the old Teatro Costanzi transformed almost beyond recognition). Around June 1928 he approached Giuseppe Belluzzo, the minister of National Economy, with a request for support, and Belluzzo then wrote to the Teatro Reale, but without achieving anything.[85] After digesting this failure, Montemezzi aimed still higher and on March 26, 1930, sent copies of *La nave* and *Paolo e Virginia* to Mussolini, with a request for an audience; he

[83] Pierpaolo Brugnoli and Bruno Chiappa (eds.), *Vigasio: Vicende di una comunità e di un territorio* (Vigasio: Comune di Vigasio, 2005), p. 306.
[84] "le molte discussioni verbali e scritte degli anni scorsi." La Scala archives. The letter is not signed.
[85] Nicolodi, *Musica e Musicisti*, pp. 412–13.

286   SUCCEEDING PUCCINI

then met the Duce on March 29.[86] He presumably made a strong case for the importance of *La nave*, and given his knowledge of the man he was talking to, probably put considerable emphasis on the patriotism and politics of the opera. Montemezzi later reported that Mussolini had been "very surprised" (*ben sorpreso*) to learn that La Scala had never revived *La nave*, possibly suggesting that he had witnessed a performance in 1918.[87] Mussolini was convinced by Montemezzi's application, or at least sufficiently convinced to promise to help. The Fascist bureaucracy took up the case, the governor of Rome, Francesco Boncompagni Ludovisi, was applied to, and he passed the matter to his deputy, Paolo d'Ancora, who headed the committee which ran the Teatro Reale. The response from the theatre committee was not encouraging, however, and the message got passed back up the chain that the opera was considered "very expensive [to produce]—but heavy and not well received." Any performance was likely to "represent a sure and unjustified loss."[88]

Montemezzi responded to this rebuff with a long, pleading letter to Mussolini of July 18, 1930, clearly written soon after his return from London, representing the decision as part of a general culture discouraging new operas, and passionately urging the claims of *La nave*:

> *La Nave* ... is my major work.
>
> I insist: my major work. I shout it to the rooftops so that I may be heard.
>
> I would really like to be understood before I die! I'm shouting because in the artist's creed, which considers art from the point of view of beauty and beauty alone, I'm sure I deserve that my *Nave* be looked upon in good faith.
>
> It was composed at a moment when everyone was looking to the other side of the Adriatic, with eyes full of tears and hope, and a heart swollen with sublime love. It was my greatest dream: to provide Italy with an opera solely and characteristically Italian which had no precedent, such as to be a modest contribution from a faithful and doting artist.[89]

Given the consensus of Italian critics that *La nave* was particularly Germanic in its musical language, it is revealingly odd that Montemezzi should call it "solely and characteristically Italian," and his assertion of the claims of "pure"

[86] Nicolodi, *Musica e Musicisti*, p. 413 and n. 5.
[87] Letter to Tito Ricordi, September 18, 1931. Chandler collection.
[88] Nicolodi, *Musica e Musicisti*, pp. 414–15.
[89] Nicolodi, *Musica e Musicisti*, p. 416.

beauty sits awkwardly beside the emphasis on the opera's patriotic significance. By now, however, it appears he was prepared to make almost any claim for the opera to help secure a revival. He had "other operas" that had been unfairly neglected too, he noted, but he did not want to name them as that might risk distracting attention from *La nave*.

A powerful irony of Montemezzi's career at this juncture is that though *La notte di Zoraima* represented a very definite break with the nationalist themes of his earlier operas, his passionate desire to see *La nave* revived on a major stage, and growing belief that this would only happen with government support, led him to increasingly emphasize its political dimension. In the summer of 1930, Montemezzi came up with the idea that a revival of *La nave* would be a particularly apt way of celebrating the tenth anniversary of the Fascist takeover of Italy—the so-called March on Rome of October 1922. He put the idea to Mussolini in a letter of September 11, 1930: "no other opera can be more suitable . . . to exalt the power of our race. And no other moment could be more opportune than the tenth anniversary of fascism."[90] Over the following year, Montemezzi was able to discuss the idea with Arnaldo Mussolini (1885–1931), Mussolini's brother and closest advisor, and found him eager to help. Arnaldo was promising to take up the case with Jenner Mataloni (1898–1968), the president of the Province of Milan, who would become general manager of La Scala in 1932. Montemezzi had also secured the support of Marcello Visconti di Modrone (1898–1964), the mayor of Milan.[91] All this presupposed a La Scala revival, of course, and it appears Montemezzi now thought he had a better chance there than at the Teatro Reale. In part this was because Tito Ricordi, after many years of retirement in Paris, had unexpectedly joined the board of La Scala in September 1931. Montemezzi had a number of conversations with Tito, who promised to recommend *La nave* for the 1932–1933 season, in accordance with "the tenth anniversary of fascism" plan. It appears there was a real chance of a revival at this point, but Arnaldo's unexpected death on December 21, 1931, and Tito's ill health the following year removed two key allies, and in the end nothing was achieved.

Montemezzi's lobbying and the scraping tone in which he sought the favor of Mussolini and other powerful people need to be judged in context. By the late 1920s, most Italian composers recognized that the only way they could

---

[90] Nicolodi, *Musica e Musicisti*, p. 418.
[91] Montemezzi to Tito Ricordi, September 18, 1931.

288   SUCCEEDING PUCCINI

advance their careers was by working within the mechanisms provided by the regime, and those mechanisms were oiled by sycophancy. Montemezzi, to his credit perhaps, though in a privileged position because of his wealth, maintained a considerably greater distance from the regime than most of his rivals and, unlike many of them, did not join the Fascist Party, dedicate any works to Mussolini, or compose anything celebrating or endorsing Fascist achievements and ambitions. In fact, it would soon become clear, he quietly harbored distinctly anti-regime views.

An odd comment on Montemezzi's musical ambitions at this time is that in the summer of 1932 he published a brief *Elegia* for cello and piano with Casa Ricordi.[92] His motivation for composing this work, so unlike the rest of his music, is unclear, but it was perhaps written specifically for its first performers, the celebrated Milanese cellist Enrico Mainardi (1897–1976) and the pianist Guido Agosti (1901–1989), who included it in a concert at the Venice Biennale on September 7. A working sketch among the Donadelli family documents shows that Montemezzi's original title was *Invocazione*, and he clearly only changed his mind very late, for the clean manuscript score submitted to Ricordi has this earlier title scratched out and substituted with the more neutral and atmospheric *Elegia*. An almost religious intention seems to linger over the three-minute composition, a sort of wordless prayer, a *Lied ohne Worte*, based on a single rocking idea which postpones the stress until the second beat of each bar. It proceeds with a steady pace, with little emotional scope, not exceeding, until the more emotional Reprise, the melodic range of an 11th, the piano loyally and discreetly accompanying the cello. The piece is structured in an ABA form, with a 15-bar main section, a central 29-bar contrasting one, a 26-bar Reprise, and a 14-bar Coda which oddly opposes a blatant, solemn, albeit short-lived *fortissimo* opening with the *pianissimo sottovoce e intimamente espressivo* with which the *Elegia* ends *perdendosi*.

The *Elegia* quietly closed a period which had seen the composition of the new prelude for *L'amore dei tre re*, *Paolo e Virginia*, and *La notte di Zoraima*. Over a decade would now pass before another Montemezzi composition was premiered: a gulf in his creative career comparable to the one succeeding *La nave*.

---

[92] Montemezzi to Carlo Clausetti and Renzo Valcarenghi, July 28, 1932, promises to send them the score. Archivio Storico Ricordi.

9

"A world torn up by war"

L'incantesimo, 1933–1942

The 1930s saw a definite shift in Montemezzi's creative ambitions. The turn in his career that we traced to around 1926, the year of the premiere of *Turandot*—the turn which saw Montemezzi focusing on getting his older operas revived, rather than creating new work—became more and more pronounced. The belief that he could compose another major opera, sustained through the 1920s, now largely disappeared. Montemezzi's most noteworthy professional achievement in his final Italian years was bringing about important, acclaimed revivals of *Héllera* and *La nave*.

This is not the whole story, though, for Montemezzi remained eager to compose new operas, even if on a more modest scale than in the past. In 1933 he obtained the untitled, one-act libretto from Sem Benelli—the only purpose-written libretto Benelli ever attempted—that eventually became *L'incantesimo*.[1] This was again a project Montemezzi embarked on independently of Casa Ricordi, and it seems far more likely that the composer approached Benelli with a request for a libretto than that the writer unexpectedly volunteered one. He probably agreed a fee for the libretto itself, something he could easily afford, and also agreed to pay Benelli twelve percent of any future profits from the opera.[2]

Montemezzi's wish to work with Benelli again is highly significant on two fronts. First, the libretto of *L'amore dei tre re* had been widely praised, even receiving some ecstatic acclaim, while the librettos of Montemezzi's other operas had all been severely faulted, that of *La notte di Zoraima* most of all. The composer, it would seem, was now eager to rekindle his 1910s inspiration by again setting Benelli's glowing poetry. It is possible that he specifically asked for something akin to *L'amore dei tre re*, or that Benelli sensed a

---

[1] Enid A. Haupt, "Enchanting Fabric," *Philadelphia Inquirer*, November 14, 1943, p. 4.
[2] Montemezzi to Sem Benelli, June 1, 1946. Archivio Sem Benelli, Biblioteca della Società Economica di Chiavari.

Succeeding Puccini. David Chandler and Raffaele Mellace, Oxford University Press. © Oxford University Press 2025.
DOI: 10.1093/9780197761373.003.0010

290 SUCCEEDING PUCCINI

preference for this kind of material, for *L'incantesimo* is clearly linked to the earlier opera, as discussed later in this chapter. Second, choosing to work with Benelli at this time was a political gesture, the significance of which should not be underestimated.

Benelli, who had played a notable part in the Fiume affair, accepted Mussolini's invitation to stand in the controversial 1924 election and was elected to the Chamber of Deputies. But his comfortable relationship with the regime was short-lived; after the notorious murder of the anti-Fascist politician Giacomo Matteotti on June 10, 1924, Benelli quickly distanced himself from Mussolini and in September that year founded the Lega Italica, a nationalist, but anti-Fascist political movement aiming, vaguely, at a "new spiritual unity" for all Italians, emphasizing the importance of the freedom of the individual. Although the Lega only lasted three months, it made Benelli a marked man: he was placed under police surveillance, his writings were routinely censored, in many cases by Mussolini himself, and performances of his plays were often disrupted by Fascist protestors.[3] In 1925, Benelli signed Benedetto Croce's "Manifesto of the Anti-Fascist Intellectuals." In 1929, he began a series of petitions to Mussolini, for several years unanswered, requesting an end to the persecutions he received as a writer.[4] In the 1930s, Benelli regularly described himself as feeling like an exile and prisoner in Italy. Montemezzi must have been aware of some of this, so in soliciting a libretto from the aggrieved author he was making his own quiet political statement. Yet when actually faced with the libretto, his inspiration largely failed. There are very few references to *L'incantesimo* in the documentary record, but it is clear that as late as June 1935, Montemezzi was still requesting changes to the libretto, and when Benelli wrote, promising them "in a few days," he mentioned the composer's "pain and exasperation."[5] Later comments suggest that Montemezzi made little progress on *L'incantesimo* before his move to the United States in 1939, something that, in hindsight, he blamed on the uncongenial political situation in Italy. The fact that Benelli's libretto is a veiled critique of Mussolini's oppressive reign was perhaps as much an impediment as a spur to composition.

---

[3] For the Lega Italica, and its consequences for Benelli, see Sandro Antonini, *Sem Benelli: Vita di un poeta: dai trionfi internazionali alla persecuzione fascista* (Genoa: De Ferrari, 2007), pp. 63–69.
[4] Antonini, *Sem Benelli*, p. 97.
[5] "fra pochi giorni"; "il tuo dolore e la tua esasperazione." Benelli to Montemezzi, June 10, 1935. Donadelli family documents.

L'INCANTESIMO, 1933–1942   291

This is one of the least-documented periods in Montemezzi's career and an obvious inference is that, as he approached his sixtieth birthday, he was not particularly active. He and Katherine continued to mix with Milanese high society, though, and at one of their dinner parties hosted Crown Prince Umberto (1904–1983), the future Umberto II, the last king of Italy.[6] In some respects, Montemezzi's connection with the United States seemed to be weakening. As noted in the previous chapter, he did not cross the Atlantic for the New World premiere of *La notte di Zoraima*, and while Katherine made annual summer visits to New York in the early 1930s, he did not. On these occasions, Montemezzi tended to spend a few weeks in Vigasio, attending the Arena Opera Festival in Verona and giving Marco the chance to play with his younger relatives. In 1935, for a change, the whole family traveled to the United States for an extended stay, arriving in New York on July 6. Upon landing, Montemezzi announced that he "expect[ed] to spend a few weeks in Elberon, N.J., and later tour the United States."[7] He reported that he was working on his new opera, which still lacked a "definite title," and "smilingly predicted that it would be finished 'when it is complete'"—a rare reference to early work on *L'incantesimo*.[8] The intention was apparently to start the visit in Katherine's old family home on Jerome Avenue: an appropriate way to introduce Marco to the United States, American life, and his "other" family. But it turned out a very unfortunate time to be away from Italy, for Montemezzi's mother died unexpectedly in the early morning of August 9. A funeral was arranged for August 11 and Elisa was buried without her son and his family present. This was an enormous blow to Montemezzi and may well explain why he seems to have maintained a low profile during this long American stay. There were no revivals of *L'amore dei tre re* to tempt him into the limelight, and he seems to have avoided the press. At the beginning of November, the Montemezzis rented a house on Brazilian Avenue, Palm Beach, Florida, and stayed there until March, Marco being placed in a local private school.[9] It is probable that Katherine considered this nine-month visit to the United States a trial run for the family's possible relocation there, given the fast-deteriorating political situation in Europe.

---

[6] Information from Renata Donadelli.

[7] "Montemezzi, Composer, Here," *New York Times*, July 7, 1935, p. N4.

[8] "Montemezzi, Here for Visit, Writing Opera," *New York Herald Tribune*, July 7, 1935, p. 14.

[9] "Palm Beach Socialite in Real Estate Field," *Palm Beach Post*, November 15, 1935, p. 8; "Palm Beach Notes," *Palm Beach Post*, December 28, 1952, p. 2.

292 SUCCEEDING PUCCINI

The loss of his mother appears, initially, to have had a negative impact on Montemezzi's composition of *L'incantesimo*. We consider the claims concerning the opera made by Gastone Benettoni soon after Montemezzi's death important, because they obviously draw on a source close to the composer, most likely Katherine.[10] Benettoni states emphatically that Montemezzi started work on the opera in 1936, on the old upright piano in his "rustico studio" in the Vigasio house. It is hard to believe that nothing had been composed prior to this juncture, but it seems to have been a decisive restart, with earlier drafts perhaps abandoned or destroyed. Clearly, on his return from the United States in the spring of 1936, Montemezzi would have both wanted and needed to go to Vigasio, to sort out his mother's affairs. He would have been back in the house where he composed his finest operas, and he would have been full of memories of the past, while also feeling, presumably, that a new epoch in his life had begun. Even if the inspiration did not last long, this demonstration of the potency of the old "studio" perhaps influenced his and Katherine's decision to retain the house as a much-loved second home.

The Montemezzis' lives revolved around opera to a considerable extent, and they would go to some trouble to see favorite works. One such effort in particular was highlighted by Katherine when she later summarized her life with the composer: "Once, she recalled, they motored from Budapest to Vienna—a five or six-hour drive—just to catch a performance of 'Rosenkavalier.'"[11] We are tempted to date this effort to September 1936, and to see special significance in it. Montemezzi was certainly in Budapest in August 1936, presumably just for a vacation, as there was no performance of *L'amore dei tre re* to tempt him there.[12] We also know that the Montemezzis visited the salt mines at Hallein, Austria, on August 25, 1936, the occasion of a rare family photograph (Figure 9.1). Assuming that they traveled to Budapest via Hallein, and back to Italy via Vienna, they could have seen Strauss's opera staged at the Wiener Staatsoper on September 14, conducted by Hans Knappertsbusch. Earlier in the year, Knappertsbusch had been dismissed from his post as music director at the Bavarian State Opera by the Nazis; after this crisis, he was picked up by the Wiener Staatsoper, and if the Montemezzis made a special effort to see his *Rosenkavalier*, it may have been, in part at least, a gesture of political solidarity. If it was, it anticipates

---

[10] Gastone Benettoni, "Incantesimo," *Epoca*, July 19, 1952, p. 77.
[11] Norman Frisch, "Widow Loved Montemezzi and His Operas," *Daily News* (Los Angeles), October 19, 1952, p. 28.
[12] Autograph signature for an unknown admirer. Chandler collection.

Figure 9.1 Marco, Katherine, and Italo Montemezzi in Hallein, Austria, August 25, 1936. *Donadelli family documents.*

294   SUCCEEDING PUCCINI

an intriguing episode in the summer of 1938, when Montemezzi traveled to Lucerne to attend a concert of Wagner's music conducted by Toscanini. The conductor was very much persona non grata with the Fascist regime, and Italians who crossed the border to attend the concert had their license plates recorded by the police and were subsequently named and shamed in pro-Fascist newspapers.[13]

Professionally speaking, much of Montemezzi's energy continued to go into lobbying for a revival of *La nave*. In 1932 he seems to have largely suspended such efforts, perhaps disillusioned, or even embarrassed, by the failure of his scheme to have the opera revived to mark "the tenth anniversary of fascism." But on May 11, 1933, he opened a new campaign with another long letter to Mussolini, reminding him of earlier correspondence and reaffirming that *La nave* was "without doubt, my major work ... [the one] to which I gave the best part of myself."[14] La Scala was again the desired forum, and the authorities now made efforts to nudge the theatre into reviving the work, but it was rejected on basically economic grounds, as it had been at the Teatro Reale in 1930. Montemezzi maintained the pressure, however, and finally things began to turn in his favor when Serafin was nominated artistic director of the Opera di Roma, the resident company at the Teatro Reale, in July 1934. This gave Montemezzi a powerful ally in the operatic world, yet the situation now became more complicated, for Serafin, with Montemezzi's support, proposed a revival of *Héllera*. The composer had declared in favor of the earlier opera, having persuaded the renowned tenor Beniamino Gigli to sing the role of Adolfo. In 1929, as noted in the previous chapter, Montemezzi had described *Héllera* as "liv[ing] all the time at the top of my heart," and there can be no doubt that, after *La nave*, it was the opera he most wanted revived. In May 1935 he revised the score for a final time.

A lavish Teatro Reale revival of *Héllera* was to prove the great "might-have-been" event of Montemezzi's 1930s. Though it is impossible to say whether it would have launched the opera into the repertoire, as Montemezzi predicted, it would surely have led to a fairly definitive verdict on its merits. It was provisionally selected for the 1934–1935 season with Gigli and Claudia Muzio in the main roles. Unfortunately, it was then dropped on what were said to be economic grounds: a decision Montemezzi described as "a stab in the back" when he wrote to Mussolini, complaining about the situation, on October

---

[13] Harvey Sachs, *Music in Fascist Italy* (New York: Norton, 1987), pp. 230–32.

[14] Fiamma Nicolodi, *Musica e musicisti nel ventennio fascista* (Fiesole: Discanto, 1984), p. 419.

29, 1934.[15] On April 6, 1935, when a plan to stage *L'amore dei tre re* in Genoa had also fallen through, he wrote even more bitterly:

> Nothing anywhere! For those who are in command I do not exist: it would seem that I have never contributed anything to the art. My operas, of which much has been said and written, are ignored in the Country I adore, and any request of mine is persistently refused. I bang my head against a wall and find myself humiliated, hurt in my own heart, in an unequal struggle.[16]

"*La Nave, L'Amore dei tre Re,* and *Héllera* ought to be welcomed by the Theatre Directors with great confidence to refresh their repertoires, of which there is so much need," Montemezzi urged—the order in which he names his operas perhaps reflecting his judgment on their relative value. The letter states, poignantly, that repeated "injustice" "paralyzes me in my work and makes my life unbearable." This feeling doubtless goes some way toward explaining why he was unable to make much progress on *L'incantesimo*. Serafin proposed *La nave* for the 1935–1936 season, but again unsuccessfully. At this point, Montemezzi took off for his long visit to the United States, and his lobbying efforts were suspended for a year or so.

In 1936, however, Montemezzi began lobbying again, hoping to see *La nave* revived at La Scala[17] and *Héllera* in Rome. A decisive breakthrough seemed to have been made when Serafin got *Héllera* firmly scheduled for the Teatro Reale's 1937–1938 season. Gigli again accepted the role of Adolfo; Maria Caniglia, who had sung Manuela in *La notte di Zoraima*, as well as Fiora, and who often sang opposite Gigli, was chosen for the title role. It is not clear what happened next, but in the summer of 1937 Serafin traveled to Argentina to conduct a season of opera and in his absence *Héllera* was dropped. As Montemezzi later explained the situation, "while Serafin was at the Colon [*sic*] in Buenos Aires in the summer, some rascal from the Management of the Reale removed the opera from the bill."[18] He clearly believed that, had Serafin been in Italy, the revival would have gone ahead. For Montemezzi, embittered by years of unsuccessful attempts to get one of

---

[15] Nicolodi, *Musica e musicisti*, p. 422.

[16] Nicolodi, *Musica e musicisti*, p. 424.

[17] Montemezzi to Guido Pesenti (the mayor of Milan), June 25, 1936. Chandler collection.

[18] "mentre Serafin in estate si trovava al Colon di Buenos Aires, qualche farabutto che apparteneva alla Direzione del Reale, ha levato l'opera dal cartellone," Montemezzi to Alfredo Colombo, April 16, 1951. Chandler collection.

296   SUCCEEDING PUCCINI

his "other" operas staged, this was heartbreaking and something of a final straw. On November 3 he wrote to Mussolini, asking for a second audience with the dictator. By now his years of appeals and flatteries appear to have genuinely interested Mussolini in his case, and a meeting was speedily arranged for November 11. Marco Montemezzi would later recall how, on this occasion, his tyrannical schoolteacher congratulated him on his father's access to power with a fulsome "complimenti!"[19]

The main subject of this second meeting between Montemezzi and Mussolini seems to have been *Héllera*, but no doubt broader injustices were evoked, and presumably the composer took the opportunity to say something about *La nave*. At this point things moved surprisingly quickly; just one week later, Montemezzi, now sounding much happier, was writing to Osvaldo Sebastiani, Mussolini's secretary: "His Excellency the Head of Government has, with much goodness, taken an interest in my case and, as a first result, we will have my *Héllera* on the Radio this 12 and 14 December."[20] This radio broadcast from Rome was not a substitute of equal value for the abandoned Teatro Reale production, but it was something, and the most significant career event since the premiere of *La notte di Zoraima* seven years earlier. The RAI orchestra was conducted by Fernando Previtali, and the production featured Franca Somigli (1901–1974) in the title role, Pau (Paolo) Civil (1899–1987) as Adolfo, and a young Tito Gobbi (1913–1984) as Schauwalki.

Before considering the response to the 1937 *Héllera*, it is worth noting that by this juncture, radio had done a good deal to keep Montemezzi's lesser-known operas in the public ear. It was a medium he highly approved. When in the United States in 1925 he heard a broadcast of *Cavalleria rusticana* and wrote enthusiastically to the radio station (WGBS):

> It is with the utmost pleasure that I send my congratulations for the excellent result of such an extraordinary project as the reproduction of an entire opera by wireless. "Cavalleria Rusticana" has thus been heard by numerous people who may perhaps never have the opportunity of being present at its production in a theatre.[21]

---

[19] Email from Steven Schot, Marco's supervisor at American University, December 13, 2010.
[20] Nicolodi, *Musica e Musicisti*, p. 426.
[21] Quoted in "Opera Now Being Adapted for Presentation by Radio," *New York Times*, April 5, 1925, p. 14.

L'INCANTESIMO, 1933–1942 297

On May 6, 1926, Attilio Parelli's *I dispettosi amanti*, aired from Milan, became the first opera to receive a complete broadcast in Italy. A little over two years later, *L'amore dei tre re* was broadcast from Milan on July 1 and 5, 1928, with plans for a secondary broadcast from Stuttgart, though the latter had to be abandoned due to weather conditions.[22] Montemezzi missed these broadcasts, however, as he was in Le Touquet at the time. As noted in the previous chapter, he did have the chance to hear Act 3 of *L'amore dei tre re* on the radio in London in 1930. *Giovanni Gallurese* was aired from Turin on November 15, 1931, *L'amore dei tre re* from Rome on September 26, 1934, and *La notte di Zoraima* from Turin on August 2, 1936 (with Giuseppina Cobelli returning to the title role).[23]

The broadcast of *Héllera* was far more significant because the opera had not been heard since 1909 and had never been performed in its revised form. None of the critics reviewing it in 1937 had heard it before. As discussed in Chapter 3, Montemezzi extensively revised the work immediately after witnessing its comparative failure on stage. In 1919, he returned to it, and made further revisions. And in May 1935, probably on the assumption that Serafin was about to revive the opera, he revised it again. Casa Ricordi issued a new edition of the libretto in 1936 and a new vocal score in 1937.[24] The result of the first broadcast was highly gratifying. Several critics went to some trouble to champion the opera and to express their incredulity at what L.F.L. in *Il Giornale d'Italia* called its "twenty-nine years of undeserved oblivion": "That . . . the composer of *L'Amore dei tre re* had to appeal to the radio to return his opera *Héllera* to the opera house is quite amazing and [the fact is] even more amazing after listening to this opera, the fate of which is among the strangest."[25] The anonymous critic for *La Tribuna* found the opera "generous, genuine, and rich in inspiration, lyricism, as well as in powerful and persuasive drama," and demanded "reparation," touching a political note which echoes some of Montemezzi's complaints to Mussolini:

---

[22] Casa Ricordi to Montemezzi, July 4, 1928. Archivio Storico Ricordi, Copialettere.

[23] For more details of these 1930s broadcasts, see Giorgio Gualerzi and Carlo Marinelli Roscioni, *50 anni di opera Lirica alla Rai 1931–1980: Le produzioni liriche delle Sedi di Milano, Napoli, Roma e Torino* (Turin: Edizioni RAI, 1981), pp. 37, 50, 63.

[24] It is also worth noting that in 1931 Ricordi published two fantasias derived, respectively, from Act 1 and Act 2 of *Héllera*, by the minor composer Illuminato Culotta (1892–1979). This kind of derivative work was usually based on well-known scores, so this publication may represent an earlier attempt by the publisher to renew interest in the forgotten opera.

[25] L.F.L., "'*Héllera*' di Montemezzi," *Il Giornale d'Italia*, December 16, 1937, p. 3.

298 SUCCEEDING PUCCINI

if we want our composers to find in the fascist atmosphere, generator of art and life, a spur and incitement to produce and to give Italy new expressions of their geniuses, it is first of all necessary to show that such high efforts meet with a full and sincere acknowledgment.[26]

Best of all was a very positive review from Raymond Hall of the *New York Times*, who happened to be in Italy. He found it a "splendid libretto, one of the finest of Luigi Illica," and judged:

one can only approve the Veronese maestro's faith in this youthful work. The music is wholly worthy of the fine subject. Here is a work of acute psychological penetration, of moving dramatic truth, and of the distinction one would expect from the aristocratic composer of the "Three Kings."
    What is more important from the public's standpoint, the score is an inexhaustible fountain of melody. In its fresh, beautifully modelled flow, the melodic declamation of "Héllera" is invariably adherent to the characters and the situations. In its chief climaxes—and the score is a long succession of such moments of aspiring spirituality, of amorous exaltation, of grueling torment or tragic conclusion—the music often attains an authentic state of grace. One could even say "inspired" with propriety.[27]

The broadcasts reached a large part of Europe: Herbert F. Peyser, in Vienna, appears to have enjoyed good reception and was impressed by what he heard.[28]
    The critical consensus was that *Héllera* had proved itself, Montemezzi had suffered a clear injustice, and the opera needed to return to the stage. Years later, the composer recalled: "I have never forgotten that the following day [after the first broadcast], Caniglia, who had listened to the opera, came to me fervently begging me to give to her, before anybody else, that [title] role when the opera should be staged. She was enthusiastic."[29] Yet *Héllera* never did return to the stage. It was obviously too late to schedule it for the 1937–1938 season, and when news got out that a magnificent revival of

---

[26] "'Héllera' di Montemezzi alla Radio," *La Tribuna*, December 16, 1937, p. 3.

[27] Raymond Hall, "'Hellera' [sic] Revived," *New York Times*, January 16, 1938, p. X7.

[28] Herbert F. Peyser, "An Appreciation of L'Amore dei Tre Re," *Musical America*, February 1949, p. 14.

[29] "Non ho mai dimenticato che il giorno dopo la Caniglia, che aveva sentito l'opera, venne da me a pregarmi fervidamente di dare a lei, prima di tutte, quel ruolo quando si fosse rappresentata l'opera. Era entusiasta." Montemezzi to Alfredo Colombo, April 16, 1951.

La nave was planned for the following season, it probably convinced theatre managements to wait. Then Montemezzi's departure from Italy in early 1939, and the advent of war, meant that momentum was wholly lost.

The *Héllera* broadcasts represent a definite upturn in Montemezzi's career, and the revival of *La nave* which followed was still more encouraging. On March 21, 1938, he could report to Sebastiani with considerable pride that:

> the great opera season at the Teatro Reale di Roma will open this coming December with *La Nave.*
>
> I am proud that my work of art and of Adriatic Propaganda has been chosen for the grand opening, and that I might give in this way my humble contribution to the commemoration of our Great Poet-Soldier.[30]

D'Annunzio had died on March 1. It is not clear whether this, or earlier reports of the poet ailing, influenced the decision, but in either case there is no doubt that *La nave* suited the imperialistic mood of the times. Italy's brutal victory in the Second Italo-Abyssinian War of 1935–1936 had consolidated an African empire and fostered the myth that a Roman era was returning. Mussolini was now intensely interested in establishing Italy as the dominant power in the Mediterranean. Within four months of the revival of *La nave*, Italy would invade Albania: another remarkable literalization of the opera's message about redeeming the Adriatic.

As in 1918, the preparations for putting *La nave* on stage were necessarily extensive, and the press started showing considerable interest as the opening of the 1938–1939 season neared. The director was Carlo Piccinato, there were new stage and costume designs by Cipriano E. Oppo, and Serafin was again conducting. Gina Cigna (1900–2001) was cast as Basiliola, opposite the Marco Gràtico of Pau Civil, who had sung in *Héllera*. Montemezzi made some slight adjustments to the score for them, "lowering by a half tone or tone some parts of the soprano and tenor."[31] He later reported that "the chorus rehearsed this music [*La nave*] and nothing else for a full month."[32] The original plan was for *La nave* to open the Teatro Reale season on December

---

[30] Nicolodi, *Musica e Musicisti*, p. 426.

[31] "abbassare di un mezzo tono o di un tono qualche pezzo della soprano e del tenore." Montemezzi to Alfredo Colombo, letter postmarked April 9, 1946. Ricordi Collection, Music Library, Northwestern University.

[32] Quoted in Alfred Frankenstein, "Three Kings and One Composer," *San Francisco Chronicle*, October 26, 1941, p. 25.

300 SUCCEEDING PUCCINI

8, a very prestigious scheduling; unfortunately, Cigna fell ill, so the first performance had to be replaced with *Tannhäuser*, leading to an odd conspiracy theory that the Vatican had proscribed the production.[33] This must have been an exceptionally painful moment for Montemezzi, after years of campaigning to see the opera revived. Fortunately, Cigna recovered quickly and the second performance on December 14 went ahead on schedule. It was a grand event:

> This was the audience of the great occasions, with big names in politics, the aristocracy, great minds, and of high society, diplomats and party officials (*gerarchi*); with ladies wearing low-necked dresses and bejewelled according to the latest fashion, supplying a harmony of delicate colors beside the smart uniforms of the Army and the Party and the tailcoats. It was a show only Rome has the ability to offer.[34]

Montemezzi was present and saw much in the result to vindicate his faith in his most ambitious work. All the critics agreed that the opera had been received very favorably: "The composer was called out, on his own and with the other artists, uncountable times amid general acclamations."[35]

The critics were mostly friendly, several of them supporting Montemezzi's view that the opera had been unjustly neglected for far too long.[36] *La nave* was an "unappreciated and underestimated masterpiece," Alceo Toni told readers of *Il Popolo d'Italia*, an opera drawing "on the confluence of the two big streams of Verdian and Wagnerian romanticism."[37] Bruno Barilli, the cult critic, rhapsodized in its praise: "Montemezzi writes what he feels: and he feels on a large scale, with justice and truth."[38] On the other hand, Pizzetti was positively spiteful: "it seems to me that it [*La nave*] presents no aesthetic character of its own, nor any boldness, nor any innovation."[39] Adriano Lualdi was led to perhaps the most profound critical response, finding a way to both praise the opera and to explain how it had lost its way in the 1920s:

---

[33] See "Vatican Protest? Banned Play Withdrawn," *Catholic Herald*, December 16, 1938, p. 7.

[34] s. s., "'La Nave' di Montemezzi al Teatro Reale dell'opera," *La Stampa*, December 15, 1938, p. 5.

[35] s. s., "'La Nave' di Montemezzi," p. 5.

[36] Seven reviews of the 1938 *La nave*, in English translation, are collected in David Chandler (ed.), *Essays on the Montemezzi-D'Annunzio 'Nave,'* 2nd edition (Norwich: Durrant Publishing, 2014).

[37] Alceo Toni, "'La Nave' di Italo Montemezzi al Reale dell'Opera," *Il Popolo d'Italia*, December 15, 1938, p. 4.

[38] Bruno Barilli, "La Nave," *Omnibus*, December 24, 1938, p. 11.

[39] Ildebrando Pizzetti, "La 'Nave' di Montemezzi al Reale," *La Tribuna*, December 16, 1938, p. 6.

It [*La nave*] doesn't yet *feel* the Italian musical Renovation that in 1917 and 1918 had already been taking place for some years. But of a particular trend (the one that looked to the North) of the late 1800s, of the most informed and cultivated trend that summarizes and stylizes with great skill and taste, it must be said that this *Nave* offers all the best and all that (in the matter of procedures, architecture, modes of expression that, here too, generically speaking, reflect the composer's predilection for Wagner, although attenuated in comparison to *L'Amore dei tre re*) deserves to be saved of the old inheritance.[40]

This observation perhaps explains better than anything else how the younger composers had come to view Montemezzi as a major end-of-an-era figure; his producing so little new music since 1918 supported the view that his career had run aground on "the Italian musical Renovation" that had brought other composers into prominence.[41]

These Roman nights must have given Montemezzi very mixed feelings. The opera he considered his masterpiece, the one he had fought so long to see revived, was being acclaimed by crowded audiences and he was, in a sense, the man of the hour, an artist who had presciently caught the mood of 1938 twenty years earlier. The success of *La nave* suggested that patriotism, Fascism, and the imperialist longings of the time could form one great, intoxicating whole. Yet it is almost certain that Montemezzi knew he was about to leave Italy. Katherine was already in the United States and had no intention of coming back. It is easy to suppose that Mussolini's official adoption of anti-Semitism in July 1938, to please Hitler, had been decisive for her. Sometime late in 1938, Montemezzi was having dinner in the house in Vigasio when the telephone rang; it was Katherine, calling from New York. Returning to the table visibly shaken, he announced that she had decided the family should relocate to the United States.[42]

On February 22, 1939, Montemezzi and the twelve-year-old Marco accordingly sailed on the *S. S. Rex* from Genoa, arriving in New York on March

---

[40] Adriano Lualdi, " 'La Nave' di d'Annunzio e Montemezzi al Reale," *Il Giornale d'Italia*, December 16, 1938, p. 5.

[41] Another intriguing glimpse of how his contemporaries understood Montemezzi's place in Italian music at this time is supplied by Respighi. When planning a series of concerts and conferences in Buenos Aires in 1935, he categorized Montemezzi, together with Puccini, Zandonai, and Catalani, among the "Post-Verdian composers," distinguishing them from the "New symphonic and operatic school" that included Alfano, Pizzetti, and Respighi himself. Elsa Respighi to Casa Ricordi, January 23, 1935. Archivio Storico Ricordi.

[42] Information from Renata Donadelli.

302 SUCCEEDING PUCCINI

2. It would prove an epochal voyage in both their lives: the father would never again consider Italy his home; the son would spend the rest of his life in the United States and become a U.S. citizen. The initial plan, according to the ship's manifest, was to stay with Katherine's mother at the Ambassador Hotel.[43] But the Montemezzis quickly moved to their own apartment in the luxurious Hotel Dorset on West 54th Street. Montemezzi wrote from the Dorset on March 10 to thank Edward Ziegler of the Metropolitan Opera for helping organize the delivery of a Knabe piano.[44] The piano may have helped restore an air of normalcy, but it is hard to resist the conclusion that Montemezzi had found leaving Italy traumatic and that his health suffered. The *Saratogian*, a local newspaper for Saratoga Springs, reported on October 20, 1939: "At the Viasana from Italy are Mr. and Mrs. Stalo [*sic*] Montemezzi of Rome [*sic*]."[45] The place in question was the Viasana Convalescent Rest Home, run since 1923 by two registered nurses. The major European conflict Katherine had feared had erupted the previous month, with Germany invading Poland and Britain and France promptly declaring war on Germany.

It would have seemed natural for the Montemezzis to settle in the New York area, and that would presumably have been Katherine's first choice, but Montemezzi disliked the New York climate, which he complained "seems to be going from bad to worse,"[46] and in October, presumably immediately after leaving the Viasana, they moved to California. Reports soon reached the press that "Montemezzi, Italy's greatest living composer of opera and his American wife have settled down in Beverly Hills."[47] Initially, they rented 703 North Alpine Drive, where they lived until summer 1940, but they soon bought a luxurious eleven-room house at 714 Walden Drive, built in 1926. This was prime real estate: when the house came on the market in 1980, it was priced at over $1.5 million.[48] Here the Montemezzis set about reestablishing the high standard of living, with domestic staff, that they had enjoyed in Milan. When Katherine put the house up for sale in 1957, it was described as having four bedrooms, a maid's room, "Beau[tiful] plantings," and "Exquisite c[ar]p[e]ts & drapes"; it stood on a lot of some 14,400 square

---

[43] Ellis Island records.
[44] Chandler collection.
[45] Jean McGregor, "Tea Table Chat," *Saratogian*, October 20, 1939, p. 5.
[46] "Montemezzi Prepares for Debut at Opera," *New York Times*, February 2, 1941, p. X7.
[47] George Ross, "Broadway," *Pittsburgh Press*, November 29, 1939, p. 15.
[48] *Los Angeles Times*, April 26, 1980, "At Home" section, p. 15.

L'INCANTESIMO, 1933–1942   303

feet and came with a three-car garage.[49] Visitors were impressed; in 1951, Lydia Lane found a "beautiful living room filled with bowls of jasmine and long stem roses."[50] Marco entered the Beverly Hills High School. In the early summer of 1940, Montemezzi and Marco drove over into Mexico, then re-entered the United States through San Ysidro on June 5.[51] This was a move to confirm their eligibility as permanent residents by obtaining Immigrant Identification Cards, prompted by the Senate Judiciary Committee's move toward legislating the registration of foreign citizens that soon afterward produced the Alien Registration Act, effective from June 28.

Although fiercely pro-war in 1915, this time Montemezzi hoped, until hope became impossible, that Italy would avoid the conflict. On February 3, 1940, he wrote to Alfredo Colombo: "We hope that Italy's neutrality, which is a stroke of genius, does not get undermined and swept away in the dreadful whirl of the war."[52] Four months later, on June 10, that hope was extinguished when Italy declared war on France and Britain. The war quickly began affecting the Montemezzis personally, for immediately after Italy's entry into the conflict, the Germans began establishing a system of military attachés and liaison staff throughout the peninsula, initially with a view to enabling military cooperation, though ultimately facilitating the buildup of the massive German presence in Italy that proved so costly to the host nation three years later.[53] The municipality of Milan requisitioned the Montemezzis' apartment for use by German military personnel. Pia, the Montemezzis' housekeeper, arranged for the valuables and some of the furniture to be shipped to neutral Switzerland, but soon after the consignment arrived there the plan changed, and it was sent on to the house in Vigasio. Part of the shipment was lost en route. Later in the war, the Vigasio house was occupied by German troops and the Montemezzis' valuables had to be moved again, this time to an attic in a Donadelli relative's house, which was then walled shut, a precaution which proved providential: the house was subsequently searched by German soldiers, but the hidden storage space was not discovered.[54]

[49] *Los Angeles Times*, August 4, 1957, Classified Part 2, p. 25.
[50] Lydia Lane, "Star Cautions Against Excesses," *San Antonio Express*, March 18, 1951, p. D17.
[51] U.S. Citizenship and Immigration Services C-File C6489317.
[52] "Noi speriamo che la neutralità dell'Italia, che è un colpo di genio, non venga intaccata e travolta nel turbine spaventoso della guerra." Ricordi Collection, Music Library, Northwestern University.
[53] See Gerhard Schreiber, "Political and Military Developments in the Mediterranean Area, 1939–40," trans. Ewald Osers, in *Germany and the Second World War*, Volume III: *The Mediterranean, South-East Europe, and North Africa 1939–1941* (Oxford: Clarendon Press, 1995), pp. 250–51.
[54] Information from Renata Donadelli.

304   SUCCEEDING PUCCINI

There was still the question of how the United States would respond to the war. "For a year and a half, from June 10, 1940 to December 7, 1941," writes John P. Diggins:

> Italian-American sentiment hung suspended between hope and fear; hope that somehow the United States could remain out of the war; fear that once the country entered the war, Italians in America would be compelled to fight against their own *parentela*.[55]

It was surely an uncomfortable time for Montemezzi. After his decade of writing scraping letters to Mussolini, he was now surrounded by incessant media attacks on the dictator, and after June 10, 1940, even Italian Americans turned strongly against Italy's ruler, many of them feeling compelled to make public statements of their undivided allegiance to the United States.[56] From that date, if not earlier, Montemezzi would have sought to distance himself from any suspicion of sympathy with Mussolini's regime.

If the political situation was bleak, there was not much for Montemezzi to feel positive about in terms of his American career either, in the summer of 1940. A revival of *La nave*, *Giovanni Gallurese*, or *La notte di Zoraima* was not to be expected, and even *L'amore dei tre re*, though still revered by most of the U.S. critics, no longer commanded the stage as it had in the 1910s and 1920s. Many of the singers who had brought it so vividly to life in the past were retired, and suitable replacements were yet to be found. The Metropolitan Opera's 1939 revival, which Montemezzi presumably read about, highlighted how things had deteriorated, with critics particularly scathing about Gennaro Papi's spiritless conducting. Montemezzi's response was to pursue opportunities to conduct the opera himself. To this end, he made common cause with his old friend Grace Moore, who had long wanted to sing Fiora, and who was now something of a superstar, thanks to her movies. She took the leading role in negotiations with operatic managements, and by November 1940 was writing of the efforts she had "made in *all* directions to re-establish this opera [*L'amore dei tre re*]," seeking to "take away the stigma of last year's performances."[57] The proposal of Montemezzi conducting and Moore starring was hard to refuse: a single

---

[55] John P. Diggins, *Mussolini and Fascism: The View from America* (Princeton, NJ: Princeton University Press, 1972), pp. 350–51.

[56] Diggins, *Mussolini and Fascism*, pp. 349–50.

[57] Letter to Edward Ziegler, November 17, 1940, Metropolitan Opera Archives.

L'INCANTESIMO, 1933–1942   305

performance was arranged for November 23, 1940, in Chicago, then three performances at the Met in February 1941, and a further performance in Boston, with the Met company, on April 3. In all five performances Charles Kullman took the role of Avito; in Chicago the roles of Archibaldo and Manfredo were taken by Virgilio Lazzari and Carlo Morelli, and on the East Coast by Ezio Pinza and Richard Bonelli.

Montemezzi appears to have coached Moore more intensively than any other singer. He had worked with her on an aria from *Giovanni Gallurese* in 1925, as discussed in Chapter 7, and when she visited him in California in the summer of 1940, they "worked extensively" on the role of Fiora.[58] Moore was also taking advice on the role from Mary Garden. Then, for some ten days before the Chicago performance in November, "the soprano, the composer, Mr. Kullman, and Virgilio Lazzari . . . [were] virtually inseparable, living, breathing, eating and drinking 'The Love of Three Kings.'"[59] It is probable that on no previous occasion had Montemezzi been able to stamp his own ideas so thoroughly on a production of *L'amore dei tre re*. Those ideas were endorsed in a series of very positive reviews. The Chicago performance was judged a "huge success," with Montemezzi making "a very fine leader":

> Grace Moore surprised everyone by her very remarkable singing and acting as Fiora. She has never been seen nor heard to greater advantage and surpassed even her own former achievements. . . . it is to be hoped that we shall see her again in a character she so well understands, and which revealed the fact that she is a deep student of feminine psychology.[60]

Moore herself considered the result a "triumph," and felt that her performance, combined with the critical verdicts, had brought "Fiora back to operatic life."[61] The acclaim continued in New York and Boston. For Oscar Thompson, the New York performances were in a wholly different league from those of the previous season:

> What a difference the conductor does make! In the pit at the Metropolitan last night Italo Montemezzi worked such magic with the orchestra as

---

[58] "Montemezzi Prepares for Debut," p. X7.

[59] Cecil Smith, "Great Day at Opera Coming Up Saturday," *Chicago Daily Tribune*, November 19, 1940, p. 17.

[60] "The Love of Three Kings," *Musical Leader*, December 14, 1940, p. 7.

[61] Grace Moore to Clara Marafioti, December 10, 1940. Chandler collection.

306   SUCCEEDING PUCCINI

to rekindle the fires that lit his "L'Amore dei Tre Re" in the days when Toscanini, Polacco and Marinuzzi taught our opera habitues how it should sound.... if some had begun to doubt the validity of their old enthusiasms for the work itself, what Mr. Montemezzi accomplished must have left them more than a little ashamed....

"L'Amore" has never sounded more consistently of a piece than it did last night. One could say again what was said of it at the time of its Metropolitan premiere on January 2, 1914, that in its workmanship here was the finest operatic score that had come out of Italy since the last operas of Verdi, not excepting the successive "hits" of Puccini.[62]

As Moore was recognized as a Fiora of the Garden variety, she divided critical opinion on the East Coast. Interestingly, Lucrezia Bori, who for many East Coast critics remained the supreme exponent of the role, attended one of the performances. Bori, in general very reluctant to criticize other singers, made her views plain: "She [Moore] looked lovely and she has temperament, but the aching strain of this young woman torn between conflicting emotions was not quite there. Perhaps it will come with time."[63]

The second New York performance was broadcast internationally, bringing Montemezzi the biggest audience of his career. On the radio, the opera was introduced by Milton Cross as "the newest of all the operas that have found a more or less permanent place in the Metropolitan's repertory."[64] Recordings of the broadcast were made and quickly began to circulate among collectors. This is the earliest complete recording of *L'amore dei tre re* available today and preserves an invaluable record of how Montemezzi wanted his opera played.

The 1940–1941 season also saw the international premiere of *Paolo e Virginia* at Carnegie Hall on March 6. The concert began with the New York Philharmonic's regular conductor, John Barbirolli, leading Vaughan Williams's *Fantasia on a Theme by Thomas Tallis*, then Montemezzi took over to conduct his own work, and after an interval Barbirolli returned to direct Beethoven's Seventh Symphony. *Paolo e Virginia* was warmly applauded, but the New York critics felt the same lack of enthusiasm as their Rome counterparts in 1930 and expressed themselves in similar terms. Miles

---

[62] Oscar Thompson, 'Montemezzi Leads "L'Amore," ' *New York Sun*, February 8, 1941, p. 28.
[63] Lanfranco Rasponi, *The Last Prima Donnas* (New York: Knopf, 1982), p. 440.
[64] Cross's introduction is preserved on the 2003 Guild Historical release of the performance (GHCD 2234/5).

Kastendieck, who the previous month had judged *L'amore dei tre re* the finest of all modern operas, memorably found "a lotus-eating atmosphere in which everything always appeared to sound the same."[65] A year later, on March 26, 1942, Montemezzi conducted *Paolo e Virginia* again as part of a concert at the Auditorium, Los Angeles.

In the 1941–1942 season, the San Francisco Opera staged *L'amore dei tre re*, again with the composer conducting and a cast substantially the same as at the Met. A performance was given in San Francisco on October 29, 1941, and a second one in Los Angeles on November 7, both obtaining very positive reviews. In connection with these performances, Alfred Frankenstein of the *San Francisco Chronicle* interviewed Montemezzi and found him "possess[ing] enormous enthusiasm for many things, and first of all for the business of living even in a world torn up by war." Yet, despite this personal enthusiasm, Montemezzi took a gloomy view of politics and art:

> He does not know when, if ever, he will go back [to Italy]. The European situation he regards with hopeless pessimism, an attitude that applies also to his view of art at the present time. "The world is too heavily politized," he said, "too much cut up by cross-currents of sect and faction. The faith that produces art is not with us anymore, and perhaps it never will return."[66]

Fortunately, *L'incantesimo* allowed Montemezzi to resolve some of his complicated political feelings into art. As noted earlier, he had obtained the libretto in 1933, and probably restarted work on it in 1936, but had been able to make little progress in Italy, something he later blamed on the political situation. However, once comfortable in Beverly Hills, Montemezzi returned to *L'incantesimo* and found "creative difficulties vanishing excepting for delays caused by the allergy to letter-writing of Benelli."[67] He wanted to consult with Benelli "regarding certain small changes" to the text,[68] but was unable to get a reply, and in fact could not re-establish contact with the librettist

---

[65] Miles Kastendieck, "Montemezzi Conducts at the Philharmonic," *Brooklyn Eagle*, March 7, 1941, p. 9. For Kastendieck's judgment on *L'amore dei tre re*, see "Montemezzi Achieves Success For His Opera," *Brooklyn Eagle*, February 25, 1941, p. 9.

[66] Frankenstein, "Three Kings and One Composer," p. 25.

[67] Haupt, "Enchanting Fabric," p. 4.

[68] "Montemezzi Prepares for Debut," p. X7.

308 SUCCEEDING PUCCINI

until 1946.[69] Montemezzi told Frankenstein that he had "just completed" the new opera; the manuscript short score is dated June 2, 1941, but the orchestration came later and continued into 1942.

The best place to start assessing the dramatic and political implications of *L'incantesimo* is the synopsis published ahead of the work's eventual broadcast, for this was almost certainly prepared, or at least approved, by Montemezzi, and it clarifies a few details not clear in the libretto itself:

> The action takes place in the Middle Ages, in the castle of Folco, at the foot of the Italian Alps. Folco and his young wife Giselda have just finished dinner in the great hall. Folco inquires of a servant if Count Rinaldo has arrived. Giselda asks if her husband doubts her love, that he has invited her former suitor after so long a silence. Folco replies that he merely wishes to ask Rinaldo about his magician, Salomone, and whether he can interpret something strange that has befallen.
>
> Rinaldo arrives with Salomone, to whom Folco tells his story. During a hunt he had followed a wolf and killed him. Then he saw a hind, and was about to kill her, when the face of the hind turned into the face of Giselda. Too late, he struck. What, he asks Salomone, does this portend?
>
> Salomone interprets it by saying that Folco is full of pride and ignores the real meaning of love. As Folco protests, Salomone declares he can prove his love by digging up the hind he has killed and, if he finds Giselda's corpse instead, he must carry it through the storm to the castle. Folco leaves to do this.
>
> Rinaldo tells Giselda he still loves her, but Giselda is not convinced. However, as Rinaldo continues to plead his love, Giselda declares that if he can make Spring appear during this Winter storm she will believe and be his.
>
> The scene darkens, Giselda is afraid. Outside Folco's voice is heard, and Rinaldo has disappeared. Folco enters and asks Salomone where Giselda is. Salomone points to her, but Folco sees only the hind where his wife is standing.
>
> Suddenly the call of Spring is heard, Folco and Salomone disappear and as the Spring dawns outside, Giselda sings a hymn in praise of love.[70]

---

[69] Montemezzi to Sem Benelli, June 1, 1946.

[70] Viva Liebling, "News and Previews of Radio, Stage and Screen," *Musical Courier*, October 5, 1943, p. 8.

The story, though largely original, appears to draw on Celtic mythology. In an influential study of Celtic deer cults, published in 1932, J. G. McKay noted "several tales in which a hunter, who has been stalking deer, observes, when putting up his gun to take aim, that the animal has changed into a woman."[71] Given the date, there is a fascinating possibility that Benelli was directly inspired by McKay's account. Or he may have encountered a comparable idea elsewhere. In Madame d'Aulnoy's 1698 fairytale, "La Biche au bois," for example, the hero, a prince, fires arrows at a doe who is in fact his fiancée in a state of enchantment. The parallels with *Bianca* are also notable, and one can reasonably wonder whether Montemezzi had told Benelli about his first opera.

For Montemezzi and Benelli, though, the most important source must have been *L'amore dei tre re*. The two operas are clearly and significantly connected, *L'incantesimo* representing a sort of "reversal" of *L'amore dei tre re*, moving from premises strikingly similar but developing them in a way that leads to a totally dissimilar outcome. The two dramas share the same basis: a setting in a castle in a generic Middle Ages; a pivotal female figure in an otherwise male cast (with, again, a tenor, baritone, and bass); the men's contest for the woman; and a restless, expectant atmosphere. The drama again begins *in medias res*, in a similarly unpretentious fashion, with Folco (comparable to Fiora's father-in-law Archibaldo rather than her husband Manfredo) anxiously asking his servant about the snow, just as Archibaldo had asked his servant about the door of Fiora's bedroom. Even apparently different situations show unexpected correspondences and are given similar musical settings. For example, Rinaldo's arrival (no. 6) is celebrated by Folco, even though the two men are rivals, and the euphoric orchestral commentary is comparable to that of Manfredo's entrance in Act 1 of *L'amore dei tre re*, as his arrival is celebrated by his blind father as the advent of light. Folco's long, crucial hunting tale (no. 11) similarly corresponds to Archibaldo's celebrated account of the conquest of Italy in his youth, though it offers more dramatic tension. Salomone's interpretation of the dream, concluding that pride prevails over love in Folco— "Trovi Amore soltanto nella Morte" (You find Love only in Death)—and comparing Giselda to a gift locked in a treasure chest that her husband

---

[71] J. G. McKay, "The Deer-Cult and the Deer-Goddess Cult of the Ancient Caledonians," *Folklore* 43/2 (June 1932): p. 155.

310 SUCCEEDING PUCCINI

is unable to unlock, perfectly applies to the characters of Archibaldo and Fiora.[72]

There are equally significant differences between *L'amore dei tre re* and *L'incantesimo*, of course. The rivalry for Giselda is much more traditional, paling in comparison to the husband/lover/father-in-law contest in the earlier opera. Salomone, the bass, is the impartial wise man his name suggests, and is not a contender for Fiora's affections. Folco shares Archibaldo's vehemence, as the stage direction *con impeto* (vehemently) insistingly emphasizes, but he is often more melancholic and anxious than furious and vengeful. The glorious sharp-key-dominated episode, where Salomone gives Folco instructions to test the truth of his love (no. 28), implies that the latter's love is at least felt as authentic—an illusion Folco corroborates with a convincing declaration of romantic longing: "Io volerò! . . . / Fammi ancora vedere gli occhi tuoi" (I will fly! . . . / Let me once more see your eyes). Montemezzi translates Folco's knightly stand here into enthusiastic vehemence supported by the finest Straussian orchestration, both in the passionate tide and in instrumental details: this passage shows Folco at his best—a side Archibaldo could never have shown. Most importantly, *L'incantesimo* represents the elegiac version, or even *conversion*, of the earlier masterpiece. The profound tragedy of *L'amore dei tre re* is replaced with a redemptive, uplifting plot. Giselda personifies the happy fulfillment of Fiora's destiny—a fulfillment Fiora longed for but could not achieve, being condemned to much harsher conditions. In the finale of *L'incantesimo*, the men literally fade away, in a scene the opposite of the all-male carnage ending *L'amore dei tre re*. Giselda stands alone on the stage, living the inconceivable experience of being born again, in a sort of "interior regeneration."[73] In this perfect *art nouveau* finale, Giselda identifies with flowers: with life, not death, ironically fulfilling a destiny implied in Fiora's name, and establishing herself as her predecessor's more fortunate sister.

What are the political implications? If Fiora had represented Italy, and if Giselda is read as a sort of second Fiora, then *L'incantesimo* paints a picture of an Italy wedded to a brutal master and in need of redemption through a return to an earlier, more gracious, generous love. It is easy to understand Folco as a paranoid Mussolini figure and his story as figuring

[72] There is no published vocal score of *L'incantesimo*. Quotations here are from the autograph full score in the Archivio Storico Ricordi.

[73] Cesare Orselli, "Montemezzi dà voce a un incanto d'amore," in liner notes for the compact disc recording of Italo Montemezzi, *L'incantesimo* (Bongiovanni, 2019), p. 9.

the successive stages of Fascist violence, first directed at what seemed a legitimate target (the wolf), then at an innocent one (the hind), and finally at what it professed to love (Giselda). In this sense, Salomone challenges Folco/Mussolini to recognize the destruction of innocence as intrinsically self-destructive: but Folco/Mussolini cannot be saved by achieving a higher level of self-awareness and sees only what he has killed, not what he has lost. By contrast, Rinaldo can be read as based on Benelli himself, the poetic, imaginative founder of the Lega Italica, longing to reclaim Italy. The opera does not have to be interpreted politically, of course, but the psychological complexity of the plot invites a search for deeper meetings: it is a world away from the simplistic melodrama of *La notte di Zoraima*. The libretto was clearly conceived by Benelli as symbolic theatre: a choice which may have seemed outdated by 1933, and even more so by 1943, when the opera was first broadcast, but one totally consistent with his overall poetics, which had seen him enjoy his greatest successes in the first decade of the century.

Some critics of *L'incantesimo* subsequently found insufficient dramatic vitality in the opera, and this is a legitimate criticism, though also a case of misunderstanding the work's nature. Apart from Folco, the characters offer little individual psychological insight and scarcely possess any past. Rinaldo is quite inconsistent, and physically fades away at the end. His only reason for existing is to let Giselda become aware of her true nature and aspirations. We know very little even of Giselda herself, much less than we do about Fiora. If the *dramatis personae* are generally less interesting than in *L'amore dei tre re*, the biggest loss is that of a character such as Manfredo, whose complexity is only partially compensated by Folco's contradictory nature. The focus of *L'incantesimo* is elsewhere: in the suggested landscape, the natural conditions where the action takes place, the living elements of nature that symbolize the characters' interior lives. The allegorical scheme of winter versus spring, night and snow versus May flowers, develops against the background of forest mystery and symbolic animals. The characters themselves are symbols as much as dramatic personages: their mutual relationships are devoid of any real consistency, the opposite of what we would expect in traditional opera. The value of the score lies in Montemezzi's effective evocation of a fairy-tale world where realism has no place, and where human beings express their inner feelings through the life in nature. In this respect, the similarities with *Bianca*, which shares the romantic themes of nature, hunting, and magic, are fascinating, and the fact that *L'incantesimo* turned

312   SUCCEEDING PUCCINI

out to be Montemezzi's last opera gives his overall operatic career a revealing sense of shape.

The orchestral prelude to *L'incantesimo*, flowing into the dialogue between Folco and the servant, stands as an explicit poetical declaration. The ostinato quaver quadruplets played by the first horn, signifying the regular fall of the snow, are equivalent to the far more menacing horse-ride ostinato in *L'amore dei tre re*. They are set against a large-note-value melody in the first violins, supported by a seven-part muted string orchestra, which does more than picture the Alpine landscape: it introduces a fantastic world, comparable to that in the prelude to *Lohengrin*, though differently constructed (Example 9.1).

Benelli's experience as a playwright is evident in the structure of *L'incantesimo*. A masterful and somewhat surprising example of this is the second part of the one-act drama, at the turning point of Folco's departure. In a flowing movement perfectly appropriate to the symbolic nature of the opera, Salomone withdraws into the background and "rimane immobile come il Tempo" (remains motionless as Time); following her dialogue with Rinaldo, Giselda crouches, "si rannicchia atterrita" (cowering in terror); Rinaldo mysteriously disappears; Salomone emerges from the background to confront Folco, who is not able to see Giselda, and then they too "nell'oscurità, spariscono" (disappear in the darkness). Giselda is now left alone on stage, and in a world devoid of men is finally able to take possession of her life and youth, symbolized by spring, as the scene changes to a garden and her ecstasy is projected by an offstage chorus. Montemezzi responds with a magnificent, relatively expanded symphonic page (nos. 30–32) covering Folco's exit, Salomone's withdrawal, and Giselda and Rinaldo being left alone, before they start their dialogue: a bright, major-mode, euphonic, full-orchestral bridging episode conveying a chivalric atmosphere, extending to the other characters the good intentions Folco has just expressed as he leaves the party to put himself to the test.

As always, Montemezzi's careful orchestral writing is remarkable, and arguably the most impressive feature of the score, as several early reviews emphasized. Oscar Thompson, for example, detected a "symphonic structure," "a web that is the main fabric of [the] score."[74] The critics disagreed on how Wagnerian this is, but as with Montemezzi's earlier operas, Wagner

---

[74] Oscar Thompson, "New Montemezzi Opera Has Radio Premiere," *Musical America*, October 1943, p. 13.

Music Example 9.1 *L'incantesimo*, bars 1–18.

Velario

Apparisce la stanza di un castello medievale in Italia a piè dell'Alpi.
Di faccia una grande vetrata. A destra un camino acceso. A sinistra
una porta. Seggioloni qua e là. Armi d'ogni genere ai muri e negli
angoli. Sulla sinistra una tavola apparecchiata.
Folco e Giselda hanno cenato allora: ma sono sempre a tavola.
I servi fermi nel fondo aspettano ordini.

Music Example 9.1 Continued

is undoubtedly a model in the extended, multi-sectional love duets. The one between Giselda and Rinaldo is definitely not one of Montemezzi's finest achievements, though, mainly because of the often blurred and not particularly inspired melodic invention for the tenor, who fails to gain much advantage even from the repeated refrain "Amore tutto può" (Love can do anything; no. 40), or, much earlier, from the occasional accompaniment of a solo violin, as at "L'amore fu" (It was love; no. 21). Much more impressive is again the expansive writing for the strings, some motifs evocative of *Tristan und Isolde* soaring from the orchestra as at Rinaldo's "Morirete per lui" (For him you will die; no. 38), or when, with a funereal pace, Giselda commences her final lines in the duet *più lento*, in G-minor (no. 40). Another Wagnerian feature reminiscent of *L'amore dei tre re* is Montemezzi's tendency to match each line of the libretto with a sparing, short-breathed, but meaningful orchestral comment, significantly contributing to the tension of each situation by means of small motivic fragments or expressive intervals. A good example is the miniature clarinet and oboe prelude introducing Giselda's question "Che dite voi?" (What are you saying?; no. 35). Or there is the solemnity of Salomone's statement "Amore tutto muta. Anche il Destino" (Love changes everything.

Even destiny; no. 27), accompanied by an ominous chorus of trumpets, trombones, tuba, and timpani, which recalls his sinister entrance music, led by trombones, tuba, and timpani, and supported by bassoons, contrabassoon, cellos, and basses (no. 10). This entrance music notably sounds like a personal variation, with different means, on Fasolt and Fafner's entrance music in *Das Rheingold* (Example 9.2).

As in *L'amore dei tre re*, and perhaps to an even greater extent, the pivotal character in *L'incantesimo* is the soprano. She is given some of the finest music in the score, starting with her initial musical evocation in a soaring, lyrical melody in the first violins, animating the strings for the first time since the still outset of the opera (no. 1) (Example 9.3). Even before that, the lyrical melody performed by the violins in the prelude (Example 9.1) and resumed as Folco addresses Giselda, "Bella mia sposa" (My beautiful bride; no. 3), can be understood as standing for Giselda, or rather the mystery she

Music Example 9.2 *L'incantesimo*, no. 9, bar 13–no. 10, bar 6.

Music Example 9.3 *L'incantesimo*, no. 1, bars 3–7.

represents.[75] The undeniable melodic quality critics praised in *L'incantesimo*, often emphasizing its Italianate nature, what Thompson called its "sensuous lyricism,"[76] is chiefly associated with her character. It situates Montemezzi in a line directly descending from Ponchielli and Catalani, and not so distant from the Mascagni of *L'amico Fritz*. Good examples of this "sensuous lyricism" include the introduction on the harp when Rinaldo first addresses Giselda (no. 7), or as she briefly comments "E il mio?!" (And mine?!), cautiously alluding to her mystery "*quasi scherzosa*," or almost jokingly (no. 9). But perhaps the best example is found in Folco's hunting tale, as the story of the wolf mutates into that of the hind, introduced by a vast, arching melody in the high strings (no. 15, *Poco più sostenuto*) which bridges the cruel realism of the former and the fairy-tale enchantment of the latter. The sudden, unexpected appearance of the hind/Giselda (*Più lento*; no. 16) materializes in the orchestra as a gorgeous lyrical oasis, recruiting both strings and woodwinds (Example 9.4): a lengthy section (eight pages of the orchestral score) notably unbroken even when Folco recounts the hind's death. The main motif of Giselda's mystery (Example 9.1), complete with the typical horn quadruplets which opened the score, makes its most crucial reappearance as she describes her life as a restless state of expectation, happiness consisting of "aspettare un angiolo che annunzi / un'alba nuova" (waiting for an angel to announce / a new dawn; no. 25). This omnipresent state of suspense is something Giselda shares with Fiora.

---

[75] Giselda later says "Son chiusa / in un'arcana ansia di mistero" (I am locked / in a secret anxiety of mystery, no. 25).
[76] Thompson, "New Montemezzi Opera," p. 13.

Music Example 9.4 *L'incantesimo*, no. 16, bars 5–10.

The "angel" Giselda is waiting for materializes in the miracle of spring crowning the opera, the magical nature of that experience unmistakably announced by the evocative, soaring melody performed by the first violin as Giselda urges Rinaldo to achieve the prodigy of a May garden on a "notte tremenda di neve" (dreadful snowy night), *Lentamente* (no. 41). The melody strongly recalls the celebrated Méditation from Massenet's *Thaïs* (1894), which equally hints at a miracle: the transfiguration of Thaïs's corrupted soul (Examples 9.5a and 9.5b). Giselda's more prominent solo before the finale touches a melodic climax, mentioning the flowers in the garden "tutto in fiore" (all blossoming) on a high B flat, and gains new momentum from the lyrical tide of the violins supporting the section evoking the singing of the birds as she promises she will belong to Rinaldo (no. 43). Rinaldo's voice, and most of all Salomone's, crown the duet, promising that Giselda will experience the spring. After Folco's brief appearance, the "successful, resounding Finale"[77]

---

[77] Gino Bertolaso, "Pubblico commosso e acclamante alla prima mondiale di 'Incantesimo,'" *L'Arena*, August 10, 1952, p. 5. Bertolaso comments on the public approval shown to the conclusion of the opera.

Music Example 9.5a *L'incantesimo*, no. 41, bars 6–13.

announced by Salomone starts. The scene progressively changes as winter is transformed into spring, symbolizing the power of youth of which Giselda is finally able to take possession (no. 48). Thirty-second notes blossom on the flutes and clarinets, with violins, harp, and celesta signifying the ecstasy

Music Example 9.5b Jules Massenet, *Thaïs*, Méditation, bars 3–10.

of love. Giselda, singing with her full voice and supported by the entire orchestra, is given the kind of final apotheosis that, each in her own way, Isolde, Salome, and Elektra had voiced in their operas, but that had been denied Fiora by her early, sudden death. As Giselda sings "O Primavera eterna, mi dono a te!" (O eternal Spring, I give myself to you; no. 50),[78] a seven-part, D-flat major, offstage choir, not envisaged by Benelli but a clear expression of Giselda's self-awareness, is introduced, its vocalizing on the exclamation "Ah!" to be performed *sempre molto sentito* (always very heartfelt).[79] An organ adds to the overall impact of this final peroration in the last three bars. Whether or not Montemezzi felt that this scene of sheer euphoria might represent his operatic swan song, it is hard not to feel that it brings down the curtain on his stage career in a particularly appropriate manner.

Perhaps a certain defiant note, too, can be heard in the conclusion of *L'incantesimo*. The final stage of Montemezzi's work on the opera coincided with what must have been a very difficult period for him personally, and he surely worried that the opera might never be performed. His world really was "torn up by war" when, to the horror of Italian Americans, Japan attacked the United States on December 7, 1941, and then, four days later, Italy declared war. Immediately after the attack on Pearl Harbor, all Italians in the United States were categorized as enemy aliens, and the arrests began of those considered potentially dangerous. By December 10, 147 Italians had been arrested, including 48 in Los Angeles, as "the Italian community

---

[78] The score departs slightly from the printed libretto here.
[79] Cesare Orselli finds the possible influence of Debussy's *Sirènes* in this choral addition: Orselli, "Montemezzi dà voce," p. 12. Montemezzi's autograph vocal score, dated June 2, 1941, contains at pp. 60–63 an alternative version of this chorus, substituting the vocalizations with words derived from a selection of Giselda's final lines, exalting the "eternal Spring." Intriguingly, in 1929, Montemezzi had accepted a commission for three *vocalizzi* for Casa Ricordi's collection of *Vocalizzi nello Stile Moderno* (1929), but never supplied them. Casa Ricordi to Montemezzi, March 27, 1929. Archivio Storico Ricordi, Copialettere.

320 SUCCEEDING PUCCINI

in Los Angeles observed . . . in stunned silence."[80] Over the following months
Montemezzi would have been subject to an increasing range of restrictions,
culminating in the Public Proclamation No. 5 of March 24, 1942, imposing
a curfew. Like other Italians in Southern California, he was now required to
be at home from 8 p.m. until 6 a.m. each day, and to travel no more than five
miles from his place of residence.[81] Onerous as this must have seemed, he
would have known that he was comparatively lucky; in many coastal areas of
California, enemy aliens were required to evacuate their homes, and nearby
Orange County decided to exclude all enemy aliens in February.[82] Moreover,
the Montemezzis would have been well aware that many groups in the United
States were calling for all enemy aliens to be placed in concentration camps.
In the atmosphere of early 1942, even speaking Italian could be viewed with
suspicion, and many Italian Americans thus voluntarily relinquished the use
of their native language for the duration of the war.[83]

How Montemezzi dealt with the trauma of 1942 is unclear, as there are
no letters from this period. There is some intriguing evidence, though, that
he may have turned to "light" forms of composition, perhaps mainly as a di-
version. On May 20, 1942, he completed a short symphonic "Serenata," a
"serenade" to which he gave the Spanish title *A ti, hermosa!* (To you, beautiful!). The work survives in manuscript full score, with a full set of parts and
a piano reduction.[84] The parts suggest that there may have been some sort
of private performance, but we have been unable to trace any performance
prior to its inclusion in a concert in Verona in 2003.[85] *A ti, hermosa!* might
be described as a light-hearted symphonic piece in a neoclassical style that
recalls Prokofiev's *Classical Symphony* (the *Larghetto* of which shares several
features) and looks back to the Haydnesque model of the *Allegretto scher-
zando* from Beethoven's Eighth Symphony. A mood of sheer entertainment
is established as the steady, regular beat of the winds hosts a light-hearted
melody in the upper strings, introduced by cellos and basses. Organized
in an irregular rondo structure (ABACD), the piece proposes as a contrast

[80] Gloria Ricci Lothrop, "The Untold Story: The Effect of the Second World War on California
Italians," *Journal of the West* 35/1 (1996): p. 9.
[81] Lothrop, "The Untold Story," p. 12.
[82] Lothrop, "The Untold Story," p. 12.
[83] See Nancy C. Carnevale, "'No Italian Spoken for the Duration of the War': Language, Italian-
American Identity, and Cultural Pluralism in the World War II Years," *Journal of American Ethnic
History* 22/3 (2003): pp. 3–33.
[84] Donadelli family documents.
[85] Conducted by Enzo Ferraris, it was recorded on June 7, 2003, and was released by the Comune
di Vigasio in 2004 (IM002).

first a lyrical melody in the violins (B, no. 2), then a more sentimental episode, the most colorful and harmonically expressive in the score (C, no. 4). *A ti, hermosa!* ends with an ecstatic, effective D-flat-major final episode (D, no. 6), dominated by the liquid arpeggios of the harp and celesta, among other instruments, the latter being given the last word.

Another composition, seemingly from this period, is the song *Per star con te!* (To be with you!). In this case there is a working sketch, two fair copies of the score, and an English translation of the lyric (with corrections).[86] The music paper matches that used for the vocal score of *L'incantesimo* and *A ti, hermosa!*. *Per star con te!*, titled *Serenata al vento* (Serenade to the wind) in the working sketch, is a chamber song in a light-hearted pop idiom, again with a retrospective flavor, this time recalling the turn-of-the-century romances by Francesco Paolo Tosti (1846–1916). The text, a very banal romantic declaration, expresses the speaker's love for his lady, asks her whether this is reciprocated, and concludes with the promise of eternal love. The E-flat song is structured as a classical ABA *Liedform*. A coquettish piano ostinato (the short piano introduction, missing in the working sketch, was added later) introduces the full-voice melody for the tenor, culminating in the melodic peak on "bella come il sol" (beautiful as the sun). A G-flat-major episode offers only a restrained contrast, before the song returns to the original E-flat-major for the final declaration: "T'amo tanto, e sol vivrò, mio grande amor, per star con te!" (I love you so much and only live, my great love, to be with you!). We have found no record of any performance.

Toward the end of 1942, the political situation began to improve. With a presidential election approaching in November, Franklin D. Roosevelt realized there was a real danger of Italian Americans withdrawing their support from the Democratic Party. Consequently, on October 12, 1942—symbolically, Columbus Day—it was announced that from October 19, Italians would no longer be classed as enemy aliens, and that most restrictions would be lifted. The news was greeted with euphoria in Italian American communities. Montemezzi had already been scheduled to conduct *L'amore dei tre re* in San Francisco on October 23, and must have obtained a special travel permit, but in the end this was not needed. This time Moore was unavailable, and Jean Tennyson proved an inferior substitute. "What a shocking thing that Montemezzi permitted his beautiful opera to be so crucified," Moore commented spitefully, almost certainly failing to realize just how

---

[86] Donadelli family documents.

322 SUCCEEDING PUCCINI

relieved the composer would have been to be able to travel and conduct at this juncture.[87] It was, in fact, to be the last performance of *L'amore dei tre re* in the United States for over two years, a period in which a story portraying Italy as the innocent victim of foreign aggression hardly struck the right political note.[88] But now Montemezzi at least had the much more appropriate *L'incantesimo* to start promoting.

---

[87] Grace Moore to Clara Marafioti, January 7, 1943. Chandler collection.
[88] *L'amore dei tre re* largely disappeared from the international stage in the later war years, though there was a notable revival at the Teatro Colón, Buenos Aires, in July 1944, conducted by Ettore Panizza.

10

"The same Italianate song"

Italia mia! Nulla fermerà il tuo canto!, 1943–1952

As 1943 commenced, Montemezzi probably began feeling more comfortable in his personal circumstances, even if the international situation remained grim, with no obvious end to the war in sight. As with much of his life, it is difficult to get a sense of how he passed the time, but he provided some clues in an interview with Enid A. Haupt toward the end of this year: "Montemezzi keeps in condition by long walks which have replaced the drives he enjoyed before gas rationing. With his American-born wife, Katherine Leith, he plays golf, bridge and gin-rummy."[1] This suggests a leisurely lifestyle perhaps built around regular routines. There was a good amount of entertaining and socializing, generally organized by Katherine. The fullest account of this, and a valuable portrait of the Montemezzis in the early 1940s, is by Evelyn Barbirolli, wife of the conductor John Barbirolli:

> We used to go to lunch occasionally at the Montemezzis. Italo Montemezzi, a charming Venetian [*sic*] composer, loved to talk Venetian with John. . . . Montemezzi's wife, Catherine [*sic*], was a vigorous New Yorker who felt strongly that Italo had never had the success which was his due, and she tried hard to remedy this. Italo didn't mind at all: he lived comfortably and adored playing golf. I had the impression that he no longer bothered to compose (I think Catherine was wealthy). He was likeable and attractive. Catherine's lunches were well-known, and she often invited famous people in the hope that they would do something for Italo's music. The lunches always took place out of doors (it hardly ever rained in that part of California, so planning could be done well in advance without risk). The table was long and very narrow so that you could talk comfortably to your opposite neighbour as well as the one next to you. I remember one luncheon when

---

[1] Enid A. Haupt, "Enchanting Fabric," *Philadelphia Inquirer*, November 14, 1943, p. 4.

Succeeding Puccini. David Chandler and Raffaele Mellace, Oxford University Press. © Oxford University Press 2025.
DOI: 10.1093/9780197761373.003.0011

324   SUCCEEDING PUCCINI

> Stravinsky was sitting opposite John; he looked even more dour and dismal
> than usual and was taking no part in the conversation.[2]

The description is most useful for its suggestion that Montemezzi had developed an appearance of indifference to the fate of his music. It was certainly just an appearance, as his letters make clear, but to people who knew him only superficially, he must have decided to strike an unconcerned pose, perhaps in recognition of the fact that he was, on the whole, in a very privileged position. The reference to Stravinsky's visits is also fascinating; it is not clear what Robert Craft wanted to imply when he wrote that "Stravinsky's connection with Italo Montemezzi ... was purely social."[3]

Montemezzi's principal professional goal was now to get *L'incantesimo* performed. It had been composed independently of Casa Ricordi, who were very likely still unaware of the opera's existence, and certainly in no position to help launch it. This was a new situation for Montemezzi, and he conceived the idea of a radio broadcast, believing, perhaps optimistically, that in this way "millions of people could hear it."[4] He made a "special request" to Samuel Chotzinoff, music director of the National Broadcasting Company (NBC): "Long an admirer of the NBC Symphony Orchestra, he expressed a wish that his new creation be performed with this orchestra. NBC acceded with enthusiasm."[5] Montemezzi was paid a fee of $1,000.[6] It is entirely possible that even before this juncture he had come to think of *L'incantesimo* as particularly suited to radio performance, for the opera's dramatic weakness, the fact that the scenes with Folco in the snow are narrated rather than enacted, becomes something of a strength in a purely aural medium. The idea of an opera specially for radio was about a decade old. The first Italian example appears to have been Riccardo Pick-Mangiagalli's *L'ospite inatteso*, a "radiophonic" opera first broadcast on the Milan-Turin-Genoa network on October 25, 1931; the first American example was Charles Wakefield Cadman's *The Willow Tree*, broadcast on October 3, 1932. The early examples were quickly forgotten, however, and at the time of the war, the only one to

---

[2] Evelyn Barbirolli, *Life with Glorious John* (London: Robson Books, 2002), p. 84.

[3] Robert Craft, *An Improbable Life: Memoirs by Robert Craft* (Nashville, TN: Vanderbilt University Press, 2002), p. 139.

[4] "New Montemezzi Opera Saturday," *New York Evening Post*, October 5, 1943, p. 28.

[5] Viva Liebling, "News and Previews of Radio, Stage and Screen," *Musical Courier*, October 5, 1943, p. 8.

[6] Montemezzi to Sem Benelli, June 1, 1946. Archivio Sem Benelli, Biblioteca della Società Economica di Chiavari.

ITALIA MIA! NULLA FERMERÀ IL TUO CANTO! 325

have really registered in America's musical consciousness was Gian Carlo Menotti's *Old Maid and the Thief* of 1939, to this day sometimes misleadingly described as the first radio opera.

In the run-up to the first performance of *L'incantesimo*, Montemezzi appears to have deliberately associated the opera with resistance to Mussolini's regime. The *Musical Courier* reported, presumably on his authority, that the composer was "a stanch enemy of Fascism" and Benelli "as ardent an anti-Fascist as Montemezzi."[7] This formula was, at the least, the wrong way around, given how much Benelli suffered for his political views, but it was not demonstrably untrue and Montemezzi could now congratulate himself on having collaborated with such an author, and on having an opera that must have seemed more relevant in 1943 than it had in 1933, in its call for a renewal of Italy. *L'incantesimo* was broadcast between 1:30 and 2:30 p.m. on Saturday October 9, 1943, with Montemezzi himself conducting the work before an audience in Studio 8-H, Radio City, New York, the studio from which *The Old Man and the Thief* had been broadcast four years earlier. Montemezzi was "insistent" about having Alexander Sved (Sándor Svéd, 1906–1979), an old friend, take the part of Folco.[8] Vivian Della Chiesa (1915–2009) sang Giselda, Mario Berini sang Rinaldo, and Virgilio Lazzari, celebrated for his performances of Archibaldo, took the role of Salomone. There was a slight, and slightly ironic, echo of the coincidence of art and politics which had marked the premiere of *La nave* a quarter of a century earlier. After the opera had reached its ecstatic conclusion, there came "the second after . . . the announcement of important, gratifying and murderous war news."[9] This news is most likely to have concerned the Allied advance into Italy, against stiff German opposition, which was dominating headlines at the time. Mussolini, who had already largely lost power, was head of the two-week-old Italian Social Republic purely by courtesy of the Germans.

Olin Downes of the *New York Times* was the most enthusiastic of the critics. A great lover of *L'amore dei tre re*, he had been unimpressed by *Giovanni Gallurese* and had condemned *La notte di Zoraima*, but he welcomed *L'incantesimo* as a return to form:

---

[7] Liebling, "News and Previews," p. 8.
[8] "Montemezzi Opera Premiered by NBC," *Musical Courier*, October 20, 1943, p. 7.
[9] Olin Downes, "Montemezzi Opera in Radio Premiere," *New York Times*, October 10, 1943, p. 48.

326 SUCCEEDING PUCCINI

It is evident that in his score Mr. Montemezzi has said nothing that is new since the score of "L'Amore dei tre re"—a similar theme. His lyricism has the same ardent pulse and sweep of line—a lyricism less coarse and vital, perhaps, than that of Puccini or other Italian realists, but wholly poetical in color and exaltation, without grease, and superbly vocal. In other words, we have in the finest pages of "L'Incantesimo" the same priceless melodic substance, so scarce today in music; the same Italianate song in terms of translated symphonism, which made "L'Amore"; the same freedom from dross[;] and poetic sentiment. Just some more of it, which is splendid, and likely to be of wide popular appeal.[10]

Marion Bauer, the distinguished American composer, was also very impressed, judging the broadcast a historic event: "For the first time an opera by a composer of his [Montemezzi's] rank has been given its world premiere by radio." She found in the new opera "Montemezzi's finest style of beautiful lyricism, rich harmonization and splendid orchestration. . . . this work is sincere and natural music . . . the entire effect is beautiful and noble."[11] Oscar Thompson, who reviewed the work for the *New York Sun* and *Musical America*, was not quite as positive, emphasizing that *L'incantesimo* would not work in the theatre. He denied charges of Wagnerianism, judging that:

if its lyric blood is that of Mascagni, Leoncavallo and Puccini, it runs a more aristocratic course, both in its basic inspiration and in the employment of a technique superior to theirs in the refinements of the musical art. Like that of "L'Amore," the music of "L'Incantesimo" has a patrician cast.[12]

Although some critics found the opera lacking in impact, the reviews as a whole made far happier reading than those of *La notte di Zoraima* by the same critics, and Montemezzi also received many letters and telegrams from friends and acquaintances praising the new opera.[13]

The problem with *L'incantesimo* was the question of what would happen next. NBC understood the live broadcast as a one-off prestigious event and did not broadcast it again; on the other hand, several critics joined

[10] Downes, "Montemezzi Opera," p. 48.
[11] Marion Bauer, "Montemezzi's New Opera," *Musical Leader*, November 1943, p. 7.
[12] Oscar Thompson, "New Montemezzi Opera Has Radio Premiere," *Musical America*, October 1943, p. 13.
[13] Donadelli family documents.

ITALIA MIA! NULLA FERMERÀ IL TUO CANTO! 327

Thompson in questioning its suitability for staging, and late 1943 was not a good time to be launching a new opera, especially without the help of a publisher. Indeed, *L'incantesimo* was never staged in Montemezzi's lifetime—a situation seemingly encouraged by its entering America's musical memory as a classic radio opera. When, in early 1946, *Musical America* conducted the third of their polls about radio music with "music editors and critics of the daily newspapers in the United States and Canada," they included the question:

> 2. Are you in favor of more operas written especially for radio—operas in which the composer takes into account radio's unique advantages as well as its limitations—like the works of Gian Carlo Menotti and Italo Montemezzi given in recent years?[14]

A resounding 83% of respondents answered "Yes." Both question and answer represent a powerful endorsement of *L'incantesimo*, but by coupling it with Menotti's *Old Maid and the Thief*, specifically composed as a radio opera to an NBC commission, *Musical America* was pressing a misleading, albeit flattering case that *L'incantesimo* was also, as the question put it, "written especially for radio" (*The Old Maid and the Thief* had been staged by 1946, so the category did not necessarily preclude subsequent stage performance). Herbert F. Peyser also insisted that *L'incantesimo* was a "radio opera"—the best he had heard—and claimed that both Benelli and Montemezzi intended it as such: "Any attempt to objectify the work in conventional stage form would almost certainly involve modifications that would mar its authors' aims."[15] Private recordings of the 1943 broadcast were soon circulating among collectors and have continued to do so to the present day; they have an aura which perhaps continues to work against exploration of the opera's theatrical possibilities.[16] Yet Montemezzi clearly wanted to see *L'incantesimo* staged.

Around the period when *L'incantesimo* was broadcast, Montemezzi embarked on what proved his last known composition: a second symphonic

[14] "Matters of Opinion," *Musical America*, May 1946, p. 6.
[15] Herbert F. Peyser, "An Appreciation of L'Amore dei Tre Re," *Musical America*, February 1949, p. 142.
[16] At the time of writing, there have been just three stagings: at Verona, soon after Montemezzi's death (discussed in our Epilogue), by the Opera Theater of Pittsburgh in 2010, and by the Latvian National Opera in 2019. There have also been concert performances in New York in 2007 and Milan in 2018.

328 SUCCEEDING PUCCINI

poem. Though originally performed as *My Italy! Nothing will stop your Song!*, this is usually known by its Italian title, *Italia mia! Nulla fermerà il tuo canto!*. Montemezzi had some difficulty deciding on the second part of the title.[17] It was completed on July 14, 1944, as the decisive Battle of Normandy was raging in Europe. Zandonai may have offered a model with his *Autunno fra i monti—Patria lontana*, composed in 1917–1918 when he was exiled from his native Trentino. Formally, *Italia mia!* strikes an interesting balance between narrative development and classical symmetries derived from absolute music. The overall theme can be identified as the struggle between Italy's lyrical vocation—a destiny of art, peace, love—and the threat of war. The overall structure, clearly if not symmetrically organized, has a large introductory section establishing Italy's longing for peace and beauty (nos. 1–3); the core of the composition then juxtaposes contrasting evocations of war and peace, the juxtaposition repeated and varied three times, each ending with a short-lived *tranquillo* episode (nos. 4–7, 8–10, 11–18); finally the conflict is resolved in a peaceful coda (no. 19).

The first section is clearly inspired by the last movement of Beethoven's Ninth Symphony, its *recitativo* by cellos and basses dramatically posing, right from the abrupt start, a wordless question answered by the *appoggiatura* of three muted solo violins, oboes, and English horn (Example 10.1). This becomes an essential gesture which plays a crucial role in the first section, seemingly symbolizing the possibility of relief, a promise fulfilled as the full sections of strings, woodwinds, harp, celesta, and horns establish, with a fluid *animando un poco* dominated by triplets, a sentimental atmosphere recalling *Paolo e Virginia* (no. 2). The soaring melodic *élan* of the violins in the upper register evokes a sort of acoustic paradise where woodwinds twitter (no. 3). The growing tension leads, however, to the central part of the score (no. 4). The warlike atmosphere relies, as in *L'amore dei tre re*, on a rhythmic invention: the steady, dull ostinato of semiquavers performed by second violins in their mid-register, backed by all the strings, dominating a martial *Mosso (non troppo)* section (Example 10.2) energized by the fanfares of trumpets and horns, enhanced by the roll of timpani and steel drum, and culminating in a violent brass chorale. Then the solo oboe suddenly fantasizing *tranquillo* against the silence of the orchestra is answered by arcane Wagnerian-sounding chords from the woodwinds before activating

---

[17] The manuscript sketch among the Donadelli family documents shows the composer wavering between *Nessuno fermerà il tuo canto*, *Nulla mai fermerà il tuo canto*, and *Nulla fermerà mai il tuo canto*, before settling on the final version.

Music Example 10.1 *Italia mia! Nulla fermerà il tuo canto!*, bars 1–6.

Music Example 10.2 *Italia mia! Nulla fermerà il tuo canto!*, no. 4, bars 1–3.

330 SUCCEEDING PUCCINI

a broad, soaring melody of the first violins involving the entire orchestra, hinting at a different, albeit very short-lived perspective (no. 7). The *Mosso* section makes another appearance (no. 8), again contrasted with a bright, D-major melody of *unisono* violins (no. 9), then for a third time contradicted by the martial, minor-key episode (no. 11), dominated by the brass chorale and the inescapable sound of the steel drum. Once the climax of the tension has been reached (no. 13), a *diminuendo* reduces the texture to a constant dotted rhythm of cellos and basses, the tremolo of upper strings and steel drum. The melancholic solo oboe resumes its *tranquillo* song on the aforementioned evocative woodwind chords, leading to a final *Largamente* (no. 15), recruiting the full sections of strings and woodwinds *piano, espressivo e crescendo poco a poco*, supporting a beautiful soaring melody of the first violins, as the *appoggiaturas* from the opening section return in bright B-flat major. In this culminating section preceding the Coda, Montemezzi's music attains a strong Straussian flavor, and can hardly help sounding as a continuing declaration of faith in Belle Époque modernism some thirty years after its heyday. This intense lyricism is wound down in the Coda (no. 19), characterized by a widespread pattern of semiquavers suggesting the suspension of motion and leading to the final, surprise effect of bells sounding "*come se venissero da una chiesa lontana*" (as if from a distant church). In this nostalgic ending, the powerful sense of distance aptly conveys the personal significance of Montemezzi's last composition, in its combined spatial and temporal aspects: the object of his longing is not just Italy, but the Italy of 1913, the year of his greatest triumph just before the land which nurtured him was shaken to its foundations by two world wars.

In the background, of course, was the ongoing international conflict. In June 1944, Montemezzi wrote to Bruno Zirato that he did not "feel well morally" with the world still at war and his son about to commence military service.[18] Marco Montemezzi had entered the California Institute of Technology in 1942, but was called up for military service in August 1944, entering the U.S. Navy and training at Naval Station Treasure Island, San Francisco.[19] On Treasure Island, Marco developed a close friendship with Walter Couture, from a wealthy family in Jamestown, New York; Walter became a frequent visitor to the Montemezzi home.[20] On May 8, 1945,

---

[18] Bruno Zirato to Montemezzi, June 19, 1944, New York Philharmonic archives.
[19] Montemezzi to Alfredo Colombo, December 22, 1945. Ricordi Collection, Music Library, Northwestern University.
[20] "Round About Town," *Jamestown Post-Journal*, January 19, 1949, p. 26.

ITALIA MIA! NULLA FERMERÀ IL TUO CANTO! 331

Victory In Europe Day, and just in time for his nineteenth birthday, Marco relinquished his Italian citizenship and became a naturalized American.[21] The significance of this cannot be overstated, for there was no requirement for foreign-born servicemen to naturalize, though military service allowed them an expediated route to do so, and between July 1, 1942, and June 30, 1945, over 9,000 Italians in the U.S. Armed Forces took advantage of it.[22] Marco's naturalization was a clear statement that the family saw its future in the United States, not Italy. The end of the war meant that he did not see active service, and he left the Navy in July 1946, returning to Caltech from which he graduated in 1949 with a bachelor of science degree.

There were, no doubt, regular trips to New York in these years, for most of Katherine's family still lived in the New York area and there were significant family events, with Katherine's nieces getting married and having children.[23] Montemezzi witnessed the passing of an older generation, too, when Katherine's mother died on February 8, 1946; this brought a considerable accession to their wealth, Marinda's estate having a gross value over $700,000.[24] This probably explains why, in the spring of 1946, the Montemezzis were "in New York for a few weeks, and therefore extremely busy."[25] Members of the new generation of the family born in the 1940s later remembered seeing Montemezzi as an elderly, white-haired man at family events, but nothing more of him. His English was never very good and as most of the family knew no Italian, communication must have been limited.

The premiere of *My Italy!* finally took place on July 30, 1946, in a Hollywood Bowl concert also including Mozart's *Don Giovanni* overture, Beethoven's Seventh Symphony, and a new work by José Iturbi, with Leopold Stokowski conducting his recently founded Hollywood Bowl Symphony Orchestra. Montemezzi was able to attend the rehearsals. He and Katherine were boxholders at the Bowl, and Montemezzi admired the acoustics there. *My Italy!* made only a mild impression, and critics heard different things in

---

[21] U.S. Citizenship and Immigration Services C-File C6489317.

[22] Watson B. Miller, "Foreign Born in the United States Army During World War II, with Special Reference to the Alien," *Monthly Review—Immigration and Naturalization Service* 6/4 (October 1948): p. 53.

[23] Alice C. Conreid (1912–2010), the oldest niece, daughter of Margaret, gave birth to her first child, Henry Glendon Walter III, in 1940, and a daughter, Margaret Wendy Walter, a year or two later. Dorothy's first child, Muriel B. Brown (1920–2009), married Sylvan Barnet in 1941; they had two children, Peter Barnet, born 1943, and Bruce Barnet, born 1945.

[24] "Two Deal Residents Share Leith Estate," *Asbury Park Evening Press*, April 24, 1948, p. 10.

[25] "a New York per alcune settimane, e perciò straoccupati." Montemezzi to Francesco Donadelli, May 14, 1946. Donadelli family documents.

332   SUCCEEDING PUCCINI

it. Richard Drake Saunders judged it "sonorous nothings in the operatic style of the last century."[26] Mildred Norton considered it "a fervent musical apostrophe . . . a pleasantly concocted tonal mélange, full of swirling Straussian orchestration, and while it is turgid in spots, without direction, and overlong, it has some nice moments."[27] In contrast, Patterson Greene found the work "rich in the melodic phraseology of the country to which it is dedicated. Its themes, though they never develop into forthright tunes, are suffused with the essential quality of Italian popular melodies. They are well integrated, and the orchestration is sensuous."[28] None of the critics, notably, detected any kind of program. "It went very well, and in winter it will be performed in New York and many other cities in the United States," Montemezzi reported.[29] However, we have found no records of further performances in his lifetime, and by 1946 it was clearer than ever that none of his other music would emerge from the gigantic shadow cast by *L'amore dei tre re*. He never renounced composition entirely, and in 1948 was telling Verna Arvey that he was "looking ahead and planning future works," and "eager to visit Italy, if only to find there a good libretto."[30] In April 1952, the month before he died, Montemezzi was trying to obtain a copy of the one-act comedy *Spacca il centesimo* (1931) by the famous actor and playwright Peppino De Filippo (1903–1980), presumably because he thought it had operatic potential.[31] Nevertheless, *My Italy!* was Montemezzi's last premiere, and if any music was composed subsequent to 1944, it does not appear to have survived.

In the postwar period, *L'amore dei tre re* entered the sunset of its fame, but there was little sign yet that it would soon start dropping out of the international repertoire. It was chosen to open the third opera festival held in Dayton, Ohio, on May 15, 1945: fortuitously, exactly a week after Germany surrendered. A more significant production was mounted the following year when the Cincinnati Opera, founded in 1920, included it in their Silver Jubilee season (they had missed a season in 1925) and invited Montemezzi to conduct. He was reluctant, because of the summer heat, and joked that he

---

[26] Richard Drake Saunders, "Los Angeles," *Musical Courier*, September 1946, p. 35.

[27] Mildred Norton, "Music Review," *Daily News* (Los Angeles), July 31, 1946, p. 19.

[28] Greene's review, "New Music at Bowl," from the *Los Angeles Examiner*, is preserved in the Los Angeles Philharmonic Archives. Page numbers are not recorded.

[29] "Andò benissimo, ed in inverno si eseguirà a New York e in parecchie altre città degli Stati Uniti." Montemezzi to Francesco Donadelli, August 27, 1946. Donadelli family documents.

[30] Verna Arvey, "Visits to the Homes of Famous Composers No. XIV: Italo Montemezzi," *Opera and Concert*, November 1948, p. 15.

[31] Angelo Ghiro to Montemezzi, April 10, 1952. Donadelli family documents.

would have to perform "in a swimming costume," but in the end agreed.[32] The Montemezzis arrived in Cincinnati on July 3, only a few days before the first performance, and there was apparently no time for a full dress rehearsal with the staging in place. This led to a comic episode, for Adam Bruehl had arranged an unorthodox stage for Act 2, with Armand Tokatyan's Avito on the far side, rather than the near side, of the wall on which Lily Djanel's Fiora was to stand. Montemezzi only became aware of this arrangement on the night of the first performance, July 9, and expressed his dissatisfaction in no uncertain terms. He refused to proceed unless the wall could be reduced in height, and this led to a forty-five-minute delay which made front-page news in the local press.[33] Despite this, the performance was a sensation. There was "[w]ild applause" and critics judged it "the greatest triumph of the season" to that date: no mean accolade given that it followed *Otello*, *La traviata*, *Tannhäuser*, *Madama Butterfly*, *Carmen*, and *Aida*. Lazzari, returning to the role of Archibaldo, was especially admired.[34] Montemezzi felt it was "a truly sensational success."[35]

The 1946 Cincinnati production was in fact so successful that the management repeated it the following year, again with Montemezzi conducting. This time Mary Leighton reported to *Musical America*:

> Because of its dramatic potency, and [the] fresh and vital quality of the score, Montemezzi's The Love of Three Kings, with the composer conducting, hit the peak of the week.... Virgilio Lazzari repeated his sensational triumph of last season (when the opera was revived) as the blind king, Archibaldo, receiving what will doubtless be the biggest ovation of the season.[36]

The "week" in question had included *Lohengrin*, *Carmen*, *Aida*, *Madama Butterfly*, and *Il trovatore*, so again it was clear that *L'amore dei tre re* could compete on perfectly equal terms with operas that have gone on being stalwarts of the repertoire. Such demonstrations of enthusiasm, and the corresponding critical verdicts, obviously gave Montemezzi a great deal of pleasure.

---

[32] "in costume da bagno." Montemezzi to Alfredo Colombo, letter postmarked April 9, 1946. Ricordi Collection, Music Library, Northwestern University.

[33] "Opera Obstacle: Scenery Shifting Delays Opening," *Cincinnati Post*, July 10, 1946, p. 1.

[34] Eleanor Bell, "Opera: Love of 3 Kings," *Cincinnati Post*, July 10, 1946, p. 16.

[35] "un successo veramente clamoroso." Montemezzi to Francesco Donadelli, August 27, 1946.

[36] Mary Leighton, "Cincinnati's Summer Opera Season Opens Auspiciously with Lohengrin," *Musical America*, July 1947, p. 16.

334   SUCCEEDING PUCCINI

The San Francisco Opera followed Cincinnati's lead and asked Montemezzi to conduct *L'amore dei tre re* for them later in 1947, with Dorothy Kirsten (1910–1992) singing Fiora for the first time. He spent a good deal of time coaching Kirsten, perhaps seeing her as a natural successor to Grace Moore, who had been tragically killed in a plane crash that January. Kirsten considered this a "good fortune" and "privilege": "[w]orking with Montemezzi was certainly another high point in my career."[37] The greatest benefit, she believed, was the opportunity "to learn firsthand everything there is to know about the character." She was informed that the opera "is an entirely symbolic drama. Fiora represents Italy." Montemezzi paid great attention to every aspect of the performance. In Act 2, for example, when Fiora has to stand on the ramparts and wave the veil, Kirsten found that:

> Montemezzi wanted it done to a certain tempo and also at special places clearly marked in the score. I tried different fabrics until I found one that floated in the slight breeze created by an electric fan placed behind the scenery. The fan kept the veil afloat against the sky for just the right number of beats before it was drawn back for another wave.[38]

Kirsten judged the biggest challenge of singing under Montemezzi to be the extended phrasing he wanted:

> Charles Kullmann, who had sung the opera with Montemezzi before, warned me to be prepared for slower tempos and stretched-out phrases. I was grateful for that tip, because the vocal line that Montemezzi wanted without an interfering breath was already very long. It was truly a tour de force.... Later, when I sang the opera with other conductors, including Tullio Serafin, it was a much easier task.[39]

The performance itself was another great success. Arthur Bloomfield remembered:

> a thrilling performance, with the white-maned Montemezzi himself in the pit. The climax of the second act ... was so exciting that the oft-reserved Regular Series audience applauded vigorously and long.[40]

[37] Dorothy Kirsten, *A Time to Sing* (New York: Doubleday, 1982), p. 189.
[38] Kirsten, *A Time to Sing*, pp. 190–91.
[39] Kirsten, *A Time to Sing*, p. 133.
[40] Arthur Bloomfield, *The San Francisco Opera: 1922–1978* (Sausalito, CA: Comstock Editions, 1978), p. 99.

The San Francisco production was taken on to Los Angeles where, on October 24, Montemezzi conducted his opera for the last time. Again there was enthusiastic applause and reviews.

The broader critical climate was also encouraging. In July 1947, *Musical America* ran the editorial quoted in our Introduction, lamenting the increasing tendency of American opera companies to repeat the same dozen or so favorite operas, though adding: "This is not to intimate that the average operatic organization ought to consider it a sworn duty to perform, along with its Traviata or its Faust, something like Tristan, Pelléas, Rosenkavalier or L'Amore dei Tre Re."[41] The implications do not need spelling out. In the same year, Donald Jay Grout's soon-to-be-classic *Short History of Opera* delivered its resounding verdict, also quoted in our Introduction: "[*L'amore dei tre re*] is without doubt the greatest Italian tragic opera since Verdi's *Otello*."[42] In January 1949, *Opera News* devoted a special issue to *L'amore dei tre re*, in conjunction with what turned out to be the Met's last revival of their old favorite. Here the young Jane Phillips (1926–2013)—later, as Mary Jane Phillips-Matz, the author of major biographies of Verdi and Puccini—delivered perhaps the most positive assessment of all: "it takes its place in tragedy's highest ranks. It is the best, not only of opera, but of drama and poetry, not only for today but for all people in all time."[43] The following month, *Musical America* published a long, enthusiastic, richly illustrated essay on Montemezzi by Peyser, suggesting that "one might almost say" *L'amore dei tre re* belonged to the United States "by adoption," and that it was "only fitting" that the composer had made California his home.[44] Montemezzi and Katherine had many friends with musical interests, so it is certain that such acclaim was brought to his attention, and it doubtless helped endear him to life in the United States.

L'amore dei tre re was returning to the stage in other countries, too. Most satisfying for Montemezzi was a revival at La Scala, with three performances, directed by Sem Benelli, commencing on October 12, 1948. On August 3 he wrote to Mario Labroca, the artistic director at La Scala, offering to assist at the rehearsals and to attend the performances; Labroca somewhat tersely replied that Montemezzi was welcome to attend, but made it clear his advice

---

[41] "Towards More Variety in the Operatic Diet," *Musical America*, July 1947, p. 7.

[42] Donald Jay Grout, *A Short History of Opera*, 2 vols. (New York: Columbia University Press, 1947), vol. 2, pp. 444–45.

[43] Jane Phillips, "Ay, Every Inch a King," *Opera News*, January 10, 1949, p. 31.

[44] Herbert F. Peyser, "An Appreciation of L'Amore dei Tre Re," *Musical America*, February 1949, p. 14.

336 SUCCEEDING PUCCINI

was not wanted.[45] Montemezzi must have been hurt by this rebuff, so different from his recent experiences with American companies, but nevertheless finally decided to return to Italy.

Perhaps the biggest biographical question posed by Montemezzi's final decade is why it took him until 1948 to make this decision. During the war, Ezio Pinza had been a regular visitor in Beverly Hills, and the two men liked to talk "about politics, especially about going back to Italy."[46] As early as December 22, 1945, Montemezzi had written to Alfredo Colombo: "I shall return to Italy as soon as it is possible; that is when there is a certain arrangement for travels."[47] On March 28, 1947, he was more specific: "Between 1st June and the end of September, I will choose a period of a couple of months to come to Italy."[48] Yet despite such statements regularly appearing in his letters, the summer of 1948 had arrived without any return, or definite plan for one. The only credible explanation would seem to be that Montemezzi was afraid of what he would find. He had read and heard much about the wartime devastation and reacted with horror: "I was cut to pieces by the dismal descriptions, concerning my poor Italy!"[49] His own world had been transformed and he almost certainly sensed that there was no possible return to his and Katherine's pre-war lifestyle. Of the valuables and furniture sent from the Milan apartment first to Switzerland, then on to Vigasio, a considerable part did not arrive, and was never subsequently recovered. Of the items left in the apartment at the time the German military occupied it, a great many had disappeared. Pia, the Montemezzis' servant, had been able to enter the apartment in January 1946, and she drew up a list of what was missing, including eight paintings and "13 antique chairs." It was a depressingly long list, and she added that everything still there was "half ramshackle."[50] The apartment had now been requisitioned by the Allied Military Government. Yet more possessions had been stolen from the Vigasio house. Montemezzi,

---

[45] Montemezzi's letter to Labroca was sold by Roger Gross in 2010. A copy of Labroca's reply, dated August 20, is in the La Scala archives.

[46] Robert Croan, "Opera Theater Under Montemezzi's 'Spell,'" *Pittsburgh Post-Gazette*, February 10, 2010, p. D3.

[47] "Io ritornerò in Italia appena si potrà; vale a dire quando ci sarà una certa sistemazione per i viaggi." Ricordi Collection, Music Library, Northwestern University.

[48] "Io, tra il 1° di giugno e l'ultimo di settembre, sceglierò un periodo di un paio di mesi per venire in Italia." Montemezzi to Alfredo Colombo, Ricordi Collection, Music Library, Northwestern University.

[49] "rimasi massacrato dalle lugubri descrizioni riguardanti la mia povera Italia!" Montemezzi to Alfredo Colombo, March 28, 1947.

[50] "13 sedie antiche," "mezzo sgangherato." Pia's report is included in Montemezzi to Francesco Donadelli, November 7, 1946. Donadelli family documents.

extremely upset about all this, tried hard to pursue claims for compensation, including inviting the Italian consul for dinner in Beverly Hills.[51] These claims were initially rejected in 1957, on the grounds that Katherine and Marco were no longer Italian citizens, then, after appeal, finally rejected in 1978.[52]

Montemezzi was also much concerned about the damage inflicted on his musical legacy by the war. He was appalled to learn that Casa Ricordi's headquarters on Via Berchet had been struck by Allied bombs in August 1943. As the details became clear, after the cessation of hostilities, it was revealed that while Ricordi still possessed performance materials for *L'amore dei tre re*, *Giovanni Gallurese*, and *La notte di Zoraima*—parts for the latter two having been retained in the United States—those for *Héllera* and *La nave* had been destroyed. This was a terrible blow, the two operas Montemezzi had tried so hard to see revived in the years before the war now being effectively unavailable for performance. In a series of letters, he urged Casa Ricordi to reconstruct performance parts using his autograph scores (which had survived) and the vocal scores, but the publisher clearly felt there was more urgent business needing attention. The performance materials for *La nave* were only finally reconstructed in 2012, when Teatro Grattacielo of New York offered to arrange a concert performance. Those for *Héllera* are still unavailable at the time of writing.

Other factors too may have made Montemezzi reluctant to return to Italy. He was concerned about the unstable political situation, and possibly inclined to depressive feelings. "The fact is that life today is, in my opinion, a great disappointment. When I think of Italy, and as you can imagine I always think about it, I no longer have peace. Let's not talk about it!" he wrote gloomily on December 12, 1946.[53] He had apparently supported the successful republican side in the great institutional referendum of this year, writing, "The King is also finished. It is right to say: He who breaks pays!,"[54] yet he must have known that such a view was hard to reconcile with some of his earlier political positions. Another possible factor, affecting him personally, was the collapse in the value of the lira. Rampant inflation in the later war years meant that by 1945 the urban cost of living was over twenty

---

[51] Montemezzi to Francesco Donadelli, December 12, 1946. Donadelli family documents.

[52] Unaddressed letter from the office of the Minister of the Treasury, June 5, 1978.

[53] "Quando penso all'Italia, e come immaginate ci penso sempre, non ho più pace. Non ne parliamo!" Montemezzi to Francesco Donadelli. Donadelli family documents.

[54] "Il Re ha anche lui finito. È il caso di dire: Chi rompe paga!" Montemezzi to Francesco Donadelli, June 19, 1946. Donadelli family documents.

338 SUCCEEDING PUCCINI

times what it had been in 1939.[55] Particularly relevant to the Montemezzis was the transformed exchange rate. Before the war, the lira traded at 19 to the United States dollar. In June 1945, an attempt was made to fix it at 100 to the dollar, but the massive black market refused to accept this valuation, and the following January the rate was revised to 225 lire to the dollar, and in November 1947 changed again to 575 lire to the dollar.[56] How much this affected the Montemezzis is unclear, but it tilted their wealth far more toward the dollar and Katherine's trust fund than had been the case before the war. Montemezzi had left some, and possibly most, of his money in the Banca Commerciale, Verona, and had collected rental income and paid taxes in Italy throughout the war years,[57] but whatever portion of his wealth was held in lire was now massively devalued. In 1946 he was persuaded to join a scheme that would ensure his landholdings by the Tartaro River benefited from a planned new irrigation system. He calculated that this would cost him around 127,000 lire and wrote: "Good heavens!!... That little money, earned in many, many years of hard work, is now going away like smoke in the wind!!"[58] Yet he must have realized that in 1946-dollar terms it was cheap.

With all this in the background, Montemezzi finally returned to Italy in October 1948. Whereas in the past he had traveled by ship, this time he flew with Trans World Airlines, which had started offering transatlantic flights in 1946. If Montemezzi was concerned about his reception, it seems he had reason to be. La Scala took some photographs of his visit to the theatre, and it is clear he appeared on stage, but astonishingly, of the nine known reviews, only one (in *Il Popolo*) mentions his presence at this significant revival of *L'amore dei tre re*.[59] The audience was described as responding enthusiastically to the opera, but while only two of the reviews were mostly negative, none of them struck the wholly admiring note that Montemezzi could take for granted in the United States, and there was much talk of "Wagnerianism" and "eclecticism." Supporting the assumption that Milan made no special acknowledgment of Montemezzi's return is the feature that Teodoro Celli

---

[55] P. Scholliers and V. Zamagni (eds.), *Labour's Reward: Real Wages and Economic Change in 19th- and 20th-Century Europe* (Aldershot, UK: Edward Elgar, 1995), pp. 231–32.

[56] Rainer Masera, "Inflation, Stabilization and Economic Recovery in Italy After the War: Vera Lutz's Assessment," *Banca Nazionale del Lavoro, PSL Quarterly Review* 36 (1983): pp. 35–36.

[57] Montemezzi's Italian accounts for the years 1939 to 1948 are preserved among the Donadelli family documents.

[58] "Apriti cielo!!... Quei pochi soldi guadagnati in tanti e tanti anni di fatiche, adesso se ne vanno come fumi al vento!!" Montemezzi to Francesco Donadelli, November 19, 1946. Donadelli family documents.

[59] The nine reviews are preserved in the Scala Archives.

ITALIA MIA! NULLA FERMERÀ IL TUO CANTO! 339

(1917–1989), a Wagnerian critic, wrote on this occasion. Celli, who lived in Milan, put great emphasis on Montemezzi's warm reception in Vigasio, remarking incidentally, and as though a point of merely sociological interest, "in villages they still act with a warmth and an enthusiasm that we from the cities have not seen for a long time."[60] Reading between the lines, it would seem that Montemezzi's return to Milan produced no such displays of affection as an admiring feature could chronicle, and there is reason to suppose this was a disappointment to him, and that it helps explain why another three years would pass before he returned to Italy again. It is easy to understand why some members of Milan's musical and media establishment might have had mixed feelings about the reappearance of a man who had missed all the suffering of the war years in comfortable, self-imposed exile, and then only returned so belatedly for his opera's new staging at La Scala. Possibly questions were asked about his politics, too. If his reception at La Scala was a disappointment, so too must have been Montemezzi's visit to the apartment at Via Maggiolini 1. As noted previously, after the war this had passed into the hands of the Allied Military Government, and it was subsequently passed on to the Italian Air Force, probably in 1946; it was still occupied by Air Force officers. The apartment was now in an "awful state of conservation," and the Montemezzis subsequently decided to sell it.[61]

But if there was disappointment in Milan, there was joy in Vigasio. Here Montemezzi was a "simple man of the land" returning to his birthplace:

> It was wonderful . . . that the people of Vigasio demonstrated so much enthusiasm for their fellow villager Italo Montemezzi, that is for a man who is not a sporting champion, nor a politician, but simply a musician. At the railway station they went to welcome him with a procession of cars, and Montemezzi, astonished, had not yet had time to get over the surprise when he was lifted bodily, thrust into a car, and carried to his home. There a large crowd acclaiming him was waiting, and the musician couldn't escape the hundreds of handshakes and the duty of an occasional little speech crowned at the end with enthusiastic applause. Dear village cordiality. It was the time of the festival, which involves fireworks and various celebrations. Those celebrations and illuminations had been immediately

---

[60] Teodoro Celli, "Lo Accolsero in Paese con Petardi e Luminarie: Vigasio ha un grosso debito col musicista Montemezzi," *Oggi*, October 24, 1948, p. 21.

[61] "in pessimo stato di conservazione." Notary act 25681, September 29, 1951. Agenzia delle Entrate, Servizio di Pubblicità Immobiliare di Milano 3.

340   SUCCEEDING PUCCINI

redirected toward the new objective (*obbiettivo*): a nice printed sign, stuck on the walls of his house, welcomed the illustrious son of Vigasio who has come back to his homeland, and announced that those celebrations and those "fires of joy" were for him, or at least for him as well.[62]

When Montemezzi was finally sitting in his old house, he was asked "what he wanted most, now he was finally in Italy, [and] he answered, after thinking about it for a while: 'A soup of rice and beans! [*Una minestra di risi e fasòi*].'"[63] Presumably such an attitude did much to endear him to his old neighbors. There was also a "particularly friendly and nostalgic evening" organized in Verona, apparently on November 6 and seemingly by Luigi Tretti, a lawyer and the president of the city's Liceo Musicale.[64] On this occasion, Aldo Fedeli, the mayor of Verona, presented Montemezzi with an album of Veronese prints, "In remembrance of an unforgettable evening."[65] Montemezzi flew back to the United States from Rome, arriving in New York on November 20.[66]

Montemezzi later made an astonishing report to Silvio Bertoldi concerning this 1948 return to Vigasio: "he [Montemezzi] found everything unchanged, as it was before: his old house . . . his desk made of two planks resting on trestles, the upright piano with the help of which he wrote his most famous music, the usual yellowed papers."[67] This suggests that his Vigasio relatives had made a great effort to give the house an air of normalcy, but Montemezzi's willingness to sustain the illusion probably speaks of deep psychological needs, and an unwillingness to face the reality of his situation. On the whole, the evidence suggests that the 1948 trip was rather painful, for despite his regular assertions of undying love for his country, Montemezzi was clearly in no hurry to make a second return. It is difficult to understand how the myth started that he actually moved back to Italy in 1948, which appears in several later reference works.

Life in the United States was quieter now that Montemezzi was no longer conducting, and in his last years he engaged little with the American press. But the Montemezzis continued to entertain. Mary Garden notably stayed with

---

[62] Celli, "Lo Accolsero," p. 21.

[63] Silvio Bertoldi, "A Vigasio cessano i rumori per non disturbare Montemezzi," *Oggi*, May 15, 1952, p. 44.

[64] Luigi Tretti, "Glorie musicali di Montemezzi," in *Omaggio a Italo Montemezzi*, edited by Piergiorgio Rossetti (Vigasio: Amministrazione Comunale di Vigasio, 2002), p. 44.

[65] "A ricordo di una indimenticabile serata." Inscription on the album, dated November 6, 1948. Donadelli family documents.

[66] Air Passenger Manifest. Ancestry.com.

[67] Bertoldi, "A Vigasio," p. 43.

ITALIA MIA! NULLA FERMERÀ IL TUO CANTO! 341

them in 1949, 1950, and 1951, in the course of her lecture tours of the country. There were more formal events, too, such as the "surprise dinner party" at the Montemezzis' home on September 9, 1950, presumably arranged by Katherine, at which the composer, in a belated celebration of his seventy-fifth birthday, was awarded the recently created Stella della Solidarietà Italiana (Star of Italian Solidarity) by the Italian consul, Mario Ungaro.[68] Pinza and the conductor Richard Hageman were among those attending the event. Much of the burden of such occasions doubtless fell on the Montemezzis' Texas-born maid, Lenora Ready, a widow, recorded as living with them in the 1950 census.[69]

Even when wartime hostilities were over, Montemezzi seems to have realized that there was virtually no chance of an American company staging *La nave*. He therefore attempted to promote a revival of *Héllera* instead, with the opportunity for an American premiere still going begging. "As to Héllera, I have been doing everything to revive it," he wrote in April 1946.[70] The Metropolitan Opera and the Chicago Opera Company had both expressed interest, he claimed, and he was about to meet Gaetano Merola, general director of the San Francisco Opera, to discuss possibilities there. Yet though Montemezzi was still a major name in the United States, none of these possible revivals actually took place. When Renata Tebaldi (1922–2004) made her first appearance in the United States in September 1950, having been contracted to sing Aida by the San Francisco Opera, he changed tack. Tebaldi was one of the great stars of postwar opera and Montemezzi managed to have a lengthy conversation with her in the course of her visit to California. Having heard her sing, he was convinced she could be the perfect Héllera, and that her star power could finally launch the opera into the repertoire:

> She has all the qualities to interpret that role, exactly as I intend it. . . . Tebaldi, with regard to her voice, pronunciation, interpretation of the character, expression, and figure, is one hundred percent of what is necessary. Héllera is sentiment, drama, dynamism, and not being difficult to prepare, it will be practical and will travel the world.[71]

[68] "Italy Honors Composer at Dinner Here," *Los Angeles Times*, September 10, 1950, p. 19.

[69] Beverly Hills E. D. 19–161, sheet 7.

[70] "Riguardo ad Héllera io faccio di tutto per farla rivivere." Montemezzi to Alfredo Colombo, letter postmarked April 9, 1946.

[71] "Ha tutte le qualità per interpretare quel ruolo, proprio come intendo io. . . . la Tebaldi, come voce, come pronuncia, come interpretazione del personaggio, come espressione e come figura, è un cento per cento di quello che occorre. Héllera è sentimento, dramma, dinamismo, e non essendo di difficile preparazione, sarà pratica e girerà il mondo." Letter to Alfredo Colombo, April 16, 1951. Chandler collection.

342   SUCCEEDING PUCCINI

Tebaldi expressed an interest in singing the role but seems to have argued that there was a better chance of a revival in Italy. Montemezzi accepted this, and thus his final campaign to restore his most ill-fated opera to the stage commenced. It appears from his letters to Casa Ricordi during 1951 that the publisher, though not against the idea, did not consider it an urgent matter either. Unfortunately, time was no longer on Montemezzi's side, and though momentum gradually built up, his unexpected death meant there was never to be a Tebaldi *Héllera*.

Perhaps the most significant event in this final stage of Montemezzi's career was the appearance of the first complete commercial recording of *L'amore dei tre re*. As noted in Chapter 5, the very integrated nature of Montemezzi's operas meant that little of his music was recorded in the 78 era. However, with the advent of the long-playing record in the summer of 1948, a compact and popular opera like *L'amore dei tre re* became an attractive proposition, and a recording was made in Milan on September 3, 1950, with Arturo Basile conducting the RAI orchestra. It was released early the following year and obtained many very positive reviews. Montemezzi himself found "the tempi . . . too brisk from the beginning to the end," but judged the recording in other respects "successful."[72] He was eager to promote it and quick to take advantage of the fact that it made the opera much easier to broadcast. He traveled to New York in March 1951 to record an interview with Dario Soria, the founder of the Cetra-Soria label which was pressing and distributing the recording in the United States. It appears the interview and extracts from the recording were broadcast sometime in March, and there were further broadcasts in both San Francisco and Los Angeles in April.[73] On May 12, the entire recording was broadcast on Soria's weekend "Festival of Opera" for the WOR station, an ambitious project to popularize opera that had commenced on March 24 with a broadcast of *The Barber of Seville*. A sure sign of its success was that it made a second appearance on the "Festival of Opera" as early as August 24, the fact that it could be accompanied by some of Montemezzi's own commentary perhaps adding to its appeal. Altogether, the American radio audience had plenty of chances to hear *L'amore dei tre re* in 1951, and encouraged by this, Montemezzi hoped Cetra-Soria would release a studio recording of *L'incantesimo* too.[74] The company was interested in the idea; again, however, his unexpected death meant it was never realized.

[72] "i tempi sono troppo mossi dal principio alla fine." Letter to Colombo, April 16, 1951.
[73] Montemezzi to Alfredo Colombo, April 16, 1951.
[74] Edgardo Trinelli to Montemezzi, November 29, 1951. Donadelli family documents.

ITALIA MIA! NULLA FERMERÀ IL TUO CANTO! 343

Montemezzi was excited by the possibilities offered by new media, especially film. As early as 1941, he was reporting:

I would like to do a movie opera, and I have one that could be ideally adapted. It is my one-act piece called "La Notte di Zoraima." . . . But movie opera would have to be dynamic and specially constructed; just to film people singing arias wouldn't do, but they don't seem to see that in Hollywood. Not yet, anyhow.[75]

It is intriguing to find Montemezzi recommending *La notte di Zoraima* for treatment as a film. Perhaps he regarded this opera, in particular, as offering strong scenographic possibilities, but it is just as likely that he felt it did not have much of a future on stage. In 1946, Montemezzi recommended both *La notte di Zoraima* and *L'amore dei tre re* as strongly suited to cinematic treatment.[76] However, no tangible offer to film his music reached him until 1950, when Rudolph Polk and Bernard Luber's World Artists planned to devote one of their twenty-five-minute feature films to Dorothy Kirsten. Kirsten wanted to include the Act 1 duet between Fiora and Avito from *L'amore dei tre re* and Montemezzi helped in negotiations with Ricordi.[77] In the end, unfortunately, it appears the film was never made, as Kirsten was too busy filming *The Great Caruso*.[78] Montemezzi, who was "not really enthusiastic" about the Kirsten film, had by this time decided that "[t]he most beautiful thing would be making a great film of the whole of L'Amore dei tre re, also according to my intention; and I hope we'll get there."[79] He did not live to see such a thing, but the NBC television version of 1962 demonstrated how effective his masterpiece could be on screen.

Having given power of attorney to Montemezzi's Vigasio cousin, Francesco Donadelli (1894–1979), the Montemezzis finally sold their Milan apartment in September 1951 for 3.1 million lire.[80] The great devaluation of the Italian currency meant this was, in dollar terms, less than half the sum

[75] Quoted in Alfred Frankenstein, "Three Kings and One Composer," *San Francisco Chronicle*, October 26, 1941, p. 25.

[76] Montemezzi to Alfredo Colombo, letter postmarked April 9, 1946.

[77] Montemezzi to Alfredo Colombo, September 20, 1950. Ricordi Collection, Music Library, Northwestern University.

[78] "On the Sound Track," *Billboard*, October 7, 1950, p. 16.

[79] "Io non ne sono veramente entusiasta. . . . La cosa più bella sarebbe di fare un grande film di tutto L'Amore dei tre re, secondo anche il mio intendimento; e spero che un giorno ci si arriverà." Montemezzi to Alfredo Colombo, September 20, 1950.

[80] Notary act 25681, September 29, 1951.

344 SUCCEEDING PUCCINI

Katherine had paid for it in 1923, and it was an inconsequential addition to their wealth. The long-delayed sale was perhaps driven most of all by a desire to simplify the family's financial affairs.

Around this time, Italy finally began to recognize Montemezzi as a national treasure. With the deaths of Zandonai in 1944, Mascagni in 1945, Giordano in 1948, and Cilea in 1950, he and Alfano had become the grand old men of Italian opera, the oldest composers who had written really popular operas. Yet there was a feeling in Italy that Montemezzi had never been properly appreciated there, despite all the acclaim from the United States. The first evidence of a change of mood was a campaign to revive *La nave* at the Arena di Verona Festival the following year. In August 1951, Montemezzi reported excitedly: "We can be sure that 'La Nave' will be performed in the Verona Arena next summer, because I know that a considerable campaign will be prepared. And it is about time!"[81] Soon there was even more to feel good about. In the autumn of 1951 a "Comitato Onoranze a Italo Montemezzi" was set up. It was, initially, a Veronese scheme led by Tretti and the distinguished poet Lionello Fiumi (1894–1973), but soon became a national project under the patronage of Luigi Einaudi, Italy's second president, and reporting more directly to Antonio Segni, the minister for education (and a future president). The committee planned the publication of an *Omaggio* volume devoted to Montemezzi and his music; the issuance of a commemorative medal, and the construction of some busts, both by Maria Trevisani Montini (1907–2001), a sculptor from Vigasio; and some related ceremonial and musical events.

In connection with these initiatives, Montemezzi made a second return to Italy; he was in Vigasio by October 4 and returned to New York on December 9, flying out of Milan.[82] The main purpose of this trip appears to have been to prepare for an even more extended visit the following year, but he was also able to see a revival of *L'amore dei tre re* in Bologna in November, and no doubt took every opportunity of lobbying for a revival of *Héllera* with Tebaldi. Not much is recorded of the 1951 trip, but it was then, in the old house in Vigasio, that Montemezzi gave an account of his life to Giuseppe Silvestri, to be included in the *Omaggio* volume. This has, until now, served as the main reference biography of the composer. In his old house, too, he was photographed surrounded by relatives and neighbors (Figure 10.1). It is almost certain that Montemezzi

---

[81] "Si può essere sicuri che 'La Nave' verrà rappresentata nell'Arena di Verona la prossima estate, perché so che si preparerà una campagna non indifferente. Ed è ora!" Montemezzi to Alfredo Colombo, August 17, 1951. Ricordi Collection, Music Library, Northwestern University.
[82] Air Passenger Manifest.

Figure 10.1 Montemezzi in his Vigasio home, October 15, 1951. *Chandler collection.*

sat for Trevisani Montini in the course of this visit to Vigasio. Telling Silvestri, "I'll return here in spring,"[83] he then continued to Rome, where he hoped to persuade Guido Sampaoli (1889–1977), artistic director of the Teatro dell'Opera (the former Teatro Reale dell'Opera, where he had worked under Serafin), to stage *L'incantesimo*. Montemezzi had brought an LP record of the 1943 broadcast with him and was keen for Sampaoli to hear it; the latter appears to have been genuinely interested in producing the work, which would have added very significantly to the planned celebrations.[84] However, during the winter of 1951–1952 the Arena Festival dropped the plan to stage *La nave* and substituted *L'incantesimo*, with Sampaoli relinquishing any interest he had in the latter work. This substitution had the merit of presenting an opera never staged before, but there can be no question that *L'incantesimo* was far less suited to the vast, open-air stage of the Arena. Nevertheless, it seems likely that Montemezzi supported, and possibly even encouraged, the change, as he now had bigger plans for *La nave*.[85]

---

[83] Giuseppe Silvestri, "Vita e opera: vocazione e volontà," in *Omaggio a Italo Montemezzi*, edited by Piergiorgio Rossetti (Vigasio: Amministrazione Comunale di Vigasio, 2002), p. 35.
[84] Montemezzi to Sampaoli, October 4, 1951. Chandler collection.
[85] In a letter to Montemezzi of May 14, 1952, Renzo Bianchi argued that *La nave* was more suited to the Arena Festival and *L'incantesimo* to the "celebrated theatre" (*celebre teatro*), presumably La Scala. It is hard to be certain, but the implication seems to be that Montemezzi had made the opposite argument to Bianchi. Donadelli family documents.

346   SUCCEEDING PUCCINI

Montemezzi's final visit to Italy saw him and Katherine first flying to Portugal on March 10, 1952, where, three days later, they were guests of honor at the first of two performances of *L'amore dei tre re* at the Teatro Nacional de São Carlos, Lisbon. They flew on to Rome on March 15, where they stayed at the luxurious Hotel Excelsior. Here a conversation of some significance occurred: "upon returning to Rome, Mme. Montemezzi asked her Italian-born husband if he would like to live there. 'I think not, I love America,' was his reply."[86] After "a most pleasant visit to Rome, Naples, and Capri,"[87] they arrived in Milan on April 24, where they stayed at the Grand Hotel Continentale until May 8.[88] Katherine, who had not been there since 1938, was dismayed by the state of the city, which she found "so awful."[89]

Presuming a good deal on his newfound status in Italy, Montemezzi had developed an exceptionally ambitious plan that he explained to Nicola De Pirro (1898–1979), the general secretary for entertainment, in a letter drafted on April 20:

> My plan is to be able to have my opera Héllera, or La Nave, staged in the 1952–53 season at La Scala in Milan, at the Teatro dell'Opera in Rome, and at the San Carlo in Naples.... an agreement between those three great houses regarding the scenes, the costumes etc., would enormously facilitate the realization of the project....
>
> I believe this project of mine will be realized, and we will certainly do a good service to Art. You can imagine, dearest signor De Pirro, with what great eagerness I await this realization, after many, many years of unfair oblivion.[90]

Montemezzi's movements on this 1952 trip were shaped a good deal by his desire to lobby for this project. In Rome, he talked to Sampaoli again and found him enthusiastic about the idea; he also hoped to meet De Pirro. In Naples, he talked to Pasquale Di Costanzo, manager of the Teatro di San

---

[86] Judy Jennings, "Composer's Widow Here," *Philadelphia Inquirer*, January 7, 1956, p. 8.

[87] "una piacevolissima visita a Roma, Napoli e Capri." Montemezzi to Sampaoli, April 28, 1952. Chandler collection.

[88] Hotel receipt. Donadelli family documents.

[89] Marco Montemezzi to his parents, April 22, 1952. Donadelli family documents.

[90] "Il mio progetto è di poter far rappresentare nella stagione del 1952–53 una delle mie la mia opera Héllera, oppure La Nave, alla Scala di Milano, al teatro dell'Opera di Roma e al San Carlo di Napoli.... un'intesa fra quei tre grandi teatri riguardo alle scene, ai costumi ecc., faciliterebbe enormemente la realizzazione del progetto. . . . / Questo mio progetto credo che si realizzerà, e certamente renderemo un buon servizio all'Arte. Lei puoi immaginare carissimo signor De Pirro come ansiosamente ciò con quale ansia io attenda questa realizzazione, dopo tanti e tanti anni di ingiuste dimenticanze." Donadelli family documents.

ITALIA MIA! NULLA FERMERÀ IL TUO CANTO! 347

Carlo, and found him eager to pursue the idea as well; in Milan, he talked to Antonio Ghiringhelli (1903–1979), general director of La Scala.[91] He also lobbied La Scala through the composer Renzo Bianchi (1887–1972), one of the directors. Montemezzi met Tebaldi in Milan and found her still excited at the idea of singing *Héllera*; she apparently made her own appeal to La Scala, for Bianchi reported that "the well-known singer played her part with great passion."[92] It is difficult to assess whether there was any real chance of attaining the ambitious co-production that Montemezzi wanted, and Bianchi was certainly doubtful about La Scala's involvement. But it was clear that any such co-production would need both the composer's participation and a connection to the larger celebration of his career that was being planned.

The Montemezzis moved on to Vigasio on May 8, now, if not earlier, joined by Louise Roos, Katherine's cousin, and a leading socialite in San Francisco. Soon afterward, and clearly not earlier than May 9, Montemezzi gave his last interview to Silvio Bertoldi, a young journalist from Verona, who was preparing a feature for *Oggi* magazine. Bertoldi found him looking "much younger" than he really was and less like a "venerable musician" than "an old sportsman, a gentleman keen on horse racing and a breeder of thoroughbreds. This characteristic is accentuated by his face, tanned by the sun, under his fully snow-white hair and by his clothes of British fabric and cut, of the kind usually typical of country gentlemen."[93] Montemezzi did not say anything very remarkable on the occasion, but reviewed some of the events of his life, including a few little titbits of information not found elsewhere which have been incorporated into the present book. A photograph was taken of him sitting in the garden.

Bertoldi's feature was published on May 15. It is not clear whether Montemezzi could have seen it. That day, he and Katherine went shopping in Verona, before returning to the Vigasio house late in the afternoon. It was the thirty-third anniversary of her father's death, so there may well have been some talk of mortality. Montemezzi went to sit in the garden, intending to write a letter, but soon afterward had a heart attack. Katherine found him "slumped over in his chair," unable to explain what had occurred. His last words which can be firmly authenticated are: "I was writing and the pen fell

---

[91] Montemezzi to Sampaoli, April 28, 1952.

[92] "la nota cantante ha fatto la sua parte con molta passione." Bianchi to Montemezzi, May 14, 1952. Donadelli family documents.

[93] Bertoldi, "A Vigasio," p. 43.

348   SUCCEEDING PUCCINI

from my hand. I can't imagine what happened."[94] He was led into the house and put to bed; a doctor and priest were summoned. He may, at this point, have said, "Now I feel fine again; it was nothing."[95] A few minutes later he was dead. The poet Fiumi, one of the editors of the *Omaggio* volume, found something appropriate in this death in the old family home:

> under *his* roof, like the tired swallow, he [Montemezzi] came to die. He had always expressed a wish to be buried in his land, near his family, and that, if the scythe were to strike him beyond the seas, his mortal remains should be returned to a small patch in the cemetery of Vigasio. Fate, at least on this occasion, was kind to him. . . . He died surrounded by the objects he had held dear in his childhood, the beating of his heart stopping like one of those industrious clocks which, just here, in the same rooms, his clockmaker father used to construct.[96]

[94] These details are from Susan Smith, "Mrs. Robt. Roos Sends Word of Europe Travels," *San Francisco Examiner*, June 13, 1952, p. 14. This appears to be the best authenticated account of Montemezzi's death, given that Roos was staying with the Montemezzis at the time, and was Katherine's main companion in the weeks that followed.

[95] Silvestri includes this detail but cites no source and as his account is obviously poeticized we do not consider it particularly reliable. See Silvestri, "Vita e opera," p. 36.

[96] Lionello Fiumi, "Montemezzi 'veronese,'" in *Omaggio a Italo Montemezzi*, edited by Piergiorgio Rossetti (Vigasio: Amministrazione Comunale di Vigasio, 2002), p. 40.

Epilogue

"The shining path"

A funeral was arranged for May 17, most of the arrangements undertaken by the Comune of Vigasio, which wanted it to be the grandest such event the town had ever seen. Letters and telegrams of condolence poured in from all over Italy, as well as from abroad. On the afternoon of May 17, the shops and businesses in Vigasio closed, and at 4:30 p.m. an "interminable" procession set out from Villa Montemezzi, conveying the composer's mortal remains first to the church, then to the cemetery. A number of large wreaths were carried, one of which had been sent by Mary Garden, and prominent in the procession itself was Maria Callas. At 5:30 p.m., the procession reached the cemetery, where a number of speeches were made, and Montemezzi was then buried beside his parents.[1]

On June 3, back in the United States, Montemezzi was "honored with a Solemn High Mass . . . at St. Peter's Italian Church [in Los Angeles] by members of the Federated Italo-Americans of Southern California."[2] Marco, who had been unable to attend his father's funeral in Italy, led the mourners.

On June 28, Katherine was invited to a ceremony at the Palazzo Barbieri in Verona. The Comune of Vigasio presented one of Trevisani Montini's bronze busts of Montemezzi to the City of Verona, which in turn gave it to the Conservatorio Evaristo Felice Dall'Abaco, where the concert hall was subsequently named after Montemezzi (it is now L'Auditorium Nuovo Montemezzi). Katherine was presented with a gold medal presumably originally intended for her husband.[3] She returned to the United States soon afterward, but kept the house in Vigasio, and for several years made annual visits there in the course of more extended European trips. This surely bespeaks a happy marriage.

---

[1] Details of the funeral are from "I funerali di Italo Montemezzi a Vigasio," in *Omaggio a Italo Montemezzi*, edited by Piergiorgio Rossetti (Vigasio: Amministrazione Comunale di Vigasio, 2002), pp. 88–90.

[2] "Italians Here Pay Honor to Memory of Composer," *Los Angeles Times*, June 4, 1952, p. 27.

[3] "La cerimonia commemorative a Palazzo Barbieri, a Verona" in Rossetti (ed.), *Omaggio a Italo Montemezzi*, p. 90.

Succeeding Puccini. David Chandler and Raffaele Mellace, Oxford University Press. © Oxford University Press 2025.
DOI: 10.1093/9780197761373.003.0011

350   EPILOGUE

Many tributes to Montemezzi were published in the international press. Tullio Serafin was unequivocal in his verdict: Montemezzi was the "[g]reatest of contemporary Italian composers." He also paid generous tribute to his friend's character: "Only those who knew him . . . have an idea of the great humanity of the man, Montemezzi. He was the most simple, the best of men. . . . Your problems were his problems and he considered them all with gravest concern. The sincerity which is felt through all his music was typical of his life."[4] In 1955, Serafin conducted his old friend's music for the last time, half a century after the premiere of *Giovanni Gallurese*, leading two performances of *L'amore dei tre re* for the recently founded Lyric Opera of Chicago.

Montemezzi's death had come unexpectedly and cast a long shadow over the events planned for the summer: "the homage to the living Maestro had, unfortunately, to transform itself into a solemn remembrance of his memory."[5] In August, *Omaggio a Italo Montemezzi* was published in Verona. As well as essays on the composer's life and work, it contained many brief tributes from prominent figures in the musical world, all written before Montemezzi's death. Among the most touching is one from Franco Alfano, his old rival at Casa Ricordi: "I will be happy and very honored to be part of the Committee preparing worthy honors for Italo Montemezzi, a magnificent musician and an old and very dear friend of mine."[6] Another significant figure of this generation paying his respects was Vittorio Gnecchi (1876–1954), the composer of *Cassandra* (1905):

I consider Italo Montemezzi preeminent among Italian composers of this century.

"L'Amore dei tre re" is, in my opinion, the modern opera most deeply worthy of being considered a continuation of the shining path marked by Verdi.[7]

Also in August, the Arena di Verona Festival staged *L'incantesimo* for the first time as part of an implausible triple bill with *Cavalleria rusticana* and the Offenbach ballet *Gaîté Parisienne*. Three performances were given, on August 9, 12, and 15, with Carla Gavazzi as Giselda, Enzo Mascherini as Folco, Francesco Albanese as Rinaldo, and Giuseppe Modesti as Salomone;

---

[4] Tullio Serafin, "Italo Montemezzi—An Appreciation," *Opera News*, January 19, 1953, pp. 10, 31.
[5] Luigi Tretti, "Glorie musicali di Montemezzi," in Rossetti (ed.), *Omaggio a Italo Montemezzi*, p. 42.
[6] Rossetti (ed.), *Omaggio a Italo Montemezzi*, p. 75.
[7] Rossetti (ed.), *Omaggio a Italo Montemezzi*, p. 79.

EPILOGUE   351

the conductor was Francesco Molinari Pradelli. The incorporation of Mascagni and Offenbach into the program might suggest some doubt as to whether the Arena could be otherwise filled, but whether or not this was the case, on August 9 the venue was "packed, jammed and out of hand."[8] The performance of *L'incantesimo* was delayed by some commemorative speeches and a boisterous crowd, then unfortunately interrupted by a long rain delay when "almost over."[9] Much of the effect was lost and though reviewers were appreciative, they were not enthusiastic. This appears to have been the last occasion in the twentieth century when any of Montemezzi's "other" operas were staged. Italian interest in *L'incantesimo* was not exhausted, however, and a much larger audience had the chance to hear it on the evening of December 16, 1953, when RAI's Programma Nazionale broadcast a radio performance conducted by Arturo Basile. Mascherini and Albanese returned to their roles, and Giselda was sung by Adele Sticchi, and Solomone by Franco Calabrese. This time it was programmed, rather more appropriately, with Antonio Savasta's brief one-act opera *Galatea* (1920), and Italians could experience it as Americans had a decade earlier.

Any study of Montemezzi's reputation should consider the impact of his unexpected death on performances of his works. It is hard to be sure, but in our understanding, it was a negative one. There was undoubtedly a great upsurge of interest in Montemezzi in Italy in 1951–1952, reinforced by his newfound willingness to be there promoting his work and involving himself in productions. A successful, epic-scaled *Nave*, or a *Héllera* with Tebaldi, may have allowed Montemezzi to shrug off the "single opera" stigma once and for all. Had he lived longer and continued on the course he had embarked on in 1951–1952, it is hard to believe that one or other of these operas would not have returned to the stage in Italy: this would have required Casa Ricordi to produce performance parts, in turn facilitating further productions. But with Montemezzi's death, the main impulse for revival, and the commercial value of his presence at revivals, immediately disappeared. In the United States, too, where he had always been so esteemed, it is hard to believe there would not have been more revivals of *L'amore dei tre re* at least had he been available to attend them.

---

[8] Claudia Cassidy, *Europe—On the Aisle* (New York: Random House, 1954), p. 187.

[9] Cassidy, *Europe—On the Aisle*, p. 188. For very circumstantial accounts of the interrupted performance, see Cassidy's account here, as well as her article, "Visit to Montemezzi's Opera on Verona Stage a 'Comedy of Errors,'" *Chicago Sunday Tribune*, August 24, 1952, Part 7, pp. 9–10.

352 EPILOGUE

As it was, the first American performances to register Montemezzi's absence were the San Francisco company's revivals of *L'amore dei tre re* in San Francisco and Los Angeles in October 1952—he had been expected as the guest of honor.[10] It may be that this left the company with a particular sense that they should keep his flame burning, and they brought the opera out again in 1959 and 1966. But elsewhere, the old war horse was being retired: the Met staged it for the last time in 1949, Chicago in 1955, the Teatro Colón, Buenos Aires, in 1955. La Scala staged it in 1953, with de Sabata conducting—the last time he conducted an opera—and then did not revive it until 2023. To some extent, an era was closing, and Montemezzi's death must have added to that sense, but *L'amore dei tre re* was too powerful a work to simply disappear, and in the 1960s it found its largest audience yet thanks to the National Broadcasting Company (NBC). The NBC Opera's television version of *L'amore dei tre re*, sung in English and broadcast in color on February 25, 1962, and then again on January 27, 1963, was advertised with the statement: "millions more people will watch this single performance of 'The Love of Three Kings' than have seen it since its premiere in 1913." The NBC Opera's television director, Kirk Browning (1921–2008), believed *L'amore dei tre re* was a "good opera" that would make a "good television show," and that it "contains the most passionate love scenes in all opera."[11] The production, conducted by Alfred Wallenstein, a protégé of Toscanini, and featuring Phyllis Curtin as Fiora, Giorgio Tozzi as Archibaldo, Richard Torigi as Manfredo, and Frank Porretta as Avito, was a critical and popular success. Winthrop Sargeant (1903–1986), the influential music critic for the *New Yorker*, claimed it had converted him to the idea of television opera: "the opera proved so gripping that it must have left many of its auditors limp, if not actually in tears. . . . Musically, it is a marvel, written in the final flush of the post-Wagnerian tradition, with a score far richer in hypnotic power than that of 'Pélleas,' and full of the noblest sort of expressiveness."[12] Had the NBC Opera not been forced to dissolve in 1964, because of financial difficulties, *The Love of Three Kings* may well have been broadcast on further occasions and done much to keep Montemezzi's masterpiece in the public eye, at least in the United States. A second complete recording of the opera

[10] Arthur Bloomfield, *The San Francisco Opera: 1922–1978* (Sausalito, CA: Comstock Editions, 1978), p. 128.

[11] Quoted in Harold Stern, "NBC Opera 'Season' Tomorrow," *Evening Press* (Binghamton), February 24, 1962, p. 3.

[12] Winthrop Sargeant, "Of Kings and Giants," *New Yorker*, March 3, 1962, p. 121.

EPILOGUE 353

was released in 1972 and a third—for many the definitive recording, with Plácido Domingo as Avito and Nello Santi conducting—in 1976.

Katherine Montemezzi continued to live in Beverly Hills for several years before selling 714 Walden Drive in 1957 and moving back to New York, where she lived at 525 Park Avenue and died on August 15, 1966. She continued to do what she could to promote interest in her husband's music. In 1954 the Opera Guild of Southern California opened an Opera Museum Collection, intending subsequently to move its exhibits "to the future Los Angeles Opera House," and "[t]he first exhibit was dedicated to the memory of the late Maestro Italo Montemezzi and the late Maestro Gaetano Merola, both of whom were so vitally associated with opera productions in Los Angeles." "One case was completely filled with mementos of Maestro Montemezzi and articles given by singers associated with performances of his opera *The Love of Three Kings*. A gift most cherished by the Opera Guild came from Madame Montemezzi, the bronze bust of the Maestro, a duplicate of the one in Italy" (Figure E.1).[13] Unfortunately, the present whereabouts of these items is unclear; they never became, as intended, part of a Los Angeles Opera House collection. Katherine stayed in touch with Mary Garden and nurtured contacts with younger opera singers. When, in 1963, Robert Lawrence suggested to her that Callas "might be the definitive Fiora," he found her in ready agreement, reporting: "I've spoken to Callas, and she's waiting for an opportunity."[14] On this Lawrence commented, surely correctly, "The rest of a top-notch ensemble might come automatically, once a decision was reached to give the work another major revival." Sadly, the opportunity never came; Callas sang on stage for the last time in July 1965. In 1963, Katherine wrote to La Scala, encouraging the theatre to stage a revival of *L'amore dei tre re* to mark the opera's fiftieth anniversary; the response was that "composers of this period [Montemezzi's] do not, at this time, particularly interest either the public or the critics"—Zandonai and Alfano were cited as other examples.[15]

Unlike his mother, Marco Montemezzi appears to have done little to extend his father's legacy, and with him the major opportunity to collect together family papers and artifacts and entrust them to a public collection

---

[13] "Memorabilia for Los Angeles," *Opera News*, March 8, 1954, p. 29.

[14] Robert Lawrence, "Figures on the Battlements," *Opera News*, January 4, 1964, p. 7.

[15] "i compositori di questo periodo non destano, in questo momento, particolare interesse né nel pubblico né nella critica." "Promemoria per il sovrintendente," March 6, 1963, La Scala Archives. Katherine's undated letter is also in the La Scala Archives.

Figure E.1 Katherine and Marco Montemezzi presenting Montemezzi's bust to the Opera Guild of California, 1954. *Metropolitan Opera Archives.*

was lost. When he inherited Villa Montemezzi in due course, he sold it to his Vigasio relative, Renata Donadelli, and her husband Leonello Sartori. After obtaining his B.Sc., he became a teacher of mathematics. In the early 1970s, he decided to pursue his interest in mathematics more seriously and studied for an M.A. and Ph.D. at American University, where he also taught part-time until his retirement in 1986. Marco did not need to work, for his

EPILOGUE 355

mother had set up a trust fund which paid him around $80,000 a year.[16] In the last years of his life he was persuaded to underwrite the JMA Head Injury Foundation in Washington, D.C., founded in 1987 by his friend Julien Dilks. This eventually left him bankrupt, as a result of which he committed suicide on August 24, 1992. Most of Marco's possessions had to be sold off to pay his debts; the family papers and photographs he had retained were inherited by the residual beneficiary of his estate, Maureen Polsby.

In 1976, the organizers of a concert performance of *L'amore dei tre re* with piano accompaniment in Toronto discovered, in the interval after the second act, that Marco was in the audience. He told them he "went to every performance of his father's opera, wherever it was in the world," and at the end he was persuaded to go on stage to take a bow: "He was charming and he was kind enough to say that it was one of the best performances of the work he had ever heard."[17] This anecdote, suggesting remarkable filial piety, sits oddly besides evidence of a rather different attitude. In 1981, the Washington Opera (now the Washington National Opera) revived *L'amore dei tre re* and asked Marco to contribute an essay on his father to their magazine, and then to attend as a guest of honor. Marco accordingly furnished a piece printed with the misleading title "Italo Montemezzi: A Son Remembers."[18] In fact, rather extraordinarily, there is no personal reminiscence at all: most of the essay is taken, without acknowledgment, almost word for word from Verna Arvey's 1948 article for *Opera and Concert* with a very long quotation from Montemezzi's own account of how he came to write *L'amore dei tre re* added. Psychoanalysis could no doubt say interesting things about these seemingly contradictory attitudes toward his father and his work. Renata Donadelli, Marco's distant cousin, suggested there was "a lack of feeling" between Marco and his father, though they shared a love of Wagner and Marco was a fine pianist. Marco would often claim that his father had "adored" him.[19]

Since the 1960s, *L'amore dei tre re* has appeared regularly, if not often, on the stage. On these occasions, reviewers have often expressed wonder, rather like Sargeant's in 1962, at the power of an opera they may not even have heard

[16] Information from Maureen Polsby.
[17] Stuart Hamilton, *Opening Windows: Confessions of a Canadian Vocal Coach* (Toronto: Dundurn, 2012), pp. 121–22. It is worth noting that Hamilton, who played the piano in the concert, judged *L'amore dei tre re* "a score of incomparable orchestral richness and a truly haunting melodic invention" (p. 121).
[18] Marco A. Montemezzi, "Italo Montemezzi: A Son Remembers," *Washington Opera Magazine* 8/3 (Spring 1981): pp. 18–20. Reprinted in Rossetti (ed.), *Omaggio a Italo Montemezzi*, pp. 162–64.
[19] Information from Maureen Polsby.

356 EPILOGUE

of before. In the period 2000–2023, it was performed a total of eighty-one times in eight different countries, twenty-nine of those performances being in the United States.[20] Particularly satisfactory for lovers of the opera is the way it has shown a remarkable ability to impress audiences in places where its original impact, for whatever reason, was limited. Reviewing a 1992 revival in Kassel, Germany, for example, the veteran reviewer James Helme Sutcliffe was stunned by its effect on him and the rest of the audience, who "went berserk": "by Act 2 Montemezzi's soaring, galloping, grinding score had taken possession of everyone present. I'd hate to count the years since opera so thrilled me."[21] Similarly, the five performances staged by Theater Lübeck in 2022 proved so successful that it was brought back the next year for eight more. Revivals at Opera Holland Park, London, in 2007 and 2015, had a comparable impact, and the final judgment quoted in this book is that of Michael Volpe, the former general director of Holland Park, whose company has done so much to revive lesser-known Italian operas from the period 1890 to 1930: "perhaps only one is, in my view, an unimpeachable masterpiece, and that is Italo Montemezzi's L'amore dei Tre Re [sic]."[22]

L'amore dei tre re may have become a sort of "cult classic," but for thousands of opera devotees around the world it still burns as bright as ever it did in its early 1900s heyday.

---

[20] Data from Marco Mazzolini, General Manager, Casa Ricordi.
[21] James Helme Sutcliffe, "Cassel [sic]," Opera 43/7 (July 1992): pp. 833, 834.
[22] Michael Volpe, "Raiders of the Lost Aria," Guardian, July 21, 2011, film & music, p. 12.

Select Bibliography

Manuscript Sources

Four principal collections of manuscript material are drawn on in this book. The Archivio Storico Ricordi, Milan, holds the manuscript full scores of all Montemezzi operas apart from *Bianca*, as well as those of *Paolo e Virginia* and *Italia mia! Nulla fermerà il tuo canto!*. It also contains hundreds of letters, reports, and contract documents related to Montemezzi and his librettists. The Donadelli family documents, currently still held in Villa Montemezzi, Vigasio, are another invaluable manuscript resource. These include a good deal of manuscript music, most importantly the score of *Bianca*, many letters to and from Montemezzi, and various other documents, cited here where relevant. A third, very useful archive is the Ricordi Collection in the Music Library at Northwestern University, containing much of Montemezzi's correspondence with Casa Ricordi from 1940 onward. Finally, in the course of writing this book, it has become clear that much important Montemezzi material is still widely scattered in private collections, with significant new documents regularly coming up for sale. Since 2010, David Chandler has been able to acquire most of the significant Montemezzi-related material to have reached the market; this is cited as the Chandler collection.

Of the smaller archival collections, particularly notable are those of the Conservatorio Giuseppe Verdi, Milan (including some of Montemezzi's student compositions, most importantly the *Frammento del Cantico dei Cantici di Salomone*), La Scala, Milan (both the Archivio Storico and the Museo Teatrale), and the Metropolitan Opera, New York.

Printed Sources

Adami, Giuseppe. "In attesa de 'L'Amore dei tre re' di Italo Montemezzi." *La Sera: Giornale politico, finanziario, illustrato*, April 7, 1913, p. 2.

Alberti, Nino. "Giovanni Gallurese di Italo Montemezzi." *Radiocorriere*, November 14–21, 1931, p. 11.

Alberti, Nino. "La Stagione Lirica dell'Eiar." *Radio Corriere*, August 2–8, 1936, p. 6.

Anonymous. *Italo Montemezzi* (Milan: Ricordi, 1933).

Anonymous. "La nostra musica. I. Montemezzi." *Musica e musicisti* 60/10 (1905): pp. 658–59. (Sometimes attributed to Giulio Ricordi.)

Anonymous. "Notizie liriche e drammatiche." *La Sera: Giornale politico, finanziario, illustrato*, November 13, 1905, p. 3.

Arvey, Verna. "Visits to the Homes of Famous Composers No. XIV: Italo Montemezzi." *Opera and Concert*, November 1948, pp. 14–15, 28–29.

Bassi, Adriano (ed.). *Caro maestro (D'Annunzio e i musicisti)* (Genoa: De Ferrari, 1997).

Bertoldi, Silvio. "A Vigasio cessano i rumori per non disturbare Montemezzi." *Oggi*, May 15, 1952, pp. 43–44.

Brugnoli, Pierpaolo, and Bruno Chiappa (eds.). *Vigasio: Vicende di una comunità e di un territorio* (Vigasio: Comune di Vigasio, 2005).

Bucci, Vincenzo. "'La Nave' nel Cantiere. Un Varo alla Scala di Milano." *Emporium* 48 (October 1918): pp. 171–79.

358   SELECT BIBLIOGRAPHY

C., L. "'Hellera' del M° Montemezzi: Un'intervista coll'autore." *La Gazzetta del Popolo*, March 2, 1909, p. 5.

Celli, Teodoro. "Lo Accolsero in Paese con Petardi e Luminarie: Vigasio ha un grosso debito col musicista Montemezzi." *Oggi*, October 24, 1948, pp. 21–22.

Celli, Teodoro, and Giuseppe Pugliese. *Tullio Serafin: il patriarca del melodramma* (Venice: Corbo e Fiore, 1985).

Ceriani, Davide. "Italianizing the Metropolitan Opera House: Giulio Gatti-Casazza's Era and the Politics of Opera in New York City, 1908–1935." PhD dissertation, Harvard University, 2011.

Chandler, David (ed.). *Americans on Italo Montemezzi* (Norwich: Durrant Publishing, 2014).

Chandler, David (ed.). *Essays on the Montemezzi-D'Annunzio 'Nave,'* 2nd ed. (Norwich: Durrant Publishing, 2014).

Downes, Olin. "The Quest of a Drama to Sing—Montemezzi and 'Three Kings.'" *New York Times*, March 9, 1924, p. X6.

Dryden, Konrad. *Franco Alfano: Transcending "Turandot"* (Lanham, MD: Scarecrow Press, 2010).

Dryden, Konrad. *Riccardo Zandonai: A Biography* (Frankfurt: Peter Lang, 1999).

Fiumi, Lionello. "Montemezzi 'veronese.'" In *Omaggio a Italo Montemezzi*, edited by Piergiorgio Rossetti, pp. 37–41.

Frisch, Norman. "Widow Loved Montemezzi and His Operas." *Daily News* (Los Angeles), October 19, 1952, pp. 28–29.

Gatti, Guido M. "Gabriele D'Annunzio and the Italian Opera-Composers." *Musical Quarterly* 10/2 (April 1924): pp. 263–88.

Guarnieri Corazzol, Adriana. "Sem Benelli e il libretto dell'*Amore dei tre re*." In *L'amore dei tre re*, program book, edited by Raffaele Mellace, pp. 57–62.

Halperson, Maurice. "How 'Gallurese' Saved an Impresario from Bankruptcy." *Musical America*, February 21, 1925, pp. 3, 27.

Haupt, Enid A. "Enchanting Fabric." *Philadelphia Inquirer*, November 14, 1943, p. 4.

Keolker, James. *Last Acts: The Operas of Puccini and His Italian Contemporaries from Alfano to Zandonai* (Napa, CA: Opera Companion Publications, 2000).

Lawrence, Robert. "Figures on the Battlements." *Opera News*, January 4, 1964, pp. 6–7.

Mallach, Alan. *The Autumn of Italian Opera: From Verismo to Modernism, 1890–1915* (Boston: Northeastern University Press, 2007).

Mariani, Renato. *Verismo in musica e altri studi*, edited by Cesare Orselli (Florence: Olschki, 1976).

Mellace, Raffaele. "Prolegomeni a una lettura della 'Nave': Una collaborazione tra d'Annunzio, Montemezzi e Tito Ricordi." *Chigiana* 47 (2008): pp. 417–53.

Mellace, Raffaele. "Su le soglie del lido: Spazio e paesaggio nella 'Nave,' tra d'Annunzio e Montemezzi." *Archivio d'Annunzio* 3 (2016): pp. 81–96.

Mellace, Raffaele (ed.). *L'amore dei tre re*, program book (Milan: Teatro alla Scala, 2023).

Meltzer, Charles Henry. "Montemezzi and His Music." *The Review* 1/27 (November 15, 1919): pp. 587–88.

Montecchi, L. R. "'L'amore dei tre re': Conversando con l'Autore alla vigilia d'armi." *La Maschera* 6/16 (April 17, 1910): pp. 1–4.

Montemezzi, Italo. "Come scrissi la musica per 'La Nave.'" *Scenario* 7 (April 1938): pp. 217–18.

Montemezzi, Italo. "Reminiscences of *L'Amore dei Tre Re*." *Opera News*, February 10, 1941, pp. 16–17.

Morini, Mario. "Carteggi inediti di Montemezzi, Illica e Giulio Ricordi per *Héllera*." *Ricordiana*, new series 2/5 (May 1956): pp. 233–38.

Navarra, Ugo. *Noterelle critiche sulla tragedia lirica di Gabriele D'Annunzio La Nave ridotta da Tito Ricordi per la Musica di Italo Montemezzi* (Milan, 1918).

Nicolodi, Fiamma. *Musica e musicisti nel ventennio fascista* (Fiesole: Discanto, 1984).

SELECT BIBLIOGRAPHY 359

Orselli, Cesare. "Montemezzi dà voce a un incanto d'amore." Liner notes for the compact disc recording of Italo Montemezzi, *L'incantesimo* (Bongiovanni, 2019), pp. 4–12.

Paoletti, Matteo. *A Huge Revolution of Theatrical Commerce: Walter Mocchi and the Italian Musical Theatre Business in South America* (Cambridge: Cambridge University Press, 2020).

Paoletti, Matteo. *Mascagni, Mocchi, Sonzogno: La Società Teatrale Internazionale (1908–1931) e i suoi protagonist* (Bologna: Alma Mater Studiorum, 2015).

Peyser, Herbert F. "An Appreciation of L'Amore dei Tre Re." *Musical America*, February 1949, pp. 14–15, 142, 144, 300–301.

Peyser, Herbert F. "For Deeper Enjoyment of *L'Amore dei tre Re*." *Opera News*, January 10, 1949, pp. 4–6, 30–31.

Peyser, Herbert F. "'Let simplicity be the composer's constant objective,' Abjures Italo Montemezzi." *Musical America*, November 22, 1919, pp. 3–4.

Phillips, Jane. "Ay, Every Inch a King." *Opera News*, January 10, 1949, pp. 12, 14, 31.

Pougin, Arthur. "Semaine théâtrale." *Le Ménestrel*, May 2, 1914, p. 139.

r., r.d. "Montemezzi parla delle sue opere." *Il Giornale d'Italia*, March 9, 1929, p. 3.

Rindom, Ditlev. "Bygone Modernity: Re-imagining Italian Opera in Milan, New York and Buenos Aires, 1887–1914." PhD dissertation, University of Cambridge, 2019.

Rossetti, Piergiorgio (ed.). *Omaggio a Italo Montemezzi* (Vigasio: Amministrazione Comunale di Vigasio, 2002).

Roth, Olaf. *Die Opernlibretti nach Dramen G. d'Annunzios* (Frankfurt: Peter Lang, 1999).

Sachs, Harvey. *Music in Fascist Italy* (London: Weidenfeld and Nicolson, 1987).

Sala, Emilio. "Registro vocale e funzione attanziale: turbamenti del triangolo nell'*Amore dei tre re*." In *L'amore dei tre re*, program book, edited by Raffaele Mellace, pp. 51–55.

Serafin, Tullio. "Italo Montemezzi—An Appreciation." *Opera News*, January 19, 1953, pp. 10–11, 31.

Silvestri, Giuseppe. "Vita e opera: Vocazione e volontà." In *Omaggio a Italo Montemezzi*, edited by Piergiorgio Rossetti, pp. 16–36.

Tomelleri, Luciano. "La nave (D'Annunzio e Montemezzi)." In *Gabriele d'Annunzio e la musica*, edited by Alfredo Casella et al. (Milan: Fratelli Bocca, 1939), pp. 40–46. Reprinted in *Rivista musicale italiana* 43 (1939): pp. 200–6.

Tretti, Luigi. "Glorie musicali di Montemezzi." In *Omaggio a Italo Montemezzi*, edited by Piergiorgio Rossetti, pp. 42–59.

Tretti, Luigi, and Lionello Fiumi (eds.). *Omaggio a Italo Montemezzi* (Verona: Ghidini and Fiorini, 1952). Reprinted, with additional materials, in Piergiorgio Rossetti (ed.), *Omaggio a Italo Montemezzi*.

Uras, Lara Sonja. "Un personaggio per Italo Montemezzi: Giovanni Gallurese tra storia e mito." In *Scapigliatura e Fin de Siècle: Libretti d'opera italiani dall'Unità al Primo Novecento*, edited by Johannes Streicher et al. (Rome, ISMEZ: 2006), pp. 553–69.

Index

Adami, Giuseppe, 7, 146–47, 152, 156, 180, 235–36, 241, 244, 245, 246, 261–62
Aleardi, Aleardo, 18
Alfano, Franco, 6, 8, 20–21, 75, 78, 94–96, 109, 179, 184, 234–35, 246, 251–53, 263, 344, 350, 353
    La leggenda di Sakùntala, 208–09, 246
    Madonna Imperia, 263
    Il Principe Zilah, 95–96, 109
    Second String Quartet, 252
    L'ultimo Lord, 8
    and Rostand's *La princesse lointaine*, 234–35
Anfossi, Giovanni, 33–34, 36
Antona-Traversi, Giannino, 48
Argentina
    performance and reception of IM's music, 166–67
Australia
    performance and reception of IM's music, 177–78

Basile, Arturo, 342, 351
Bel Geddes, Norman, 213, 223
Benelli, Sem, 110–18, 176, 190, 218, 289–90, 307–08, 309, 311, 312, 325, 327, 335
    La cena delle beffe, 110, 111, 112, 241
Berg, Alban
    Wozzeck, 122
Bernardin de Saint-Pierre, Jacques-Henri, 5, 236, 254
Beverly Hills (as residence of IM), 2, 302–03, 323–24, 340–41, 353
Bignotti, Angelo, 30
Boito, Arrigo, 64, 146
Bonaparte, Maria Letizia, 70, 92
Bonetti, Vincenzo, 37
Bonetti Competition, 37, 46, 62
Bori, Lucrezia, 159, 161, 165, 226, 229, 306
Brazil
    performance and reception of IM's music, 168

Caldanzano, Luigi Emilio, 128, 157–58
Callas, Maria, 349, 353
Caniglia, Maria, 279, 284, 295, 298
Caramba. *See* Sapelli, Luigi
Casella, Alfredo, 251, 252, 282
Catalani, Alfredo, 38, 94, 223, 316
    Loreley, 38
Cavara, Otello, 235
Chicago Opera, 174, 216, 223–25, 341
Cilea, Francesco, 88, 252, 344
    Adriana Lecouvreur, 88, 96
cinema, 83, 90, 343
Clausetti, Carlo, 216
Constant, Benjamin
    Adolphe, 80–81, 97
Costa, Enrico, 52
Croce, Benedetto, 158, 290
Curubeto Godoy, María Isabel, 246

D'Angelantonio, Francesco, 48–51
    Il regno delle ballerine, 48–49, 51
D'Annunzio, Gabriele, 39, 56, 119, 142, 179, 185–91, 209, 210, 214, 217–19, 223, 247, 299
    Alcyone, 39, 197
    Lettera ai Dalmati, 217
    La nave, 185, 187–88
    Poema paradisiaco, 56
D'Annunzio, Ugo Veniero, 229–30
Dargomïzhsky, Alexander, 118–19
D'Arienzo, Marco, 30
Da Venezia, Franco, 62
De Angelis, Nazzareno, 152, 166, 168
Debussy, Claude, 118–20, 145, 166, 223
    Pelléas et Mélisande, 1, 2, 118–20, 131, 145, 352
Delius, Frederick, 63
Della Corte, Andrea, 263, 281
D'Erasmo, Alberto (IM's tutor), 21, 33, 37
De Sabata, Victor, 165, 352
Didur, Adamo, 159, 165, 178, 229

362 INDEX

Donadelli, Elisa (IM's mother), 12–13, 240, 291
Donadelli, Renato (IM's cousin), 218–19, 285
Dvořák, Antonín, 33
  New World Symphony, 33
  Rusalka, 39

Ferrari-Fontana, Edoardo, 152, 159, 161, 174, 175
Ferroni, Vincenzo, 24–25, 33, 47
Fiume (Rijeka), 218–19
  IM visits, 219
Fiumi, Lionello, 190, 344, 348
Fontana, Ferdinando, 64, 94
Forzano, Giovacchino, 235, 241
  Sly, 241
France
  performance and reception of IM's music, 162–65
  IM's visits to, 20, 162–63, 237, 249, 277
Franchetti, Alberto, 26, 119, 146, 179
  La figlia di Iorio, 119, 185
Futurism, 90

Galeffi, Carlo, 153, 167
Garden, Mary, 115, 165, 225–29, 249, 305, 340–41, 349, 354
  as Fiora, 226–29
Gatti-Casazza, Giulio, 158, 238, 243–44
Germany
  performance and reception of IM's music, 175–76
Ghisalberti, Mario, 263–64, 273, 282
Ghislanzoni, Antonio, 28
Gigli, Beniamino, 165, 294, 295
Gilman, Lawrence, 57, 170, 248, 284
Giordano, Umberto, 88, 110, 236, 240, 241, 246, 252, 344
  Andrea Chénier, 88, 96
  Fedora, 88
Gnecchi, Vittorio, 252–53, 350
Grout, Donald Jay, 1, 3, 6, 8, 335

Hale, Philip, 1, 119–20
Henderson, W. J., 136, 160
Hoffmann, E. T. A., 38
Hubbard, William L., 188, 223–25, 227

Illica, Luigi, 78–80, 81–82, 84, 88, 93–94, 97, 101, 109, 161, 179–80, 298
  Italia, 179–80
  Maria Antonietta, 78, 81
  La Perugina, 109
Interdonato, Stefano, 30

Johnson, Edward, 211, 212

Kirsten, Dorothy, 334, 343
Krehbiel, Henry E., 159–60

Lazzari, Virgilio, 167–68, 227, 305, 325, 333
Lehár, Franz, 89–90
  The Merry Widow, 89–90
Leoncavallo, Ruggero, 67, 70, 221, 326
Leone, Evasio, 34
Leopardi, Giacomo, 56, 62
Literaturoper, 1, 118–20, 180
Loti, Pierre
  Ramuntcho, 79, 81
Lualdi, Adriano, 172, 188–89, 219, 252, 281, 300–01

Mahler, Gustav, 143
Marinuzzi, Gino, 168, 306
Mascagni, Pietro, 7, 22, 26, 30, 47, 78, 90, 119, 137, 221, 240, 246, 252, 316, 326, 344
  L'amico Fritz, 137, 316
  Cavalleria rusticana, 47, 49, 50, 52, 54, 57, 296, 350–51
  Guglielmo Ratcliff, 119
  Parisina, 119, 180, 185
Massenet, Jules, 24, 26, 47, 317
  Thaïs, 317
Mendelssohn, Felix, 28, 33, 133
  Overture to *A Midsummer Night's Dream*, 133–36
  Scottish Symphony, 33
Menotti, Gian Carlo, 325, 327
  The Old Maid and the Thief, 325, 327
Messina earthquake, 88–89
Metropolitan Opera House, 1, 107, 159, 173, 283, 305–06, 341, 353
Mexico
  performance and reception of IM's music, 167–68
Milan (as residence of IM), 78, 238–40
Monaldi, Gino, 156–57
Montefiore, Tommaso, 110, 241
Montemezzi, Bortolo (IM's father), 11–12, 13–14, 15, 16, 20, 240
  military career, 12, 16
  as musician, 16
Montemezzi, Elisa (IM's mother). *See under Donadelli*

Montemezzi, Italo: **Key Biographical Events**
  birth, 13
  schooling, 16, 18

INDEX 363

first attempt to enter the Royal Conservatory
of Music, 19
enters the Royal Conservatory, 22
graduates from the Royal Conservatory, 36
signed by Casa Ricordi, 75–76
conscription, 190
first visit to the United States, 220–32
marriage, 237
parenthood, 249
move to the United States, 301–02
death, 348
funeral, 349
Montemezzi, Italo: **Character**, 14–15, 17, 25,
152, 221–22, 350
Montemezzi, Italo: **As Conductor**, 2, 33–34,
223–24, 279, 304–07, 321–22, 332–35
Montemezzi, Italo: **Lobbying Activities**, 151,
249–50, 253, 285–88, 294–96, 341–42,
344–45, 346–47
Montemezzi, Italo: **WORKS** (*1. Completed
Operas; 2. Other Operatic Projects; 3.
Other Compositions 1875–1900; 4. Other
Compositions 1901–1952*)

1. Completed Operas
L'amore dei tre re, 1–6, 8, 31, 53, 83, 110–46,
148–82, 197, 217–18, 222, 225–29,
242–43, 259, 266, 267, 278, 284, 289–90,
295, 304–06, 312, 314–15, 321–22, 326,
328, 332–36, 343, 344, 350, 351–53,
356–57
story and meaning, 113–16
responses to the spoken play, 116–18
conceived as a *Literaturoper*, 118–20
libretto, 120–22
music, 122–45
premiere, 153–54
critical reception, 154–57, 159–73, 175–78,
227–29, 278, 305–06, 307, 333, 335, 338,
350, 352, 355–56
recordings, 178, 306, 342, 352–53
radio broadcasts, 278, 297, 306, 342
relationship to *L'incantesimo*, 309–11
television version, 343, 353
Bianca, 37–46, 53, 309, 311–12
date, 37
libretto, 37–39
music, 40–45
Giovanni Gallurese, 4, 47–74, 82–83, 243–44,
259, 266
one-act version, 49–50
story, 51–52
libretto, 52–53

music, 53–62
private performance, 64
sponsorship, 66–67
premiere, 68–70
critical reception, 70–72, 82–83, 248
published, 76
first Milan production, 82
New York production, 247–48
radio broadcast, 297
Héllera, 4, 80–81, 83–88, 91–109, 116, 149, 151,
181, 259–61, 289, 295, 337, 351
source, 80–81
composition, 83–84
IM's commentary (including plot summary),
84–88
premiere, 92–93
critical reception, 93–94, 297–98
financial loss, 94
revision and publication, 96, 107, 297
music, 96–107
campaigns to revive, 294, 295–96, 341–42,
344, 346–47
radio broadcast, 108, 296, 297–98
L'incantesimo, 31, 289–90, 291, 292, 295, 307–19,
322, 345
story and meaning, 308–12
relationship to *L'amore dei tre re*, 309–11
music, 312–19
radio premiere, 324–25
critical reception, 325–26
stage premiere, 350–51
La nave, 4, 5, 123, 185–218, 222, 227, 246–47,
249–50, 259, 266–67, 270, 285–87, 289,
295, 299–301, 325, 337, 344, 345, 351
inspiration and source, 185–87
libretto, 187–89
composition, 190–92
music, 192–209
premiere, 211–12
critical reception, 212–14, 224–25, 282
Chicago production, 223–24
campaigns to revive, 246–47, 249–50, 285–87,
294, 295–96, 346–47
Rome production, 299–301
La notte di Zoraima, 8, 263–77, 279–84, 311,
343
origins, 263–65
story and significance, 265–67
music, 267–77
premiere, 279–81
critical reception, 281–84
New York production, 283–84
radio broadcast, 297

364 INDEX

2. Other Operatic Projects
La Dogaressa, 261–62, 263, 265
Paolo e Virginia, 5, 79, 236, 238, 240–42, 243,
    244–46, 248, 253, 262, 266
La principessa lontana, 182–85, 234–35, 261, 262

3. Other Compositions 1875–1900
Il canto di Mignon, 28–30
Una croce in camposanto, 30
"Fosco . . . e chiamommi" (scena), 31
Frammento del Cantico dei Cantici di Salomone,
    34–36
fugue exercises, 27
Gelosia (scena), 31–33
"Mi soccorri, o madre" (madrigal), 28
"Ornando, come suole" (madrigal), 28
polka, 17
"Qui attenderla in segreto" (scena), 30
Scherzo, 27–28
"Se un giorno mi vedrai, angelo pio," 30
Sinfonia in E minor, 33–34
Sonata per piano e violino, 28

4. Other Compositions 1901–1952
A ti, hermosa!, 320–21
Elegia, 288
Italia mia! Nulla fermerà il tuo canto!, 327–30,
    331–32
Paolo e Virginia (symphonic poem), 245, 253–59,
    285, 328
    performances, 277, 306–07
*Per le Onoranze ad Amilcare Ponchielli nel
    25° Anniversario della sua Morte. Cantata*,
    146–47
Per star con te!, 321

Montemezzi, Katherine (formerly Leith) (IM's
    wife), 144, 229–33, 236–40, 291, 301, 323,
    331, 346, 349, 353
    family background and wealth, 230–32
    in love with IM, 232–33, 236–37
    becomes Italian citizen, 238
    pregnancy and motherhood, 248–49
    regains U.S. citizenship, 285
Montemezzi, Marco (IM's son), 16, 249, 291,
    296, 301–02, 330–31, 349, 354–56
    dedicatee of *La notte di Zoraima*, 277
    becomes U.S. citizen, 331
Moore, Grace, 226, 243–44, 304–6, 321–22, 334
Moranzoni, Roberto, 162, 165
Mostra del '900 musicale italiano (1927), 252–53
Mozart, Wolfgang Amadeus
    Le nozze di Figaro, 45

Musical America, 1, 248, 327, 333, 335
Mussolini, Arnaldo, 287
Mussolini, Benito, 251–52, 282, 285–88, 290,
    294–96, 304, 310–11, 325
Mussorgsky, Modest, 59, 156, 208
    Boris Godunov, 59, 208
    Khovanshchina, 208
Muzio, Claudia, 174, 229, 294

Nappi, Giovanni Battista, 82, 152, 153–54,
    155–56, 210
Newman, Ernest, 248, 278
Nogarola, Antonio (IM's godfather), 13
Nogarola, Lodovico Violini, 20, 66–67

Omaggio a Italo Montemezzi (1952), 8, 344, 350
operetta, 89–90, 95
Orefice, Giacomo, 119, 144, 214

Parker, H. T., 162, 170–72, 184
Peyser, Herbert F., 25, 158, 160–61, 220–23,
    284, 298, 327, 335
Pinza, Ezio, 278, 305, 336
Piontelli, Luigi, 65–66, 67–68
Pizzetti, Ildebrando, 63, 119, 170, 186, 188, 209,
    246, 251, 252, 300
    Fedra, 119, 185
Polacco, Giorgio, 167, 306
Ponchielli, Amilcare, 5, 30, 146–47, 316
    La Gioconda, 146–47
Ponselle, Rosa, 278–79, 283, 284
Pougin, Arthur, 46, 51, 163–64
Pozza, Giovanni, 82, 92–93, 154–55
Pozzali, Temistocle, 91–92
Puccini, Giacomo, 4–9, 22, 28, 30, 63–64, 74,
    75, 76, 78, 94, 136, 146, 160, 161, 170, 174,
    176, 177–78, 180, 182, 221, 236, 237, 246,
    248, 306, 326
    La Bohème, 4, 6, 26, 66, 81
    Edgar, 4, 94
    La fanciulla del West, 5, 8, 107
    Madama Butterfly, 5, 75, 236
    Manon Lescaut, 4, 76
    La rondine, 5, 180
    Tosca, 5, 6, 26, 53, 54, 203
    Il trittico, 5, 235
    Turandot, 6, 8, 122, 235, 240–41, 246, 249–50
    Le Villi, 4, 47, 63–64, 74

radio, 278, 296–97, 306, 324–25, 326, 327, 342, 352
Raisa, Rosa, 223–24
Ravinia Opera, 174
Respighi, Ottorino, 251, 252, 301

INDEX 365

Ricordi (company), 4, 64, 66, 72, 75, 91, 94–95,
    108, 147–48, 181–82, 261, 265, 337, 342,
    351, 353
  IM's contracts and payments, 75–76, 147–48,
    178, 181–82, 245, 254, 263, 265
Ricordi, Giulio, 68, 72, 74, 75, 78–79, 81, 83–84,
    85, 111, 148, 150, 236
Ricordi, Tito, 95, 96, 104, 108–09, 117–18, 119,
    148, 149–50, 158, 179–80, 181, 183–84,
    186–88, 212, 216, 287
Rostand, Edmond, 182–84, 234
  La princesse lointaine, 182–85, 234–35
Royal Conservatory of Music (Milan), 19, 21–22,
    23–24

Saladino, Michele, 22–23, 23–24
San Franciso Opera, 2, 174, 307, 321–22,
    334–35, 341, 352
Sapelli, Luigi, 97
Scala, La, 25–26, 150, 151, 172, 173, 209–10,
    242, 249–50, 265, 277, 279, 284, 285–86,
    287, 294, 335–36, 338–39, 346–47, 353
Serafin, Tullio, 14, 24, 26–27, 64–65, 66, 68, 91,
    146–47, 210, 211–12, 214–15, 217, 247,
    294, 295–96, 350
  conducts IM's works, 68–69, 91, 146–47,
    152–53, 166–67, 211–12, 214–15, 247, 283,
    299, 334, 350
Serra, Renato, 158
Simonetta, Tomaso Castelbarco Visconti, 48, 66
Simoni, Renato, 179, 212–13, 235–36, 240–41,
    244, 246
Smareglia, Antonio, 38
Smith, John Christopher, 118
Società Teatrale Internazionale, 90–92
Solazzi, Ugo, 76, 147
Sonzogno (company), 4, 47, 74, 91
  Casa Sonzogno's 1884 competition, 4, 47,
    63–64
  Casa Sonzogno's 1890 competition, 47
  Casa Sonzogno's 1904 competition, 4, 47,
    49–50, 62–63
Strauss, Richard, 118, 128, 155, 165–66, 214,
    253, 259, 310, 330
  Der Rosenkavalier, 1, 166, 292
  Salome, 118, 214
Stravinsky, Igor, 142, 324
Sweden
  performance and reception of IM's music,
    282–83

Tansini, Ugo, 68
Tasso, Torquato, 38

Taylor, Deems, 79n.14, 226, 248, 283
Tebaldi, Renata, 341–42, 347, 351
Thompson, Oscar, 248, 305–06, 312, 316, 326,
    327
Toscanini, Arturo, 26, 27, 29, 35–36, 146, 158,
    159, 214–15, 219, 249, 294, 306
  conducts IM's works, 35–36, 159, 161, 172,
    249

United Kingdom
  performance and reception of IM's music,
    165–66, 277–78
  IM's visit to, 277–79
United States of America
  performance and reception of *L'amore dei tre
    re*, 1–2, 159–62, 170–74, 226–29, 242–43,
    304–06, 307, 332–35, 352
  performance and reception of IM's other
    music, 223–25, 247–48, 283–84, 304,
    306–07, 324–27, 331–32
  IM's visits to, 220–32, 242–44, 247–48, 291

Valcarenghi, Renzo, 216, 234
Vanni Marcoux, 162–63, 165
Verdi, Giuseppe, 4, 5, 6, 7, 46, 75, 144, 156, 159,
    162, 163, 164, 176, 199, 300, 350
  Aida, 3, 61, 217, 281
  Don Carlo, 61
  Ernani, 54, 61
  I masnadieri, 31
  Otello, 1, 3, 6, 144, 156, 159, 162
  La traviata, 97, 137, 138
  Il trovatore, 53, 266, 270
Vigasio (IM's birthplace), 10–11, 47, 76–78,
    291, 338, 339–40, 349
Villa Montemezzi, 14, 76–77, 120, 149, 265, 292,
    340, 344–45, 347–48, 349, 354
Visconti di Modrone, Uberto, 151, 210

Wagner, Richard, and Wagnerianism, 26, 42,
    131, 136, 141, 142, 144, 163, 164, 168,
    170, 176, 214, 259, 281, 294, 300, 301,
    312–15, 328
  Lohengrin, 26, 33, 60, 312
  Das Rheingold, 195–96, 315
  Der Ring des Nibelungen, 26, 42
  Siegfried, 42–43, 145
  Tristan und Isolde, 1, 2, 26, 131, 137, 144, 314
Weber, Carl Maria von, 38
  Der Freischütz, 38, 45
Wilson, Woodrow, 216–18
Witkowski, Georges Martin, 235
Wolf-Ferrari, Ermanno, 65, 241, 252, 264

366 INDEX

World War II
  impact on the Montemezzis, 303–04, 319–20, 321–22, 330–31, 336–37, 338

Zandonai, Riccardo, 6, 8, 21, 63, 95, 150, 168, 179–80, 182, 183, 221, 235, 241, 246, 252, 328, 344, 353
  Autunno fra i monti–Patria lontana, 328

Conchita, 95, 150
Francesca da Rimini, 119, 161, 166, 173, 179, 185, 186
Il grillo del focolare, 95
Una partita, 8
La via della finestra, 180, 216
Zuppone Strani, Giuseppe, 37–38, 39, 63